Praise for the Second Edition

In the second edition of *New Directions in the American Presidency*, Lori Cox Han and her colleagues address a range of key issues, challenges, and opportunities confronting presidents. The essays, firmly grounded in the evolution of the presidency and its interplay with the broader U.S. political system, combine the latest political science scholarship and contemporary illustrations with keen analytical insight and engaging narratives. Readers will welcome the volume's balance, its probing examination, and its thought-provoking assessment.

Karen M. Hult, *Virginia Tech*

In this superlatively written and thoroughly updated second edition, Lori Cox Han has brought together some of the field's most insightful scholars to deliver an eminently analytical volume for any course on the U.S. presidency. Highly recommended.

Richard S. Conley, *University of Florida*

This new edition of *New Directions in the American Presidency* is timely and broad-ranging, featuring the latest analyses by leading scholars of the presidency. This collection succeeds in addressing major long-standing questions – and suggests directions for future work – in the field. Well-written and very balanced, this volume should be of equal interest to students of and experts on the presidency.

Mark J. Rozell, *George Mason University*

Lori Cox Han's new edition of *New Directions in the American Presidency* assesses executive branch politics comprehensively and highlights the most recent research in this area. In focusing on the presidency, the book covers the larger political landscape that chief executives interact with, including Congress, the courts, and the media. Essays by leading experts will inform and engage both new students and seasoned scholars who are seeking to gain a broader understanding about presidential power and leadership.

Adam L. Warber, *Clemson University*

New Directions in the American Presidency features clear, concise analyses of how the presidency currently functions and fruitful suggestions for new research directions in the field. With important contributions by leading experts, this book will have a comfortable home in classrooms and be kept close at hand by junior and senior scholars alike.

Daniel E. Ponder, *Drury University*

New Directions in the American Presidency

Especially coming out of the landmark presidential elections of 2008 and 2016, the study of the American presidency—both as a political institution and of those who have held the office—is one of the most fascinating and dynamic fields of study within American government. *New Directions in the American Presidency* takes a current look at the various issues facing the contemporary presidency and provides a "state of the art" overview of current trends in the field of presidency research.

This volume of original chapters by leading presidential scholars is designed to include all the essential topics covered in an undergraduate-level presidency course or a graduate-level seminar while also bringing together key disciplinary debates and treatment of important current real-world developments. Each chapter is written with students in mind so that it remains accessible, interesting, and engaging.

New to the Second Edition

- New key chapters on presidents, political parties, and presidential leadership (essential following the 2016 presidential election).
- A fresh approach to the president and the Constitution and the president and domestic policymaking are provided by new authors for these foundational chapters.
- All chapters have been revised with updates coming out of the 2016 election, especially in relation to presidential campaign politics, media, and the Supreme Court.

Lori Cox Han is Professor of Political Science at Chapman University.

New Directions in American Politics

The Routledge series *New Directions in American Politics* is composed of contributed volumes covering key areas of study in the field of American politics and government. Each title provides a state-of-the-art overview of current trends in its respective subfield, with an eye toward cutting-edge research accessible to advanced undergraduate and beginning graduate students. While the volumes touch on the main topics of relevant study, they are not meant to cover the "nuts and bolts" of the subject. Rather, they engage readers in the most recent scholarship, real-world controversies, and theoretical debates with the aim of getting students excited about the same issues that animate scholars.

Titles in the series:

New Directions in American Political Parties
Edited by Jeffrey M. Stonecash

New Directions in the American Presidency
Edited by Lori Cox Han

New Directions in Campaigns and Elections
Edited by Stephen K. Medvic

New Directions in Congressional Politics
Edited by Jamie L. Carson

New Directions in Interest Group Politics
Edited by Matt Grossmann

New Directions in Judicial Politics
Edited by Kevin T. McGuire

New Directions in Media and Politics
Edited by Travis N. Ridout

New Directions in Public Opinion
Edited by Adam J. Berinsky

New Directions in the American Presidency

Second Edition

**Edited by
Lori Cox Han**

Routledge
Taylor & Francis Group

NEW YORK AND LONDON

Published 2018
by Routledge
711 Third Avenue, New York, NY 10017

and by Routledge
2 Park Square, Milton Park, Abingdon, Oxon, OX14 4RN

Routledge is an imprint of the Taylor & Francis Group, an informa business

© 2018 Taylor & Francis

The right of the editor to be identified as the author of the editorial material, and of the authors for their individual chapters, has been asserted in accordance with sections 77 and 78 of the Copyright, Designs and Patents Act 1988.

First edition published by Routledge 2011

Library of Congress Cataloging in Publication Data
Names: Han, Lori Cox, editor.
Title: New directions in the American presidency / edited by Lori Cox Han.
Description: Second Edition. | New York: Routledge, 2018. | Series: New Directions in American Politics | "First edition published by Routledge 2011"—T.p. verso. | Includes bibliographical references and index.
Identifiers: LCCN 2017028281 | ISBN 9781138739086 (hardback) | ISBN 9781138739093 (paperback) | ISBN 9781315184395 (ebook)
Subjects: LCSH: Presidents—United States. | United States—Politics and government.
Classification: LCC JK516 .N495 2018 | DDC 352.230973—dc23
LC record available at https://lccn.loc.gov/2017028281

ISBN: 978-1-138-73908-6 (hbk)
ISBN: 978-1-138-73909-3 (pbk)
ISBN: 978-1-315-18439-5 (ebk)

Typeset in Times New Roman
by codeMantra

For Tom, Taylor, and Davis

Contents

Figures and Tables

Figures

Tables

Acknowledgments

The study of the American presidency is constantly evolving, and it is never boring. As the president and his administration continue to dominate so much of the day-to-day political life as well as the policy agenda in American society, political scientists (as well as scholars in numerous other academic disciplines) find themselves confronted with endless questions about the president as a political actor and the presidency as a political institution. The current presidency of Donald J. Trump, as well as the three most previous presidencies of Barack Obama, George W. Bush, and Bill Clinton, provides many avenues of research involving complex questions about governing and politics. As this volume shows, cutting-edge and innovative research has become the mainstay in presidential studies. Each of the contributors is a leading expert in their respective field, and each is also an accomplished classroom instructor. As a result, the perspectives and analyses provided in each chapter show the depth and breadth of our current understandings of the presidency, as well as future areas of research in this dynamic subfield. In addition, each chapter is written with the student of the presidency in mind as a way of introducing the topic to students at all levels, letting the reader know that "this is what political scientists know" about each relevant topic.

As with any book project, the finished product represents the hard work of many people from start to finish. First and foremost, I wish to thank the contributors who made this volume possible by generously sharing their time, as well as their knowledge and expertise on the presidency. Their work, here and in numerous other venues, sustains the subfield of presidential studies and has enlightened countless students and colleagues alike. Thanks also to those who commented on an earlier version of the project: Matthew R. Miles, Brigham Young University-Idaho; Daniel E. Ponder, Drury University; Barry L. Tadlock, Ohio University; and Adam L. Warber, Clemson University. I would also like to thank Jennifer Knerr at Routledge for her enthusiasm and support in publishing a second edition of this volume, as well as Ze'ev Sudry for his support in completing the project. At Chapman University, I am grateful for all the help provided by Erin Berthon, no matter how small or large the request. I would also like to thank President Daniele Struppa for his continued support of my research agenda, and for creating a culture on our campus where both research and teaching are valued. The best part of my job at Chapman is my time spent in the classroom with our amazing students, who constantly remind me why I chose this profession in the first place. Finally, I am eternally grateful to my husband, Tom Han, and my children, Taylor NyBlom and Davis Han, for their continued love, support, and patience every time I embark on a new book project.

Contributors

Randall E. Adkins is Professor of Political Science and Associate Dean of the College of Arts & Sciences at the University of Nebraska at Omaha. He teaches courses on the presidency, Congress, political parties, and campaigns and elections. He is the editor of *The Evolution of Political Parties, Campaigns, and Elections*; *Cases in Congressional Campaigns*, and is the author of numerous articles and chapters in edited volumes on the presidency and campaigns and elections. His research has appeared in *American Politics Quarterly, American Politics Research, American Review of Politics, the Journal of Political Marketing, Political Research Quarterly, Presidential Studies Quarterly, PS: Political Science & Politics, and Publius*. He is also a former American Political Science Association Congressional Fellow where he worked for the Hon. David E. Price (NC-4). He received his Ph.D. from Miami University.

Julia R. Azari is Associate Professor of Political Science at Marquette University. She is the author of *Delivering the People's Message: The Changing Politics of the Presidential Mandate* and the co-editor of *The Presidential Leadership Dilemma: Between the Constitution and a Political Party*. Her work has appeared in *The Annals of the American Academy of Political and Social Science, Social Science Quarterly, Presidential Studies Quarterly*, and *Perspectives on Politics*. She writes about presidential politics and political parties for The Mischiefs of Faction on Vox.com and FiveThirtyEight.com. She received her Ph.D. from Yale University.

Meena Bose is Executive Dean for Public Policy and Public Service Programs in Hofstra University's Peter S. Kalikow School of Government, Public Policy, and International Affairs, and Director of Hofstra's Peter S. Kalikow Center for the Study of the American Presidency. She is the author of *Shaping and Signaling Presidential Policy: The National Security Decision Making of Eisenhower and Kennedy*, and editor of the reference volume *The New York Times on the Presidency*. She has edited several volumes in presidency studies and a reader in American politics. She is third author for both the

American Government: Institutions and Policies textbook, 16th ed., and *The Paradoxes of the American Presidency*, 5th ed. She taught for six years at the United States Military Academy at West Point, where she also served as Director of American Politics. She received her Ph.D. from Princeton University.

Matthew J. Dickinson is Professor of Political Science at Middlebury College. Previously he taught at Harvard University, where he also received his Ph.D. under Richard E. Neustadt. He is the author *of Bitter Harvest: FDR, Presidential Power, and the Growth of the Presidential Branch*, co-editor of *Guardian of the Presidency: The Legacy of Richard E. Neustadt*, and has published numerous articles on the presidency, presidential decision making, and presidential advisers. His current book project, *The President and the White House Staff: People, Positions and Processes, 1945–2012*, examines the evolution of the White House staff in the post-FDR period. His blog, Presidential Power, can be found at http://sites.middlebury.edu/presidentialpower/.

Matthew Eshbaugh-Soha is Department Chair and Professor of Political Science at the University of North Texas. He is the author of two books and over two dozen scholarly articles published in a variety of journals including *American Journal of Political Science, Political Research Quarterly, Political Communication*, and *Presidential Studies Quarterly*. He received his Ph.D. from Texas A&M University.

Victoria A. Farrar-Myers is a Senior Fellow and the Director of the Tower Scholars Program at The John Goodwin Tower Center for Political Studies at Southern Methodist University in Dallas, Texas. Among her many publications, she is the author of *Scripted for Change: The Institutionalization of the American Presidency*, co-author of *Legislative Labyrinth: Congress and Campaign Finance Reform* and *Limits and Loopholes: The Quest for Money, Free Speech and Fair Elections*, and co-editor of *Corruption and American Politics* and *Controlling the Message: New Media in American Political Campaigns*. During 1997–1998, she served as an American Political Science Association Congressional Fellow in the U.S. House of Representatives, and in 2014 she served as the Fulbright Distinguished Chair in American Politics at Flinders University in Adelaide, Australia. She received her Ph.D. in Political Science from SUNY Albany.

Lori Cox Han is Professor of Political Science at Chapman University. An expert on the presidency, media and politics, and women and politics, she is the author of several books including *Presidents and the American Presidency*, 2nd ed. (with Diane J. Heith), *Women, Power, and Politics: The Fight for Gender Equality in the United States* (with Caroline Heldman), *In It to Win: Electing Madam President, A Presidency Upstaged: The Public Leadership of George H.W. Bush*, and

Governing From Center Stage: White House Communication Strategies During the Television Age of Politics. She is also editor of *Hatred of America's Presidents: Personal Attacks on the White House from Washington to Trump* and co-editor of *Rethinking Madam President: Are We Ready for a Woman in the White House?*, *The Presidency and the Challenge of Democracy*, and *In the Public Domain: Presidents and the Challenge of Public Leadership*. She is past president of the Presidency Research Group, an organized section of the American Political Science Association devoted to the study of the presidency. She received her Ph.D. from the University of Southern California.

Diane J. Heith is Professor of Government and Politics at St. John's University. She is the author of several works on the presidency, public opinion, and the media including *Presidents and the American Presidency*, 2nd ed. (with Lori Cox Han), *The Presidential Road Show: Public Leadership in an Era of Party Polarization, Polling to Govern: Public Opinion and Presidential Leadership*, and is co-editor of *In the Public Domain: Presidents and the Challenges of Public Leadership*. Her work has appeared in the journals *Public Opinion Quarterly, Presidential Studies Quarterly, Political Science Quarterly, The Journal of Health Politics, Policy and Law, The Journal of Women, Politics and Policy, White House Studies* and *Congress and the Presidency*. She received her Ph.D. from Brown University.

Nancy Kassop is Professor of Political Science at the State University of New York at New Paltz. She is a contributing scholar to the White House Transition Project (2016) and co-author of the essay on "The Office of the White House Counsel" at www.whitehousetransition project.org, and the author of articles and book chapters on the presidency and law, with recent works including "Law Versus Politics in the Counterterrorism Policies of the George W. Bush Administration: The Sacrifice of One for the Other?" in Meena Bose, ed.; *The Constitution, Politics and Policy-Making in the George W. Bush Presidency* (2016); "Executive Branch Legal Analysis for National Security Policy: Who Controls Access to Legal Memos?" *Presidential Studies Quarterly* (2014); and "Rivals for Influence on Counterterrorism Policy: White House Political Staff vs. Executive Branch Legal Advisors," *Presidential Studies Quarterly* (2013). She is co-editor of the book review section of *Presidential Studies Quarterly* and a past president of the Presidency Research Group organized section of the American Political Science Association. She received her Ph.D. from New York University.

Brandon Rottinghaus is Professor of Political Science at the University of Houston. His primary research and teaching interests include the presidency, the media, public opinion, executive-legislative relations and research methods. He is the author of *The Provisional Pulpit: Modern Conditional Presidential Leadership of Public Opinion*, *The Institutional Effects of Executive Scandal*, and *The Dual Executive: Unilateral Orders in a Separated and Shared Power System*, and his work has also appeared in several journals and edited volumes. He is also the founding designer of the Presidential Proclamations Project at the University of Houston, an online resource documenting presidential use of unilateral powers through executive proclamation. He received his Ph.D. from Northwestern University.

Jeremy L. Strickler is Assistant Professor of Political Science at the University of Tennessee, Chattanooga. His research and teaching interests are in political institutions, policy history, and American political development. His current book project utilizes archival evidence from presidential libraries to examine the historical dynamic between the modern presidency, war, and domestic policymaking in the mid-twentieth century. He is also working on a presidential history of the war on drugs in the United States. He received his Ph.D. from the University of Oregon.

Justin S. Vaughn is Associate Professor of Political Science at Boise State University, where he also directs the Center for Idaho History and Politics. He has published five books including *Czars in the White House: The Rise of Policy Czars as a Presidential Management Tool* and the award-winning *Women and the White House: Gender, Popular Culture and Presidential Politics*. His current research focuses on determinants of presidential greatness as well as new dimensions of presidential rhetoric. He received his Ph.D. from Texas A&M University.

1   Introduction

Studying Presidents and the Presidency

Lori Cox Han

On January 20, 2017, Donald J. Trump took the oath of office as the 45th president of the United States. Trump won the presidency in what was perhaps the most negative presidential campaign on record, and he entered office with the lowest approval rating (45 percent)[1] of any president since the advent of public opinion polling in the 1930s. Historically, a presidential inauguration represents an important political ritual for American citizens, as it serves as a time of renewal of faith in the U.S. constitutional system to witness the peaceful transition of power from one leader to the next. Presidents look to the inauguration, and in particular the inaugural address, as an opportunity to set the tone for their tenure in office with both the public and other political actors, and most use the event as an opportunity to talk about broader political principles and their vision for the country. Aside from the constitutional requirement that presidents must take the oath of office, inaugurations are one of the many symbolic acts in which a president engages, and it is the first time that they address the American public—the national constituency that they uniquely represent within the political system—as president. Each president also faces unique circumstances on the day they take office, and therefore may have different strategies and goals that they and their advisors are attempting to achieve.[2]

For Trump, the political environment at the start of his presidency was marked by a deep partisan divide as well as shock and even hatred among his political opponents that the unconventional—and at times controversial—business man with no political experience had won the White House. Striking a populist tone, similar to his messaging throughout the 2016 presidential campaign, Trump stated that:

> What truly matters is not which party controls our government, but whether our government is controlled by the people. January 20th 2017, will be remembered as the day the people became the rulers of this nation again. The forgotten men and women of our country will be forgotten no longer. Everyone is listening to you now.[3]

Despite protests (some violent) over Trump's election, the constitutional requirements of the inauguration had been met, and the government continued to function. Once again, the United States had seen a peaceful transition of power, no matter how contentious the election had been.

In addition to the political, constitutional, and symbolic significance of presidential inaugurals, the start of a new presidential administration also serves as a milestone for those who study the presidency—a brand new president and administration to assess and analyze. The study of the American presidency, both as a political institution along with those who have held the office, is one of the most fascinating and dynamic fields of study within political science. While the framers of the U.S. Constitution may have envisioned coequal branches among the legislative, executive, and judiciary, the powers of the presidency have expanded throughout the past century as contemporary American presidents, for better or worse, have often been the driving force behind policymaking at both the national and international levels. As such, the actions of the current administration, as well as other recent administrations, raise numerous questions for scholars to consider about the powers of the office, the complex nature in which presidents shape the policy agenda, and various other aspects of governing.

Trump and his three most recent predecessors—Barack Obama, George W. Bush, and Bill Clinton—have opened myriad avenues of analysis regarding a broad spectrum of issues for presidency scholars, both as individual political actors as well as the institutional implications of their actions while in office. For example, Obama took office at a time of economic crisis, as the United States faced the most daunting economic downturn and recession since the Great Depression of the 1930s. In addition, the new commander in chief inherited two wars in Iraq and Afghanistan, both initiated by his immediate predecessor as part of the War on Terror. Expectations for Obama's presidency were high—his supporters expected him to fix the economy, bring home American troops from the Middle East, reform health care, and heal the partisan divide in the nation as part of a new post-racial era in American politics. However, Obama left office in 2017 with a mixed record—major initiatives on health care and the environment had been enacted, though devastating losses for the Democratic Party at all levels of government during Obama's time in office meant a likely reversal for many of the accomplishments. For George W. Bush, one major component of his eight years in office will forever be linked to the expansion of presidential war powers in the aftermath of the September 11, 2001 terrorist attacks. In addition, the Bush years will also be remembered for an increasing budget deficit, the prominence of a socially conservative policy agenda, and an escalation of partisanship at the national level. While Bill Clinton may have left office with a budget surplus, his time in office was marked by six years of divided government, an impeachment, and his ability to politically outmaneuver his political opponents through strong political and communication skills (which also contributed to the partisan divide in Washington).

These presidencies and related topics are just a sampling of issues that animate current research on the American presidency. That research, in turn, also animates how presidency courses are taught at both the undergraduate and graduate levels. While presidential studies itself is considered a subfield within the discipline of political science, numerous subfields within presidential studies have also emerged as part of the growing literature on both presidents and the presidency. For example, presidential/congressional relations, presidential powers, the executive branch as a political institution, and the public aspects of the presidency are just a few of the areas where scholars have focused their attention in an effort to better understand (and sometimes predict the actions of) the president, his staff, and/or other relevant political actors within the executive branch. In addition, interdisciplinary research on the presidency has merged the growing literature in political science with that of psychology, history, communication, economics, and sociology, among others. As a result, both the quality and quantity of research devoted to presidents and the presidency continues to grow.

This chapter provides an overview of presidential studies and the current state of presidency research. Having a better understanding of topics such as the different eras usually associated with the presidency and the methods of study used by presidency scholars can aid students in learning about the various facets of the institution of the presidency as well as those who have held the office. This chapter considers the general categories used to organize presidents and their presidencies by historical eras, which provides a sense of how the institution itself, along with the day-to-day job responsibilities of the president, has evolved throughout U.S. history. Next, the state of presidency research is considered, including how the various methodological tools now available to presidency scholars have greatly expanded our understanding of presidents as political actors and the presidency as a political institution. Finally, the plan of the book explains how the essays in this volume illustrate the new and emerging trends within presidential studies and how that research provides both a guide and a basis for analysis of the presidency for students. If the 2016 presidential election and the early days of the Trump administration show us nothing else, it is that the presidency continues to challenge the conventional wisdom of presidency scholars while forging new areas of research and exploration.

Presidential Eras

The American presidency remains one of the most fascinating institutions in history, and the powers and intricacies of the office seem to defy comparison to anything before or since. Individual presidents have come and gone, serving their country with varying degrees of success, but the presidency as an institution remains a focal point of political power both nationally and internationally. The presidency of the eighteenth century, as outlined by the framers of the U.S. Constitution, may seem weak compared to the powers that had emerged by the start of the twenty-first century, but the essential characteristics of the American presidency are as recognizable today as they were 230 years ago. Despite wars, scandals, economic turbulence, and even assassinations, the presidency has endured and is one of the most resilient political structures ever created. Still, the powers of the office, along with the public presence of presidents themselves, have varied at different times due to different circumstances (political and otherwise). Generally, the history of the presidency can be divided into three eras: the traditional presidency, the modern presidency, and the postmodern/contemporary presidency.[4]

The traditional presidency includes those presidents from the late eighteenth century until the turn of the twentieth century who "performed within modest limits and largely with unmemorable results." The most notable presidencies during this time include George Washington (1789–1797), Thomas Jefferson (1801–1809), Andrew Jackson (1829–1837), and Abraham Lincoln (1861–1865), all of whom are "towering exceptions" during an era when presidential powers remained modest and limited.[5] Truth be told, the presidency was not a coveted prize for most founding-era politicians, nor was the associated role of commander-in-chief. Particularly during the late eighteenth century, talented public officials had little incentive to seek an office whose risks and uncertainties outweighed the potential benefits, as the presidency offered modest prestige, narrow authority, and meager resources. In most cases, governors of politically prominent states, such as New York, Massachusetts, and Virginia, wielded more power and prestige than the nation's presidents. Although American presidents of the early republic were honored and respected by their fellow Americans, not least because of their service and contributions prior to 1789, they occupied an office that was unassuming and limited, which is just what the framers of the Constitution had intended. Similarly, throughout the nineteenth century, most presidents merely carried out the laws passed by Congress, which assumed the role of the dominant policymaking branch. Despite the political reforms of the 1820s and 1830s, which opened the electoral process to middle- and lower-income voters and eased restrictions on office holding, presidents, for the most part, remained passive participants in national policymaking.

The potential power of the presidency, particularly in shaping the national agenda, waging wars, and connecting with the American public, would not be tapped until the twentieth century. The development of the modern presidency, with all its power and bureaucratic machinery, laid waste to the modestly crafted, humble office erected by the framers. Of the three branches of government, the executive has traveled farthest from its origins and least resembles the intent of its creators. Theodore Roosevelt

(1901–1909) and Woodrow Wilson (1921–1929) were its "architects, as asserters of bold undertakings in domestic and foreign affairs, as gifted mobilizers of public opinion, as inducers of congressional concurrence."[6] With the election of Franklin D. Roosevelt in 1932, a dramatic expansion of the size and power of the federal government began. FDR's presidency (1933–1945) brought with it important changes that would define the modern presidency: enhanced presidential staff resources, a greater presidential role in policymaking, a stronger relationship with the mass public, and a greater presence in the foreign policy arena. Two themes also emerge in explaining the modern presidency, including an increase in expectations for presidential leadership and increased presidential capacity to lead.[7]

These changes were a direct result of FDR's New Deal as well as U.S. involvement in World War II. During this time, the presidency surpassed Congress and political parties as the "leading instrument of popular rule."[8] Harry Truman (1945–1953) and Dwight Eisenhower (1953–1961) continued the influence of the presidency as the lead actor in domestic and international affairs due in part to the Cold War as well as the growth of the U.S. economy. The public presidency would also continue to expand, especially as John F. Kennedy (1961–1963) ushered in the use of television as a potential governing tool.[9] This era is also marked by U.S. dominance as a global and economic superpower, which allowed presidents to pursue extensive domestic policy agendas (such as Lyndon Johnson's (1963–1969) Great Society and the War on Poverty) as well as foreign policy objectives (containing the spread of communism). Yet, the failure of U.S. containment policy in Vietnam would call into question the powers of the modern presidency; both Johnson and Richard Nixon (1969–1974) would be labeled "imperial" presidents for their actions in Vietnam and for Nixon's involvement in and eventual resignation due to Watergate.[10]

By the mid-1970s, with Nixon's resignation and the end of the Vietnam War, the modern presidency had been diminished as necessary resources for presidential power fell "well short of the tasks [presidents were] expected to perform and the challenges to be faced."[11] Some scholars began to argue that the American presidency had entered a new "postmodern" or "contemporary" phase.[12] By the 1980s, not only had divided government become more common (with the White House controlled by one political party and at least one house of Congress controlled by the other), but increasing budget deficits and a rising national debt left presidents fewer opportunities to pursue an aggressive domestic agenda through new federal programs. Instead, Ronald Reagan's (1981–1989) electoral success and popularity was based in part on his promise to reduce the size and power of the federal government. In addition, as the Cold War ended, cooperation in what George H.W. Bush (1989–1993) called "the new world order" became more important than protecting the United

States from the spread of communism and the imminent threat of a nuclear war with the Soviet Union.

The challenges faced by Bill Clinton (1993–2001), George W. Bush (2001–2009), and Barack Obama (2009–2017) represent both the increased powers and diminished capacities of governing that have evolved in recent decades. All three administrations faced trying economic circumstances that severely limited presidential powers over the domestic policymaking agenda. However, Bush expanded presidential war powers with military actions in both Afghanistan and Iraq to preempt and prevent potential threats to national security (known as the Bush Doctrine). In addition, all three presidents had to contend with a political environment dominated by hyper-partisanship and fueled by unyielding, yet fragmented, news media coverage,[13] a situation that has grown worse in the aftermath of the 2016 presidential election and Trump's inauguration in 2017.

President-Centered Approaches

In 1977, Hugh Heclo published a report for the Ford Foundation on the state of research devoted to the presidency, concluding that while the topic itself was "probably already overwritten," there existed "immense gaps and deficiencies" stemming from a lack of empirical research and too much attention paid to topics such as presidential power, personalities, and decision making during a crisis.[14] At the time, many presidency scholars were focusing much of their attention on the presidencies of Eisenhower, Kennedy, Johnson, and Nixon, and topics such as the Cold War, the Cuban Missile Crisis, the Vietnam War, and Watergate fell nicely into the familiar research categories prominent by the mid-1970s. The same categories and themes had been present since the 1825 publication of *The Presidency of the United States* by Augustus B. Woodward, a small pamphlet considered to be the first study of the presidency as a social and political institution. Those categories of study included (1) the man, (2) public politics, (3) Washington politics, (4) executive politics, and (5) didactic reviews (attempts to synthesize the other categories and draw lessons from the presidency).[15] Heclo argued that the field of presidential studies needed more reliance on primary documents, a better understanding of how the presidency works day-to-day (in order to help it perform better), and a broader, more interdisciplinary approach.[16] Despite several "well-intentioned publications" on the presidency, "presidential studies have coasted on the reputations of a few rightfully respected classics on the Presidency and on secondary literature and anecdotes produced by former participants."[17]

Following Heclo's lead, by the early 1980s, presidency scholars began reassessing the trends of their research. Different types of presidential scholarship had emerged during distinct periods, including studies that focused on the formal powers of the executive office, a psychoanalytic approach to understanding the behaviors of presidents, and the informal power structure within the White House and its impact on presidential leadership.[18] Presidential research also tended to focus on a "political-actor perspective," a president-centered approach that often relied on descriptive analyses or anecdotal comparisons between presidents, and suffered from what many scholars referred to as the infamous "n = 1" syndrome.[19]

In 1983, George C. Edwards III and Stephen J. Wayne published *Studying the Presidency*, an edited volume analyzing the state of the sub-field and its various methodological approaches. At the time, presidency scholars were just beginning to grapple with the question of how to more systematically study both presidents and the presidency in a method more befitting the social sciences, generally and political science, specifically. More "theoretically sophisticated and empirically relevant" work was necessary to expand the presidency literature to keep pace with the "phenomenal growth of the presidency: the expansion of its powers, the enlargement of its staff, the evolution of its processes."[20] Challenges in studying the presidency had often come from the unavailability of data, the lack of measurable (particularly quantitative) indicators, an absence of theory, and a lack of transparence for scholars in the behind-the-scenes day-to-day White House operations, all of which "impede the collection and analysis of data, thereby discouraging empirical research." As a result, little about the presidency had lent itself to quantitative and comparative study, other than public opinion, voting studies, and legislative scorecards.[21]

By the early 1990s, a robust discussion had emerged among presidency scholars on how to develop a more rigorous and systematic approach more befitting the traditions of political science to study both the president and the presidency. According to Gary King and Lyn Ragsdale,

> We believe that scholars must concentrate on two important steps to understand the American presidency more fully. First, scholars must move from anecdotal observation to systematic description.... Second, anecdotal observation leaves citizens and scholars without a reliable basis for comparison and analysis.... Presidency watchers of all kinds have an interest in eliminating anecdotal observation and thus reducing the chasm between information and meaning.[22]

Many scholars have maintained an emphasis on presidential leadership and its importance in understanding the role of the president in both policymaking and governing, yet, at the same time began to change the direction of research by relying on a broader theoretical perspective and including extensive data for comparative analysis. Many still rely on Richard Neustadt's classic work *Presidential Power*, first published in 1960, for at least a starting point in their research, while also recognizing the limitations that an individual president can face in effecting political change.[23]

Specific topics contributing to the growing literature on presidential leadership consider changes in the political environment,[24] the institutionalization of and leadership within the executive branch,[25] policymaking and the president's relationship with Congress,[26] and the public presidency and changes in White House communication strategies.[27] For example, according to Samuel Kernell, presidents of the modern era began to "go public," a strategy where the president sells his programs directly to the American people. Going public, which Kernell argues is contradictory to some views of democratic theory, became more common as a result of a weakened party system, split-ticket voting, divided government, increased power of interest groups, and the growth of mass communication systems.[28] More recent scholarship has expanded on Kernell's work, and in doing so has questioned its accuracy due to recent changes in the political and media environment. Edwards argues that presidential messaging is not always successful in changing public opinion on certain issues.[29] And, Jeffrey Cohen argues that the polarization of political parties and the growth and fragmentation of media sources now force presidents to develop innovative public strategies to target key constituencies, a dramatic shift from the more simplified view of going public to a national audience as first argued by Kernell in the 1980s.[30]

Leadership style and presidential personality have also remained salient topics of research. According to Fred Greenstein, the presidential "difference," that is, determining the effect that a president can have on the many facets of his administration, can be best understood by understanding the following factors: public communication skills, organizational capacity, political skill, policy vision, cognitive style, and emotional intelligence.[31] The relevance of James David Barber's work on presidential character is still debated due to its categorization based on psychology and personality types—levels of activity as either active or passive, and affect (or feelings) toward activity as either positive or negative, which point to a president's deeper layers of personality and how that will determine his success or failure.[32] Seeking to better understand the effect of a president's personality on his administration's successes and failures, along with the notion of "presidential greatness," represents another line of inquiry among those scholars interested in the president-centered approach.[33] Perhaps presidential leadership is best summed up by Bert Rockman, who argues that as a topic of study, it is both fascinating and complex that presidents may vary in temperaments, but all are confronted with similar pressures while in office—"it is the manipulable factor in a sea of largely nonmanipulable forces."[34]

Presidency-Centered Approaches

In contrast are scholars who support an institutional approach to studying the presidency, arguing that it is the institution itself—and not individual presidents—that shapes presidential behavior and political outcomes. Many scholars argue that the presidency became institutionalized and politicized throughout the twentieth century, leaving the president as an individual mostly irrelevant in most decision-making processes. Therefore, scholars should rely on a methodological approach, such as rational choice modeling of presidential theory building, as opposed to wasting time trying to understand the role of presidential leadership.[35] For example, Terry Moe explains how presidents are unique in having considerable resources and strategies at their disposal in their job of governing day-to-day. Congress, in comparison, cannot match these executive branch resources in terms of expertise, experience, and information, while the president can act unilaterally in some instances, as well as more swiftly and decisively. Presidents can also make sure that appointees within the executive branch are loyal to him (similar to political patronage), and can also centralize decision making within the White House to increase his own power (policy decisions and implementation, such as through executive orders).[36] Other quantitative approaches have emerged to better understand specific aspects of the presidency as an institution, including unilateral actions by presidents,[37] public appeals,[38] presidential control of the bureaucracy,[39] and war powers.[40]

Other institutional approaches include "new institutionalism," which looks beyond institutions to also include an analysis of the ideas and people that influence those institutions. For example, Stephen Skowronek provides a theory of "political time" by offering a cyclical explanation of presidential power. When a president takes office, the political environment that he encounters is due in part to the actions of his predecessors as well as recent national and world events. As such, the president's circumstances, or the "political time," in which he finds himself in office, will determine how much opportunity he has to enact policy changes.[41]

Louis Fisher has provided an extensive analysis on the legal and constitutional aspects of the presidency, including presidential war powers and the separation of powers between the president and Congress. He argues that the presidency as an institution and the powers that belong to individual presidents are best understood by recognizing that both the presidency and Congress operate within a political environment that also includes the judiciary, the bureaucracy, independent regulatory commissions, political parties, state and local governments, interest groups, and other nations. A president's power, therefore, is determined by cooperation and/or resistance from Congress, the Courts, or other political institutions with whom the president and the executive branch must share power.[42]

Lyn Ragsdale's research relies on three dimensions to explain the presidency as an institution: organization, behavior, and structure. Presidents can make marginal changes to the organization of the presidency, but the office is not reinvented with each new occupant in the White House. She argues that it is through rigorous data analysis across several presidencies that can explain the president's role within the institution of the presidency; ultimately, "the institution of the presidency shapes presidents as much as presidents, during their short tenures, shape the institution."[43]

Erwin Hargrove provides a compelling discussion of how to maintain the debate over the relevance of presidential leadership while still moving forward in developing better research patterns for the discipline. The individuality of the president himself is still an important consideration, including the effect on events and institutions, but only if historical situations and other environmental factors are considered as well. Therefore, individuals do make a difference, but Hargrove wants to know under what conditions this occurs, since the "relative importance of leaders varies across institutions and across time and place." A president, then, deals with practices that are institutionalized, as well as those that are not. These two approaches allow for the consideration of presidential leadership while still providing explanations about the institutional nature of the presidency.[44]

While every significant work on the presidency cannot be included here, it is important to note that since the discussion began more than four decades ago on how to improve the study of the presidency within political science, many notable contributions to the literature have been made by scholars relying on a variety of methodological and/or theoretical perspectives. In addition, the debate among presidency scholars now has the depth and breadth that was missing several decades ago, and healthy disagreements exist on not only what questions should be asked, but how they should be answered. In 2009, an issue of *Presidential Studies Quarterly* included a symposium on the state of presidency research, which highlighted the progress made, touting some of the most influential works being done within the subfield. Broadly speaking, key areas of current research include the president's influence, if any, over public opinion,[45] presidential war powers and other constitutional concerns,[46] presidential control (or lack thereof) over executive branch agencies and the policy agenda,[47] and the president's relationship with the news media,[48] to name just a few. While presidency scholars may disagree on how to approach these and other relevant questions, most would agree that the evolution within presidential studies has had a positive effect on our understanding of the dynamic political institution that is the presidency. As Kenneth R. Mayer puts it,

> We have theories that are useful in analyzing presidential policy making, unilateral action, legislative strategy, and institutional

structure. We have hypotheses, data, and tests. We have unanswered questions. And perhaps most importantly, we have challenges to the conventional wisdom, all of which make the subfield a far more interesting place.[49]

Plan of the Book

This volume takes a current look at the various issues facing the presidency and provides a "state-of-the-art" overview of current trends in the field of presidency research. The collected essays represent concise and engaging discussions on relevant topics within presidency research (and those topics most commonly covered in courses on the presidency) written by some of the leading scholars in the field of presidency research. Each chapter provides a discussion that tells readers "this is what political scientists know" from the perspective of current issues and challenges facing the current and most recent administrations. The goal of the book is to bring together disciplinary debates (for example, the presidency-centered v. president-centered approach to studying the presidency) along with current-event driven discussions about the contemporary presidency.

To begin, Victoria A. Farrar-Myers considers the president's relationship to the Constitution in Chapter 2, and concludes that the recent expansion of presidential powers will continue to provoke controversy about the president's role within a separated system for years to come. The next four chapters look at the president's connection to the political system as well as the public. In Chapter 3, Randall E. Adkins assesses presidential campaigns and elections in the aftermath of the 2016 presidential campaign, and analyzes key changes (including campaign finance, the front-loading of the primary process, and overall candidate strategies) to the process since the early 1970s. In Chapter 4, Julia R. Azari analyzes the connection of presidential governance to political parties, and concludes that the president–party relationship is perhaps currently undergoing a major transformation. Matthew Eshbaugh-Soha explains, in Chapter 5, the lengths that presidents and their advisors now go to in an attempt to shape news coverage and the overall public image of the presidency, yet even the most skilled communicators still face many challenges in this regard. And in Chapter 6, Diane J. Heith shows how presidents now rely on public opinion polls to enhance their leadership of the American public, yet explains how the trend of constant polling in recent White Houses may also constrain a president's ability to lead.

Next, we consider the relationship between the presidency and the other two branches of government. In Chapter 7, Brandon Rottinghaus considers recent trends in the executive-legislative relationship, and concludes that one branch is not completely dominant over the other since each can hold a political advantage at different times and in using unique governing tools. Nancy Kassop explains in Chapter 8 that the relationship between the president and the federal judiciary has many legal as well as political facets, especially when considering the importance of making a lifetime appointment to the Supreme Court. Those who work within the White House, as well as the executive branch as an institution, also offer compelling areas of research. Matthew J. Dickinson considers the crucial link between presidential power, White House staff, and executive branch effectiveness in Chapter 9, showing the challenges that presidents face in managing the many agencies and personnel that make up the federal bureaucracy.

The president's role in the policymaking process at both the national and international levels is considered in the next two chapters. Regarding domestic policy, Jeremy L. Strickler concludes in Chapter 10 that presidents may have expanded their role in recent years as the chief domestic policymaker, yet many political challenges exist that limit the president's ability to implement a domestic policy agenda. And in Chapter 11, Meena Bose shows the evolution of presidential power regarding foreign policy, and suggests that while presidents bear primary responsibility in this area, Congress still maintains an important constitutional function in pursuing foreign policy objectives. Finally, in Chapter 12, Justin S. Vaughn concludes the volume with an analysis of presidential leadership—how it is defined, how presidents attempt to lead, and whether such endeavors make any difference in the day-to-day role of governing.

Notes

1 Lydia Saad, "Trump Sets New Low Point for Inaugural Approval Rating," *Gallup*, January 23, 2017, www.gallup.com/poll/202811/trump-sets-new-low-point-inaugural-approval-rating.aspx?g_source=position1&g_medium=related&g_campaign=tiles.
2 Karlyn Kohrs Campbell and Kathleen Hall Jamieson, *Deeds Done in Words: Presidential Rhetoric and the Genres of Governance* (Chicago, IL: University of Chicago Press, 1990), 14–27.
3 "The Inaugural Address," January 20, 2017, www.whitehouse.gov/inaugural-address.
4 Louis W. Koenig, *The Chief Executive*, 6th ed. (New York: Harcourt Brace, 1996), 2–3. See also Lori Cox Han and Diane J. Heith, *Presidents and the American Presidency*, 2nd ed. (New York: Oxford University Press, 2018), Chapter 1.
5 Koenig, 2.
6 Ibid., 3.
7 Jeffrey Cohen and David Nice, *The Presidency* (New York: McGraw-Hill, 2003), 53–59; and Sidney M. Milkis and Michael Nelson, *The American Presidency: Origins and Development, 1776–2014*, 7th ed. (Washington, DC: CQ Press, 2016), 301–304.
8 Milkis and Nelson, 302.
9 See Lori Cox Han, *Governing From Center Stage: White House Communication Strategies During the Television Age of Politics* (Cresskill, NJ: Hampton Press, 2001), Chapter 2.

10 The term "imperial president" is most often associated with the book of the same title by historian Arthur Schlesinger, Jr. in which he discusses the modern presidency. See Schlesinger, *The Imperial Presidency* (Boston, MA: Houghton Mifflin, 1973).

11 Koenig, 4.

12 For example, see, Ryan Barilleaux, *The Post-Modern Presidency: The Office after Ronald Reagan* (New York: Praeger, 1988); Richard Rose, *The Postmodern President*, 2nd ed. (Chatham, NJ: Chatham House, 1991); and Steven Schier, ed., *The Postmodern Presidency: Bill Clinton's Legacy in U.S. Politics* (Pittsburgh, PA: University of Pittsburgh Press, 2000).

13 Joseph A. Pika, John Anthony Maltese, and Andrew Rudalevige, *The Politics of the Presidency*, 9th ed. (Washington, DC: CQ Press, 2017), 1.

14 Hugh Heclo, *Studying the Presidency: A Report to the Ford Foundation* (New York: Ford Foundation Press, 1977b), 5–6.

15 Ibid., 7–8.

16 Ibid., 31–45.

17 Ibid., 30.

18 George C. Edwards III, John H. Kessel, and Bert A. Rockman, *Researching the Presidency: Vital Questions, New Approaches* (Pittsburgh, PA: University of Pittsburgh Press, 1993), 3–5.

19 Lyn Ragsdale, *Vital Statistics on the Presidency: George Washington to George W. Bush*, 3rd ed. (Washington, DC: CQ Press, 2009), 1–3.

20 Stephen J. Wayne, "An Introduction to Research on the Presidency," in *Studying the Presidency*, eds. George C. Edwards III and Stephen J. Wayne (Knoxville, TN: University of Tennessee Press, 1983), 4.

21 Ibid., 5–6.

22 Gary King and Lyn Ragsdale, *The Elusive Executive: Discovering Statistical Patterns in the Presidency* (Washington, DC: CQ Press, 1988), 2–5.

23 Early examples include works such as George C. Edwards III, *At the Margins: Presidential Leadership of Congress* (New Haven, CT: Yale University Press, 1989); Mark A. Peterson, *Legislating Together: The White House and Capitol Hill from Eisenhower to Reagan* (Cambridge, MA: Harvard University Press, 1990); and Samuel Kernell, *Going Public: New Strategies of Presidential Leadership* (Washington, DC: CQ Press, 1986).

24 For example, see John H. Kessel, *Presidents, the Presidency, and the Political Environment* (Washington, DC: CQ Press, 2001); and Thomas E. Cronin and Michael A. Genovese, *The Paradoxes of the American Presidency* (New York: Oxford University Press, 1998).

25 For example, see John Burke, *The Institutional Presidency* (Baltimore, MD: Johns Hopkins University Press, 1992); Thomas J. Weko, *The Politicizing Presidency: The White House Personnel Office, 1948–1994* (Lawrence, KS: University of Kansas Press, 1995); and Shirley Anne Warshaw, *The Keys to Power: Managing the Presidency* (New York: Longman, 2000).

26 For example, see Charles O. Jones, *Separate but Equal Branches: Congress and the Presidency*, 2nd ed. (New York: Chatham House, 1999); Jeffrey E. Cohen, *Presidential Responsiveness and Public Policy-Making: The Public and the Policies That Presidents Choose* (Ann Arbor, MI: University of Michigan Press, 1997); and William W. Lammers and Michael A. Genovese, The *Presidency and Domestic Policy: Comparing Leadership Styles, FDR to Clinton* (Washington, DC: CQ Press, 2000).

27 For example, see Samuel Kernell, *Going Public: New Strategies of Presidential Leadership*, 4th ed. (Washington, DC: CQ Press, 2007); Jeffrey K. Tulis, *The Rhetorical Presidency* (Princeton, NJ: Princeton University Press, 1987); Roderick P. Hart, *The Sound of Leadership: Presidential Communication*

in the Modern Age (Chicago, IL: University of Chicago Press, 1987); Mary E. Stuckey, *The President as Interpreter-in-Chief* (Chatham, NJ: Chatham House, 1991); John Anthony Maltese, *Spin Control: The White House Office of Communications and the Management of Presidential News*, 2nd ed., rev. (Chapel Hill, NC: University of North Carolina Press, 1994); and Han, *Governing From Center Stage.*

28 Kernell, *Going Public*, 4th ed., 10–11.

29 See George C. Edwards III, *On Deaf Ears: The Limits of the Bully Pulpit* (New Haven, CT: Yale University Press, 2003).

30 See Jeffrey E. Cohen, *Going Local: Presidential Leadership in the Post-Broadcast Age* (New York: Cambridge University Press, 2010).

31 See Fred I. Greenstein, *The Presidential Difference: Leadership Style from FDR to Barack Obama*, 3rd ed. (Princeton, NJ: Princeton University Press, 2009b).

32 See James David Barber, *The Presidential Character: Predicting Performance in the White House*, rev. 4th ed. (New York: Prentice Hall, 2008).

33 For example, see Cronin and Genovese. See also Robert K. Murray and Tim H. Blessing, *Greatness in the White House: Rating the Presidents from George Washington Through Ronald Reagan*, 2nd ed. (University Park, PA: Pennsylvania State University Press, 1994); Arthur M. Schlesinger Jr., "The Ultimate Approval Rating," *New York Times Magazine*, December 15, 1996, pp. 46–51; and Brandon Rottinghaus and Justin S. Vaughn, "Measuring Obama against the Great Presidents," Brookings, February 13, 2015, www.brookings.edu/blog/fixgov/2015/02/13/measuring-obama-against-the-great-presidents/.

34 Bert A. Rockman, "The Leadership Style of George Bush," in *The Bush Presidency: First Appraisals*, eds. Colin Campbell and Bert A. Rockman (Chatham, NJ: Chatham House, 1991), 2.

35 Examples of this approach include Terry M. Moe, "The Politicized Presidency," in *The New Direction in American Politics*, eds. John E. Chubb and Paul E. Peterson (Washington, DC: The Brookings Institution, 1985); Moe, "Presidents, Institutions, and Theory," in *Researching the Presidency*; Burke, *The Institutional Presidency*; and Weko, *The Politicizing Presidency.*

36 For an excellent discussion of Moe's work in this area, see Cohen and Nice, *The Presidency*, 57–59.

37 For example, see William G. Howell, *Power without Persuasion: The Politics of Direct Presidential Action* (Princeton, NJ: Princeton University Press, 2003); and Ryan J. Barilleaux and Christopher S. Kelley, eds., *The Unitary Executive and the Modern Presidency* (College Station, TX: Texas A&M University Press, 2010).

38 For example, see Brandice Canes-Wrone, *Who's Leading Whom?* (Chicago, IL: University of Chicago Press, 2006); and B. Dan Wood, *The Politics of Economic Leadership: The Causes and Consequences of Presidential Rhetoric* (Princeton, NJ: Princeton University Press, 2007).

39 For example, see Andrew Rudalevige, *Managing the President's Program: Presidential Leadership and Legislative Policy Formation* (Princeton, NJ: Princeton University Press, 2002); and David E. Lewis, *The Politics of Presidential Appointments: Political Control and Bureaucratic Performance* (Princeton, NJ: Princeton University Press, 2008).

40 For example, see Douglas L. Kriner, *After the Rubicon: Congress, Presidents, and the Politics of Waging War* (Chicago, IL: University of Chicago Press, 2010).

41 See Stephen Skowronek, *The Politics Presidents Make: Leadership from John Adams to George Bush* (Cambridge, MA: Belknap Press, 1993).

42 See Louis Fisher, *The Politics of Shared Power: Congress and the Executive*, 4th ed. (College Station, TX: Texas A&M University Press, 1998).

43 Ragsdale, 7–13.

44 Erwin C. Hargrove, "Presidential Personality and Leadership Style," in *Researching the Presidency, Vital Questions, New Approaches* (Pittsburgh, PA: University of Pittsburgh Press, 1993), 69–72.

45 For example, see Edwards, *On Deaf Ears*; Canes-Wrone, *Who Leads Whom?*; and Diane J. Heith, *Polling to Govern: Public Opinion and Presidential Leadership* (Stanford, CA: Stanford University Press, 2003).

46 For example, see Louis Fisher, *Presidential War Power*, 2nd rev. ed. (Lawrence, KS: University Press of Kansas, 2004), and William G. Howell and Jon C. Pevehouse, *While Dangers Gather: Congressional Checks on Presidential War Powers* (Princeton, NJ: Princeton University Press, 2007).

47 For example, see Rudalevige, *Managing the President's Program*; and Kenneth R. Mayer, *With the Stroke of a Pen: Executive Orders and Presidential Power* (Princeton, NJ: Princeton University Press, 2001).

48 For example, see Jeffrey E. Cohen, *The Presidency in the Era of 24-Hour News* (Princeton, NJ: Princeton University Press, 2008); Martha Joynt Kumar, *Managing the President's Message: The White House Communications Operation* (Baltimore, MD: Johns Hopkins University Press, 2007); Diane J. Heith, *The Presidential Road Show: Public Leadership in an Era of Party Polarization and Media Fragmentation* (Boulder, CO: Paradigm, 2013); and Lori Cox Han, *A Presidency Upstaged: The Public Presidency of George H.W. Bush* (College Station, TX: Texas A&M University Press, 2011).

49 Kenneth R. Mayer, "Thoughts on 'The Revolution in Presidential Studies,'" *Presidential Studies Quarterly* 39 (2009): 781–785.

2 Presidents and the Constitution

Victoria A. Farrar-Myers

"The executive Power shall be vested in a President of the United States of America." With these 15 words, the framers of the U.S. Constitution established the foundation of presidential power and authority in the American political system. Although the Constitution set out the structure of the presidency, the institution's function has become different than what the framers might have foresaw. Two different models of presidential power and authority have encapsulated the role of the presidency in the American political system since the nation's founding, and frame the transition of the presidency over time. This chapter will examine the constitutional and theoretical foundations of each model, the transition in the role of the presidency over time and its implications, and some of the "shades of gray" found in modern day political struggles involving the president and the Constitution.

Before doing so, however, a brief discussion regarding what is meant by "power" and "authority" herein is warranted. The concept of "power" in political science has been defined from many different approaches, but perhaps none as simply elegant as Robert Dahl's classic "intuitive idea of power" that "A has power over B to the extent that he can get B to do something that B would not otherwise do."[1] To develop a better sense of power as a relation among people, one would need to include references to (a) the "source, domain, or *base*" of one's power; (b) "the *means* or instruments" used by one "to exert power"; (c) "the *amount* or extent" of one's power over another; and (d) "the range or scope" of one's power.[2] With respect to the presidency, the "source, domain, or base" of power varies, including *enumerated power* expressly granted in the Constitution; *implied power* that can be inferred from an enumerated power; *inherent power* held by virtue of the office of the presidency; and *prerogative power* to act in the public good without direction from, and possibly against, existing laws. Once one accepts any of these sources of power as legitimate, the scope of constitutionally permissible presidential action becomes broader.

The concept of "authority" used herein is defined as "the power to affect change and the perceived right to do so."[3] Such a definition incorporates both the formal and informal conceptions of power referenced above as well as a set of shared understandings of expected behavior, or norms, about who or which institution should act in any given context.[4] As with the above, once a shared set of expectations regarding how the presidency should function in the American political system is established, a president would have greater range of what would be seen as constitutionally permissible behavior. Given these conceptions of presidential power and authority, we can now begin to examine the relationship of the presidency and the Constitution.

Article II and the Framers

Article II of the Constitution contains the primary provisions related to the presidency. It starts with the vesting clause set out above, which should be contrasted against the vesting clause for Congress contained in Article I. Where Article II spoke of the executive power, Article I referenced "All legislative Powers." The use of "powers" in Article I combined with the specific and lengthy list of specific legislative powers enumerated for Congress in Article I, Section 8 connote that Congress' authority was limited to the specific grants identified within the Constitution. Such a connotation is consistent with the framers' view that Congress, not the presidency, would be the vortex of power within the American political system drawing power from the other institutions, and thus its powers needed to be contained.

By comparison, the less precise term of "executive power" coupled with the more general description of types of executive powers elsewhere in Article II implies that the presidency would have authority inherent in the nature of the institution. The structural limits of the presidency's authority derived from the vesting clause has received mixed treatment in the judicial branch, as well as remaining an active matter of academic debate.[5] Compare, for example, Chief Justice (and former president) William Howard Taft's majority opinion in *Myers v. United States*, referencing the "unitary and uniform execution of the laws which Article II of the Constitution evidently contemplated in vesting general executive power in the President alone"[6] with Justice Robert H. Jackson's concurring opinion in *Youngstown Sheet & Tube Co. v. Sawyer*, contending that a broad interpretation of the vesting clause results in the equivalent of totalitarianism.[7] Within the structural limits of what constitutes constitutional and unconstitutional presidential action, however, lies a great deal of flexibility and capacity for authority in the functional exercise of "the executive power."

As noted above, Article II contains references to various elements of the executive power, including, most notably, that of Commander-in-Chief, the power to pardon, treaty making and appointment powers, the foundations of the legislative presidency, and the faithful execution clause. Similar to the vesting clause, by comparison to Congress' enumerated powers, the examples of the executive power referenced in Article II are open-ended and less specifically defined. The breadth and lack of limiting definition of these powers have also afforded the presidency greater flexibility and capacity for authority throughout U.S. history.

As will be discussed throughout this chapter, the scope of presidential power and authority has expanded in five primary roles of the presidency, but in each case the foundation for the expansion can be found in the language of the Constitution itself. These roles are:

(1) *Chief Administrator*: A role grounded in the executive power clause (Art. II, Sec. 1, cl. 1), the appointment power (Art. II, Sec. 2, cl. 2), and the power to require written opinions from the head of each executive department (Art. II, Sec. 2, cl. 1).
(2) *Commander-in-Chief*: A role expressly provided for in the Constitution (Art. II, Sec. 2, cl. 1).
(3) *Chief Diplomat*: A role that stems from the treaty-making power (Art. II, Sec. 2, cl. 2), and the power to appoint (Art. II, Sec. 2, cl. 2) and receive (Art. II, Sec. 3) ambassadors.
(4) *Chief Legislator*: A role whose constitutional basis can be found in both Article I, where the president's veto power is addressed (Art. I, Sec. 7), and Article II, where additional powers are given related to giving the State of the Union message, recommending measures to Congress, and convening and adjourning Congress (Art. II, Sec. 3).
(5) *Chief Magistrate*: A role captured by the presidential oath required under the Constitution (Art. II, Sec. 1, cl. 8): "I do solemnly swear (or affirm) that I will faithfully execute the Office of President of the United States, and will to the best of my Ability, preserve, protect and defend the Constitution of the United States."

The *Federalist Papers* offer insight into the framers' perception of the presidency within the American political system, albeit one particular view—that of Alexander Hamilton. Hamilton wrote all 11 of the papers (*Federalist 67–77*) dedicated to the executive. These papers covered all aspects of the Constitution's provisions related to the presidency, including the executive department generally (*Federalist 67*), the mode of electing the president (*Federalist 68*), the president's duration in office (*Federalist 71–72*), and each of the specific executive powers referenced in Article II (*Federalist 73–77*). For the purposes herein, the most relevant papers addressing the presidency are *Federalist* 69 on "The Real Character of the Executive," and *Federalist* 70 entitled "The Executive Department Further Considered." Table 2.1 summarizes each of these papers and includes key quotations from each.

Taken together, these two papers reflect upon what the presidency is not (*Federalist* 69) and what it is (Federalist 70). Hamilton demonstrated in *Federalist* 69, and other papers as well, that the presidency is and will be different than a monarch; that the president will not be a king. His evidence was intended to show the structural limitations on the scope

Table 2.1 Key *Federalist* Papers Regarding the Presidency

#69 (Hamilton)	#70 (Hamilton)
Expounds on the character of the presidency by comparing it with the king of Great Britain.	Makes an argument for unity of the executive and for energy.
Key phrases:	**Key phrases:**
Elected for four years as opposed to "perpetual and heredity prince."	"Energy in the executive is a leading character in the definition of good government."
One has a "qualified negative upon the acts of the legislative body; the other has an absolute."	"A feeble executive implies a feeble execution of government."
One has "right to command the military ... the other in addition to this right, possesses that of declaring war, and of raising and regulating fleets and armies by his own authority."	"The ingredients which constitute energy in the executive are unity; duration; an adequate provision for its support; and competent powers."
"The one would have a concurrent power with a branch of the legislature in the formation of treaties; the other is the sole possessor of the power of making treaties."	"The ingredients which constitute safety in the republican sense are a due dependence on the people, and a due responsibility."
	Unity—"decision, activity, secrecy, and dispatch will ... characterize the proceedings of one man ..."

Source: Alexander Hamilton, *The Federalist Papers: No. 69*, http://avalon.law.yale.edu/18th_century/fed69.asp; Alexander Hamilton, *The Federalist Papers: No. 70*, http://avalon.law.yale.edu/18th_century/fed70.asp.

and power of the executive contained in the Constitution, particularly when compared to the absolute and unchecked authority and power of the King of England. Standing in contrast to *Federalist* 69, showing what the president cannot do, *Federalist* 70 highlights the role that the presidency can serve in the new American political system. More importantly, the foundation for what the presidency became over time can trace its roots to the characteristics that Hamilton analyzes.

The phrase "Energy in the executive is a leading character in the definition of good government" is perhaps both Hamilton's most famous statement on the nature of the presidency and the most critical element of the presidency to explain its growth in power and authority over time. As the American political system faced social, political, cultural, and technological changes, the federal government needed energy to adapt and to grow so it could respond to these changes. The presidency came to be the primary source of the required energy, and, as a result, obtained greater authority to affect change in the American political system.

The *Federalist Papers* are frequently seen as a collective view of the framers' intent regarding the Constitution. Yet, as noted above, Hamilton wrote all the papers specifically addressing the executive. The difference between Hamilton's views and those of James Madison, the primary author of most of the *Federalist Papers*, was not fully exposed in writing until a dispute over President George Washington's 1793 Proclamation of Neutrality declaring the United States' neutrality in the conflict between France and Great Britain. Stemming from a Cabinet-level difference of opinion between Secretary of the Treasury Hamilton and Secretary of State Thomas Jefferson, Hamilton wrote a series of seven essays under the pseudonym *Pacificus*, supporting the president's authority to issue such a proclamation. In response, Jefferson requested that Madison author a response to the *Pacificus* essays. Madison, in coordination with Jefferson who reviewed drafts and provided Madison inside-Cabinet information, penned his own set of five essays under the pseudonym *Helvidius*.

Although Hamilton and Madison addressed the issue of the Neutrality Proclamation from multiple perspectives, for the purposes here, the most fundamental question was, as Hamilton stated in *Pacificus* No. 1, "whether the President in issuing [the Proclamation] acted within his proper sphere, or stepped beyond the bounds of his constitutional authority and duty." Table 2.2 includes key statements related to the presidency's constitutional authority that Hamilton and Madison each made in their respective first essays. After dismissing the legislative and judicial branches as having authority to issue a neutrality proclamation, Hamilton builds his case for why the executive branch has the constitutional authority to do so relying heavily on the authority of the "Executive power" granted under the Article II vesting clause discussed above. Hamilton then reaches the conclusion that "If the Legislature have a right to make war on the one hand—it is on the other the duty of the Executive to preserve Peace till war is declared."[8]

By responding to the *Pacificus* essays, Madison was in a position of trying to refute Hamilton's arguments rather than independently setting out his conception of presidential authority. Nevertheless, from Madison's response, one can discern a much more limited conception of the presidency than what Hamilton articulated. Connecting the presidential action of issuing a neutrality proclamation to tyranny and a prerogative afforded only to the British monarchy, Madison contended that the requisite authority— while to some degree shared among institutions under the Constitution—fell squarely to the legislative branch. Madison's view of presidential authority on this issue is best captured in a statement from his fourth *Helvidius* essay:

> As the constitution has not permitted the Executive singly to conclude or judge that peace ought to be made, it might be inferred from that circumstance alone, that it never meant to give it authority, singly, to judge and conclude that war ought not to be made.[9]

As evidenced in Madison's and Hamilton's separate writings in the *Federalist Papers* and the *Pacificus-Helvidius* essays, the Madisonian and Hamilton models of the presidency were vastly different (see Table 2.3).

Table 2.2 Key Statements from the Pacificus-Helvidius Debates

Hamilton *Pacificus No. 1 (June 29, 1793)*	Madison *Helvidius No. 1 (August 24, 1793)*
"It appears to be connected with [the executive] department in various capacities, as the organ of intercourse between the Nation and foreign Nations—as the interpreter of the National Treaties in those cases in which the Judiciary is not competent, that is in the cases between Government and Government—as that Power, which is charged with the Execution of the Laws, of which Treaties form a part—as that Power which is charged with the command and application of the Public Force." "The enumeration [of certain types of executive powers, such as the treaty-making power] ought rather therefore to be considered as intended by way of greater caution, to specify and regulate the principal articles implied in the definition of Executive Power; leaving the rest to flow from the general grant of that power, interpreted in conformity to other parts ⟨of⟩ the constitution and to the principles of free government. The general doctrine then of our constitution is, that the EXECUTIVE POWER of the Nation is vested in the President; subject only to the exceptions and qu[a]lifications which are expressed in the instrument."	"If we consult for a moment, the nature and operation of the two powers to declare war and make treaties, it will be impossible not to see that they can never fall within a proper definition of executive powers. The natural province of the executive magistrate is to execute laws, as that of the legislature is to make laws. All his acts therefore, properly executive, must pre-suppose the existence of the laws to be executed." "From this view of the subject it must be evident, that although the executive may be a convenient organ of preliminary communications with foreign governments, on the subjects of treaty or war; and the proper agent for carrying into execution the final determinations of the competent authority; yet it can have no pretensions from the nature of the powers in question compared with the nature of the executive trust, to that essential agency which gives validity to such determinations. It must be further evident that, if these powers be not in their nature purely legislative, they partake so much more of that, than of any other quality, that under a constitution leaving them to result to their most natural department, the legislature would be without a rival in its claim."

Sources: Alexander Hamilton, "Pacificus No. I, [29 June 1793]," Founders Online, National Archives, http://founders.archives.gov/documents/Hamilton/01-15-02-0038, [Original source: *The Papers of Alexander Hamilton*, Vol. 15, June 1793–January 1794, ed. Harold C. Syrett (New York: Columbia University Press, 1969), 33–43]; and James Madison, "'Helvidius' Number 1, [24 August] 1793," Founders Online, National Archives, http://founders. archives.gov/documents/Madison/01-15-02-0056, [Original source: *The Papers of James Madison*, Vol. 15, 24 March 1793–20 April 1795, ed. Thomas A. Mason, Robert A. Rutland, and Jeanne K. Sisson (Charlottesville, VA: University Press of Virginia, 1985), 66–74.]

The Madisonian model focuses on the constitutional structure of the presidency. It foresees a stable institutional design over time in which the executive is clearly the second branch of the federal government whose primary constitutional purpose is to serve as a check on Congress. Under

Table 2.3 Madisonian vs. Hamiltonian Models of the Presidency

Madisonian Model	Hamiltonian Model
Constitutional (enumerated) power	Authority (implied or inherent power)/ Vesting clause
Constitution venerated	Constitution is a living document
President as presider	President as leader/energized executive
Second branch (as check)	Potential of unitary executive for growth
Stable institutional design	Room for individual impact on growth of institution
Pre-modern	Modern presidency (Post-modern?)

this model, presidential power is limited to those powers enumerated within the Constitution, and the president serves as a presider who implements the laws enacted by Congress.

Hamilton's model, on the other hand, serves as the foundation for the functional development of the presidency over time. Drawing upon the broad scope of authority implied in the term "the executive power" in the Article II vesting clause and a perception of the Constitution as a living document, the Hamilton model foresees the president as an energized executive and national leader. The institution of the presidency has room for growth in many directions and from many sources. The presidency does not just draw upon the powers enumerated in the Constitution, but also on powers inherent in the presidency and a dynamic conception of authority granted to the institution.

Despite their vastly different conceptions of the presidency, the Madisonian and Hamiltonian models have one fundamental characteristic in common—each is grounded in and stems from the Constitution. Although they emphasize different elements of the Constitution and utilize differing interpretations of the same clauses, neither approach could be considered "unconstitutional." In the words of the early preeminent presidency scholar, Edward S. Corwin,

> In short, the Constitution reflects the struggle between conceptions of executive power: the conception that it ought always to be subordinate to the supreme legislative power, and the conception that it ought to be, within generous limits, autonomous and self-directing.[10]

How this struggle has played out and continually underlies presidential action throughout American history is critical for understanding the institution of the presidency.

The Development of the Presidency as an Institution

Throughout the first century following the ratification of the Constitution, most presidents tended to adhere to the Madisonian model. The nineteenth century saw a litany of presidents—names like Martin Van Buren, Millard Fillmore, Franklin Pierce, James Buchanan, Rutherford B. Hayes, or Chester Arthur, for example—who did little to distinguish their presidency from others. Certainly, exceptions existed, such as Abraham Lincoln, whose exercise of leadership and presidential powers during the Civil War occurred during and in response to a time like no other in American history. Arguments can reasonably be made that presidents like Andrew Jackson or James Polk sought to do more with the presidency than serve as mere presiders, or that the Monroe Doctrine or Jefferson's purchase of the Louisiana Territory pushed the boundaries of a strict construction of the Constitution. These notable presidents, however, were the exception rather than the rule during the 1800s. During this time, Congress reigned as the first branch of government, as contemplated in the Madisonian structure of the Constitution, and the president generally took a secondary, and sometimes almost non-existent, role in addressing the major political events and policy issues facing the national government.

The period of the late nineteenth century and early twentieth century saw a number of changes in the nation. Among many other changes, the industrial revolution created economic opportunities and migration to the cities, but also led to greater disparities in wealth between capitalists and the labor force, as well as unsafe working conditions. Increased immigration brought to the United States the tired, poor, and huddled masses seeking the American dream, and led to new cultural and social strains on the nation. The emergence of the United States as an actor in the international sphere enabled the country to play greater roles in areas of national and economic interest, but also resulted in entangling alliances and the commitment of troops abroad in new ways.

These changes led to greater demands on the federal government, as well as opened up new policy areas in which the government could legislate or regulate. Congress and the presidents during this era could have continued to follow the Madisonian model of congressional dominance. However, several factors started to tip the balance toward the presidency in its path of functioning as the leading branch of government.

First, actions by individual presidents pushed the boundaries of what had previously constituted acceptable behavior by the Chief Executive. Theodore Roosevelt was the most active president during this era in this regard, but others, such as Grover Cleveland and Woodrow Wilson, who book-ended this era, undertook actions designed to broaden the scope of presidential authority. Even William McKinley, who as a member of the House of Representatives led the congressional efforts to revise the nation's tariff policy under the tariff act that bears his name, carved out a role for the presidency in setting the policy direction of what became the Dingley Tariff, which President McKinley signed into law.[11]

On the other end of Pennsylvania Avenue, Congress played its own role in facilitating the growth of presidential authority during this era

throughout many institutional interactions between the presidency and
Congress. In some instances, Congress would acquiesce to presidential
action, either through its silence in the wake of such action or affirma-
tively supporting the president. Other times, Congress would delegate
or cede its authority to the presidency. One must note that Congress
cannot delegate its constitutional powers, but allowing the presidency
to exercise authority in situations when Congress would have the constitutional basis to act as well is a different matter.[12] Consider, for example,
that Congress cannot delegate its power to declare war to the president,
but it can stand by or expressly support the president if the Commander-in-Chief commits troops in a military engagement abroad. In doing so,
Congress would effectively be ceding authority to the presidency. A third
way in which Congress would enhance presidential authority would be to
codify the requirement for executive action through legislation, even in
areas where the president was not previously expected to act.[13]

Rather than through one or a group of specific actions, the growth
of presidential authority during this era occurred in iterations from one
interaction between Congress and the presidency to another. The constitutional structure of the presidency had not changed, but rather a set
of norms began to develop around shared understandings of expected
behavior; around circumstances and in situations in which the president,
regardless of the individual in office, was expected to act. As those shared
understandings were carried out in practice time after time, they became
more ingrained in the institution of the presidency and supported presidential actions, often without question, where a decade or two before the
similar actions would have been inconceivable or at least met with great
resistance.[14]

The presidency of Theodore Roosevelt is sometimes viewed as a point
of demarcation between the "pre-modern president" and the "modern
president" (although others may point to Franklin D. Roosevelt or
perhaps Woodrow Wilson as the first "modern president").[15] Within the
context of the analysis herein, this era represents a transition from the
Madisonian Model to the Hamiltonian Model of presidential leadership
in the American political system, as coming out of this era the American
political system increasingly became centered around an energized, unitary executive leading the nation rather than Congress.

This era also represents a transition from a constitutional theory of
the presidency to a stewardship theory. The constitutional theory, much
like the Madisonian Model, views presidential power as strictly limited.
The presidency only has powers that are either enumerated in the Constitution or granted by Congress under its constitutional powers. The
stewardship theory, on the other hand, posits that the president can do
anything not explicitly forbidden by the Constitution or by laws passed
by Congress under its constitutional powers. Interestingly, Roosevelt
may have been the first occupant of the Oval Office whose presidency

was predicated on the stewardship theory, while his successor, William Howard Taft, may be one of the last presidents ardently adhering to the constitutional perspective.

The stewardship theory shares many perspectives with the Hamiltonian model, but also draws upon an even more expansive view of executive power conceived by John Locke, a political theorist who greatly influenced the founders. More specifically, under this conception, the executive has the prerogative "to act according to discretion for the public good, without the prescription of law, and sometimes even against it."[16] This perspective would permit a president to do anything not forbidden, but also may allow presidential action in ways that are or would seem explicitly forbidden when done in the national interest as determined in the president's discretion.

Although presidents following Roosevelt and Taft may from time to time draw on elements of each of the constitutional, stewardship, and prerogative theory, or tended to one approach or another, without a doubt all presidents since that era have exercised (to varying degrees) more expansive presidential power supported by a greater scope of presidential authority compared to presidents during the nineteenth century. Throughout the twentieth century, the role of the presidency and the institution's powers and authority continued to expand.

The Budget and Accounting Act of 1921, for example, established a central role for the presidency within the budgetary legislative process, where none formally existed before, and helped enhance the president's role as Chief Legislator.[17] FDR's presidency during the two successive crisis periods of the Great Depression and World War II broadened the role of the presidency in both domestic and international affairs, and perhaps, most importantly, cemented a shared understanding that placed the presidency at the center of the American political system. Also emerging from this era, the president's staff specifically and the federal bureaucracy generally, each under the president's leadership as Chief Administrator and Chief Magistrate, expanded greatly, and thus gave the president a broader set of tools to affect policy. Even attempts to restrain the presidency resulting from perceived abuses of presidential power during the Vietnam and Watergate eras can be seen to contribute to the institution's growth. Consider, for example, the Case-Zablocki Act of 1972, or the War Powers Resolution of 1973. Each of these congressional actions was intended to increase congressional checks on the presidency in the areas of international executive agreements and the commitment of troops respectively. Instead, they provided express authorization of certain presidential actions that previously relied upon informal bases of presidential authority, and also provided no effective mechanism to check the presidency if the president did not recognize the restraints as legitimate.[18] Rather than checking presidential authority, these provisions coupled with congressional acquiescence to the presidency in the areas of executive agreements and commitment of troops bolstered presidential authority as chief diplomat and Commander-in-Chief.

The Unilateral Presidency

The presidency's authority continued to grow in the late twentieth century, continuing into the twenty-first century, albeit in a somewhat controversial fashion through the expansion of the unilateral presidency. The unilateral presidency refers to an approach and the tools used in which a president creates, implements, shapes, and generally acts alone with respect to national policy without the involvement of Congress.[19] The tools of the unilateral presidency[20] include executive orders,[21] executive agreements,[22] signing statements,[23] presidential memoranda,[24] presidential proclamations,[25] and national security directives. As one scholar observed, "[t]o pursue a unilateral strategy, of course, presidents must be able to justify their actions on some blend of statutory, treaty, or constitutional; and when they cannot, their only recourse is legislation."[26] Such an objective assessment of the unitary executive, however, does not always play out with such clarity of understanding in the world of presidential politics.

The George W. Bush administration argued that the use of presidential unilateral powers was necessitated by the War on Terror following the terrorist attacks on September 11, 2001. What has been referred to as the "Bush Doctrine" reflected a constitutional interpretation that "would allow the President to take whatever actions he deems appropriate to preempt or respond to terrorist threats from new quarters" but not permit Congress to

> place any limits on the President's determinations as to any terrorist threat, the amount of military force to be used in response, or the method, timing, and nature of the response [because] [t]hese decisions, under our Constitution, are for the President alone to make.[27]

Such an expansive view of presidential authority pushed, and in some critics' eyes exceeded, the boundary of constitutionally permitted presidential action. Yet, even in taking this approach to presidential authority, Bush sought and obtained congressional support for undertaking military operations against Iraq.

One senator who voted against the Iraq measure was Barack Obama, who succeeded Bush as president. Political scientist Robert Spitzer contrasted the "constitutional presidencies" of Bush and Obama, particularly with respect to presidential exercise of the war power.[28] The use of the military in Libya in 2011 saw Obama openly violate two provisions of the War Powers Resolution without any resulting action by Congress seeking to check this exercise of presidential authority. The dichotomy of principled beliefs and executive action between Bush, whose administration argued for unabashed presidential unilateral action, and Obama, the constitutional law scholar, led Spitzer to conclude:

> Nevertheless, in constitutional terms, Bush had the congressional authorization he needed; Obama did not. Ironically, the grotesque scale of, and web of deception surrounding, the Iraqi war suggest that its precedential value for future presidents may be limited, whereas the precedential consequences of Obama's actions ... are more likely to encourage future presidents tempted to engage in unilateral limited military actions.

This insight captures the gray world of constitutional theory and practical politics in which the exercise of presidential authority exists in the twenty-first century.

The Modern Use of the Tools of the Presidency

The use of the tools of the presidency by Obama in the last portion of his tenure in office and by Donald J. Trump during the first 100 days of his administration offers additional evidence of the difficulty in assessing what is appropriate presidential action under the Constitution in light of the real-world policy and partisan battles any president must face. For example, compare each president's approach toward the use of force against Syria for its utilization of chemical weapons against Syrian citizens. Obama characterized such use as a "red line" threat, yet sought congressional approval before authorizing military action. In the end, he did not use military force and instead deferred to a Russian-led diplomatic approach. Trump, on the other hand, authorized a military strike following the Syrian government's use of chemical weapons against its citizens without seeking congressional approval. Despite taking opposite approaches to the same issue, both presidents were criticized: Obama for seeking congressional authority when critics contended none was needed; Trump for acting unilaterally without first seeking congressional approval.

Obama's and Trump's approach toward the legislative presidency on the issue of health care reflect that the earlier discussion herein regarding the Madisonian and Hamiltonian models remains relevant in modern politics. Obama initially sought to take a Madisonian approach to health care, one that relied heavily on Congress' constitutionally mandated legislative process in which Obama sought only to set out principles to help guide the process. When congressional action stalled, Obama switched to a Hamiltonian approach and immersed himself in the legislative process to provide the necessary energy for the Democratic majorities in both chambers of Congress to pass legislation that would become the Affordable Care Act, more commonly known as Obamacare. Trump's approach to health care initially followed that of Obama's, in which after congressional action stalled during the Republican congressional majority's first attempt at legislation designed to repeal and replace Obamacare, Trump sought to energize the process by using his "art of the deal" business negotiation tactics to persuade Republicans. However, when Speaker of the House Paul Ryan (R-WI) pulled the issue from a floor vote due to lack of support, Trump eschewed both his party leader and institutional leadership roles, and placed the legislation and its failure on Speaker Ryan. In saying he did "all he could do," Trump effectively invoked the Madisonian model and its primary role for Congress in the American political system as the underlying cause for an unsuccessful initial attempt at passing health care legislation.

Conclusion

Obama's and Trump's respective approach to executive orders demonstrates the various ways in which presidents can use this tool. Obama used executive orders in lieu of legislative action to advance policy goals and to pressure Congress. In perhaps one of the most defining statements of the latter part of his presidency, Obama proclaimed, "I've got a pen and I've got a phone—and I can use that pen to sign executive orders and take executive actions and administrative actions that move the ball forward."[29] Some saw the statement as arrogant while others contended it stemmed from the partisan realities of having a Republican-controlled Congress not interested in Obama's legislative agenda. Either way, this statement presents a clear reflection of the president's ability in some cases to unilaterally make law to the extent legislation cannot be passed. Another benefit to the presidency afforded by executive orders is their immediacy of action, something that Trump made use of in his first 100 days in office. For Trump, executive orders were agenda setting tools that could immediately establish the framework for future executive branch action and perhaps legislative branch action.

Obama and Trump each continued to use the tools of the presidency, although with different styles and different policy objectives. Such continued use bolsters the institution of the presidency as the center of the American political system, particularly if any objections to such use appear to be on policy or partisan grounds, and not on the authority of the institution for the president to employ each tool. One could even argue that in the waning stages of the Obama presidency and the early term of the Trump administration, Congress has missed an opportunity to reassert itself in legislative-executive institutional interactions. Certainly, if there ever were an opportunity in which Congress could reign in and check the exercise of presidential authority, it would be during a time in which Congress is facing a perceived "lame duck" president followed by a politically inexperienced successor. Yet, Congress' unwillingness to utilize its constitutionally granted power to chip away at the informal authority and set of expectations that has come to define the presidency serves only to further ensure that the presidency will continue to function as the predominant institution in the American political system, even if the formal structure of the Constitution seems as if it was designed to have the president serve a different role.

Notes

1 Robert A. Dahl, "The Concept of Power," *Systems Research and Behavioral Science* 2 (1957): 201–215.
2 Ibid., 203.
3 Victoria A. Farrar-Myers, *Scripted for Change: The Institutionalization of the American Presidency* (College Station, TX: Texas A&M University Press, 2007), 8.
4 Ibid., 3.
5 For comparison, see Saikrishna B. Prakash and Michael D. Ramsey, "The Executive Power of Foreign Affairs," *Yale Law Journal* 231 (2001): 231–356; Curtis A. Bradley and Martin S. Flaherty, 2003, "Executive Power Essentialism and Foreign Affairs: A Critique of the Vesting Clause Thesis," Fordham University School of Law, Fordham Law Faculty Colloquium Papers, Paper 3, 2003, www.pegc.us/archive/Unitary%20Executive/vesting_clause_crit.pdf.
6 *Myers v. United States*, 272 U.S. 52, 135 (1926).
7 *Youngstown Sheet & Tube Co. v. Sawyer*, 343 U.S. 579, 641 (1952) (Jackson, J., concurring).
8 All quotations in the above paragraph are attributable to: Alexander Hamilton, "Pacificus No. I, [29 June 1793]," Founders Online, National Archives, http://founders.archives.gov/documents/Hamilton/01-15-02-0038. [Original source: *The Papers of Alexander Hamilton*, Vol. 15, June 1793–January 1794, ed. Harold C. Syrett (New York: Columbia University Press, 1969), 33–43.]
9 James Madison, "'Helvidius' Number 4, [14 September] 1793," *Founders Online,* National Archives, http://founders.archives.gov/documents/Madison/01-15-02-0070. [Original source: *The Papers of James Madison*, Vol. 15, *24 March 1793–20 April 1795*, ed. Thomas A. Mason, Robert A. Rutland, and Jeanne K. Sisson (Charlottesville, VA: University Press of Virginia, 1985) 106–110.]
10 Edward S. Corwin, "The Presidency in Perspective," *The Journal of Politics* 11 (1949): 7–13.
11 Farrar-Myers, *Scripted for Change*, 117–137.
12 The Supreme Court has noted that, "The true distinction, therefore, is, between the delegation of power to make the law, which necessarily involves a discretion as to what it shall be, and conferring an authority or discretion as to its execution, to be exercised under and in pursuance of the law. The first cannot be done; to the latter no valid objection can be made." *J. W. Hampton, Jr. & Co. v. United States*, 276 U.S. 394, 407 (1928).
13 For example, Congress passed the Interstate Commerce Act of 1887 to help regulate the railroad industry, and this act, in part, granted the president the authority to appoint commissioners to the newly created Interstate Commerce Commission. Prior to the act, the Chief Executive had no formal means to influence railroad rate regulation, but as a result of this legislation,

"the president's ability, as set forth in the act, to appoint commissioners and remove them with reason provided the presidency with the opportunity to influence the direction of the commission." Quoted in Farrar-Myers, *Scripted for Change*, 88.

14 For an analysis of the growth of the presidency during this era, see Farrar-Myers, *Scripted for Change*.

15 For a general discussion regarding both traditional and alternative views regarding the start of the "modern presidency," see David K. Nichols, *The Myth of the Modern Presidency* (University Park, PA: Pennsylvania State University Press, 2010).

16 John Locke, *Second Treatise of Civil Government*, Sec. 160 (Of Prerogative), 1690, http://press-pubs.uchicago.edu/founders/documents/a2_1_1s1.html.

17 As Berman noted, "Prior to 1921 ... [t]he President played only a limited role in formulating the national budget" (p. 3), but following the legislation the president, through the newly created Bureau of the Budget whose head was a personal assistant to the president and not subject to Senate confirmation, played a central role in coordinating and revising the budgetary estimates from each separate department in the government's bureaucracy. See Larry Berman, *The Office of Management and Budget and the Presidency, 1921–1979* (Princeton, NJ: Princeton University Press, 1979).

18 For a discussion of executive agreements, see Kiki Caruson and Victoria A. Farrar-Myers, "Promoting the President's Foreign Policy Agenda: Presidential Use of Executive Agreements as Policy Vehicles," *Political Research Quarterly* 60 (2007): 631–644. For a discussion of the War Powers Resolution, see Victoria A. Farrar-Myers, "Transference of Authority: The Institutional Struggle over the Control of the War Power," *Congress & the Presidency* 25 (1998): 183–197.

19 For example, see William G. Howell, *Power without Persuasion: The Politics of Direct Presidential Action* (Princeton, NJ: Princeton University Press, 2003).

20 William G. Howell, "Unilateral Powers: A Brief Overview," *Presidential Studies Quarterly* 35 (2005): 417.

21 For example, see Kenneth Mayer, *With the Stroke of a Pen: Executive Orders and Presidential Power* (Princeton, NJ: Princeton University Press, 2002).

22 For example, see Caruson and Farrar-Myers, "Promoting the President's Foreign Policy Agenda."

23 For example, see Christopher S. Kelley and Bryan W. Marshall, "The Last Word: Presidential Power and the Role of Signing Statements," *Presidential Studies Quarterly* 38 (2008): 248–267.

24 For example, see Phillip J. Cooper, "Presidential Memoranda and Executive Orders: Of Patchwork Quilts, Trump Cards, and Shell Games," *Presidential Studies Quarterly* 31 (2001): 126–141.

25 Brandon Rottinghaus and Jason Maier, "The Power of Decree: Presidential Use of Executive Proclamations, 1977–2005," *Political Research Quarterly* 60 (2007): 338–343.

26 Howell, "Unilateral Powers," 417.

27 John C. Yoo, "The President's Constitutional Authority to Conduct Military Operations against Terrorists and Nations Supporting Them (Memorandum Opinion for the Deputy Counsel to the President)," 2001, www.justice.gov/sites/default/files/olc/opinions/2001/09/31/op-olc-v025-p0188_0.pdf.

28 Robert J. Spitzer, "Comparing the Constitutional Presidencies of George W. Bush and Barack Obama: War Powers, Signing Statements, Vetoes," *White House Studies* 12 (2013): 125–146.

29 Barack Obama, "Remarks by the President before Cabinet Meeting," January 14, 2014, https://obamawhitehouse.archives.gov/the-press-office/2014/01/14/remarks-president-cabinet-meeting.

3 Presidential Campaigns and Elections

Randall E. Adkins

The fundamental goal of political parties is to win public office. Bill Clinton once contrasted the two major parties stating, "Democrats want to fall in love, and Republicans just fall in line."[1] *Under normal circumstances* winning in contemporary presidential campaigns follows a blueprint that includes finding the best candidate available, raising as much money as possible, hiring the most qualified campaign staff possible, surveying the public to determine the best issues on which to run, and communicating that message to voters.

The 2016 election cycle, however, was far from normal. Previous presidential candidates of the two major parties have typically held high elective office such as governor or senator, been reelected to that office at least once, developed significant political experience and policy expertise, and possess a national-level following among the public-at-large. In 2016, however, 17 Republicans declared their intention to run for president, including nine former or current governors, five current or former senators, two business executives, and one neurosurgeon. From that group, caucus-goers and primary voters chose Donald J. Trump, a real estate executive that never held political office, had little political experience and policy expertise, and had developed a national reputation as a reality television star. Karl Rove, former political strategist for George W. Bush, was right when he told New Jersey Governor Chris Christie in 2012 that "clear paths to the nomination were a thing of the past" for Republicans.[2] On the Democratic side, the eventual nominee, Hillary Clinton, received a serious threat from a 74-year-old political independent. Bernie Sanders served in either the House of Representatives or the Senate continuously since 1991, and he most definitely possessed the policy expertise necessary to run for president, but he was not a leader in the Democratic Party—he had never registered as a Democrat.

Sometimes polls are quite revealing. In August 1971, a pollster asked voters for the first time, "Do you feel that things in this country are generally going in the right direction today, or do you feel that things have pretty seriously gotten off on the wrong track?" Generally, the response to that question is upside-down, meaning that more people think the country is off on the wrong track than headed in the right direction.

However, there were three time periods when a majority of the public felt that the country was headed in the right direction for a sustained period. The first was during the Ronald Reagan administration in the mid-1980s, and the second was during the Clinton administration in the late 1990s when the economy was growing after a recession. The third time was during the Bush administration in the months after 9/11. In many respects, Barack Obama did not serve in normal circumstances. In fact, he was elected to the presidency during a financial crisis when answers to the right direction/wrong track question were at historic lows. During Obama's second term, the majority of responses to this survey question were on the wrong track side of the equation, and at one point, in October 2013, by more than a 50 percent difference.[3] High levels of dissatisfaction can foster demonstrations, protests, or radical swings in election outcomes as the electorate seeks to send a message to those in governmental leadership. Whether public officeholders are reelected or defeated, turnover in the nation's capital often leads to policy change and procedural reform.

One way to characterize the presidential selection process in the United States is as an epic struggle between the remarkable influence of party leaders versus individual candidates and their supporters. In the 1820s, the congressional caucus system of party nominations that emerged when George Washington decided not to run for a third term as president broke down as Eastern and Western states decided to each nominate their own "favorite son" candidate. As a result, none of the four candidates vying for the presidency won a majority of the Electoral College, but the bargain struck in the Congress that elected John Quincy Adams infuriated Andrew Jackson and his supporters, and resulted in Jackson winning an overwhelming victory in 1828. By 1832, party nominees were selected by delegates at national nominating conventions, which were seen as a more democratic alternative to the congressional caucus system. The elites soon regained control over the process by gaining control over who were selected as delegates. For example, by 1920 the Associated Press reported that a small group of leaders or "bosses" within the Republican Party traveled to Chicago and met behind-the-scenes at the Blackstone Hotel in a "smoke-filled" room to plan the strategy for the nomination of Senator Warren Harding (R-OH) for president. Meetings like this were the norm for choosing the presidential nominees of both major parties, and this continued for the next few decades. In 1960, however, a junior senator from Massachusetts outmaneuvered Democratic Party leaders and won the nomination over a group of more established candidates. John F. Kennedy entered and won the West Virginia primary to demonstrate that a Catholic could win a heavily Protestant state. This turned the conventional wisdom on its head and convinced party leaders and convention delegates that candidates that could win in the primaries were more electable in the general election. Kennedy's success was soon followed by other major reforms in how presidential candidates are selected in the United States.[4]

By the 1970s, the presidential selection process was clearly candidate-driven.[5] While candidates might still court party elders behind-the-scenes, the road to the party nomination was a long and grueling marathon won by traveling from state to state to visit with small groups of voters over coffee or large groups of voters in high school gymnasiums, running television ads to attract those voters that stayed at home, and raising and spending millions of dollars to fund it.[6] The candidates nominated tended to be the candidates that understood how the process had evolved, recognized the changes in the process, and adjusted their campaign strategies accordingly. Candidates that focused on courting party elders to win the nomination simply lost. In describing the winner of the Democratic nomination in 1976, Kamarck (2009) wrote that Jimmy Carter ultimately "got it."[7] While the one-term former governor of Georgia quickly grasped how the presidential nomination process had changed, more experienced politicians, including Senator Lloyd Bentsen (D-TX), former party chair and Senator Fred Harris (D-OK), former Vice President Hubert Humphrey, Senator Ted Kennedy (D-MA), and Alabama Governor George Wallace, fundamentally did not grasp what was happening. The impact of the reforms was historic. Courting voters became more important than courting party elders. Candidates needed to sell themselves to voters in order to persuade party leaders of their electability in the general.

After the reforms of the 1970s, candidate-centered politics forced candidates to become entrepreneurs in order to be competitive. This means that campaigns start earlier, candidates must raise campaign funds themselves, they must construct sophisticated campaign organizations in individual states to compete in multiple caucuses and primaries, and they must survey the public using polls in order to develop issue positions and campaign strategies that differentiate themselves from the field of candidates while simultaneously resonating with voters. Three big alterations to the nominating environment fueled the emergence of the candidate-centered presidential campaign. These included reforms to the rules of the national and state parties governing how delegates to the national nominating conventions were selected, changes in campaign finance regulation at the federal level, and developing new strategies for reaching voters.

Selecting Delegates

Historically, the process used to select convention delegates was relatively decentralized, with power residing in state parties for the most part, but the methods by which convention delegates were selected changed considerably in the 1970s, and has undergone modest changes since then.[8] As early as 1912, the parties allowed a few states to choose a small number of delegates through preference primaries, but party leaders generally relied on state party conventions to choose most of the national party convention delegates, thereby maintaining a form of informal, but tight control over the nomination process. In 1968, however, the process fell apart. President Lyndon Johnson announced in March that he would "not seek nor accept" the Democratic Party's presidential nomination, and in June the new frontrunner for the Democratic nomination, Senator Robert Kennedy of New York, was assassinated on the evening that he won the California primary. Thus, the Democrats convened that summer at their convention in Chicago without consensus on a nominee, which led party leaders to select a party elder, Vice President Hubert Humphrey. Humphrey was not on the ballot in any of the primaries, which infuriated the anti-establishment faction of the Democratic Party and led to public protests that resulted in police action. The party chairman, Senator Fred Harris, created a commission to make recommendations on reforms in the process for selecting presidential nominees, which was formally known as the Commission on Party Structure and Delegate Selection. Senator George McGovern of South Dakota and Representative Donald Fraser of Minnesota led the commission, which recommended that the delegate selection process be made more open and inclusive. Most states chose to promote openness by selecting convention delegates through binding primaries and caucuses, and both parties in almost every state did so by the early 1980s. Promoting inclusiveness in the Democratic Party led to a change in the demographics of convention delegates from mostly older, white, male, public officeholders or labor union officials, to something that more closely matched the demographics of the party as a whole. Overall, the outcome was that a nomination process once central-ized informally in the hands of the party elites was now decentralized.

The reforms of the McGovern-Fraser Commission started the parties down the road to additional changes. While both major parties estab-lished nominal rules or guidelines for selecting delegates to the national nominating conventions, each party's rules are different and may change from one election cycle to another. For example, following the 2004 pres-idential election, Senate Majority Leader Harry Reid of Nevada success-fully argued that his state should switch to holding caucuses rather than a primary election, and in 2008 Nevada was given the important posi-tion of becoming the first Western state on the nomination schedule. Of course, this forced the Hillary Clinton and Barack Obama campaigns to focus their attention on the Silver State early in the campaign season. In order to gain efficiencies within states such as a common date for primary elections for all federal and state offices in both parties, state party lead-ers often codified the preferred procedures into state law when the ma-jority party held large majorities in their state legislature. Additionally, state parties are permitted to set their own rules governing the process of delegate selection within the state. For example, the Democratic Party has always supported states allocating delegates in proportion to the percentage of the vote a candidate received, but the Republican Party traditionally supported allocating all of the delegates to the candidate that won a plurality of votes in the state. Republicans started to move away from winner-take-all allocation in 2012, and in 2016 those states holding caucuses and primaries prior to March 15 were expected to be proportional with winner-take-all thereafter.[9] Overall, the decentralized nature of the party rules and state laws governing presidential selection offers candidates the chance to think "outside the box" to find the opportunity to think entrepreneurially and seek some competitive advantage over the other candidates.

One of the most controversial issues that resulted from the reforms of the nomination process was the fear among party leaders that reliance on caucuses and primaries would result in the nomination of highly ideological candidates that would be less appealing in the general election. Voter turnout in caucuses and primaries is typically much lower than it is in the general election, and in caucuses and primaries, stronger partisans are typically more likely to turn out to vote than weak partisans. Taken together, these facts understandably generate a recipe for picking presidential nominees that tend to be more ideological or more partisan. Additionally, scholars concluded it was likely that more ideological candidates would defeat the more moderate candidates as weaker candidates leave the race and the field of contenders narrowed.[10] In 1972, one of the more liberal members of the U.S. Senate, George McGovern (D-SD), won the Democratic Party nomination. In turn, Richard Nixon soundly defeated McGovern in the general election and the Democrats quickly became sensitive to the issue of electability. In 2016, Senator Bernie Sanders (I-VT) won many important victories over the frontrunner, Hillary Clinton, in 22 states, including New Hampshire, Michigan, Minnesota, and Wisconsin. Although he trailed Clinton in pledged delegates heading into the convention in Philadelphia, Sanders hoped to convince enough convention delegates to switch their vote. The more centrist Clinton prevailed even though her public approval ratings were weak.

Concerned about the electability of their party's presidential nominees and many other issues, the Democrats created a commission led by North Carolina Governor James Hunt to explore the problem. In the words of Hunt, the major recommendation of the Commission was, "We must also give our convention more flexibility to respond to changing circumstances and, in cases where the voters' mandate is less than clear, to make a reasoned choice."[11] This meant creating a new form of delegates called "superdelegates," who were chosen from among party officials or party officeholders in each state for the purpose of tipping the balance in favor of the more electable candidate in the event that no candidate emerged with a majority of delegates prior to the convention. While many factions within the Democratic Party supported the concept of superdelegates, other factions rose in opposition because they were afraid that those appointed would be primarily white, male office-holders. Between 1980 and 1984, the percentage of female delegates to the Democratic Convention went unchanged, the percentage of Black delegates to the Democratic Convention grew by only three percent, and the percentage of Latino delegates grew by only one percent. By 2008, however, the percentage of convention delegates that were Black and Latino grew to 23 percent and 11 percent, respectively.[12] Ironically, su-perdelegates were of little consequence until the 2008 election, although they were intended to provide party leaders with the power to determine the presidential nominee.

With caucuses and primaries becoming more important to the process of selecting convention delegates, the privileged position that the Iowa caucuses and the New Hampshire primary held as the "first in the nation" events led to another important controversy. Given their relatively small population, each state has been the recipient of several benefits that are not commensurate to their size. Mayer and Busch identify at least three benefits, including increased attention from the presidential candidates and subsequently the news media, influence over the outcome of the nom-ination that is disproportionate, plus other economic and policy benefits that are more challenging to measure.[13] Being first means candidates can spend any amount of time, from a few weeks to many months, campaign-ing in Iowa and New Hampshire, engaging in a massive "ground war" as opposed to an "air war" campaign. In 2004, for example, the candi-dates for the Democratic Party nomination visited Iowa 860 times and New Hampshire 800 times altogether. By contrast, the same group of candidates traveled to the final two states to hold primaries (on June 8), a grand total of six times.[14] Not surprisingly, the news media arrive in both Iowa and New Hampshire to report on the horserace often days or weeks before the candidates do.

Even though these early states play an important "bellwether" role in determining presidential nominations in the post-reform era, they have not always chosen the candidate that eventually won the party's nomina-tion. Often, the boost a candidate gained from winning one, the other, or both early contests was enough to propel his or her reputation from national obscurity to international prominence. In 1984, Gary Hart, a little-known senator from Colorado won 37.3 percent of the vote in the New Hampshire primary, defeating the frontrunner, former Vice Presi-dent Walter Mondale. Hart was immediately considered a serious con-tender throughout the remaining caucuses and primaries, and even won many of the larger states like Florida, Ohio, and California. The effect of performing well in early states on the outcome of caucuses and prima-ries in states later in the nomination season is well documented.[15] More specifically, however, when controlling for factors such as performance in early preference polls before the primaries and campaign spending, many studies agree that doing well in the New Hampshire primary affects who eventually becomes the nominee.[16] With regard to the Hawkeye State, one study found that when controlling for the outcome of the New Hampshire primary, the Iowa caucuses were not that important in determining who becomes the nominee.[17] Another recent study that examined a broader span of time suggested that the Iowa caucuses have influenced party nomination outcomes.[18] Unfortunately, this influence was in some instances unclear because New Hampshire scheduled their primary almost immediately following the Iowa caucuses.

In the post-reform era, many candidates that went on to win their party's nomination failed to win the Iowa caucuses or the New Hampshire primary, but doing so without performing well in one or both states would be a tall order. Not including incumbent presidents, Jimmy Carter in 1976, Walter Mondale in 1984, Al Gore in 2000, John Kerry in 2004, and Barack Obama in 2008 all won the Iowa caucuses on the Democratic side. And Carter in 1976, Dukakis in 1988, Gore in 2000, and Kerry in 2004 all won the New Hampshire primary. On the other hand, only Bob Dole in 1996 and George W. Bush in 2000 won the Iowa caucuses on the Republican side, and Romney effectively tied with Rick Santorum in 2012. In addition, Ronald Reagan in 1980, George H. W. Bush in 1988, John McCain in 2008, Mitt Romney in 2012, and Donald Trump in 2016 won the New Hampshire primary. Since the reforms of the 1970s, only one eventual nominee failed to win either the Iowa caucuses or the New Hampshire primary. In 1992, then Governor Bill Clinton of Arkansas finished second in the Iowa caucuses to Iowa's favorite son, Senator Tom Harkin, and he finished second in the New Hampshire primary to former Senator Paul Tsongas who served in the neighboring state of Massachusetts. The candidates that perform poorly in either or both states generally drop out of the race soon thereafter. This "initial winnowing"[19] refers to candidates that exit the race after the early caucuses and primaries because they are having trouble raising funds, connecting with voters or local party leaders, or simply performing poorly in garnering delegates. Even though no candidate may have accumulated a majority of delegates to the national nominating convention, winnowing continues until only one candidate is left in the race—the last man or woman standing.

Another criticism of the Iowa caucuses and New Hampshire primary is the question of whether they are a good reflection of the nation. The U.S. Census Bureau estimates that in 2015 the state of Iowa was 91.8 percent White and had a median household income of $53,183. New Hampshire was 93.9 percent White and had a median household income of $66,779. The overall U.S. population, however, was only 77.1 percent White and had a median household income of $53,889. In contrast, Lewis-Beck and Squire use an extensive battery of state-level socioeconomic, political, and policy measures to empirically demonstrate that the state of Iowa is more representative than critics claim. In their study, Iowa turned out to be ranked 12th overall when comparing all 50 states on over 50 different factors.[20]

Over the years, many states that previously held caucuses and primaries in the months of April, May, and June chose to move forward in the calendar to the months of February and March to remain meaningful in the nomination process. Mayer and Busch refer to this highly contentious trend as "frontloading."[21] In essence, public officials and voters in states holding caucuses and primaries later in the campaign season grew frustrated as most, if not all but the nominee, was winnowed from the race before caucusing or voting occurred in their state.[22] Thus, voters in these states were typically presented with the choice of ratifying the eventual nominee (the candidate that mathematically wrapped up the nomination) or the eventual nominee and a "protest" or "advocacy" candidate with no mathematical chance of winning. In other words, the controversy was really that the attrition of candidates in early caucuses and primaries structured the decisions of voters in later caucuses and primaries, but the solution was just as contentious. To maintain their "first in the nation" status, every time a state moved their caucuses or primary earlier, Iowa and New Hampshire moved theirs even earlier. The overall effect of frontloading was to essentially compress most of the primary calendar into February and March.

In the 2008 cycle, the state of Iowa moved their caucuses to January 3, and New Hampshire moved their primary to January 8 (in the previous cycle Iowa scheduled caucuses on January 19 and New Hampshire scheduled their primary on January 27). That year, Florida and Michigan moved their primaries ahead of the date set by the Democratic Party for the beginning of the nominating season (February 1), forcing Iowa and New Hampshire to take extreme measures to protect their traditional first-in-the-nation status. Following the 2004 election cycle, under pressure from party leaders in many states that were resentful of the exception that the party had provided to Iowa and New Hampshire, the Democrats formed the Commission on Presidential Nomination Timing and Scheduling to study the issue. Rep. David Price of North Carolina and former Labor Secretary Alexis Herman headed this group.[23] While the Price-Herman Commission recommended that in addition to allowing Iowa and New Hampshire to continue to go first, that Nevada be permitted to hold caucuses and South Carolina permitted to hold their primary before the "window" for the primary season officially opened. The Democratic Party responded to Florida and Michigan's noncompliance by stripping both states of their delegates to the national nominating convention (one-half of the voting delegates were eventually restored). Overall, the result was a primary calendar with a similar pace to previous election cycles, but one that included a Southern state with a higher proportion of Blacks and a Western state with a higher proportion of Latinos.

Figure 3.1 shows how the cumulative percentage of delegates selected within four and eight weeks of the start of the nomination season changed over time. From 1988 to 1996, the percentage of delegates chosen to attend each party's convention within the first four weeks of the nominating season grew to about one-half of the total delegates available at the conventions. The primary reason for this was the creation of a Southern regional primary known as "Super Tuesday." In 1988, the states of Alabama, Florida, Georgia, Kentucky, Louisiana, Mississippi, Oklahoma, Tennessee, and Texas agreed to hold their primaries on March 8. The purpose in doing so was to allow the Southern states to unite in their support of a moderate to conservative Democrat who would better represent the interests of the South.[24] Unfortunately, front-runner Michael Dukakis of Massachusetts and Jesse Jackson split the vote that day with Senator Al Gore of Tennessee. Since then, other states followed the lead of the South, moving their primaries forward, either on their own or with other states in their region.[25]

Over the past four decades, the first four weeks of the primary calendar saw some volatility in the cumulative percentage of delegates selected to the national nominating conventions. However, during the first eight weeks it grew from about 30 percent in 1972 to about 70 percent by 1996, and that trend has been generally maintained ever since. In 2012, the parties spread the dates beyond the eight-week window by moving the Iowa caucuses and New Hampshire primary up to early January, and fewer states participated in Super Tuesday. By 2016, however, the parties returned to something closer to the normal pattern. Ridout and Rottinghaus observed that the frontloading strategy generally pays off for states that move their caucuses or primary up in the calendar in terms of a

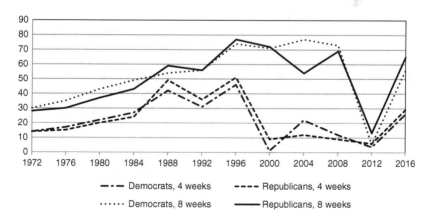

Figure 3.1 Cumulative Percentage of Delegates Selected by End of Fourth Week and End of Eighth Week during the Primary Season by Party, 1972–2016

greater number of campaign visits by candidates and increased spending on campaign advertisements.[26] Mayer and Busch found frontloading achieves the principal goal of the parties, which is to lock in the eventual nominee more quickly, but the cost of shortening the primary calendar is that campaign organization and communication suffer, which subsequently affects the quality of information that voters have to make decisions.[27]

In some election cycles, entering the caucuses and primaries in every state has been necessary. In most years, the length of presidential campaigns following the New Hampshire primary is quite short, as candidates are winnowed from the field relatively early due to poor performance in the frontloaded states. In 2008, however, for the first time since 1988, a campaign for a party's presidential nomination lasted from the Iowa caucuses all the way to the party convention. It is important to recognize that Dukakis wrapped up the nomination relatively handily even in the lengthy 1988 Democratic nomination contest because that year Jackson remained in the campaign primarily to bring attention to the issues that he believed were important for the Democratic Party to address at the convention, and possibly to earn a spot as vice president on the ticket. Traditionally, the states holding primaries later in the calendar served the function of allowing the frontrunner to consolidate or "mop up" the remaining support necessary to enter the convention with a majority of delegates, and in later years, even begin competing against the opposing candidate in the fall campaign.[28] This long "interregnum" period is clearly a product of frontloading, and has dramatically increased the need for a well-financed nomination campaign.[29]

For the Democrats in 2008, there was no time to mop up the mess of a frontloaded schedule because the remaining primaries served as a continuation of the battleground phase of the campaign. Throughout 2007, Hillary Clinton was the quintessential frontrunner, leading her closest rival Barack Obama in fundraising, endorsements from public officials, and in the preference polls. In the latter months of 2007, however, Obama quietly chiseled away at her lead in every category, and then won the Iowa caucuses by nine percent. Clinton quickly licked her wounds and flew to the Northeast, narrowly defeating Obama by 2.6 percent in the New Hampshire primary. She followed her win there with a victory in the Nevada caucuses, but Obama handily defeated her in the South Carolina primary. On Super Tuesday, Clinton won eight of 15 primaries, including California, but Obama won the remaining seven primaries and six of the seven states holding caucuses. The race was dead even, but from that point until the convention it was a horserace that Obama always led by just a nose. Clinton remained in the race and fought from behind with a campaign reminiscent of Senator Ted Kennedy's challenge to incumbent President Jimmy Carter in 1980. John McCain, on the other hand, wrapped up the Republican nomination rather quickly once the primary season started, despite troubles in his campaign in the summer of 2007.

Table 3.1 and Table 3.2 show the results of the caucuses and primaries, by state, for both parties in 2016.

Unlike 2008, in 2016, Clinton won the battle and the war. In 2008, Clinton won the battle over voters, netting approximately 200,000 more votes than Obama, but lost the war because she lost the Democratic nomination to Obama, who was better organized in caucus states.[30] Her campaign did not make that mistake again. Although her principal opponent, Bernie Sanders, crisscrossed the country speaking to large, enthusiastic crowds, Clinton won over 3.7 million more votes in Democratic primaries, won 54 percent of delegates selected in caucuses and primaries, and 84 percent of superdelegates. Like 2008, Clinton struggled in caucus states (Sanders won 12 of 14), but she won arguably the two most important, Iowa and Nevada, because they were first. Overall, she won only about one-third of convention delegates selected by states holding caucuses in 2008, but her campaign raised that to almost 45 percent in 2016.[31]

In 2012, the Republicans continued their pattern of falling in line behind their frontrunner, Mitt Romney, but that was not the case in 2016 in

Table 3.1 Results of Democratic and Republican Caucuses, 2016

		Democrats		Republicans			
	Date	Clinton	Sanders	Cruz	Kasich	Rubio	Trump
Iowa	Feb. 1	49.9	49.6	27.6	1.9	23.1	24.3
Nevada (D)	Feb. 20	52.6	47.3				
Nevada (R)	Feb. 23			21.4	3.6	23.9	45.9
Alaska (R)	Mar. 1			36.4	4.1	15.1	33.5
Colorado (D)	Mar. 1	40.4	59.8				
Minnesota	Mar. 1	38.4	61.6	29.0	5.8	36.5	21.3
Kansas	Mar. 5	32.3	67.7	48.2	10.7	16.7	23.3
Kentucky (R)	Mar. 5			31.6	14.4	16.4	35.9
Maine (R)	Mar. 5			45.9	8.0	12.2	32.6
Nebraska (D)	Mar. 5	53.3	46.7				
Maine (D)	Mar. 6	35.5	64.3				
Hawaii (R)	Mar. 8			32.7	10.6	13.1	42.4
District of Columbia (R)	Mar. 12			12.4	35.5	37.3	13.8
Wyoming (R)	Mar. 12			66.3	0.0	19.5	7.2
Idaho (D)	Mar. 22	21.2	78.0				
Utah	Mar. 22	20.3	79.3	69.2	16.8	0.0	14.0
Alaska (D)	Mar. 26	18.4	81.6				
Hawaii (D)	Mar. 26	30.0	69.8				
Washington (D)	Mar. 26	27.1	72.7				
Wyoming (D)	Apr. 9	44.3	55.7				
North Dakota (D)	Jun. 7	25.6	64.2				

Source: www.politico.com/2016-election/primary/results/map/president.

Table 3.2 Results of Democratic and Republican Primaries, 2016

		Democrats		Republicans			
	Date	*Clinton*	*Sanders*	*Cruz*	*Kasich*	*Rubio*	*Trump*
New Hampshire	Feb. 9	38.0	60.4	11.7	15.8	10.6	35.3
South Carolina (R)	Feb. 20			22.3	7.6	22.5	32.5
South Carolina (D)	Feb. 27	73.5	26.0				
Alabama	Mar. 1	77.8	19.2	21.1	4.4	18.7	43.4
Arkansas	Mar. 1	66.3	29.7	30.5	3.7	24.9	32.8
Georgia	Mar. 1	71.3	28.2	23.6	5.6	24.4	38.8
Massachusetts	Mar. 1	50.1	48.7	9.6	18.0	17.9	49.3
Oklahoma	Mar. 1	41.5	51.9	34.4	3.6	26.0	28.3
Tennessee	Mar. 1	66.1	32.4	24.7	5.3	21.2	38.9
Texas	Mar. 1	65.2	33.2	43.8	4.2	17.7	26.7
Vermont	Mar. 1	13.6	86.1	9.7	30.4	19.3	32.7
Virginia	Mar. 1	64.3	35.2	16.9	9.4	31.9	34.7
Louisiana	Mar. 5	71.1	23.2	37.8	6.4	11.2	41.4
Idaho (R)	Mar. 8			45.4	7.4	15.9	28.1
Michigan	Mar. 8	48.3	49.8	24.9	24.3	9.3	36.5
Mississippi	Mar. 8	82.6	16.5	36.3	8.8	5.1	47.3
Florida	Mar. 15	64.4	33.3	17.1	6.8	27.0	45.7
Illinois	Mar. 15	50.5	48.7	30.3	19.7	8.7	38.8
Missouri	Mar. 15	49.6	49.4	40.7	9.9	6.1	40.9
Ohio	Mar. 15	56.5	42.7	13.1	46.8	2.9	35.6
North Carolina	Mar. 15	54.6	40.8	36.8	12.7	7.7	40.2
Arizona	Mar. 22	57.6	39.9	24.9	10.0	13.3	47.1
Wisconsin	Apr. 5	43.1	56.6	48.2	14.1	1.0	35.1
New York	Apr. 19	58.0	42.0	14.5	25.1	–	60.4
Connecticut	Apr. 26	51.8	46.4	11.7	28.4	–	57.9
Delaware	Apr. 26	59.8	39.2	15.9	20.4	0.9	60.8
Maryland	Apr. 26	63.0	33.2	18.9	23.0	0.7	54.4
Pennsylvania	Apr. 26	55.6	43.6	21.6	19.4	0.7	56.7
Rhode Island	Apr. 26	43.6	54.6	10.6	24.5	0.6	63.6
Indiana	May 3	47.5	52.5	36.6	7.6	0.5	53.3
Nebraska (R)	May 10			18.4	11.4	3.6	61.4
West Virginia	May 10	35.8	51.4	9.0	6.7	1.4	77.0
Oregon	May 17	44.0	56.0	17.0	16.3	–	66.6
Washington (R)	May 24			10.5	9.8		75.8
Kentucky (D)	May 27	46.8	46.3				
California	Jun. 7	55.8	43.2	9.2	11.3	–	75.3
Montana	Jun. 7	44.6	51.1	9.4	6.9	3.3	73.7
New Jersey	Jun. 7	63.3	36.7	6.1	13.3	–	80.6
New Mexico	Jun. 7	51.5	48.5	13.3	7.6	–	70.7
South Dakota	Jun. 7	51.0	49.0	17.0	15.9	–	67.1
District of Columbia (D)	Jun. 14	78.7	21.1				

Source: http://www.politico.com/2016-election/primary/results/map/president.

Note: "–" indicates that the candidate was not listed on the ballot.

the Grand Old Party. An unusually large number of candidates declared their intent to seek the Republican nomination. Of the 17 candidates that chose to seek the Republican nomination, nine were current or former governors, five were current or former senators, two were business executives, and one was a neurosurgeon. Five of those candidates failed to gain any traction in the polls and withdrew before the primaries. Of the remaining candidates, seven withdrew prior to Super Tuesday and one immediately thereafter. Still in the race were Senator Ted Cruz of Texas, Ohio Governor John Kasich, Senator Marco Rubio of Florida, and business executive Donald J. Trump. Given his high name recognition due to his status as a reality television host, Trump made an immediate splash when he entered in June 2015. Once the voting started, Trump found it rather easy to gain a plurality of the vote in almost every state, starting with New Hampshire, Nevada, South Carolina, and seven of nine primaries on Super Tuesday. Trump did not win the majority of any state until his home state of New York on April 19, but then pulled off a series of impressive victories in Northeastern states the following week. By May 4, Cruz and Kasich exited the race, leaving Trump the presumptive nominee. Many mainstream Republicans continued to oppose Trump's nomination both before and at the convention, including Romney and former senior advisor to George W. Bush, Karl Rove. Neither George H.W. Bush nor George W. Bush ever endorsed Trump, even after he secured the Republican nomination.

As performance in caucuses and primaries became the means of nominating candidates for president, the political cues taken by voters become important to study. First, while newspaper endorsements are highly sought after by campaigns, their effect on voters appears to be marginal.[32] Second, endorsements by celebrities with a national following such as Oprah Winfrey's endorsement of Obama in 2008 or Rev. Jerry Falwell, Jr.'s endorsement of Trump days before the Iowa caucuses in 2016 sometimes matter in important ways.[33] Third, political organizations often endorse candidates, which subsequently encourages many members of the group to support the candidate endorsed.[34] In 2004, the endorsement of Democratic candidate John Kerry by the firefighters unions was important to his victory in the caucuses. Last, and more importantly, it seemed that in recent election cycles the influence of party leaders over the nomination outcomes was growing. Studies showed that candidates led in the polls reported by the news media, and endorsements by public officials clearly mattered in the minds of voters during the primaries.[35] Effectively, party leaders were reasserting their influence over the presidential nomination process during the "invisible primary" period before the Iowa caucuses. By working together, the Republicans appeared to gain control over their process much sooner than the Democrats who initially found it more difficult to fall behind a nominee. In 2012, the Republican establishment eventually fell behind Romney, in part, because the field of candidates was one of the weakest in decades. The 2016 election cycle proved to be uncommonly disciplined on the Democratic side and exceptionally unruly for Republicans. Democrats quickly fell behind Clinton as the heir apparent to Obama's legacy. Republican Party leaders were initially divided among a large field of qualified candidates and failed to coordinate their support behind any single frontrunner. As a result, they were flummoxed as Trump marched to their party's nomination, turning small pluralities in early states into strong majorities in the later states of the primary season. Noel proposes that it is possible the political environment has changed (e.g. Super PACs, new media), the divisions among Republican leaders were stronger than anticipated, or Donald Trump's entry into the race simply disrupted the normal rhythm of the race.[36]

Raising Campaign Funds

Congress fortified the candidate-centered environment with passage of the Federal Election Campaign Act (FECA).[37] This comprehensive law passed in 1971, along with subsequent amendments, limited campaign contributions from individuals and political action committees, created a public finance option for both the primaries and the general election, and established a government agency responsible for disclosure and enforcement called the Federal Election Commission. Under this law, party organizations would no longer fund presidential campaigns, because their contributions to candidate campaigns were severely limited. Instead, candidates were expected to seek contributions from individuals (up to a $1,000) and political action committees (up to $5,000) in both the primaries and the general election. This also meant that candidates needed to devote significant time and resources building up personal and political support networks to fund their campaigns. Following the passage of FECA, campaign fundraising and spending grew exponentially, and criticism of the role of campaign fundraising and spending in the presidential selection process also increased. Figure 3.2 shows the growth of campaign contributions and expenditures by campaigns since the passage of FECA.

A public finance option was also created to help level the playing field at the presidential level. In the primaries, candidates who agreed to abide by state-to-state spending caps were awarded a matching grant from the government for the first $250 of any contribution they received from an individual. During the general election, both major party presidential nominees were awarded a grant from the federal government to level the playing field (if they pledged not to raise additional funds on their own). Table 3.3 shows the total of how much candidates of both major parties have been provided in both matching funds during the primaries, for the party conventions, and in public funds during the general election dating back to 1976.

The public funding system created in the 1970s essentially collapsed between 2000 and 2012, but the antecedents of the collapse were evident as early as 1996. Senator Bob Dole of Kansas emerged as the Republican nominee from a bruising primary campaign as other candidates were winnowed from the race. Dole had little cash on hand when he

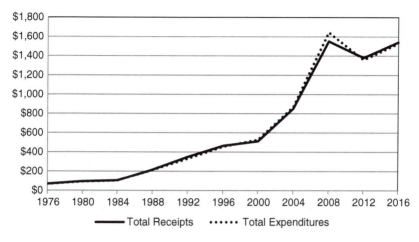

Figure 3.2 Total Contributions and Spending by Presidential Candidates (in millions), 1976–2016

Source: Numbers are from summary reports filed December 31 for each presidential campaign year. http://classic.fec.gov/press/campaign_finance_statistics.shtml

Note: Numbers are not adjusted for inflation.

Table 3.3 Total Public Funding in Presidential Elections (in millions), 1976–2016

Year	Primaries	Conventions	General Election
1976	$249,49,510.06	$41,49,629.73	$436,40,000.00
1980	$314,31,659.29	$88,32,000.00	$631,22,304.00
1984	$365,19,404.83	$161,60,000.00	$808,00,000.00
1988	$675,49,607.72	$184,40,000.00	$922,00,000.00
1992	$434,32,630.82	$220,96,000.00	$1104,80,000.00
1996	$585,38,356.15	$247,28,000.00	$1526,40,000.00
2000	$622,61,373.56	$295,46,690.00	$1477,33,452.00
2004	$284,33,885.61	$298,48,000.00	$1492,40,000.00
2008	$217,28,501.14	$336,41,520.00	$841,03,800.00
2012	$0.00	$364,96,600.00	$0.00
2016	$10,88,929.29	–	$0.00

Source: http://classic.fec.gov/press/bkgnd/fund.shtml.

Notes: In the primaries, eligible candidates may receive up to $250 in public funds to match each individual contribution. If candidates accept public funds in the primaries, they are limited in spending to $10 million plus a cost-of-living adjustment over the base year of 1974. The Democratic and Republican candidates that win the party nominations are eligible to receive grants to cover all expenses in the general election. If the Democratic and Republican nominees accept these public funds, then they are limited to spending $20 million plus a cost of living adjustment over the base year of 1974, and must agree not to raise additional private contributions. On April 3, 2014, President Barack Obama signed legislation to end the public funding of presidential nomination conventions.

mathematically wrapped up the nomination because he accepted federal matching funds, and candidates that accept federal matching funds during the primaries must abide by state-by-state spending limits. The total of those state-by-state spending limits for all 50 states effectively created a national cap on what Dole could spend during the primary season. Thus, his campaign operated on fumes through the interregnum period, from mid-March until the party convention in San Diego in August.[38] That year the state-by-state limits totaled $37.1 million (plus campaigns could raise additional sources for legal and accounting expenses), but Dole's campaign needed every bit of it just to win the nomination, and he emerged with a substantial campaign debt that was tough to eliminate. In contrast, the incumbent president, Bill Clinton, faced no opposition for the Democratic nomination and emerged with a healthy war chest, which his campaign used during the interregnum to attack an effectively defenseless Dole.

That same year, however, the Democratic and Republican Parties were searching for innovative ways to spend a relatively untapped form of campaign funds called "soft money."[39] An amendment to FECA in 1979 permitted political parties to raise funds for "party-building" activities such as get-out-the-vote efforts. The amendment was intended to reverse the consequences of the 1974 amendment that weakened political parties by limiting campaign contributions to and from political parties. Soft money could be raised in large sums from fewer individuals because the funds were not subject to contribution limits. Along with the FEC's administrative rulings regarding how campaign advertisements were classified (electioneering or issue-oriented), soft money established a new category of campaign fundraising for both parties. The combined total of soft money spent by the Democratic and Republican parties combined expanded from $88.1 million in 1992, to $243.6 million in 1996, to $456.9 million in 2000. The Bipartisan Campaign Reform Act (BCRA) passed in 2002 prohibited the national parties from raising or spending soft money on federal elections. The BCRA also more clearly defined electioneering and issue advertisements, making it more challenging for the parties to spend soft money on issue-oriented advertisements created to look and sound like electioneering advertisements. Before BCRA, it was as simple as creatively avoiding the magic words "vote for" or "vote against."

The collapse of the public funding system continued in the 2000 election cycle. In the primary season, the state-by-state spending limits totaled $40.5 million. The campaign of George W. Bush, governor of Texas, determined that if they did not accept federal matching funds, then they could raise substantially more than their competitors. Subsequently, they could also spend more because spending limits would not apply to their campaign. By the end of July, the Bush campaign had raised $94.5 million to spend on the primaries, which was more than double the amount raised by Senator John McCain, his closest rival for the Republican nomination. In fact, of McCain's approximately $45 million raised, $14.5 million was from federal matching funds. On the Democratic side, Vice President Al Gore raised $49.2 million of which $15.3 million was from federal matching funds. The Bush campaign dispatched McCain soon after Super Tuesday and found they were left with quite a bit of cash on hand during the interregnum period to spend running against their Democratic rival. Democrats learned from that mistake. In 2004, John Kerry was almost able to match Bush's campaign fundraising, $234.6 million to $269.9 million. The total of federal matching funds provided to Democratic and Republican candidates that year was $28.4 million. It dropped to $21.7 million in 2008, and $0 in 2012 when no major party candidate accepted federal matching funds.

Although less public money was introduced in 2008 than any year since 1976, the crisis in campaign finance escalated.[40] Presidential campaign fundraising and spending practically doubled, growing to $1.551 billion and $1.645 billion, respectively. McCain, an original sponsor in the Senate of BCRA, which governed the public funding system, was in deep financial trouble and used the matching funds as a life-preserver. On the other hand, the Clinton and Obama campaigns decided in the early days of the campaign that they would not need the public funding system. After he won the nomination, McCain's campaign found they could raise funds more easily and backed out of their pledge to use public funds to remain competitive with the spending of Clinton and Obama as they competed through the interregnum period.[41]

Public funding of the general election also broke down in 2008. Neither of the major party candidates accepting public funding in the general election could collect $84.1 million, but the campaigns were not permitted to raise other funds. On June 19, Obama announced his campaign would decline public funding altogether, citing the advantage that the Republican National Committee (RNC) and other conservative groups would have over the Democrats. In addition to courting new donors, this allowed the Obama campaign to tap into those donors from the primaries and ask for additional donations. September turned out to be his best fundraising month, netting more than $153.1 million.[42] Under BCRA, campaigns could by law raise up to $2,300 from an individual in both the primaries and the general election. As a sponsor of the BCRA, McCain felt honor-bound to participate in the public funding of the general election, which allowed the Obama campaign to literally overwhelm the McCain camp. Obama's campaign spent money in states where Democrats had no history of spending money, such as Virginia where they spent $25.4 million on 35,461 advertisements. In contrast, McCain and the RNC spent only $12.5 million on 20,049 advertisements.[43] The Obama campaign also executed a plan to increase voter registration and turnout among core Democratic constituencies, the effect of which they expected to filter down to other Democrats running for office.

The genesis of another seismic change came in 2008 with the advent of the Super PAC, which dramatically altered the campaign fundraising landscape in 2012 and 2016.[44] Just prior to the primary season that year, a conservative non-profit organization, Citizens United, wanted to make a film critical of Hillary Clinton available through video-on-demand cable television. The Federal Election Commission felt that under BCRA the film met the definition of an electioneering communication, and expenditures on electioneering communication by corporations or unions were prohibited within 30 days of a primary. Although not decided until January 2010, the Supreme Court in *Citizens United v. FEC* struck down provisions of BCRA that prohibited corporations (including non-profit corporations) from making independent expenditures on electioneering communication. In a 5-4 decision, the majority argued that independent expenditures do not lead to corruption or the appearance of corruption, and that limitations on corporations or unions on using funds to advocate or oppose candidates restricted the organization's political speech. In July of the same year, the Court of Appeals for the District of Columbia expressly applied the *Citizens United* ruling in *SpeechNow.org v. FEC*. The Court allowed non-profit organizations to accept contributions unlimited in size from corporations, unions, and individuals, but only for independent expenditures. In other words, funds could not be transferred to other types of PACs or to individual campaigns.[45] The result of the two cases were the creation of independent, expenditure-only political action committees that could raise and spend unlimited sums of money on electioneering communication advocating for or opposing a candidate(s) for federal office if they do not coordinate with the campaigns that benefit (known as Super PACs).

In 2012, 1,310 Super PACs reported over $828 million in receipts and over $609 million in expenditures. The most prominent Super PAC supporting Obama was Priorities USA Action, which raised $79,050,419, and made $65,166,859 in independent expenditures on the President's behalf. The most prominent Super PAC supporting Romney was Restore Our Future, which raised $153,741,731, and made $142,097,336 in independent expenditures on Romney's behalf. In 2016, 2,389 Super PACs reported raising over $1.79 billion and spending more than $1.104 billion. Priorities USA Action raised $192,065,767 and spent $133,407,972 in support of Clinton. On the other side, Trump was supported by many Super PACs, the three largest of which were Get Our Jobs Back, Future 45, and Rebuilding America Now. Collectively, these three raised $97,933,263 and spent $95,468,914.[46]

Not all campaign donors are "big money" donors and not all candidates are supported by Super PACs. In 2016, the Sanders campaign wore their average donation of $27 as a badge of honor, and he only received nominal support from Super PACs because he denounced big money in campaigns.[47] Trump initially self-funded much of his early campaign that year, claiming that he would not be beholden to special interests. Given the amount of money that is available in the campaign finance system, however, candidacies of this nature will likely remain the exception and not become the rule.

Campaign Strategy

Of course, there were other controversies that arose out of the reform movement of the 1970s, but in typical fashion the candidates and their campaigns quickly adapted, continuously inventing and reinventing strategies for reaching voters. Candidates and their campaigns at the presidential level are among the most innovative. For example, in 1992 Bill Clinton's campaign organization created a rapid response "war room" for providing the news media with their own "spin" to the criticisms of his opponents. As these entrepreneurial strategies prove successful, they become the norm in the next campaign cycle.

In the 1960s, campaigns discovered that the proliferation of television offered an important new instrument for communicating directly with voters without the filter of the news media.[48] Campaign advertisements were first run during the 1952 and 1956 election cycles that pitted Adlai Stevenson, the Democratic governor of Illinois, against the Republican standard-bearer, General Dwight Eisenhower. Stevenson, who was not a fan of televised political advertising said,

> "I don't think the American people want politics and the presidency to become the plaything of the high-pressure men, of the ghostwriters, of the public relations men. I think they will be shocked by such contempt for the intelligence of the American people. This isn't soap opera, this isn't Ivory soap versus Palmolive."[49]

The public, however, was responsive to television advertising of all forms, positive and negative, and campaigns make effective us of it.

Another form of communicating directly with voters is televised debates.[50] The first televised presidential debate occurred in 1960 between John F. Kennedy, the Democratic Senator from Massachusetts, and Republican Vice President Richard Nixon. In the 1964, 1968, and 1972 election cycles Presidents Lyndon Johnson and Richard Nixon both recognized the value of television advertising as their principal means for campaign communication, though neither was interested in participating in presidential debates. In 1976, however, President Gerald Ford challenged Jimmy Carter to revive presidential debates during his acceptance speech at the Republican convention, and they have continued to be among the major events of presidential campaigns ever since. Originally, the League of Women Voters hosted the debates, but to tighten control over the timing and format of the debates, the two major parties eventually created a bipartisan organization known as the Commission on Presidential Debates to manage the events. One controversy that arose out of the creation of the debate commission was that the parties could set the threshold for third party participation, which is high. Third party candidates are required to be on the ballot in enough states that they could win a minimum of 270 Electoral College votes, and they must poll at least 15 percent in five national preference surveys.

Debates during the nominating season predate the 1960 Kennedy-Nixon debates.[51] In 1948, Republican Governors Thomas Dewey of New York and Harold Stassen of Minnesota debated each other on the radio in the days leading up to the primary in Oregon. In 1956, Stevenson debated Senator Estes Kefauver of Tennessee on television in advance of the Florida primary. Four years later, Senators Hubert Humphrey of Minnesota and John F. Kennedy debated on television before the West Virginia primary. Televised debates during the primary season were still rare in the 1970s, but began to gain serious traction in both parties in the 1980s and are quite common today. In 2016, the Democrats originally scheduled six debates and extended that number to nine due to the length of the primary season. The Republicans scheduled 12 debates (down from 20 in the 2012 election cycle), but because of the large number of Republicans running for the party nomination, the candidates were assigned to either the "main event" or the "undercard" debate depending on their standing in the polls. Early in the campaign season voter preferences can be swayed by candidate performance in the debates, particularly by candidate misstatements. For example, in 2012 Governor Rick Perry of Texas defended the decision of his state to pass a state-based DREAM Act that allowed children of illegal immigrants to pay in-state tuition rates. Prior to the debate, Perry was the frontrunner and ahead in virtually every poll by a strong margin. Taking a position at odds with a large percentage of Republican primary voters dropped him to third place within days. For candidates vying for the nomination, debates offer an opportunity to introduce themselves to voters and communicate with some level of precision, which is why candidates practice debate performance. For voters, debates offer the opportunity to make the invisible primary visible.

Aside from television, the Internet started to provide new avenues for reaching voters directly in recent election cycles. Tales from the last four election cycles reveal that many new methods of campaign communication merit serious consideration. For example, former Vermont Governor Howard Dean's rise from obscurity during the summer of 2003 to Democratic frontrunner was primarily due to the ability of his campaign to tap into networks of Democratic activists through the social networking site Meetup. In fact, Dean's grassroots Internet-based efforts outperformed many of his campaign's traditional organization endeavors.[52] While Dean was also the first candidate to effectively raise funds on the Internet, both the frontrunner campaign of Barack Obama and the advocacy campaign of Rep. Ron Paul of Texas relied heavily and successfully on the Internet to raise funds, particularly from small money donors, and to communicate and construct elaborate networks of activists in 2008. In 2016, the innovative social media technology was Twitter. Created in 2006, Twitter allows users to post messages called "tweets" that can be up to 140 characters. Trump began using Twitter on a personal and professional basis in May 2009. Over the years, Trump used his Twitter feed to criticize China, Iran, Iraq, ISIS, and Mexico, all leading up to the announcement of his candidacy and his signature issue, immigration. Trump first used the slogan "Make America Great Again" on Twitter, January 3, 2009. During the campaign season, he made great use of the medium to attack his opponents, calling Jeb Bush and Hillary Clinton "weak," Marco Rubio a "lightweight," and Ted Cruz "nasty." He also used Twitter to comment on the news media, calling Glenn Beck "dumb" and "wacko," Megan Kelly "crazy," and Karl Rove "dopey." By spring 2016, the frequency of Twitter users "liking" or "retweeting" one of his Tweets often numbered in the tens of thousands. The frequency of times he was mentioned on Twitter weekly numbered in the millions.[53] Trump effectively used Twitter to circumvent the news media and speak directly to voters. He also used Twitter to drive the news agenda by tweeting provocative comments that almost every news outlet covered in such depth that it virtually sucked the oxygen out of the news cycle.

Another important aspect of campaign strategy is the vote of the Electoral College, which in a close election cycle turns out to be more important than the popular vote. Following the Republican National Convention in July, Trump received the traditional "convention bounce" in the polls for about two days. The Democratic National Convention was scheduled for the following week, and then the polls swung about ten percent in Clinton's favor due to her convention bounce. In the weeks after the convention, Trump's poll numbers bottomed-out at about 40 percent in early August, but then slowly began to climb and in mid-September he got within about one percentage point of Clinton for a couple of days. Trump's trend-line was up and so was Clinton's, but there was still volatility in the polls.[54] Most pundits believe the volatility came from the fact that both candidates had much higher unfavorable than favorable ratings.[55]

Each campaign also faced an "October surprise." Clinton was plagued by news that during her tenure as Secretary of State she had relied on a private, family e-mail server for official government business that included classified information, which may have violated federal law. While there were never any charges in the incident, both the State Department and the Federal Bureau of Investigation looked into the matter throughout the election year. In fact, FBI Director James Comey reported to Congress in late October that the Bureau was investigating new e-mails they believed were relevant that were found on a laptop owned by Huma Abedin, a Clinton advisor whose husband was under investigation. The revelations about Trump, however, were worse. On October 7, the

Washington Post reported that the television show Access *Hollywood* had recorded a vulgar off-air conversation between Trump and host Billy Bush. During the conversation Trump readily admitted to the uninitiated touching of women that many legal experts believe met the definition of sexual assault.[56]

As the election drew near, the conventional wisdom said that Clinton would win the election handily although she never exceeded 50 percent in the polls. In contrast, Obama reached that plateau about three weeks prior to the election in 2008. With neither candidate able to achieve 50 percent in the polls, the Democrat's "blue wall" in the Electoral College took center stage. The blue wall represents those states that have consistently voted Democratic in presidential elections from 1992–2012 (see Table 3.4). Collectively, these states represent 242 votes of the minimum 270 needed to win the Electoral College vote. In 2016, Trump needed to win the 206 electoral votes in states that Mitt Romney won in 2012. Then, he needed to secure battleground states like Florida, Iowa, and Ohio, where he was competitive in the polls and which would provide him with another 53 electoral votes. That still left him at least 11 electoral votes shy of 270. Trump needed to win in one or more states where he was not polling well. If Clinton could hold onto traditionally Democratic states like Michigan, Pennsylvania, and Wisconsin, then she would likely be able to amass the minimum 270 electoral votes needed.

In the end, Clinton won almost 2.9 million more votes than Trump, but his campaign managed to peel away 98 electoral votes from the Democrats' representing states won by Obama in 2012. These states included Florida, Iowa, Michigan, Ohio, Pennsylvania, Wisconsin, and the 2nd congressional district of Maine. Maine (along with Nebraska) uses a unique plan for allocating presidential electors, whereby the candidate that wins a plurality within a congressional district wins the vote representing that district. It is not too surprising that Trump won both Florida and Ohio. Both are traditional battleground states, both states had recently elected Republican governors, the state legislature in each state was controlled by the Republicans, and Trump was competitive in the polls in each state. Iowa voted Democratic in five of the last six presidential elections, but the state had also recently elected a Republican governor and state legislature, and Trump led the polls in Iowa consistently after Labor Day. The real shock was that the Trump campaign was able to turn three states in the blue wall red, in spite of the fact that he never really led in the polls in any of the three states. Granted, voters in Michigan and Wisconsin had recently elected Republicans to the governor's office and control of the state legislature, but voters in Pennsylvania recently elected a Democrat, Tom Wolf, to the governor's office. Clinton campaign manager, Robby Mook, employed a sophisticated "big data" operation to make decisions similar to what the Obama campaign built in the 2012 cycle.[57] However, their models suggested that it was important

Table 3.4 Frequency that Democratic Presidential Candidate Carried the State, 1992–2012

0	1	2	3	4	5	6
Alabama (9)	*Arizona (11)*	*Arkansas (6)*	Colorado (9)	Nevada (6)	*Iowa (6)*	California (55)
Alaska (3)	*Georgia (16)*	*Kentucky (8)*	*Florida (29)*	*Ohio (18)*	New Hampshire (4)	Connecticut (7)
Idaho (4)	*Indiana (11)*	*Louisiana (8)*			New Mexico (5)	Delaware (3)
Kansas (6)	*Montana (3)*	*Missouri (10)*				District of Columbia (3)
Mississippi (6)	*North Carolina (15)*	*Tennessee (11)*				Hawaii (4)
Nebraska (5)		*Virginia (13)*				Illinois (20)
North Dakota (3)		*West Virginia (5)*				Maine (4)
Oklahoma (7)						Maryland (10)
South Carolina (9)						Massachusetts (11)
South Dakota (3)						*Michigan (16)*
Texas (38)						Minnesota (10)
Utah (6)						New Jersey (14)
Wyoming (3)						New York (29)
						Oregon (7)
						Pennsylvania (20)
						Rhode Island (4)
						Vermont (3)
						Washington (12)
						Wisconsin (10)

Total 2016 Electoral Votes

0	1	2	3	4	5	6
102	56	61	38	24	15	242

Source: Table 1–3, *Vital Statistics on American Politics, 2015–16.* CQ Press Electronic Library, Vital Statistics on American Politics Online Edition. Originally published in Vital Statistics on American Politics 2015–2016, edited by Harold W. Stanley and Richard G. Niemi (Washington, DC: CQ Press, 2016), http://sk.sagepub.com.leo.lib.unomaha.edu/cqpress/vital-statistics-on-american-politics-2015-2016/n1.xml.

Note: Numbers of electoral votes for 2016 are shown in *parentheses.* States won by Donald Trump in 2016 are italicized (plus one congressional district in Maine).

for the Clinton campaign to drive up the vote in core Democratic constituencies (e.g. women, Blacks, Latinos), but in the end it hurt them among
white, working-class voters that lacked a college education in those rust-
belt states who viewed Trump as strong on the economy, jobs, and national security.

The setting in which the candidates operated in both parties in 2016
was similar to recent post-reform election cycles. Given the competitive-
ness of recent elections, however, the presidential candidates and their
campaigns, the national parties, and outside groups relied on some time-
tested strategies to persuade voters, but in the case of the Trump campaign, there was a concerted effort to find alternative campaign strategies
to the previously established norms, particularly in the use of social media and their strategy for securing electoral votes. Thus, the post-reform
environment continues to characterize our presidential selection process,
but one that also evolves through innovation and entrepreneurism.

Conclusion

Typically, campaigns and elections come down to essentially the same
proven formula for success: the best candidate the party can field, strong
fundraising, a solid campaign organization, good polling, and many
innovative strategies for performing each better than the opposition.
Trump is commonly called a "disruptor." He certainly disrupted the normal cycle of electoral politics in 2016, and he is also disrupting the traditional process of government as president. Moving forward, however,
it is important to realize how the 2016 cycle impacts the formula, even if
that impact will be a marginal transition rather than the seismic earth-
quake we saw in the presidential selection process in the 1970s. First, all
signs are that the presidential nomination process will continue to be
frontloaded and that Iowa and New Hampshire will continue to play an
important role. Second, to win, candidates need to prepare for a long,
drawn-out contest, probably in both parties. In 2008, Obama's campaign
was prepared to fight for every delegate, and Clinton was better-prepared
in 2016. Assuming the Republican Party continues to allocate delegates
proportionally during the early weeks of the caucus and primary season, their candidates can expect the same. Also, it is important to note
that in two recent election cycles, superdelegates played a pivotal role
in deciding who won the Democratic Party's nomination. Without the
early support of superdelegates, neither Obama in 2008 nor Clinton in
2016 reached a majority of delegates needed to win before the convention
started. At their most recent convention, the delegates decided moving
forward that about two-thirds of delegates will be bound by the results
of the caucuses or primary in their state.[58] This will reduce the influence of superdelegates. Third, the campaign finance system created under FECA is clearly broken and unlikely to be fixed in the near future.

Fundraising will be even more important in future elections as additional candidates continue to opt out of the public funding system and outside organizations find a larger voice in the presidential selection. Fourth, both Obama's 2008 campaign and Trump's 2016 campaign demonstrated that the Electoral College map is much more competitive than imagined. Democrats will be working to win back those traditionally "blue wall" states they lost in 2016 and searching feverishly for new states to steal from the Republican column. Finally, while party leaders and party activists will continue to play an important role in the presidential selection process, the growth of the Internet and social media as a campaign tool offers a new form of activism among a new breed of political partisans who will probably create new, cutting-edge innovations for use in presidential campaigns and elections.

Notes

1 Mark Halperin and John Heilemann, *Double Down: Game Change 2012* (New York: Penguin Press, 2013), 206.
2 Ibid., 203.
3 Dean Obeidallah, "We've Been on the Wrong Track Since 1972," *The Daily Beast*, November 7, 2014, www.thedailybeast.com/articles/2014/11/07/we-ve-been-on-the-wrong-track-since-1972.
4 See Randall E. Adkins, *The Evolution of Political Parties, Campaigns, and Elections: Landmark Documents, 1787–2008* (Washington, DC: CQ Press, 2008).
5 See John Aldrich, *Before the Convention: Strategies and Choices in Presidential Nominations* (Chicago, IL: University of Chicago Press, 1980; and Martin P. Wattenberg, *The Rise of Candidate-Centered Politics: Presidential Elections in the 1980s* (Cambridge, MA: Harvard University Press, 1991).
6 See Jules Witcover, *Marathon: The Pursuit of the Presidency, 1972–1976* (New York: Viking Press, 1977).
7 Elaine Kamarck, "A History of 'Super-Delegates' in the Democratic Party," February 14, 2008, http://belfercenter.ksg.harvard.edu/publication/18072/history_of_superdelegates_in_the_democratic_party.html.
8 See Adkins, *"The Evolution of Political Parties."*
9 John Sides, "Everything You Need to Know about Delegate Math in the Presidential Primary," *Washington Post*, February 16, 2016, www.washingtonpost.com/news/monkey-cage/wp/2016/02/16/everything-you-need-to-know-about-delegate-math-in-the-presidential-primary/?utm_term=.16208e3e1631.
10 For example, see Steven J. Brams, *The Presidential Election Game* (New Haven, CT: Yale University Press, 1978).
11 Kamarck, "A History of 'Superdelegates.'"
12 "Table 1-28 Profile of National Convention Delegates, 1968–2008 (percent)," CQ Press Electronic Library, Vital Statistics on American Politics Online Edition. Originally published in *Vital Statistics on American Politics 2015–2016*, eds. Harold W. Stanley and Richard G. Niemi (Washington, DC: CQ Press, 2016), http://sk.sagepub.com.leo.lib.unomaha.edu/cqpress/vital-statistics-on-american-politics-2015-2016/n1.xml.
13 William G. Mayer and Andrew E. Busch, *The Front-Loading Problem in Presidential Nominations* (Washington, DC: Brookings, 2004).

14 Travis N. Ridout and Brandon Rottinghaus, "The Importance of Being Early: Presidential Primary Front-Loading and the Impact of the Proposed Western Regional Primary," *PS: Political Science & Politics* 41 (2008): 123–128.

15 For example, see Larry M. Bartels, *Presidential Primaries and the Dynamics of Public Choice* (Princeton, NJ: Princeton University Press, 1988).

16 Randall E. Adkins and Andrew J. Dowdle, "Is the Exhibition Season Becoming More Important to Forecasting Presidential Nominations?" *American Politics Research* 29 (2001): 283–288; William G. Mayer, "From the End of the Nomination Contest to the Start of the National Conventions: Preliminary Thoughts on a New Period in Presidential Campaign Politics," *The Forum* 2, no. 2 (2004): Article 1; Dante J. Scala, *Stormy Weather: The New Hampshire Primary and Presidential Politics* (New York: Palgrave Macmillan, 2003); and Wayne P. Steger, Andrew J. Dowdle, and Randall E. Adkins, "The New Hampshire Effect in Presidential Nominations," *Political Research Quarterly* 57 (2004): 375–390.

17 Randall E. Adkins and Andrew J. Dowdle, "How Important Are Iowa and New Hampshire to Winning Post-Reform Presidential Nominations?" *Political Research Quarterly* 54 (2001): 431–444.

18 See Christopher C. Hull, *Grassroots Rules: How the Iowa Caucus Helps Elect American Presidents* (Stanford, CA: Stanford University Press, 2007).

19 See Barbara Norrander, *Super Tuesday: Regional Politics and Presidential Primaries* (Lexington, KY: University Press of Kentucky, 1992).

20 Michael S. Lewis-Beck and Peverill Squire, "Iowa: The Most Representative State?" *PS: Political Science & Politics* 42 (2009): 39–44.

21 See Mayer and Busch, *The Front-Loading Problem*.

22 Barbara Norrander, "The End Game in Post-Reform Presidential Nominations," *Journal of Politics* 62 (2000): 999–1013; and Barbara Norrander, "The Attrition Game: Initial Resources, Initial Contests and the Exit of Candidates during the US Presidential Primary Season," *British Journal of Political Science* 36 (2006): 487–507.

23 See Adkins, *The Evolution of Political Parties*.

24 Norrander, *Super Tuesday*.

25 Ridout and Rottinghaus, "The Importance of Being Early."

26 Ibid.

27 See Mayer and Busch, *The Front-Loading Problem*.

28 Ryan J. Barilleaux and Randall E. Adkins, "The Nominations: Process and Patterns," in *The Elections of 1992*, ed. Michael Nelson (Washington, DC: CQ Press, 1993).

29 See Mayer, "From the End of the Nomination Contest"; and Mayer and Busch, *The Front-Loading Problem*.

30 Jay Cost, "What Went Wrong with the Clinton Campaign?" *RealClearPolitics*. April 10, 2008, www.realclearpolitics.com/horseraceblog/2008/04/what_went_wrong_with_the_clint.html.

31 Paul Abramson, John Aldrich, and David Rohde, *Change and Continuity in the 2008 Elections* (Washington, DC: CQ Press, 2009), 31.

32 See Michael G. Hagen and Kathleen Hall Jamieson, "Do Newspaper Endorsements Matter? Do Politicians Speak for Themselves in Newspapers and on Television?" in *In Everything You Think You Know about Politics and Why You're Wrong*, ed. Kathleen Hall Jamieson (New York: Basic Books, 2000).

33 Kathleen Hall Jamieson and Bruce W. Hardy, "Media, Endorsements, and the 2008 Primaries," in *Reforming the Presidential Nomination Process*, eds. Stephen S. Smith and Melanie J. Springer (Washington, DC: Brookings, 2009), 64–84.

34 Ronald B. Rapoport, Walter J. Stone, and Alan I. Abramowitz, "Do Endorsements Matter? Group Influence in the 1984 Democratic Caucuses," *American Political Science Review* 85 (1991): 193–203.

35 See, among others, Martin Cohen, David Karol, Hans Noel, and John Zaller, *The Party Decides: Presidential Nominations Before and After Reform* (Chicago, IL: University of Chicago Press, 2008); and Andrew J. Dowdle, Randall E. Adkins, and Wayne P. Steger, "The Viability Primary: What Drives Mass Partisan Support for Candidates before the Primaries?" *Political Research Quarterly* 62 (2009): 77–91.

36 Hans Noel, "Why Can't the GOP Stop Trump?" *New York Times*, March 1, 2016, www.nytimes.com/2016/03/01/opinion/campaign-stops/why-cant-the-gop-stop-trump.html.

37 See Adkins, *"The Evolution of Political Parties."*

38 See Mayer, "From the End of the Nomination Contest"; and Mayer and Busch, *The Front-Loading Problem.*

39 See Adkins, *"The Evolution of Political Parties."*

40 Randall E. Adkins and Andrew J. Dowdle, "Change and Continuity in the Presidential Money Primary," *American Review of Politics* 28 (2009): 319–341.

41 David Miller, "McCain Opts Out of Public Matching Funds," *CBS News*, February 11, 2008, www.cbsnews.com/8301-502163_162-3819016-502163.html.

42 Tahman Bradley, "Final Fundraising Figure: Obama's $750M," *ABC News*, December 5, 2008, http://abcnews.go.com/Politics/Vote2008/story?id=6397572 &page=1.

43 Anthony Corrado and Molly Corbett, "Rewriting the Playbook on Presidential Campaign Financing," in *Campaigning for President 2008*, ed. Dennis W. Johnson (New York: Routledge, 2009), 131.

44 Andrew J. Dowdle, Randall E. Adkins, Karen Sebold, and Patrick A. Stewart, "Financing the 2012 Presidential Election in a Post-*Citizens United* World," in *Winning the Presidency 2012*, ed. William J. Crotty (Boulder, CO: Paradigm, 2013), 158–171.

45 See Anthony Corrado, "The Regulatory Environment of the 2008 Elections," in *Financing the 2008 Election*, ed. David B. Magleby and Anthony Corrado (Washington, DC: Brookings, 2011).

46 See "Super PACs," Center for Responsive Politics, October 8, 2014, www.opensecrets.org/pacs/superpacs.php?cycle=2012;and"SuperPACs,"Centerfor Responsive Politics, www.opensecrets.org/pacs/superpacs.php?cycle=2016.

47 Philip Bump, "Bernie Sanders Keeps Saying His Average Donation is $27," *Washington Post*, April 18, 2016, www.washingtonpost.com/news/the-fix/wp/2016/04/18/bernie-sanders-keeps-saying-his-average-donation-is-27-but-it-really-isnt/?utm_term=.036464498a37.

48 See Adkins, *"The Evolution of Political Parties."*

49 Quoted in Edwin Diamond and Stephen Bates, *The Spot: The Rise of Political Advertising on Television*, 3rd. ed. (Cambridge, MA: MIT Press, 1993), 58.

50 See Adkins, *"The Evolution of Political Parties."*

51 Ibid.

52 See Michael Hindman, "The Real Lessons of Howard Dean: Reflections on the First Digital Campaign," *Perspectives on Politics* 3 (2005): 121–128; and Hull, *Grassroots Rules.*

53 "I. You. Great. Trump*," *Politico Magazine*, May/June 2016, www.politico.com/magazine/gallery/2016/04/donald-trump-twitter-account-history-social-media-campaign-000631?slide=0.

54 "General Election: Trump vs. Clinton," *RealClearPolitics*, November 2016, www.realclearpolitics.com/epolls/2016/president/us/general_election_trump_vs_clinton-5491.html.

55 "Clinton: Favorable/Unfavorable," *RealClearPolitics*, November 2016, www. realclearpolitics.com/epolls/other/clinton_favorableunfavorable-1131. html; "Trump: Favorable/Unfavorable," *RealClearPolitics*, May 2016, www. realclearpolitics.com/epolls/other/trump_favorableunfavorable-5493.html.

56 David A. Fahrenthold, "Trump Recorded Having Extremely Lewd Conversation about Women in 2005," *Washington Post*, October 7, 2016, www.washingtonpost. com/politics/trump-recorded-having-extremely-lewd-conversation-about-women-in-2005/2016/10/07/3b9ce776-8cb4-11e6-bf8a-3d26847eeed4_story. html?utm_term=.76c52ea222ec.

57 Michael Scherer, "How Obama's Data Crunchers Helped Him Win," *CNN*, November 8, 2012, www.cnn.com/2012/11/07/tech/web/obama-campaign-tech-team/.

58 Evelyn Rupert, "Democrats Vote to Overhaul Superdelegate System," *The Hill*, July 23, 2016, http://thehill.com/blogs/blog-briefing-room/news/288989-democrats-vote-to-reform-super-delegate-system.

4 Presidents and Political Parties

Julia R. Azari

On January 20, 2017, the first president to win by imposing himself on a party took the oath of office. Donald J. Trump was neither a party politician who rose through the ranks, nor an outsider recruited for the nomination like Dwight Eisenhower. His nomination and subsequent election have raised questions about the relationship between presidents and parties. Parties provide electoral organization and resources that presidents need—although Trump's 2016 election challenged these assumptions. Presidents often serve as the mouthpieces for their parties' priorities and values—but the differences between Trump and other Republican leaders have called this long-standing assumption into question.

What do political scientists know about the interdependent and often fraught relationship between presidents and parties? Its terms have shifted over time as the relative resources and challenges of each institution have evolved. Not all institutional changes have altered the president–party relationship in the same way. Media developments have allowed presidents to be more independent, while partisan polarization has deepened the link between politicians who share party labels.

History provides ample stories about how presidents have changed their parties. Franklin D. Roosevelt (mostly) molded the Democrats into a liberal, New Deal party; Lyndon Johnson made his party a civil rights party; and Ronald Reagan reshaped the Republicans around the conservative movement. Beneath the surface of each such story is a longer process of relationships among presidential candidates, social movements, and party politics. Furthermore, while accounts of presidents changing their parties have intuitive appeal, parties also constrain and, perhaps, shape presidents' priorities and stances.

Although it is commonly understood that presidents have become "more partisan" over time, the cross-institutional relationship is more complex. Presidents and parties have long been interdependent. Both institutions have their own imperatives and logics. Both inform and constrain the other. Finally, substantial evidence is emerging to suggest that the two parties do not operate in the same way; as a result, scholars would be well served to consider the president–party relationship differently depending on the president's party affiliation. Finally, this chapter

considers whether the president–party relationship will undergo a fundamental transformation in the early twenty-first century, reflected by the
nomination and election of Trump.

How Contemporary Scholars Think about the President–Party Relationship

Several frameworks exist for understanding the relationship between
presidents and parties. One of the standard frames has been one of competition and constraint. Numerous scholars have pointed out that, especially where the demands of the modern presidency are concerned,
presidents often clash with their parties, and the relationship can be one
of mutual constraint. Presidents face obligations to act like leaders of
the nation—heads of state and stewards of national values—as well as
mouthpieces for their parties' governing philosophies.[1] Classic works
of scholarship about policy-making stress the weakness of party ties for
modern presidents. David Mayhew shows that divided government produces major legislation as often as unified government.[2] George Edwards,
writing about the mid-twentieth century Democratic Party, notes that
"Presidents do not lobby for candidates for congressional party leadership positions and virtually always remain neutral during the selection
process,"[3] and as a result, may find themselves with congressional leaders who share a party label but not key policy priorities. This framework
presents parties as having limited usefulness for presidents, and sometimes posing constraints.

A second approach depicts presidents as symbolic leaders of their parties. The role of the president as the chief communicator of party ideals
goes back well into the nation's history; Andrew Jackson's early claims to
an electoral mandate rooted presidential authority in partisan electoral
victory.[4] Modern rhetoric has served a dual purpose in this regard, both
bolstering and undermining partisan leadership. Speeches have traditionally been occasions to express national values, although Republican and
Democratic presidents have not infrequently had divergent interpretations of those values. George H. W. Bush and Bill Clinton each addressed
the topic of diversity differently, representing distinct partisan perspectives on how to "make one out of many."[5] Presidents can also use the bully
pulpit to celebrate party victory and articulate its meaning, including explaining the shortcomings of opponents' ideas.[6] Richard Skinner writes
of George W. Bush, "his televised addresses attracted disproportionately
Republican audiences. The White House even welcomed conservative
talk show hosts to the South Lawn during the 2006 campaign."[7] In other
words, rhetoric and media relations reflect partisan fragmentation in U.S.
politics. At the same time, research also shows that strategic references
to bipartisanship have increased over time, illustrating the pressures on
presidents to transcend their parties as well as lead them.[8] Daniel Galvin
captures the shifting expectations about how presidents will balance

these competing pressures, describing some eras as more partisan than others. He suggests that presidents in office during less partisan eras may engage in "sub-rosa partisanship"—defined as "building their party's strength without attracting too much attention."[9] In other words, one of the main advantages that presidents enjoy as party leaders—the ability to communicate party priorities to the broader public—also conflicts with other expectations surrounding the presidency.

Finally, the president–party relationship is sometimes characterized by the insider-outsider dichotomy. In some respects, as the following sections will show, this dynamic has followed changes to the nomination system. Elite-centered processes favored presidential candidates who were, if not major party figures, at least established politicians with some relevant experience. Conventional wisdom, which later sections interrogate, suggests that opening the process to primaries may have ushered in an era of relative outsiders. Outsider politics have been especially potent at a few key moments in recent history. As Andrew Busch writes,

> The final ingredient in the cauldron of 1980 was the prominence of the archetype of the political outsider. The outsider was a figure whose political appeal rested largely on his ability to distance himself from—or even to run against—the normal workings and institutions of national politics. The outsider was almost always for "reform" and against the "establishment" and sought to present himself as an alternative to "politics as usual."[10]

Jimmy Carter had been able to take advantage of the outsider approach in 1976, but by 1980 was associated with the system as the incumbent president. After Reagan, two other governors (Clinton and Bush) ascended to the presidency by campaigning on arguments that they were separate from the "mess in Washington" and could bring a fresh perspective. Senator John McCain (R-AZ) similarly tried to present himself as a "maverick" unafraid to break with party, but his 2008 presidential bid illustrated the tensions of this strategy as he found himself moving to the right to appease core party interests.[11] Barack Obama, although a sitting senator, positioned himself as someone with reformer's instincts, and who would not succumb to the ills of Washington, DC: the "revolving door" of government and lobbying work, and the divisions between parties that rendered governing nearly impossible. Obama's reform ambitions proved difficult to put into practice, and the thirst for change remained into the 2016 election season.

How the President–Party Relationship Developed

The presidency is written into the Constitution; political parties are not. The first American presidents had no formal party affiliations, although teams formed rather quickly around the most controversial issues of the day—foreign policy, the role of the federal government, and the management of the economy. Marc Landy and Sidney Milkis refer to George Washington as an "unwitting partisan" who rejected the idea of party politics but ended up siding with Federalist perspectives on many issues.[12]

The inception of the modern party system meant that presidents were now contending with parties that were robust organizations in their own right. The Democratic Party created by Jackson and Martin Van Buren allowed for coordination among different geographic and ideological wings. Considerable scholarly controversy surrounds the exact nature of this system. Although the "party period" is often identified as one in which party conventions dominated the political scene and recruited "dark horse" political lightweights for the presidency, recent scholarship has disputed this characterization. James K. Polk biographer, Walter Borneman, points out that Polk won the 1844 nomination as an experienced politician with close ties to Jackson.[13] Lara Brown suggests that many existing narratives of the early convention system write presidential aspirants out of the story, making them the "object" rather than the subject, often downplaying years of strategy and preparation for a presidential bid.[14]

Balance among intra-party factions was key for presidential leadership in this period. Stephen Skowronek describes Polk's approach as "equal and exact justice," quoting promises made by the 1844 compromise candidate.[15] Policy informed the conflicts within the party; patronage informed the solution. Democratic delegates in Baltimore had clashed over the annexation of Texas, over tariffs, and the beginnings of the sectional crisis over slavery had even begun to rumble.[16] Polk, who won the nomination by virtue of not being Van Buren or Lewis Cass, promised to strike a satisfactory balance between these two candidates' loyalists when staffing federal positions.

Localized centers of powers and broad diversity on policy substance characterized the Democratic Party through this period. The result for the presidency was an increasingly challenging political balance leading up to the Civil War, with Democratic presidents eventually siding with the South in practice. After the Civil War, the Democratic Party frequently fell short at the national level, and despite some close elections (including 1876, in which the Democratic candidate, Samuel Tilden, won the popular vote), the party produced few presidents until the twentieth century was well under way.

The story for Republicans during the same period resembles that of the Democrats, but is not identical. For one thing, the Republican Party did not form until 1854, more than 20 years after the Democrats. The immediate forbearers of the GOP were the Whigs and the National Republicans, who reflected a distinct set of priorities about public work and public morality—but had reservations about both executive power and party functions. The Whig Party produced few presidents, and, by a strange coincidence, those who were elected under that label both succumbed to illness and did not serve out their terms. Perhaps more tellingly, both of their successors were only loosely affiliated with the Whig party. John Tyler, a former Whig, was often at odds with the party's stances on westward expansion, tariffs, and land.[17]

After the Civil War, Republican presidents navigated a party driven by many factions. These factions represented different positions on a wide range of issues, from how fiercely to pursue reconstruction after the Civil War to whether to enact civil service reforms. Furthermore, although Republicans appeared to dominate presidential elections, the reality was that party politics in the latter half of the nineteenth century was often highly competitive. Democrats made substantial congressional gains in the 1870s, and Rutherford B. Hayes won the 1876 election only after a controversial process handed him an Electoral College victory. The Democratic Party was divided and disadvantaged, but hardly a non-entity in national politics. As a result of a competitive environment, both within and across parties, Republican presidents throughout this period were often constrained in policy and politics. As with the Democrats before the Civil War, Republican presidents found themselves in the position of managing relationships within the party, from the tensions between reformers and standpatters to questions about race, civil rights, and the "lily white" effort to build the party in the South.[18]

The civil service reform question illustrates presidents' capacities to challenge the institutions upon which their parties depend. Presidents could not alter the civil service system without the help of Congress, but James Garfield's support for reform likely contributed to its success. The result was a weakening of one of the central mechanisms by which parties and presidents linked their fates. Patronage allowed those in power to reward their supporters, though the advantage this system conferred on the president was dubious. Daniel Klinghard observes, "Satisfying patronage demands also served the ambitions of congressmen better than it did those of presidents;" the informal rules and power structures that arose around federal patronage allowed stakeholders to resist presidential efforts to control the apparatus.[19] Civil service reform, as a result, created the conditions for presidents to develop their own bases of political support and set the stage for a shift in the foundations of the president–party relationship.[20]

The early decades of the president–party relationship illustrate several key points that continue to shape this cross-institutional dynamic. First, there are some differences across the two parties. The history of the president–party relationship suggests that the two party's distinct origin stories and electoral circumstances have conditioned how they have constrained and shaped presidential initiatives. Second, structure matters. Presidents' relationships with their parties are affected not only by the substance of intra-party disputes, but also by the mechanisms by which these disagreements are resolved. Patronage and the convention system formed the backbone of dispute resolution and party coordination in the nineteenth century. The dissolution of these two systems, during roughly the same period, but by different pathways, has altered the dynamic between the two institutions.

Because of these structural changes, the period roughly between 1880 and 1920 was a major transitional one for the president–party relationship. The so-called "state of courts and parties" gave way to a more fully developed administrative state.[21] Presidents and presidential candidates also began to circumvent the party to develop their own political constituencies. Institutional change was not confined to evolving campaign practices and civil service reform. The Progressive movement challenged party power through its promotion of direct primaries and a general embrace of direct democracy. At the same time, presidential power was growing along with the move toward extended federal involvement in the economy and the labor market.

The President–Party Relationship Becomes Modern

FDR's presidency represented a turning point in president–party relations. FDR was a committed Democrat, yet his presidency marked the beginning of the end of the so-called "convention era." Sidney Milkis has attributed this development to FDR's replacement of the traditional party apparatus with the administrative state.[22] By the time of FDR's inauguration in 1933, progressive politicians like Theodore Roosevelt and Wilson had attempted to weaken traditional party control and lead their parties—and the nation—from the White House. Building on decades of this kind of presidential party leadership, FDR attempted to remake the Democratic Party as a liberal New Deal party. Even a president with his political skills and favorable political conditions, however, was not able to transform his party completely. The unsuccessful 1938 "purge" attempt illustrated the limits of presidential capacity to alter ideological commitments and impose top-down discipline in a party system that had been fashioned in a bottom-up design.

It is not, therefore, entirely surprising that the next president to be elected who was not FDR's vice president was Eisenhower, who had no previous political affiliation and had previously been courted by both parties to run for office. His appeal to the electorate was personal, not ideological. Furthermore, the parties were not ideologically "sorted"— both included a range of positions on major issues. This meant that presidents often assembled bipartisan coalitions, or engaged in transactional horse-trading to pass bills.

Perhaps no two presidencies illustrate the modern president–party arrangement as well as John F. Kennedy and Lyndon Johnson. Both faced a sprawling, diverse Democratic coalition in Congress. There was considerable distrust and disagreement across party factions. For Kennedy, this problem was due to a combination of factors: the fact that senior congressional leaders had "previously outranked him"; his reputation as a liberal; and his identity as a Northern Catholic.[23] As James MacGregor Burns describes, Kennedy's path to the presidency involved appeal to liberals concerned with issues beyond the usual New Deal coalition—, including

> civil liberties, colonialism, the quality (as well as the quantity) of public education, aid to developing nations, McCarthyism, school desegregation, strengthening the United Nations and other international organizations, governmental support for the arts, and a host of other such issues.[24]

Burns also notes that Kennedy solidified his status within this wing of the party by joining the Democratic Advisory Council, a liberal organization within the DNC.[25] However, in order to govern, Kennedy needed to work with a very different congressional party. The powerful actors in Congress included figures like Wilbur Mills, who "opposed Kennedy's Medicare bill and increasingly perceived the president as a reckless spender."[26]

The tensions within the Democratic Party over spending, civil rights, and other identities (geographical, religious) are well documented.[27] Kennedy's experience also illustrates how these dynamics affected modern presidents, who, as Richard Neustadt observed, were expected to address a much wider range of policy problems than their earlier counterparts.[28] As a Democrat in the White House after eight years of Eisenhower's "modern Republicanism," Kennedy presented an agenda to extend the ideas of the New Deal. Furthermore, as the issue of civil rights became increasingly urgent and contentious, presidents found themselves at the epicenter of national action. Unlike any other actor in the American political system, the modern president can articulate national values from a platform of authority. This unilateral symbolic power is to some extent matched by the capacity to change policy; presidents including FDR, Harry Truman, and Kennedy used executive action to ban discrimination in the federal government (at least in the military and other national security positions). In 1957, Eisenhower also learned that the president's obligation to enforce laws also implicated the executive branch in the struggle over civil rights and school integration.[29]

The intersection of diverse parties, growing social movement pressure, and the imperatives of modern presidential politics shaped the president–party relations of Lyndon Johnson. In contrast with FDR, Johnson did not explicitly embrace the goal of remaking the Democratic Party. Evidence suggests that he was more concerned about his own legacy, and the oft-quoted line, however apocryphal its origins, about losing the South for a generation illustrates the stakes of his decision.[30] Johnson's use of the presidency to not only address civil rights and voting rights directly contributed to the modern notion that presidents should and do take the lead in resolving domestic policy challenges. It also forged an association between civil rights and the Democratic Party, which solidified and nationalized a shift that had long been in progress.[31] This ideological sorting has helped to reshape the president–party relationship.

The Partisan Presidency

Structural factors have also altered the president–party relationship. The era of brokered conventions forced presidential candidates to appeal to different factions within the party, without necessarily being the first choice of any faction. The modern era that produced presidents like Kennedy and Johnson rested on a hybrid system of nominations, with scattered primaries throughout the nation. The 1968 convention showed that despite some input from voters and activists, traditional party elites were still in charge. This changed with the reforms adopted in response to the McGovern-Fraser Commission, and the formal rules of the process were opened to rank-and-file voters in a new system of binding primaries and caucuses to select convention delegates.

While changes to the nomination process have altered the president–party relationship, a large body of scholarship suggests that one foundation remains in place. The "invisible primary" that takes place informally before New Hampshire voters cast their ballots and Iowans head to their caucus locations has, according to the influential book *The Party Decides*, anchored the selection process after the McGovern-Fraser reforms.[32] This informal process has ensured that nominees are broadly appealing to their party coalitions. On the Republican side, this includes endorsements from national security, economic, and social conservatives. For Democrats, labor, socially liberal groups that are pro-choice (like NARAL) or support LGBTQ rights, and organized representatives of ethnic and racial minorities are among the important "policy demanders" to whom presidential candidates must be acceptable. As Bawn et al. point out in their seminal article on political parties and policy demanders, the structure of parties and nominations can sometimes pull candidates away from the preferences of the general electorate.[33]

This insight has implications for aspirants who successfully navigate the nomination process and the general election and find themselves in the White House. Republican presidents have often been elected on promises to satisfy the demands of social conservatives, but have encountered significant obstacles from doing so once in office—or have been accused of governing in ways that are at odds with public preferences. Writing in 2006, Jacob Hacker and Paul Pierson draw on Morris Fiorina's finding that the American public has grown more "centrist" and "tolerant" on cultural issues like abortion and same-sex marriage.[34]

Yet, cultural conservatism remains an important force in the Republican Party, creating a dilemma for presidents.

For Republican presidents, this has meant navigating the demands of socially conservative interest groups during the nomination process, the general election, and in office. Reagan mustered support in the Republican Party by appealing to an emerging movement of social conservatives who opposed abortion and the Equal Rights Amendment. These groups backed Reagan against Gerald Ford—who equivocated about a constitutional abortion amendment—in 1976, and formed the backbone of his bid against George H. W. Bush and other rivals in 1980. In office, Reagan had a more difficult time carrying out these promises, disappointing supporters by neglecting social issues on the national agenda and appointing a supporter of abortion rights, Sandra Day O'Connor, to the Supreme Court.[35]

Reagan's dilemma, described by historian Gil Troy in terms of the competing imperatives between pragmatic and conservative, illustrates a fundamental struggle for presidents. The "policy-demanders" in their support coalitions can exert pressure to move in directions that is at odds with public opinion in general. For Reagan, as well as subsequent presidents, this has meant that, especially in the area of touchy social issues, presidential action has been confined to unilateral executive actions and rhetorical symbolism. For example, Republican presidents (and, in 2017, Vice President Mike Pence) have often addressed the anti-abortion March for Life, which takes place in Washington, DC, although the typical mode of messaging has been to place a phone call rather than to appear in person amongst the activists.[36]

A critical institutional development for the president–party relationship was the polarization of the American electorate. Studies produce different origin points for the phenomenon. Alan Abramowitz notes the linkages between polarization and the decline of the New Deal coalition in the 1960s, but the most visible manifestation of a polarized electorate came during George W. Bush's first term. The impact of partisan identification on feelings about Bush increased considerably between 2000 and 2004.[37] Similarly, Gary Jacobson has identified congressional elections as referenda on the sitting president, noting that congressional elections have become more "nationalized" after the close of the twentieth century.[38] The 2006, 2010, and 2014 midterm elections have been "referenda" on the Bush and Obama presidencies, rendering verdicts about national politics rather than local issues.

The turn toward ideological sorting and partisan polarization has several implications for the presidency. Although the presidency was originally designed to be a source of administration rather than a seat of political leadership, recent political conditions have placed presidents in the position of being the symbolic leaders of their parties. Polarization obviously shapes how presidents and presidential candidates interact with the public. Presidential approval has begun to reflect wide differences between how citizens perceive candidates (see Table 4.1). Hetherington and Rudolph find that, beginning sometime in the mid-2000s, partisanship also began to temper basic evaluations of economic conditions, and, as a result, governmental trust.[39] One consequence is that the mid-century paradigms of a president who commands respect across partisan lines and communicates broad values through, say, a national address, has largely faded from the political scene. Presidential polarization predates the media fragmentation brought on by the Internet and cable news age, but has most likely been exacerbated by this environment. The president is often, in this context, a central target for "incivility" like name-calling and insults.

Partisan rancor changes the political environment, but the institutional imperatives of the modern presidency remain. Presidents must respond to events, manage the White House and the federal government, and set the public agenda. Arthur Vandenberg's proclamation that "politics stops at the water's edge" has all but disappeared, but presidents remain, more than ever, the primary decision-makers in foreign affairs, and the face of the nation on the international stage.[40] Through this period, the demands on the presidency did not abate. The War on Terror, natural disasters like Hurricane Katrina, and unnatural ones like the 2010 Deepwater Horizon oil spill, all called for governmental attention, directed by the president. Domestic pressures mounted as well, with the financial collapse of 2008 defining both the end of Bush's presidency and the beginning of Obama's.

In one sense, the idea of the president "above politics" is more myth than fact.[41] Lara Brown notes the importance of parties in shaping the "opportunism" of presidential hopefuls. Presidents have long been party leaders, and American politics has perpetually featured deep and fundamental divisions. In a different sense, however, the changing partisan

Table 4.1 Presidents and Public Approval Gaps

President	Approval gap
Eisenhower	39
JFK	35
LBJ	27
Nixon	41
Ford	31
Carter	27
Reagan	52
Bush	38
Clinton	55
W. Bush	61
Obama	70
Trump	75

Source: Gallup and Pew Research Center.

environment has altered the task for presidents. One surprising manifestation of this has been the increase in the use of bipartisan appeals on the campaign trail.[42] Both Bush and Obama initially ran on some version of the promise of bipartisan compromise. Bush told audiences he would be a "uniter, not a divider." Obama promised to unite the country behind shared values. Neither delivered on this promise.

George W. Bush

Despite jokes during the 2000 election about the contest between "Gush and Bore," an echo rather than a choice, one would hardly mistake the 43rd president's leadership for that of a moderate Democrat. Even in early 2001, Bush invited criticism for having tacked hard to the right in his appointments and early priorities, especially in the context of the closely contested 2000 election, in which Bush's opponent, Al Gore, had been the winner of the popular vote. Bush highlighted a range of priorities early on, from bipartisan education reform efforts to more traditional Republican issues like tax cuts and, in a new twist on a familiar theme, faith-based initiatives to provide charitable services. Bush reinstated Reagan's "Mexico City policy" for overseas abortion funding and moved to limit stem cell research.[43] Combined with the faith-based initiative, which critics suggested was simply a way to devote public resources to religious organizations, by the time the September 11, 2001 terror attacks occurred, Bush had consolidated his credentials as a social conservative, and given opponents little reason to believe he meant his promises of unity.

What kind of party did Bush leave behind? How would we characterize Bush's relationship with his party and the ways in which his initiatives affected it? The actions that he took in office highlighted three sources of tension in the coalition. The first and perhaps most immediately evident is the difference between committed social conservatives and those who were, if not hostile to this agenda, reluctant to make it a priority. The second division was between the hawkish and libertarian wings of the party, a tension that would not animate the 2008 presidential race in the same way it would during later campaigns. The final division was one that would also not manifest clearly until some years after Bush had left office: immigration. A bipartisan immigration proposal was met by some congressional Republicans with hostility because it was perceived as too lenient toward those who had entered the country unlawfully.[44] Andrew Wroe writes, "While perhaps guilty of overselling his plan, Bush claimed it would encourage economic growth, help secure America's borders and homeland security, be compassionate towards undocumented immigrants, and protect the rights of documented immigrants." Wroe further observes that Bush and his close political advisor Karl Rove imagined building a diverse coalition for the party that included non-white Americans.[45] This contrasted sharply with immigration hardliners in

Congress, who sponsored bills to deny birthright citizenship to children of undocumented immigrants and took to the talk radio airwaves to discuss the dangers of the status quo.[46]

Each of these disagreements would become fundamental in the party's later struggles. Furthermore, each one illustrates the ways in which presidents are constrained by, but also profoundly shape, their parties. Bush's efforts led his party in a more internationally aggressive and socially conservative direction. On immigration, Bush's leadership efforts appeared to matter little to those in his party who were most conservative on that issue, even though Bush had positioned himself as a symbolic leader of the party's conservative base.

Barack Obama

Like Bush, Obama ran for office promising to unite the warring sides in American politics, and, like Bush, his window was brief. Obama's 2008 election included areas where previous Democrats might not have dared to dream about victory: Indiana, North Carolina, Virginia, and even a single Electoral College vote in Nebraska. Early interpretations of this victory perhaps revealed how party dynamics had changed since the Clinton years: Obama's victory in previously red territory was not interpreted as a signal to assemble a broad centrist coalition, as with Clinton and the "third way," but rather that a new day for Democratic politics had dawned. This interpretation was not without evidence. Obama had run at least slightly to the left of Hillary Clinton in the primary, challenging her decision to vote for the Iraq War in particular.

What kind of Democrat was Obama? Different analysts have produced different answers. One recurring characterization is Obama the pragmatist.[47] Obama's approach was also, after all, an odd fit for the job of party leader. His career had been built on circumventing party hierarchy and seniority, and his ultimate appeal as the party's standard-bearer in 2008 rested in part on his personal appeal rather than on his vision for the party. Obama's early priorities in office were consistent with this neo-Progressive pragmatism. The financial crisis created an immediate agenda for the new administration. Obama's wan efforts at working with Republicans in the creation of the stimulus package have been well documented.[48] The result would set the tone for much of the rest of Obama's presidency: A stimulus bill passed with no Republican votes in the House of Representatives.

After the passage of the Affordable Care Act, in which Obama struggled alongside congressional leaders to wrangle an unwieldy and diverse delegation, the partisan tenor shifted once again. Opposition crystallized around the new health law, the Tea Party and birther movements questioned the president's legitimacy, and, with the 2010 elections, Obama became a divided government president.

What kind of Democratic Party did Obama leave behind? Much of the literature on Obama's party leadership has taken on the disconnect between his sweeping promises of transformation and transcendence of partisanship, and the reality of his polarized and circumscribed presidency. As Sidney Milkis, Jesse Rhodes, and Emily Charnock point out, "Obama's paeans to nonpartisan unity have been joined uneasily with harsher partisan rhetoric that appeals to, and helps mobilize, his core Democratic constituencies."[49] During the campaign, Obama embraced the candidate-centered idea that he would be able to overcome partisan divisions and the challenges they posed. Instead, his presidency was defined by those divisions and the obstacles to governing posed by a polarized environment and a separated powers system.

What of Obama's mark on the Democratic Party itself? The dynamics of the 2016 primary and the aftermath of the 2016 election suggest that a substantial split has emerged over "identity politics" and economic populism. This phenomenon, of course, has many causes, but some of it can be traced to Obama's presidency. Obama's own role as a symbol of the party's embrace of racial progress set the stage, and his embrace of social issues in the second term highlighted these as central to the party's agenda.

Just as with George W. Bush, Obama's main party legacy was attempting to reshape the party and instead leaving it in a state of division over priorities and realization of ideals. While their party legacies are comparable, they are not identical. The Republican Party Bush left behind in 2009 was one with some considerable differences on policy stances; for Obama's Democrats, the differences were of degree and approach. Furthermore, while both presidents influenced their parties, the party system exercised different kinds of constraints on them. For Bush, objections from his own party held back his agenda; for Obama, intra-party divisions were a marginal concern compared to Republican obstruction.

Donald Trump

As of 2017, Trump, a party outsider, now occupies the highly polarized office of the presidency. The question of whether Trump will change the Republican Party, or whether it will change him, remains open. In one sense, Trump seems poised to pick up where the Bush era divisions left off, answering definitively where the party would come down on the question of immigration policy. At the time of this writing, Trump and other Republicans are engaged in a crucial test of whether this unexpected nominee and president will change the party, or whether the party will change him. Trump's early presidency has featured several moves that reflect standard Republican priorities, from the enactment of the "Mexico City policy" to the appointment of conservative Supreme Court Justice Neil Gorsuch. His administration has embraced positions that have been previously found within Republican discourse, such as a staunch denial of climate change, a health care bill that would reduce the number of Americans with health insurance coverage, and several extreme immigration-related measures, including the "travel ban" executive orders and the plans to build a border wall. Importantly, it remains to be seen whether Trump has effected a durable shift on the question of international trade.[50] Trump has also alarmed critics, including some Republicans, with statements during the campaign about restricting press freedom and jailing his opponent, Hillary Clinton. In office, Trump has won the support of most congressional Republicans, even while some have been critical of his approach to presidential power. Thus far, in other words, the patterns of mutual influence and constraint seem to be in effect for the Trump presidency. What seems most evident, however, is that while the Republican Party has brought Trump into line with many of its standard positions on issues, the party has not curbed his tendencies to use unilateral power or engage in illiberal rhetoric.

Party Asymmetry

As we take stock of the relationship between presidents and parties, it makes sense to consider whether Republican and Democratic presidents are subject to the same political forces and whether their experiences differ. The cross-institutional relationship between presidents and parties is typically treated as a uniform concept that applies across parties. Many of the broad institutional changes that have shaped that relationship have applied across party lines: the creation and adoption of direct primaries, the proliferation of new media, and the polarization of the political environment. However, while these shifts have applied to Republicans and Democrats alike, they have not affected them in identical ways. Primaries have empowered different groups within the Republican and Democratic coalitions, and the two parties have adapted to the original McGovern-Fraser reforms differently. The Democrats adopted a system of "super-delegates" to counterbalance the input of primary voters, while the Republican Party has thus far declined to make any institutional changes in this regard. The Democratic system of delegate apportionment allocates delegates proportionally, while the Republican National Committee allows states to adopt winner-take-all primary rules.[51]

While recent research finds that partisanship affects how American citizens evaluate national conditions, such as the state of the economy and security from international threats,[52] there is some evidence that this effect may vary by party. Many commentators, particularly on the left, noted in 2017 that Republican survey respondents were far more supportive of intervention in Syria once Trump took office. Democratic respondents, on the other hand, maintained a consistent level of support for intervention between the Obama and Trump presidencies.[53] What remains unclear at this point is whether differences like these are the result of a deep-seated asymmetry between the two parties, or whether they reflect specific circumstances. For example, it is possible that partisan attitudes about intervention in Syria measured at the beginning of Trump's presidency are not comparable to such attitudes measured in Obama's second term.

New media has altered the partisan environment in ways scholars are only beginning to understand. Available evidence suggests that the contours of "narrow-casting" are not the same on the left as on the right. A study of incivility by Sarah Sobieraj and Jeffrey Berry concludes that while liberal blogs and news shows engage in considerable incivility, their method of measuring "outrage incidents" suggests that more of it occurs in right-leaning sources.[54]

Taking an institutional view, conservative media—from the *National Review* to Rush Limbaugh to Fox News—has been a consistent part of the conservative movement. Conservative media outlets shaped opposition to the Clinton presidency and were especially critical in driving the agenda of the Tea Party, which was a principal source of opposition to Obama's presidency. In addition to Berry and Sobieraj's study of outrage, several scholars have observed the institutional power of the conservative media and its role in shaping politics on the right. Although left-leaning blogs, television shows like MSNBC's *The Rachel Maddow Show*, and the humorous news show *The Daily Show* on Comedy Central have also become part of the political discourse, they have thus far been less deeply integrated into the broader Democratic coalition.

Several studies find partisan asymmetry in presidential behavior. In an analysis of presidential party-building, Daniel Galvin finds a distinct pattern: Since Eisenhower, Republican presidents have invested in their parties, building them up as institutions; Democratic presidents since Kennedy have been "party predators," depleting their parties of resources and neglecting institution-building tasks.[55] Party differences extend to rhetorical choices as well; Republican presidents make broader and more consistent mandate claims, while Democratic presidents interpret their elections in terms of many smaller issues.[56] This discrepancy goes back as far as the Carter presidency; among presidents from FDR through Richard Nixon, the pattern actually seems to be reversed. These findings are consistent with the possibility that observed that asymmetry is rooted in political circumstances rather than fundamental differences.

Conclusion

Presidents and parties are mutually interdependent. Parties need the presidency to attain national policy goals. Presidents need parties on the campaign trail and in office. However, this is not simply a relationship of political convenience. The ways in which parties influence and constrain presidents—and vice versa—have changed as other processes and institutions evolve. The president–party relationship is also properly understood as a cross-institutional relationship; each institution has changed and operates according to its own internal logic and incentives. As a result, each institution can change the other.

More substantively, an overview of recent leaders suggests that presidents have some capacity to change their parties. At the same time, the parties' ideological commitments prove remarkably resistant to pushes from even popular and politically successful leaders. Presidents leave their parties symbolically altered, and yet they cannot dislodge fundamental beliefs or bring factions into line. The implication is that presidential party leadership is neither as sweeping as some suggest, nor as weak as skeptics claim.

When we talk about presidents and parties, it makes a difference which party we are talking about. A growing body of evidence suggests that both partisanship and party-building are stronger for Republican presidents. Democratic presidents have a different experience of party leadership, less bolstered by fierce loyalty and with less inclination to foster party organization. American politics has shown a tendency to prefer alternations in the president's party; the evidence about party asymmetry suggests that we should expect to see different patterns of president–party relationships depending on which party controls the White House.

In the second decade of the twenty-first century, it is possible that the president–party relationship is undergoing another major transformation. Contemporary politics combines a hyper-polarized environment with an "outsider" presidency that prizes reform ideas and personality. This combination means that as some forces push presidents to act independently of parties, realizing that goal will largely remain impossible. It seems likely that the relationship between presidents and parties will continue to be one of contradictions and challenges, though changes to both institutions render that future uncertain.

Notes

1 See Julia Azari, Lara Brown, and Zim Nwokora, "Between a Rock and a Hard Place," in *The Presidential Leadership Dilemma: Between the Constitution and a Political Party*, eds. Julia Azari, Lara Brown, and Zim Nwokora (Albany, NY: SUNY Press, 2013).

2 See David Mayhew, *Divided We Govern: Party Control, Lawmaking, and Investigations, 1946–2002* (New Haven, CT: Yale University Press, 2005).

3 George C. Edwards III, *At the Margins: Presidential Leadership of Congress* (New Haven, CT: Yale University Press, 1990), 77.

4 See Richard J. Ellis and Stephen Kirk, "Presidential Mandates in the Nineteenth Century: Conceptual Change and Institutional Development," *Studies in American Political Development* 9 (1995): 117–186; and Mel Laracey, *Presidents and the Public: The Partisan Story of Going Public* (College Station, TX: Texas A&M University Press, 2002).

5 See Mary E. Stuckey, "Doing Diversity across the Partisan Divide: George H.W. Bush, Bill Clinton, and American National Identity," in *In the Public*

Domain: Presidents and the Challenges of Public Leadership, eds. Lori Cox Han and Diane J. Heith (Albany, NY: SUNY Press, 2005).

6 See Julia R. Azari, *Delivering the People's Message: The Changing Politics of the Presidential Mandate* (Ithaca, NY: Cornell University Press, 2014); and Julia R. Azari and Justin S. Vaughn, "Barack Obama and the Rhetoric of Electoral Logic," *Social Science Quarterly* 95 (2014): 523–540.

7 Richard M. Skinner, "George W. Bush and the Partisan Presidency," *Political Science Quarterly* 123 (2008): 605–622.

8 Jesse H. Rhodes and Zachary Albert, "The Transformation of Partisan Rhetoric in Presidential Campaigns, 1952–2012: Partisan Polarization and the Rise of Bipartisan Posturing Among Democratic Candidates," *Party Politics*, Online first, October 2015, DOI: 10.1177/1354068815610968; Jesse H. Rhodes, "Party Polarization and the Ascendance of Bipartisan Posturing as a Dominant Strategy in Presidential Rhetoric," *Presidential Studies Quarterly* 44 (2014): 120–142; John J. Coleman and Paul Manna, "Above the Fray? Uses of Party System References in Presidential Rhetoric," *Presidential Studies Quarterly* 37 (2007): 399–426.

9 Daniel J. Galvin, "Presidential Partisanship Reconsidered: Eisenhower, Nixon, Ford, and the Rise of Polarized Politics," *Political Research Quarterly* 66 (2012a): 49.

10 Andrew Busch, *Reagan's Victory: The Presidential Election of 1980 and the Rise of the Right* (Lawrence, KS: University Press of Kansas, 2005), 26.

11 See, for example, James Ridgeway, "Last Man Standing? McCain's War with the Republican Base," *The Guardian*, February 3, 2008, www.theguardian. com/world/deadlineusa/2008/feb/03/lastmanstandingmccainsbatt.

12 Marc Landy and Sidney M. Milkis, *Presidential Greatness* (Lawrence, KS: University Press of Kansas, 2000), 38.

13 See Walter Borneman, *Polk: The Man Who Transformed the Presidency and America* (New York: Random House, 2008).

14 See Lara M. Brown, *Jockeying for the American Presidency: The Political Opportunism of Aspirants* (New York: Cambria Press, 2010).

15 Stephen Skowronek, *The Politics Presidents Make: Presidential Leadership from John Adams to Bill Clinton* (Cambridge, MA: Harvard Belknap, 1997), 161.

16 Borneman, *Polk*, 97.

17 See Dan Monroe, *The Republican Vision of John Tyler* (College Station, TX: Texas A&M University Press, 2003).

18 See Philip A. Klinkner and Rogers Smith, *The Unsteady March: The Rise and Decline of Racial Equality in America* (Chicago, IL: University of Chicago Press, 2002). For a discussion of accommodation of the "lily-white" movement under the Warren Harding administration, see Megan Ming Francis, *Civil Rights and the Making of the Modern American State* (New York: Cambridge University Press, 2014).

19 Daniel P. Klinghard, "Grover Cleveland, William McKinley, and the Emergence of President as Party Leader," *Presidential Studies Quarterly* 35 (2005): 746.

20 Ibid.

21 See Stephen Skowronek, *Building a New American State: The Expansion of National Administrative Capacities, 1877–1920* (New York: Cambridge University Press, 1982).

22 See Sidney M. Milkis, *The President and the Parties: The Transformation of the American Party System Since the New Deal* (New York: Oxford University Press, 1995).

23 Sean Savage, *JFK, LBJ, and the Democratic Party* (Albany, NY: SUNY Press, 2004), 91.

24 James MacGregor Burns, *The Deadlock of Democracy: Four-Party Politics in America* (Upper Saddle River, NJ: Prentice-Hall, 1963), 308.

25 See Sam Rosenfeld, *A Choice, Not an Echo: Polarization and the Transformation of the American Party System*, Doctoral Dissertation, Harvard University, 2014.

26 Savage, *JFK*, 112.

27 See Kari Frederickson, *The Dixiecrat Revolt and the End of the Solid South, 1932–1968* (Chapel Hill, NC: University of North Carolina Press, 2001); and Robert Mickey, *Paths Out of Dixie: The Democratization of Authoritarian Enclaves in America's Deep South, 1944–1972* (Princeton, NJ: Princeton University Press, 2015).

28 See Richard Neustadt, *Presidential Power and the Modern Presidents: The Politics of Leadership from Roosevelt to Reagan* (New York: Free Press, 1990).

29 See Jean Edward Smith, *Eisenhower in War and Peace* (New York: Random House, 2012).

30 Jason Sokol, "The Power Broker's Other Voice," *Slate*, June 13, 2011, www.slate.com/articles/arts/books/2011/06/the_power_brokers_other_voice.html.

31 See Eric Schickler, *Racial Realignment: The Transformation of American Liberalism, 1932–1965* (Princeton, NJ: Princeton University Press, 2016).

32 See Martin Cohen, David Karol, Hans Noel, and John Zaller, *The Party Decides: Presidential Nominations Before and After Reform* (Chicago, IL: University of Chicago Press: 2008).

33 Kathleen Bawn, Martin Cohen, David Karol, Seth Masket, Hans Noel, and John Zaller, "A Theory of Political Parties: Groups, Policy Demands, and Nominations in American Politics," *Perspectives on Politics* 10 (2012): 571–597.

34 Jacob Hacker and Paul Pierson, *Off Center: The Republican Revolution and the Erosion of American Democracy* (New Haven, CT: Yale University Press, 2006), 42–43.

35 Will Bunch, "Five Myths about Ronald Reagan's Legacy," *Washington Post*, February 4, 2011, www.washingtonpost.com/wp-dyn/content/article/2011/02/04/AR2011020403104.html; Skowronek, in *The Politics Presidents Make*, also outlines Reagan's "rhetorical reconstruction" as a presidency which shifted the national discourse but had a far less sweeping impact on national policy commitments.

36 See Gil Troy, *Morning in America: How Ronald Reagan Invented the 1980s* (Princeton, NJ: Princeton University Press, 2007).

37 Alan Abramowitz, *The Disappearing Center: Engaged Citizens, Polarization, and American Democracy* (New Haven, CT: Yale University Press, 2011), 28.

38 Gary Jacobson, "Barack Obama and the Nationalization of Electoral Politics in 2012," *Electoral Studies* 40 (2015): 471–481.

39 See Marc J. Hetherington and Thomas J. Rudolph, *Why Washington Won't Work: Polarization, Political Trust, and the Governing Crisis* (Chicago, IL: University of Chicago Press, 2015).

40 Robert J. Lieber, "Politics Stops at the Water's Edge," *Monkey Cage, Washington Post*, February 10, 2014, www.washingtonpost.com/news/monkey-cage/wp/2014/02/10/politics-stops-at-the-waters-edge-not-recently/?utm_term=.2524f4599147.

41 See Ralph Ketcham, *Presidents above Party: The First American Presidency, 1789–1829* (Chapel Hill, NC: University of North Carolina Press, 1987).

42 Rhodes, "Party Polarization."

43 George W. Bush, Memorandum for the Administrator of the United States Agency for International Development, January 22, 2001, https://georgewbush-whitehouse.archives.gov/news/releases/20010123-5.html; "President Discusses Stem Cell Research," August 9, 2001, https://georgewbush-whitehouse.archives.gov/news/releases/2001/08/20010809-2.html.

44 Rachel Weiner, "How Immigration Reform Failed, Over and Over," *Washington Post*, January 30, 2013, www.washingtonpost.com/news/the-fix/wp/2013/01/30/how-immigration-reform-failed-over-and-over/?utm_term=.659541ee20f7.

45 Andrew Wroe, *The Republican Party and Immigration Politics: From Proposition 187 to George W. Bush* (New York: Palgrave Macmillan, 2008), 151, 191.

46 Transcript, Congressman Tom Tancredo Discusses Immigration Reform Bills, *Washington Post Live Q&As*, March 30, 2006, www.washingtonpost.com/wp-dyn/content/discussion/2006/03/29/DI2006032901468.html.

47 Stephen Skowronek, *Presidential Leadership in Political Time: Reprise and Reappraisal* (Lawrence, KS: University Press of Kansas, 2011), 186.

48 Azari and Vaughn, "Obama's Rhetoric of Electoral Logic"; see also Jonathan Alter, *The Promise: President Obama, Year One* (New York: Simon and Schuster, 2009).

49 Sidney M. Milkis, Jesse H. Rhodes, and Emily J. Charnock, "What Happened to Post-Partisanship? Barack Obama and the New American Party System," *Perspectives on Politics* 10 (2012): 57–76.

50 Reid J. Epstein and Colleen McCain Nelson, "Donald Trump Lays Out Protectionist Views in Trade Speech," *Wall Street Journal*, June 28, 2016, www.wsj.com/articles/donald-trump-lays-out-protectionist-views-in-trade-speech-1467145538; Alexander Bolton, "Angst in GOP Over Trump's Trade Agenda," *The Hill*, February 20, 2017, http://thehill.com/policy/finance/320187-angst-in-gop-over-trumps-trade-agenda.

51 Daniel Nichanian, "Clinton's Delegate Lead Would Triple Under GOP Rules," *FiveThirtyEight*, April 28, 2016, https://fivethirtyeight.com/features/clintons-delegate-lead-would-triple-under-gop-rules/.

52 See Hetherington and Rudolph, *Why Washington Won't Work*.

53 Brian Beutler, "#Bothsides is the Most Failed, Destructive, Opportunistic, and Falsifiable Analytical Conceit in American Politics" *The New Republic*, April 2017, https://newrepublic.com/minutes/141987/bothsides-failed-destructive-opportunistic-falsifiable-analytical-conceit-american-politics; Steve Benen, "On Syria, 'Reflexive Partisanship' Doesn't Apply to Both Sides," *The Rachel Maddow Show*, April 12, 2017, www.msnbc.com/rachel-maddow-show/syria-reflexive-partisanship-doesnt-apply-both-parties.

54 Jeffrey M. Berry and Sarah Sobieraj, "From Incivility to Outrage: Political Discourse in Blogs, Talk Radio, and Cable News," *Political Communication* 28 (2011): 19–41.

55 See Daniel J. Galvin, *Presidential Party-Building: Dwight D. Eisenhower to George W. Bush* (Princeton, NJ: Princeton University Press, 2009).

56 See Azari, *Delivering the People's Message*.

5   Presidents and Mass Media

Matthew Eshbaugh-Soha

Before even taking the oath of office, then President-Elect Donald J. Trump telegraphed his strategy as president for dealing with the Washington press corps: unbridled antagonism. After one cancellation and much anticipation, Trump's first press conference began with Press Secretary Sean Spicer, then Vice President-Elect Mike Pence, and Trump, himself, criticizing the news media. Without question, they were upset about an unconfirmed report about a dossier that linked Trump to the Russian government. But their approach, to send two presidential surrogates to the podium arranged for a press conference to chastise the press, is surely unique. It also signaled quite clearly the Trump administration's antagonistic strategy for dealing with the news media furthered during Spicer's first press briefing that addressed inauguration attendance numbers, and also during Trump's first solo press conference.[1]

It may not be a surprise that Trump appears to have jettisoned the mutually beneficial relationships that most presidents have with the news media during their honeymoon in favor of an antagonistic strategy. As it stands, trust in the news media is at an all-time low, as only 32 percent of Americans in 2016 had a "great deal" or "fair amount" of trust in the news media.[2] This is down from 54 percent before the War in Iraq. Naturally, Republicans have even less trust in the news media (14 percent) than Independents (30 percent) or Democrats (51 percent), suggesting that Trump's antagonism strategy is highly likely to be a hit with his partisan base, at least.

Nevertheless, an antagonistic strategy is fraught with peril. It is rare, indeed, for presidents to be able to speak directly to the American people. Yes, Trump uses Twitter to attempt to do this, but it is not clear that tweets will move public opinion, especially given the self-selectivity that drives social media users. In all likelihood, Trump's Twitter strategy may prove as limited as other strategies presidents have used to circumvent the national news media to reach the American people. A strategy of national leadership, for example, which allows for direct outreach to the American people, illustrates the point clearly. Trump delivered his first national address to a joint session of Congress on February 28, 2017. The speech was a clear success, praised by both Democrats and Republicans as one that did not employ the antagonism found in Trump's press conferences and campaign-styled remarks. The public, at least among those who watched the address, were similarly impressed. According to a CBS News/YouGov poll conducted after the address,[3] 76 percent of Americans approved of the President's speech.[4] In addition, 82 percent of respondents believed that Trump appeared presidential, 61 percent of respondents were more optimistic having watched the address, and he enjoyed 64 percent support for each policy identified by the CBS News/YouGov poll.[5]

The speech was a defining moment among those who watched the speech, for sure, and one that had the potential to shape public perception about Trump and his policies. Yet Americans rarely tune in to presidential addresses, and Trump's first address to a joint session of Congress was no different. Nielson reported that 47.74 million viewers watched the address. Although a sizeable audience,[6] these numbers were lower in comparison to Barack Obama's first address to Congress, which 52.37 million Americans watched, a difference of 9 percent, and at a 28 percent share, down considerably from audience shares enjoyed by presidents who spoke during the golden age of presidential television.[7] It may not be a surprise, then, that public opinion barely moved after the address. In fact, despite a small bump associated with the President's address, his job approval ratings declined to their pre-speech levels within one week of the speech.[8] Moreover, more Americans than ever approved of Obamacare since Trump took office,[9] and a majority thought that it should not be repealed even after the President's national address.[10] One of Trump's top priorities is to repeal the Affordable Care Act.

The limits to using a national address to circumvent the national news media and reach the American people directly are several. First, a president's supporters are most likely to watch a national address.[11] Thus, presidents are often "preaching to the choir" when they address the nation. This generates ample post-address support among those who watched, but the president's reach remains limited, leading to less movement in support from all Americans. Second, fewer viewers simply increase the media's impact on the president's public leadership efforts. It may be more likely that news coverage after the address, not the address itself, will influence the opinions of the most Americans. Thus, if presidents cannot maintain the media's focus on a speech and message, then a president's leadership of the public will be limited. Couple that with the high probability that another news event may push the president—and policy priorities—out of the news, and presidential leadership of the public with a recalcitrant media is difficult.[12]

Arguably, presidential failures to move public opinion are due to the many difficulties each faces when speaking to the nation and is not a surprise to scholars of the public presidency (discussed in Chapter 6). Given declining viewership of presidential addresses, moreover, the president increasingly needs the media to reach the public. As such, the speech itself may be even less important than the news coverage that follows, but this does not always bode well for presidential leadership, either. In all, a textbook account of news coverage presents a news media that enjoy the negative and scandalous, prefer conflict to agreement, and favor the superficial and entertaining aspects of politics, rather than substantive discussions of policy. From this, one could easily predict that even the symbolic success of Trump's first national address would not generate the support he might need among the American people for a strategy of going public to help him achieve his policy priorities.

Of course, the Trump administration's communication strategy to chastise the media—while overbearing compared to most—is not unique to the presidency. The presidency and news media have long had an antagonistic relationship. But media are often important to presidential communication, even when they are not always reliant partners. Given that presidents must depend on a media driven more by profit and ratings than democratic norms, it is no wonder that most presidents lament the difficulties of leading the news media. This does not mean that the president is incapable of communicating effectively through speeches and other public activities, however. The president not only delivers several hundred speeches per year, the White House is also staffed with expertise and supplied with myriad resources to communicate the president's messages. The efforts to which the president and his communications organization go to shape the news—and public opinion, eventually—are extensive and may foretell great success. Yet, much research illuminates the difficulty presidents face, even amid resounding successes.

Using examples from recent presidential administrations as the foundation for illustrating what we know about the public presidency, the remainder of this chapter begins with a discussion of presidential speeches, the central focus of presidential communication efforts. Because speeches are not the sole means of public leadership, however, I also underscore the organizational resources that aid presidential communication. Next, I present evidence as to whether presidential communication efforts have a substantive impact on the news media and then conclude with what might assist presidential leadership of the news media. In short, this chapter will answer the following questions: What is the public presidency? What does news coverage of the presidency look like? Are presidents successful at influencing news coverage? And what are the prospects for leadership in light of a changing media environment that might accentuate, rather than ameliorate, existing constraints and limitations on effective presidential communication?

The Public Presidency

Notwithstanding the difficulties scholars face in defining leadership and the many versions they provide,[13] leadership is unquestionably a public effort for contemporary presidents, such that a president who speaks repeatedly about his policy priorities is attempting to lead on those issues. "Rhetorical leadership" is at the "heart" of modern presidential governance,[14] after all, and, for George C. Edwards, "leading the public is at the core of the modern presidency."[15] According to Sam Kernell, leadership constitutes "going public,"[16] whereby presidents use the tools and stature of the presidency to generate public support for their policies in an effort to achieve those goals in Congress. Still others imply that publicity is important to presidential leadership. Steven Shull sees leadership as something that requires "ideological commitment and assertiveness,"[17] while Bert Rockman conceives of leadership as "the capacity to impart and sustain direction."[18]

Presidential leadership is a public effort, and so it depends on an effective communications strategy. There are many ways that presidents may engage reporters, including interviews, press conferences, and informal exchanges. Because the president's ultimate goal may be to lead public opinion, the primary way the president communicates is through public speeches. Even so, the president can rarely reach the public directly and without the media's aid. Since the end of the golden age of presidential television, when presidents could count on a sizeable viewing audience for their primetime addresses,[19] presidents often receive audience shares much lower than their first national addresses and, what is more, deliver national addresses only rarely. Indeed, the average yearly number of national addresses between 1961 and 2016 was only about 3.4, with Richard Nixon and Ronald Reagan having offered the most national addresses. Figure 5.1 shows a clear decline in recent years, with George W. Bush and

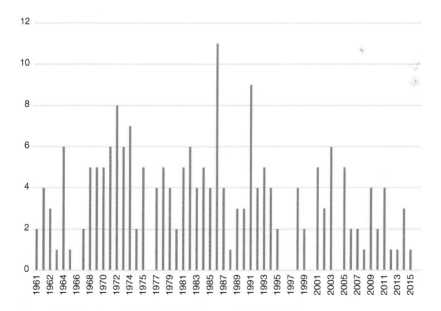

Figure 5.1 Number of National Addresses, 1961–2016

Source: Ragsdale (2014), updated by the author from the American Presidency Project.

Barack Obama averaging 2.5 speeches per year, nearly a full national address below the time series average. Given the declining frequency of direct appeals to the public, therefore, the public presidency focuses increasingly on leading media to reach public opinion through the news.[20]

Although the national address is a rare event, the presidential speech is not, as numerous studies document.[21] Figure 5.2 reveals, indeed, that all presidential speeches have increased markedly over the time frame. It reveals a peak in presidential speeches during Gerald Ford's presidential election campaign in 1976, attributable to myriad campaign-style speeches. More recently, George W. Bush delivered more speeches on average than Reagan, but fewer than Bill Clinton, producing the appearance of a declining trend in presidential speechmaking. Although Obama increased presidential speechmaking, leading to an increase since 2006, it remains unclear whether Obama's speeches represent the beginning of a long-term upward trend that will continue into the Trump administration.

Within these counts, of course, is significant variation in the focus of each speech. They include dozens of minor policy addresses that are not televised at all, or in full, but through which presidents elucidate their policy priorities. Presidents seek to generate news coverage and public

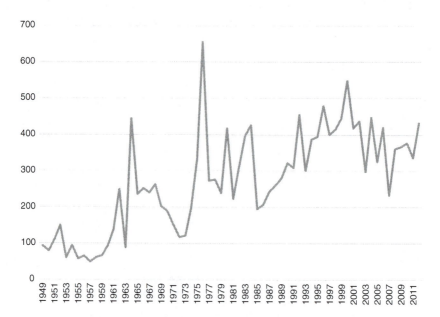

Figure 5.2 Total Number of Yearly Non-Major President Speeches, 1949–2012

Source: Data compiled from Ragsdale (2014). It is an additive measure of public appearances in Washington, DC and the United States, minor speeches, and political appearances.

Note: State of the Union Addresses are not included in the counts here.

exposure in other ways, such as by holding town hall meetings, which involve audience questions and presidents' answers. Presidents regularly attend public fundraisers, as well, although these are more common during presidential reelection and midterm election years. Even if these speeches generate substantial news coverage by local news sources,[22] national news coverage of non-televised addresses is more variable than a televised address. To maximize news coverage through these speeches, presidents work to appear newsworthy and so use the White House communications resources to present themselves in interesting and unique ways.

Among the president's arsenal of public speeches is a subset of remarks, whereby presidents travel to communities outside of Washington to generate news coverage and public support for their presidencies and policies. Called going local by some,[23] presidents have had mixed success with this public relations strategy. On the one hand, presidents generate more favorable coverage in local rather than national newspapers.[24] On the other hand, local news coverage tends to be more descriptive than substantive, limiting the president's opportunity to lead local publics to support their policy positions. In fact, even as George W. Bush influenced local newspaper coverage during his Social Security reform tour in 2006, public support for Social Security reform dropped.[25]

Another customary means of communicating to the American people, while generating modest news coverage, is the president's weekly radio address, a favorite among presidents since the Reagan administration (albeit with a brief respite during the first Bush presidency). This format transformed under the Obama administration into an Internet podcast, delivered weekly on Saturday mornings. Trump has continued to use this address in this way. Typically, news outlets cover the president's Saturday address, airing at least part of it during a Saturday afternoon news program and generating a significant increase in the amount of presidential news in newspapers.[26] But this is paired with an opposition party address and, what is more, occurs on one of the slowest news days of the week, with its potential impact limited by the few people who actually hear the president speak, whether directly on their computer or radio, or indirectly through a media summary of the speech. The radio address provides, nonetheless, an opportunity for presidents to reach out to the public through their own words and with little journalistic interpretation.[27]

Presidents are always followed by reporters, whether aboard Air Force One, as the president walks to Marine One, or when the president arrives at public speaking events throughout the nation. This provides presidents with the opportunity to answer questions quickly, giving the press their time, but not too much of it. These informal exchanges with reporters are even more plentiful than interviews, and are a reflection of personal style. Clinton averaged over 100 of these exchanges per year, whereas George H.W. Bush averaged about 50 exchanges in every year but his first. Press conferences are even fewer but they, too, reflect heavily the president's style of engaging the media.[28] George H.W. Bush held numerous afternoon press conferences in the White House briefing room, whereas Reagan held few overall, relying almost exclusively on a handful of formal evening press conferences. Although George H.W. Bush and Clinton both averaged over 33 press conferences per year during their first terms, Clinton held fewer press conferences as his second term progressed. The downward trend from Clinton's first term continued with George W. Bush, who held 89 press conferences in total during his first term in office. Although Bush held more second-term press conferences, Obama's first-term average of just under 19 press conferences was also lower than George W. Bush's average of 22.[29]

Dealing with the media directly is a different skill than speaking prepared words to an audience. Just as the president has speechwriters and media affair consultants who coordinate the president's message with his style for delivering it, so too does the president have staff who help prepare them for exchanges, research possible questions, and provide information for effective answers. Preparation is especially detailed and extensive for the president during his press conferences. Although some maintain that the press conference is a contentious event worth avoiding,[30] presidents have tremendous control over this exchange given that the president's staff can anticipate questions and prepare the president to answer them. As Martha Kumar describes, the president can

> call on the reporters he wants to recognize…in the order of his choosing. His staff prepare in advance a list of questions they believe may be asked, and senior staff members also prepare possible responses, which they discuss with the president in preparatory sessions.[31]

Undoubtedly, presidential performances vary, and presidents may perform so poorly as to avoid or limit future press conferences. The president has a honeymoon period with reporters,[32] after all, and once that ends, presidents may feel more resentment toward increasing negative news coverage of their administrations. Jimmy Carter held monthly press conferences early in his tenure, for example, but quickly curtailed them because it takes time and energy to prepare for these events to perform admirably. Clinton, likewise, appears to have reduced his press conferences throughout 1998 to avoid reporters' questions about Monica Lewinsky. Obama, well-regarded as an inspirational speaker, spoke "professorially" in press conferences, offering reflective and lengthy responses to reporters' questions. Early accounts of Trump press conferences suggest a wide-ranging style, one centered on antagonizing the media.

Even joint press conferences do not provide the president cover in the face of a major scandal, much as Clinton learned during his joint conference with British Prime Minister Tony Blair on February 6, 1998 when he was asked about his relationship with Lewinsky.[33] Ultimately, it is up to the White House staff to maximize the president's exposure in a way that presents him in the best light but also provides him an opportunity to satisfy demands on the press, reach the news, and, ultimately, the American people. Depending on circumstances and the personal style of the president, the press conference may not be the ideal scenario for the president to achieve these goals.

Some presidents prefer to hold interviews with select media outlets. George W. Bush averaged about 50 interviews with news organizations per year, while Clinton held about 46 interviews per year through his eight years in office.[34] Obama discontinued this pace, however, holding an average of only 17 interviews with network and cable news moderators, newspapers, and radio networks such as National Public Radio. It remains unclear whether Trump will prefer interviews or not. He has held several with Fox News Channel, including a high-profile Super Bowl Sunday interview with Bill O'Reilly.[35] Interviews can be valuable to presidents in leading the public and news media because they afford presidents more time to explain specific actions, situations, or criticisms of the White House.[36] A memorable example occurred when candidate Bill Clinton used a *60 Minutes* interview following Super Bowl XXVI to refute allegations concerning marital infidelity. Regardless of the means of communication, presidents directly engage the media in a variety of ways, and each approach—and especially presidential press conferences[37]—has a positive impact on presidential news coverage.

White House Communications in an Institutional Context

It is not the president alone who communicates as a part of the public presidency. It is also the institution of the presidency that allows for presidents to simultaneously lead Congress, manage the media, and reach the public. The presidency has evolved from a single elected official with a staff of less than a dozen, to an organizational entity divided into numerous task specializations with hundreds of regular staffers. Institutionalization is not relegated to communications, of course, but it has extended its reach. According to Mike McCurry, press secretary for three years during the Clinton administration:

> Twenty-five to 30 percent of the paid White House staff devotes at least two-thirds of its time to communications...but just about everybody who has any serious, consequential role at the White House...has to be...cognizant of playing a role in how are we going to communicate.[38]

Placing that in concrete numbers, and at the beginning of his second term in office, George W. Bush employed nearly 350 people in the White

House to assist the president in communicating his policies and favorably portraying his presidency.[39] Communications staff ranges from speech-writers and media affairs consultants to communications directors, the difficulties in measuring staff size notwithstanding.[40]

Although more diverse and variable by presidential administration, the two key entities involved in coordinating and communicating the president's message are the Office of Communications and the Press Office. The Office of Communications (OOC)[41] has existed more or less consistently since the Nixon administration, which created the office to facilitate communication with the media given its growing presence and importance to the public presidency. The OOC has supplied presidents with the institutional resources to maximize the effectiveness of communications strategies and respond to public expectations through myriad speeches, of course, but also other efforts to control the president's messages. These include disseminating information about the president's priorities in a timely and strategic fashion, engaging in dumps of negative information on Friday afternoon when fewer people are engaged in presidential news, and releasing trial balloons to gauge media and public response to possible administration actions. Although variable over time, the OOC now typically includes speechwriting and media affairs operations, and staff to research and coordinate strategic planning efforts.[42]

With its primary responsibility to help the president to set the public and media agendas—to engage in "merchandising" the presidency[43]—the OOC attempts to influence what about the president the media will cover in the news and, therefore, what the public thinks about the president and his policies. It does so through "barnstorming" regional media and distributing fact sheets to editors and other "opinion leaders" to build public support for the president's policies. Attempts by presidents to "go local," to target local news organizations and local publics with their policy messages, are the responsibility of this office, too, with one of the best known and most extensive efforts to do this occurring in the George W. Bush administration, and his "60 stops in 60 days" Social Security reform tour.

The Press Office also plays a central role in presidential communication efforts. In terms of influencing the media, it is perhaps even more direct than the Communications Office. It is the press secretary, through daily news briefs and morning gaggles, who provides the official record of the president and communicates it directly to reporters, mostly those who comprise the Washington press corps. Primarily, the press secretary acts as an information conduit between the president and reporters,[44] helping the president reach the media without having to do so personally as frequently. Of course, this relationship is not one-way, with the press secretary expressing the president's views for reporters to take at face value. Rather, it is one of give-and-take, whereby the president uses the press corps to communicate his messages to the public, just as the media use the president as a reliable political news source.[45] That news coverage of the presidency tends to be primarily negative[46] raises questions about the press and the OOC's ability to cultivate its relationship with the news media in a way that maximizes the president's policy success and his personal image. This appears to have been further undermined by Sean Spicer, who extended Trump's strategy of media antagonism to the daily gaggle, refusing admittance to key reporters in February 2017.

The Mediated Presidency

If the president speaks, but the media do not report it, does it make a sound? The answer appears to be that presidents can speak continuously and without interruption, but their prospects for leading publicly in the contemporary age without reaching the media first are limited. And if presidential leadership rests with the news media, it does so precariously. As Lori Cox Han writes, after all, White House reporters are interested in reporting on "suspected scandal, dissension within an administration, verbal and visual gaffes, and tactical political blunders. Few are policy experts..."[47] This raises concerns for presidential leadership of the news media, whether its amount, substance, tone, and that these stories may be mostly superficial and negative. In spite of these characteristics of news coverage, given the resources presidents expend to influence news coverage, one may expect presidents to successfully influence news coverage. But do they?

Why Media Are Important to Presidential Communication

The media are central to presidential communication and leadership for many reasons, but mainly because the president must reach the media to lead the public in the contemporary age. The media are thus vital to presidential leadership for several reasons. First, news coverage influences which issues the public considers to be important.[48] Second, media attention to policy issues affects public familiarity[49] with and the public's knowledge about those issues.[50] Third, media coverage of issues primes the public's evaluation of the president,[51] so that when the media report extensively on an issue, it is that issue that the public uses to evaluate presidential job performance. Finally, media framing matters to the public's perception about issues.[52] And although much research focuses on the relationship between hard news programs and public opinion, other research shows that even soft news programs, such as *The Oprah Winfrey Show*, may increase public exposure to important policy issues.[53]

Amount, Substance, and Tone of Presidential News

Presidents are the primary news interest of the media when compared with other political institutions. Presidents simply garner more network news time than any of the three federal branches of government. As Doris

Graber illustrates, presidents tend to average from ten to 20 stories more per month than Congress on the three major television news networks (ABC, CBS, and NBC) and approximately four times as much coverage as the U.S. Supreme Court.[54] It certainly helps the president's broader strategy of influencing the public through news coverage that public interest in presidential news is quite high, especially when compared to news of others in government.[55]

The trend in the amount of presidential news is somewhat complicated, however. Over the long haul, Jeffrey Cohen documents a clear decline in the amount of presidential news coverage on both network television and as printed in *The New York Times*.[56] Yet, Cohen shows an upward trend in presidential news coverage since 1999.[57] Tracking Graber's counts of presidential news on network television, moreover, we see that Clinton averaged about 107 stories per month between August 1994 and July 1995.[58] Although this number drops substantially to 41 stories per month between July 1999 and June 2000, it increased slightly to 45 stories for George W. Bush between July 2003 and July 2004 and during the early stages of the Iraq War. The end of the Bush administration and early Obama presidency shows an even lower average of 18 stories per month, however, reversing the slight uptick in stories.[59]

Other counts show significant differences between Obama's early news coverage in comparison with both Clinton and Bush. At least for his first 50 days in office, Obama received substantially more news coverage than either of his previous two counterparts during similar points in their tenures. The three network news programs devoted 1,021 stories, at 27 hours and 44 minutes to Obama, with a daily average of seven stories at 11 minutes. In contrast, they devoted only seven hours and 42 minutes to Bush during early 2001, down from the 15 hours and two minutes of coverage that Clinton received during his first 50 days in 1993.

If presidents are intent on generating voluminous news coverage, then going local may be an optimal strategy. For example, Andrew Barrett and Jeffrey Peake sampled 12 days in 2001 in which the president traveled throughout the U.S.[60] During this time frame, they report that local newspapers generated 119 stories, compared with only ten stories printed in the *Washington Post*. Coverage of Bush's Social Security reform tour in 2005 produces similar results, as the length of coverage in local newspapers was about 7 percent longer than in the *Washington Post*.[61] In any event, if presidents want more newspaper coverage, they should target cities with larger newspapers, which tend to print more stories about the president than smaller ones.[62]

Beyond amount, we know that news coverage does not focus on the substance of the policy priorities presidents are bent on communicating. Tom Patterson shows three trends consistent with this point: There are now more news stories (1) without a policy component; (2) that are sensational; and (3) generally soft, rather than hard.[63] This tendency toward superficial rather than substantive news coverage of the presidency is especially pronounced for news stories that are generated by local newspapers that cover the president's travels. Roughly half of Bush's front-page, local newspaper coverage of his Social Security reform tour, for example, was descriptive rather than substantive.[64]

Unquestioned is the platitude that news coverage of the presidency is negative. Of the nine years examined by Stephen Farnsworth and Robert Lichter, only one year—1989, the first year of George H. W. Bush's presidency—produced news coverage that was more than 40 percent positive.[65] These data examine each of the last four presidents' first years in office, which typically includes a honeymoon with the public, media, and Congress. If presidents cannot expect mostly positive coverage during their honeymoon period, then perhaps they should never expect more positive than negative coverage. Others report that network news organizations are more likely to report on the president's approval rating when it declines, rather than when it increases.[66] Local newspaper coverage of the president's travels produces much less negative coverage than national news does,[67] even though this coverage is less policy-driven. When local coverage is more policy-oriented, such as the Iraq War in 2003, this too produces more negative than positive.[68]

The tendency toward negative coverage of the presidency did not abate with the Obama administration. Most news coverage of Obama early in his tenure was positive. At 57 percent, this exceeds the 33 percent positive coverage George W. Bush and 44 percent positive coverage Clinton received during a comparable time in their administrations. Yet, Obama received much less than a majority—40 percent—positive coverage on his policies, with only 37 percent positive on his initial top policy priority: the economy. Foreign policy evaluations were even less positive, at 24 percent. We also know that news coverage gets worse for presidents as their tenure lengthens. This is no different for Obama, who witnessed a substantial increase in negative news coverage, with only 43 percent positive coverage from May through mid-August 2009, with "every major policy of the administration [having] received more criticism than praise from the press."[69] By engaging in an antagonistic strategy of media leadership, it is possible that Trump's news coverage will be even more negative than positive. Indeed, an analysis of Trump's first month in office shows that even a *Special Report* on Fox News Channel was more negative (25 percent) than positive (12 percent) in its coverage of the Trump administration.[70]

Does the Public Presidency Affect Media?

Whether through a national address, other speeches, or targeted efforts at going local, presidents have much opportunity to lead the news media. In the main, nevertheless, the president has much difficulty encouraging the media to cover his top policy priorities, even though the presidency garners more news coverage than any other political institution. Simply, news media have other priorities besides granting the president's words exposure on their networks. This is driven in part by media's preference for soft, entertainment and celebrity-related news, rather than hard policy-related news; and their desire for profit[71] rather than fulfilling norms of democracy. A most telling example of this occurred during Clinton's February 4, 1997 State of the Union Address, where the president actually shared the television screen with OJ Simpson's civil trial verdict.[72] Coverage tends to be quite superficial, devoid of policy content, and instead focuses on the person or in other words, the "body watch" and other types of human interest stories (e.g., the Obama's first dog, Bo, or, Trump's critique of Arnold Schwarzenegger on *Celebrity Apprentice*). Therefore, the media will not cover the president as often as he speaks, and generally may not do so substantively.

Concerning national addresses, arguably the best opportunity for presidents to generate news coverage despite the complications accentuated during the opening vignette of this chapter, we find mixed results, at best, of the president's leadership of the news media. Focusing on the obligatory and annual State of the Union Address, for example, Wayne Wanta et al. report that presidents have had only mixed success influencing what the media cover in their analysis of four State of the Union addresses since 1970, with only Nixon's 1970 Address having a clear impact on the media's agenda.[73] Oddly, Reagan's 1982 address affected newspaper coverage, but television coverage seems to have influenced the topics Reagan covered in his speech. Jeffrey Peake and Matthew Eshbaugh-Soha examine national addresses on four specific policy areas: the economy, drugs, Central America, and energy.[74] They find that although presidents were able to use their national address to increase media coverage of the issues, the percentage was low, as national addresses significantly increased national news coverage only about one-third of the time.

Others recognize that presidents speak daily, sometimes multiple times in a day, and analyze the impact of all presidential speeches on news coverage. George C. Edwards III and B. Dan Wood's study of presidential leadership of the news media finds that presidential leadership of the news media is not guaranteed.[75] Instead, presidential leadership of the media on foreign policy issues (U.S.-Soviet relations and the Arab-Israeli conflict) is virtually non-existent, a finding echoed by B. Dan Wood and Jeffrey Peake.[76] Instead, presidents tend to respond to media coverage on both issues. Although presidents lead news coverage of domestic issues, particularly health care and education, they also respond to news coverage of education and crime. Eshbaugh-Soha and Peake reveal that a presidents' economic agenda is driven by news coverage of the economy, especially when it is in recession, with fewer positive stories prompted by presidential credit-claiming during times of economic prosperity.[77]

At best, these findings demonstrate a mixed assessment of presidential leadership of the news media on domestic policy issues, and a responsive presidency on foreign policy issues.

When presidents do affect news coverage, it is typically because of their own strategic intentions to do so. Despite Edwards' and Wood's conclusion of limited presidential leadership of the news media, they concede that presidents can lead the media agenda when they act entrepreneurially and prioritize a policy not previously on the media's agenda.[78] Peake's examination of less salient foreign policy issues reveals that when presidents prioritize a unique and otherwise less newsworthy set of policies, they are best situated to increase news coverage of those issues.[79] Although national, prestige newspapers (*The New York Times* and *Washington Post*) cover the president's legislative appeals only about 40 percent of the time,[80] presidents can shape news coverage strategically by focusing extensively on a single policy in their speech. As an example, presidents who deliver a lengthy (20 paragraphs or longer) and focused policy speech can expect coverage from these newspapers over 93 percent of the time.[81] Cohen also shows a small impact of presidential speeches on the number of newspaper stories.[82] Even press conferences have a modest agenda-setting impact on network news coverage.[83]

More promising for presidents may be the strategy of going local. Here, presidents engage in domestic travel throughout the country to target local media and publics so as to generate extensive news coverage. Often, these are scripted "media events" in which the White House attempts to structure the event in such a way that there is at least the appearance of support for the president and his policies. The White House tends to have more leeway influencing the less experienced (and less cynical) reporters of local newspapers by providing less resourceful local newspapers with more information that supports its perspective. A local presidential visit is usually a positive event, besides, leading to the expectation of more positive, local news coverage, especially in areas that are predisposed to support the president.[84] Surely, the national news media will find something negative to say and it may well be the strategy itself that they criticize. More presidential speeches seem to increase negative news coverage, in any event.[85] But if the event produces little discord and we look at the local newspaper that covers the local event, then consistent with indexing theory, most coverage should reflect the tenor of the event and be mostly positive. Indeed, more quotes attributed to the president increases the positive tone of a presidential news story.[86]

The news is not entirely encouraging for presidents who rely on local media to govern. First, even when local news coverage of the president's visit is positive, it tends to be more descriptive than substantive, producing only modest references to the president's policies, even when the goal of the speech or series of speeches is to build support for that policy.[87] This complicates the president's ability to communicate his reasons why the public should support his policy agenda. Second, coverage of local visits contrasts with everyday local newspaper coverage of the presidency, which is more negative.[88] In turn, readers of local newspapers are exposed mostly to negative news of the presidency. Third, even positive local coverage may not provide any added value for presidents, as they may only be singing to the choir. Much of the evidence points to local ideology as driving the tone and amount of local newspaper coverage.[89] That is, a news organization—which desires profit—will appeal to its audience. If that audience is primarily conservative, then news coverage of a conservative president will be more positive than negative. Presidents are therefore wise to target those locales that already share their ideological views if presidents' strategy is to generate positive local news coverage. But by targeting a population that already agrees with them, presidents are not likely to build additional support for their policy solutions.

Presidents may still attempt to use local public support and newspaper coverage to their advantage, although evidence that this works is lacking. A conservative president may go local to conservative areas to put pressure on legislators from the opposition party to support his legislative priorities. George W. Bush used such a strategy to build support for tax cuts and reform Social Security. Although Congress passed a sizeable tax cut bill in 2001, Bush's travels did not shift public opinion or congressional support at all.[90] In fact, the tax cut was much smaller than Bush originally proposed. His strategy in targeting Senator Ben Nelson (D-NE) and other Democrats in "red" states to support Bush's Social Security reform efforts in 2005 summarily failed, as well.

Cable News and Other New Media

What remains to be considered, and about which current research says little, is whether the proliferation of cable news and other new media matter to presidential leadership of the news. The short answer is of course it does. Presidents are afforded additional means to communicate their message through cable television and the Internet. Even though this might stretch their reliance on traditional media, presidents have not deviated yet from attempting to lead these sources of news, and besides, the White House is well-equipped to penetrate multiple arenas of news coverage. Surely, these new media require the White House to develop and cultivate alternative strategies and considerations that may differ considerably from leading more traditional means of communication. But the White House has been quick to adjust to the fragmentation of the news media by reaching out to a wide range of formats and programs, whether "Between Two Ferns," *The View*, or by using Twitter or Facebook to communicate with followers or influence news coverage.

Indeed, limited research shows that the potential for presidential speeches to affect news coverage extends to both cable television news and online news sources.[91] To begin, cable news programs, *Special Report* (Fox) and *Hardball* (MSNBC), covered the president's speeches most frequently, on 40 of the 54 days in which the president delivered a speech. Traditional news sources covered the president an average of 22 out of 54 days the president gave a speech compared with about 20 days of coverage on online news sources (Drudge Report, Fox News, and Huffington Post). Although a potential benefit to the president, given that more of his speeches will reach a cable news audience, the president's own message could be lost in the noise of other presidential news coverage. Just as cable news covers the president nearly every day, many of those stories address aspects of an administration unrelated to the president's agenda. This, at once, shows the potential benefit that newer media afford presidential leadership of the media, but at the same time, shows a limitation to consistent presidential leadership of the news.

New Media

The long answer is that new media outlets may not make much of a difference in the overall effectiveness of presidential communications. The expectation may be that presidents should be able to reach and motivate more young people through the Internet, for example, because the nation's youth are more tech-savvy and use alternative sources of information more readily than older Americans. Obama certainly tapped into this sensation during the 2008 election by texting the announcement of his vice-presidential selection. He continued to tap the Internet as a communications source, answering questions on YouTube during the week of his 2010 State of the Union Address as one example. But do these new means of outreach matter to motivating public support or informing a relatively uninformed electorate? Although a systematic answer is impossible now, one may speculate that they would not.

Research on traditional media and public engagement in politics relies heavily on political predispositions and self-selective behavior. If American youth are not interested in American politics, then no matter how much information the Internet provides about politics and policies, one must be interested in that information to seek it out in the first place. Just because Obama speaks on the Internet does not mean that a college student is watching; they may well be surfing sports scores, posting on Snapchat, or streaming episodes of *The Walking Dead*. We certainly did not see an explosion of youth political involvement with the rise of cable television, nor did we see an increase in the level of Americans' political engagement as 24-hour news provided the potential for the greater dissemination of information.[92] At the least, the Internet's impact on political engagement appears to be slight, at best.[93]

Given self-selection, presidents may benefit, not from targeting a particular medium, but rather specific content. If a target audience, say young

Americans, are more likely to watch *The Daily Show* than *NBC Nightly News*, then presidents may wish to reach out to this type of program, much as Clinton targeted MTV and late-night talk shows during his election campaigns and presidency, or how Obama "slow jammed" news about student loan interest rates with Jimmy Fallon. Comedy and other soft news programs tend to provide a "gateway" to increased political knowledge for the politically disinterested.[94] Late night programs also increase accessibility of political information, which encourages policy learning[95] and political knowledge.[96] There may be the additional benefit of capitalizing on the agenda-setting effect that entertainment television programs have,[97] such that presidents may benefit from prioritizing a policy issue after it has been treated as a story in a courtroom or hospital drama. Just as viewer confidence in understanding politics increases, however, so too does the audience's level of political cynicism[98] undermining the potential benefits to presidents of communicating through alternative media.

Self-selection is likely to drive the impact of presidential leadership through social media, too. After all, individuals select who they might follow on social media, much like how individuals decide which partisan news programs to watch.[99] Twitter is a favorite medium of Trump and he appears to have generated much news coverage from it. From the political campaigns literature, we know that social media have limited positive and independent effects on political engagement, however.[100] Thus, much as we see supporters driving audience numbers for presidential national addresses,[101] it is likely that supporters disproportionately follow Trump on Twitter, limiting the reach of his message independent of news coverage. If news media are still the primary vehicle by which Americans understand presidential communication—whether it is a recorded or live speech or a tweet—then it remains unlikely that Twitter will allow even Trump to circumvent the news media to reach the American people.[102]

Social Media

Indeed, Trump's own reliance on Twitter and newer media may actually undermine his administration's public relations strategies. Recall the importance of the White House Office of Communications in coordinating an effective public relations campaign on behalf of presidents and their policies. Presidents who use Twitter selectively to engage the public and news media may be able to use it to supplement their larger public relations campaigns. But when Twitter is used as part of an uncoordinated strategy, this may detract from the White House's attempt to communicate a clear and unified message. Trump may see Twitter as an effective communications tool, and one vital to his antagonistic campaign strategy, but without coordination with the White House, these tweets may not help the Trump administration build a successful and well-messaged public presidency. Tweets may even discourage coverage of a well-crafted speech, simply trading news coverage of one set of remarks for 140 characters.

The bottom line is that political engagement has not increased markedly with the expansion of new media.[103] Targeting new media is hardly a guarantee of public outreach given the only roughly six million Americans who watch cable news, with Fox News Channel the ratings leader with approximately three million primetime viewers, or roughly a tenth of a percentage of the overall population. Targeting alternative programs is important for presidents who wish to lead a broader swath of the public, of course. And social media provide a way for presidents to reach supporters and speak to them without generating news coverage. It remains unlikely that presidents will be able to target only supportive cable news channels or lead through social media, given that most Americans still lack political engagement and are likely to learn about the presidency through casual media use. New media will have an impact on the presidency, to be sure, but its significance will likely occur, as Edwards wrote years ago, "at the margins."[104]

Conclusion

It remains a truism, perhaps, that despite the extent to which contemporary White Houses attempt to promote and sell the president's policy priorities, presidents experience myriad setbacks and failures in their public leadership. Scholarly research finds, indeed, that despite the level of media outreach of recent presidencies, presidents cannot always generate adequate coverage of their policies, and, even when they do, this coverage tends to be more negative than positive, or more superficial than substantive. What is more, scholarly research tends to contrast with the conventional wisdom that cultivating public opinion through the news media is the approach that modern presidents have to take to be successful. Recall Obama's lament after Scott Brown (R-MA) wrestled Ted Kennedy's Senate seat away from the Democratic party in January 2010:

> We were so busy just getting stuff done...that I think we lost some of that sense of speaking directly to the American people about what their core values are and why we have to make sure those institutions are matching up with those values.

The White House contended that this political defeat was because of a lack of effective communication. The Trump administration appears willing to blame inaccurate reporting and "fake news" for its failings. But scholarship maintains that changing the public's policy preferences is not likely in the current age of new media.

Whether this expectation will continue into the Trump presidency remains to be seen. And perhaps our scholarly expectations for presidential leadership of the news media should change in light of significant changes to the political and media environments. Much as the decentralization of Congress spurred presidents to speak more frequently to the American people,[105] so too might the fragmentation of news media encourage presidents to continue to change their media outreach strategies. Although it is unlikely that presidents can deliver more speeches than they already do, presidents may choose to target particular media sources or specific media technologies to lead the news media, much as Trump has attempted to use Twitter to do so. The specter of heightened partisanship may further adjust the extent to which presidents engage the media and public to achieve their legislative goals. As early reports reveal with Trump's handling of health care reform legislation,[106] and as suggested by recent research,[107] a more unified Congress may diminish the president's need for public leadership to achieve legislation, but rather encourage bargaining with members of Congress, especially under unified government.

At the least, we can agree that the public presidency is at the heart of contemporary presidential governance, but communicating to the public and leading the news media is no easy task. Leading the public in the contemporary age—with its fragmented media, decentralized news audiences, and diversified entertainment possibilities—requires presidents to first access the news media and then lead the media, which the White House clearly attempts to do, as we have seen. In light of this expectation of leadership and the resources devoted to cultivating news coverage, the most important power of the presidency, according to Richard Neustadt, is the "power to persuade."[108] But if successful presidential leadership requires persuading the media, then presidents are only modestly influential leaders, at best.

Notes

1 "The President's News Conference," February 16, 2017, www.whitehouse. gov/the-press-office/2017/02/16/remarks-president-trump-press-conference.
2 From the Gallup Poll, "In general, how much trust and confidence do you have in the mass media—such as newspapers, TV, and radio—when it comes to reporting the news fully, accurately, and fairly—a great deal, a fair amount, not very much or none at all?"
3 The sample, with a margin of error of ± 4.2 percent, was of 857 speech watchers. The sample leaned Republican (39 percent) and male (56 percent).
4 "In general, did you approve or disapprove of the President's speech tonight?"
5 The questions were: "In his speech tonight, did you think that Donald Trump was...presidential?; Did the speech make you feel more optimistic about what the Trump Administration will do next, more pessimistic, or didn't it change how you felt?; Based on what you heard tonight, do you favor or oppose Donald Trump's plans for...illegal immigration, improving the economy, dealing with Obamacare, etc."

6 In comparison, 111.3 million viewers watched the Atlanta Falcons' offense struggle in the second half of Super Bowl LI, losing to the New England Patriots in the Super Bowl's first-ever overtime game.

7 Foote reports a range of 62–75 percent average shares for Presidents Nixon's, Ford's, Carter's, and Reagan's televised addresses. See Joe S. Foote, "Ratings Decline of Presidential Television," *Journal of Broadcasting and Electronic Media* 32 (1988): 227.

8 Gallup's daily tracking poll shows an increase to 44 percent approval after the address, only to decline back to 41 percent by March 8, www.pollingreport.com/djt_job1.htm.

9 "Do you approve or disapprove of the health care law passed by Barack Obama and Congress in 2010?" The percentage that approve is 54 percent, according to the February 7–12, 2017 Pew Research Center Poll.

10 "Do you think Congress should vote to repeal the 2010 health care law, or should they not vote to repeal it?" 51 percent responded, "Should not repeal," during a March 6–12, 2017 sampling, Kaiser Family Foundation poll.

11 Samuel Kernell and Laurie L. Rice, "Cable and the Partisan Polarization of the President's Audience," *Presidential Studies Quarterly* 41 (2011): 693–711.

12 The news immediately after Trump's address centered on Jeff Sessions' nomination, hearing comments that he did not have any contact with Russian officials during the campaign, only to be revealed that he had. The President further stepped on a widely praised speech by tweeting several days later an accusation that President Obama had wiretapped Trump Tower during the 2016 presidential election campaign.

13 Thomas E. Cronin, "Thinking and Learning about Leadership," *Presidential Studies Quarterly* 14 (1984): 22–34.

14 Jeffrey Tulis, *The Rhetorical Presidency* (Princeton, NJ: Princeton University Press, 1987), 4.

15 George C. Edwards III, *On Deaf Ears: The Limits of the Bully Pulpit* (New Haven, CT: Yale University Press, 2003), 4.

16 See Samuel Kernell, *Going Public: New Strategies of Presidential Leadership*, 3rd ed. (Washington, DC: CQ Press, 1997).

17 Steven A. Shull, *A Kinder, Gentler Racism? The Reagan-Bush Civil Rights Legacy* (New York: Routledge, 1993), 8.

18 Bert A. Rockman, *The Leadership Question: The Presidency and the American System* (New York: Praeger, 1984), 6.

19 Matthew A. Baum and Samuel Kernell, "Has Cable Ended the Golden Age of Presidential Television?," *American Political Science Review* 93 (1998): 99–114.

20 See Matthew Eshbaugh-Soha and Jeffrey S. Peake, *Breaking through the Noise: Presidential Leadership, Public Opinion, and the News Media* (Stanford, CA: Stanford University Press, 2011).

21 Matthew Eshbaugh-Soha, "The Tone of Local Presidential News Coverage," *Political Communication* 27 (2010b): 121–140; Gregory L. Hager and Terry Sullivan, "President-Centered and Presidency-Centered Explanations of Presidential Public Activity," *American Journal of Political Science* (1994): 1079–1103; William W. Lammers, "Presidential Attention-Focusing Activities," in *The President and the Public*, ed. Doris Graber (Philadelphia, PA: Institute for the Study of Human Issues, 1982); Richard J. Powell, "'Going Public' Revisited: Presidential Speechmaking and the Bargaining Setting in Congress," *Congress & the Presidency* 26 (1999): 153–170.

22 See Jeffrey E. Cohen, *Going Local: Presidential Leadership in the Post-Broadcast Age* (New York: Cambridge University Press, 2010).

23 Ibid.; Matthew Eshbaugh-Soha and Jeffrey S. Peake, "The Contemporary Presidency: 'Going Local' to Reform Social Security," *Presidential Studies Quarterly* 36 (2006): 689–704.
24 Andrew W. Barrett and Jeffrey S. Peake, "When the President Comes to Town: Examining Local Newspaper Coverage of Domestic Presidential Travel," *American Politics Research* 35 (2007): 3–31.
25 See Eshbaugh-Soha and Peake, "The Contemporary Presidency."
26 Cohen, *"Going Local,"* 116.
27 Roderick P. Hart, Jay P. Childers, and Colene J. Lind, *Political Tone: How Leaders Talk and Why* (Chicago, IL: University of Chicago Press, 2013), Chapter 5.
28 Matthew Eshbaugh-Soha, "Presidential Press Conferences over Time," *American Journal of Political Science* 47 (2003): 348–353.
29 Lyn Ragsdale, *Vital Statistics on the Presidency*, 4th ed. (Washington, DC: CQ Press, 2014), Table 4-4.
30 See Hager and Sullivan, "President-Centered and Presidency-Centered Explanations."
31 Martha Joynt Kumar, *Managing the President's Message: The White House Communications Operation* (Baltimore, MD: Johns Hopkins University Press, 2007), 273.
32 See Michael Baruch Grossman and Martha Joynt Kumar, *Portraying the President: The White House and the News Media* (Baltimore, MD: Johns Hopkins University Press, 1981).
33 It helps, to be sure, because good journalists also want to ask about the president's policies, especially as they pertain to his guest and their meeting. Reporters asked Clinton and Blair several questions about the situation in Iraq, but several more questions concerned Monica Lewinsky and the Starr Investigation.
34 Unless otherwise noted, the following numbers for Clinton and Bush are reported by Kumar in *Managing the President's Message*, Chapter 7.
35 I cannot provide a precise number because the White House is not listing all media interviews. Although the *Public Papers of the Presidents* indicates a Westwood One Sports Radio Network (February 5, 2017), for example, there is no reference to Trump's January 25, 2017 interview with ABC News.
36 Kumar, *Managaing the President's Message*, 19.
37 Matthew Eshbaugh-Soha, "Presidential Influence of the News Media: The Case of the Press Conference," *Political Communication* 30 (2013): 548–564.
38 Kumar, *Managing the President's Message*, 4.
39 Ibid., 5.
40 Charles E. Walcott and Karen M. Hult, "White House Staff Size: Explanations and Implications," *Presidential Studies Quarterly* 29 (1999): 638–656.
41 The Office of Communications has gone by different names. For George W. Bush, communications operations were centralized according to the counselor to the president. Although slightly different organizationally, the goals remain similar across administrations (see Kumar, *Managing the President's Message*, for the most thorough discussion).
42 Ibid., Chapter 4.
43 Karen M. Hult and Charles E. Walcott, *Empowering the White House: Governance under Nixon, Ford, and Carter* (Lawrence, KS: University Press of Kansas, 2004), 63.
44 Kumar, *Managing the President's Message*, 199.
45 See Grossman and Kumar, *Portraying the President*.
46 See Jeffrey E. Cohen, *The Presidency in the Era of 24-Hour News* (Princeton, NJ: Princeton University Press, 2008).

47 Lori Cox Han, *Governing From Center Stage: White House Communication Strategies During the Television Age of Politics* (Cresskill, NJ: Hampton Press, 2001), 13.

48 See Shanto Iyengar, *Is Anyone Responsible?: How Television Frames Political Issues* (Chicago, IL: University of Chicago Press, 1991); and Shanto Iyengar, Mark D. Peters, and Donald R. Kinder, "Experimental Demonstrations of the 'Not-So-Minimal' Consequences of Television News Programs," *American Political Science Review* 76 (1982): 848–858.

49 See Benjamin I. Page and Robert Y. Shapiro, *The Rational Public: Fifty Years of Trends in Americans' Policy Preferences* (Chicago, IL: University of Chicago Press, 1992).

50 See W. Lance Bennett, *News: The Politics of Illusion,* 8th ed. (New York: Pearson, 2009).

51 George C. Edwards III, William Mitchell, and Reed Welch, "Explaining Presidential Approval: The Significance of Issue Salience," *American Journal of Political Science* 39 (1995): 108–134; Jon A. Krosnick and Donald R. Kinder, "Altering the Foundations of Support for the President through Priming," *American Political Science Review* 84 (1990): 497–512; and Iyengar, *Is Anyone Responsible?*

52 Franklin D. Gilliam Jr and Shanto Iyengar, "Prime Suspects: The Influence of Local Television News on the Viewing Public," *American Journal of Political Science* 44 (2000): 560–573.

53 See Matthew A. Baum, *Soft News Goes to War: Public Opinion and American Foreign Policy in the New Media Age* (Princeton, NJ: Princeton University Press, 2003).

54 Doris A. Graber, *Mass Media and American Politics*, 7th ed. (Washington, DC: CQ Press, 2006), 251.

55 See Herbert J. Gans, *Deciding What's News: A Study of CBS Evening News, NBC Nightly News, Newsweek, and Time* (New York: Vintage Books, 1980); and William G. Howell and Jon C. Pevehouse, *While Dangers Gather: Congressional Checks on Presidential War Powers* (Princeton, NJ: Princeton University Press, 2007), 173.

56 See Cohen, *The Presidency in the Era of 24-Hour News.*

57 Ibid., 33.

58 See Graber, *Mass Media and American Politics.*

59 See Doris A. Graber and Johanna Dunaway, *Mass Media and American Politics,* 9th ed. (Washington, DC: CQ Press, 2015).

60 Barrett and Peake, "When the President Comes to Town," 12.

61 See Eshbaugh-Soha and Peake, "The Contemporary Presidency."

62 See Cohen, *Going Local*; and Matthew Eshbaugh-Soha and Jeffrey S. Peake, "The Presidency and Local Media: Local Newspaper Coverage of President George W. Bush," *Presidential Studies Quarterly* 38 (2008): 609–630.

63 Thomas E. Patterson, *Doing Well and Doing Good: How Soft News and Critical Journalism Are Shrinking the News Audience and Weakening Democracy–and What News Outlets Can Do about It*, Joan Shorenstein Center on the Press, Politics and Public Policy, John F. Kennedy School of Government, Harvard University, 2000.

64 See Eshbaugh-Soha and Peake, "The Contemporary Presidency."

65 Stephen J. Farnsworth and Robert S. Lichter, *The Mediated Presidency: Television News and Presidential Governance* (New York: Rowman & Littlefield, 2006), 51.

66 Tim Groeling and Samuel Kernell, "Is Network News Coverage of the President Biased?," *The Journal of Politics* 60 (1998): 1063–1087.

67 See Barrett and Peake, "When the President Comes to Town"; and Eshbaugh-Soha and Peake, "The Contemporary Presidency."
68 See Eshbaugh-Soha and Peake, "The Presidency and Local Media."
69 Nikki Schwab, "Media Coverage of Obama Grows More Negative," *U.S. News and World Report*, September 14, 2009, www.usnews.com/news/washington-whispers/articles/2009/09/14/media-coverage-of-obama-grows-more-negative.
70 Roland Schatz, S. Robert Lichter and Stephen J. Farnsworth, "News Coverage of Trump is Really, Really Negative. Even on Fox News," *Washington Post,* February 28, 2017, www.washingtonpost.com/news/monkey-cage/wp/2017/02/28/news-coverage-of-trump-is-really-really-negative-even-on-fox-news/?utm_term=.a38e5a8b4bed.
71 See Jan E. Leighley, *Mass Media and Politics: A Social Science Perspective* (Boston, MA: Houghton Mifflin, 2003).
72 Francis X. Clines, "On Split Screen Night, Clinton Gets Full Attention of Congress," *New York Times*, February 4, 1997.
73 Wayne Wanta, Mary Ann Stephenson, Judy VanSlyke Turk, and Maxwell E. McCombs, "How President's State of Union Talk Influenced News Media Agendas," *Journalism Quarterly* 66 (1989): 537–541.
74 Jeffrey S. Peake and Matthew Eshbaugh-Soha, "The Agenda-Setting Impact of Major Presidential TV Addresses," *Political Communication* 25 (2008): 113–137.
75 George C. Edwards III and B. Dan Wood, "Who Influences Whom? The President, Congress, and the Media," *American Political Science Review* 93 (1999): 327–344.
76 B. Dan Wood and Jeffrey S. Peake, "The Dynamics of Foreign Policy Agenda Setting," *American Political Science Review* 92 (1998): 173–184.
77 Matthew Eshbaugh-Soha and Jeffrey S. Peake, "Presidents and the Economic Agenda," *Political Research Quarterly* 58 (2005): 127–138.
78 Edwards and Wood, "Who Influences Whom?"; and Eshbaugh-Soha and Peake, *Breaking through the Noise.*
79 Jeffrey S. Peake, "Presidential Agenda Setting in Foreign Policy," *Political Research Quarterly* 54 (2001): 69–86.
80 Andrew W. Barrett, "Press Coverage of Legislative Appeals by the President," *Political Research Quarterly* 60 (2007): 655–668.
81 Ibid., 660.
82 Cohen, *Going Local*, 116.
83 Eshbaugh-Soha, "Presidential Influence of the News Media."
84 Barrett and Peake, "When the President Comes to Town"; Eshbaugh-Soha and Peake, "The Contemporary Presidency."
85 Cohen, *Going Local*, 165.
86 Ibid.
87 Eshbaugh-Soha and Peake, "The Contemporary Presidency."
88 Matthew Eshbaugh-Soha, "The Politics of Presidential Speeches," *Congress & the Presidency* 37 (2010a): 1–21.
89 Eshbaugh-Soha and Peake, "The Presidency and Local Media."
90 See George C. Edwards III, *Governing by Campaigning: The Politics of the Bush Presidency* (New York: Longman, 2007); Senator Zell Miller (D-GA) supported the President, but had indicated his intention to do so upon Bush's inauguration.
91 Matthew Eshbaugh-Soha, "Presidential Agenda-Setting of Traditional and Nontraditional News Media," *Political Communication* 33 (2016): 1–20.
92 The discussion of how cable news failed in this regard is an important subject, but one that is well beyond the scope of this chapter. See, for starters,

William F. Baker and George Dessart, *Down the Tube: An Inside Account of the Failure of American Television* (New York: Basic Books, 1998).

93 Shelley Boulianne, "Does Internet Use Affect Engagement? A Meta-Analysis of Research," *Political Communication* 26 (2009): 193–211.

94 See Baum, *Soft News Goes to War.*

95 Michael Parkin, "Taking Late Night Comedy Seriously: How Candidate Appearances on Late Night Television Can Engage Viewers," *Political Research Quarterly* 63 (2010): 3–15.

96 Paul R. Brewer and Xiaoxia Cao, "Candidate Appearances on Soft News Shows and Public Knowledge about Primary Campaigns," *Journal of Broadcasting and Electronic Media* 50 (2006): 18–35.

97 R. Andrew Holbrook and Timothy G. Hill, "Agenda-Setting and Priming in Prime Time Television: Crime Dramas as Political Cues," *Political Communication* 22 (2005): 277–295.

98 Jody Baumgartner and Jonathan S. Morris, "The Daily Show Effect: Candidate Evaluations, Efficacy, and American Youth," *American Politics Research* 34 (2006): 341–367.

99 See Kevin Arceneaux and Martin Johnson, *Changing Minds or Changing Channels?: Partisan News in an Age of Choice* (Chicago, IL: University of Chicago Press, 2013).

100 Matthew Eshbaugh-Soha, "Traditional Media, Social Media, and Different Presidential Campaign Messages," in *Controlling the Message: New Media in American Political Campaigns*, eds. Victoria A. Farrar-Myers and Justin S. Vaughn (New York: New York University Press, 2015), 136.

101 Kernell and Rice, "Cable and the Partisan Polarization."

102 Regina G. Lawrence, "Campaign News in the Time of Twitter," in *Controlling the Message: New Media in American Political Campaigns*, eds. Victoria A. Farrar-Myers and Justin S. Vaughn (New York: New York University Press, 2015), 93.

103 See Cohen, *The Presidency in the Era of 24-Hour News.*

104 See George C. Edwards III, *At the Margins: Presidential Leadership of Congress* (New Haven, CT: Yale University Press, 1989).

105 See Kernell, *Going Public.*

106 David Weigel and Sean Sullivan, "Conservatives Meet with Trump, Who Hints That Gop Aca Fix Could Drift Further Right," *Washington Post*, March 9, 2017, www.washingtonpost.com/news/powerpost/wp/2017/03/08/conservatives-to-meet-with-trump-as-critics-pile-on-house-gop-health-care-plan/?utm_term=.8ab46e5a2ff3.

107 Ronald J. McGauvran and Matthew Eshbaugh-Soha, "Presidential Speeches Amid a More Centralized and Unified Congress," *Congress & the Presidency* 44 (2017): 55–76.

108 See Richard E. Neustadt, *Presidential Power and the Modern Presidents* (New York: John Wiley, 1960).

6 Presidents and Public Opinion

Diane J. Heith

In an interview with Jim Lehrer on PBS' *News Hour* on February 27, 2009, Barack Obama said the following about polls:

> You know, I don't—I don't make these decisions based on polls or popularity. I make the decisions based on what I think is best. This is consistent with what I said during the campaign. The fact—if anything I think people should be interested in the fact that there's been a movement in the direction of what I thought was going to be the right plan in the first place.

And on February 6, 2017, Donald Trump offered his perspective on polls at 7:01 a.m. with the following Tweet: "Any negative polls are fake news, just like the CNN, ABC, NBC polls in the election. Sorry, people want border security and extreme vetting."

Although they take a different approach to their complaints, both Obama and Trump articulate the inherent dilemma facing the modern presidency: How do you lead in a representative democracy where every miniscule decision receives a critique? Leadership seemingly requires the public to follow the leader; yet a representative democracy holds leaders accountable for their positions via elections. A public unhappy with a president's exercise of leadership will not grant that president a second term. Obama insisted, as all presidents have since the invention of public opinion polls, that he does not watch the polls. Yet, also like all presidents before him, one sentence later, he indicates knowledge of shifting public opinion, which can be obtained only by watching the polls. Trump, in contrast, embraces poll watching, while rejecting both the science and results of independent polling operations.

The twenty-first-century president lives in a world where the public's evaluation of the president, particularly whether the public approves or disapproves of the job he is doing, is constant. The continuous polling of the public seemingly offers the modern presidency a means to use the public as an extra-constitutional tool to enhance leadership opportunities. However, the unceasing evaluation defines and constrains a president's ability to lead. As both Obama and Trump learned in the transition from campaigning to governing, the public can be a tremendous asset as well as a dangerous vulnerability.

Evaluating the Presidency

Presidents take office after completing a campaign made up of a thousand strategic decisions, most notably in the electorally competitive states in their election (in recent years, the number of competitive states has been between 10 and 12). Those strategic decisions culminate in a winning, and ideally large, Electoral College outcome. In 2008, Obama earned 365 electoral votes (67 percent). In 1992, Bill Clinton received 370 (69 percent), while Ronald Reagan earned 489 (90 percent) in 1980. George Washington remains the only president to receive 100 percent of all electoral votes (and did it twice). In the modern era, Franklin D. Roosevelt came close with 523 out of 531 in 1936. The most recent close outcome in the Electoral College was the infamous 2000 election, where the Supreme Court in *Bush v. Gore* determined the outcome. George W. Bush increased his Electoral College outcome in 2004 to 53 percent, from 271 votes in 2000 to 286 in 2004.

In addition to the constitutionally mandated Electoral College votes, presidents also receive a popular vote total. All states use the popular vote total to award their Electoral College share; as a result, the summary of the state's popular votes becomes as much a mandate of support for the president as the Electoral College outcome. However, for some presidents, the discrepancy between the Electoral College outcome and the popular vote outcome persists, and is reflected in the public opinion of the president once they take office.

For presidents with close Electoral College victories, the popular vote totals typically reflect the tightness of the race. However, some presidents can win with a comfortable Electoral College outcome, but due to the distribution of voters have a narrower popular vote outcome. Moreover, winning the presidency does not guarantee public support once the candidate takes office. As Table 6.1 demonstrates, public approval on Inauguration Day (determined by the answer to the question: Do you approve of the job the president is doing?) typically correlates with the popular vote outcome, but not necessarily the Electoral College outcome. Typically, public approval of the candidate increases during their transition. With the exception of Trump, presidents since 1992 saw their approval rating significantly increase in comparison to their percentage of the popular vote.

As Table 6.1 demonstrates, the week Obama took the oath of office, his popularity stood at 67 percent. Obama was more popular on day one than almost every president taking office in the last 40 years.[1] However, Obama's popularity did not last. After just one year in office, Obama's

Table 6.1 Recent Election Outcomes and Public Approval Over Time

President	Electoral College Victory (%)	Popular Vote Actual	Popular Vote (%)[1]	Public Approval Day One (%)	Public Approval 100 Days (%)	Public Approval End of Year 1 (%)	Public Approval End of Year 4 (%)
Donald Trump 2016	304–227 (56.5)	62,980,160–65,845,06[2]	46.4–48.5	45	39	NA	NA
Barack Obama 2012	332–206 (61.7)	65,446,032–60,589,084	51–47	53	50	40	59
Barack Obama 2008	365–173 (67.8)	69,456,897–59,934,814	53–45	68	65	49	53
George W. Bush 2004	286–251 (53.1)	62,039,073–59,027,478	50–48	51	47	43	34
George W. Bush 2000	271–266 (50.37)	50,456,062–50,996,582[2]	47.9–48.4	57	62	85	49
Bill Clinton 1996	379–159 (70)	45,590,703–37,816,307	49–40	59	54	55	66
Bill Clinton 1992	370–168 (68.7)	44,908,254–39,102,343	43–37	58	48	47	57

Sources: Electoral College and Popular vote data from 270towin.com; Public Approval Data from the American Presidency Project, www.presidency.ucsb.edu.

1 Does not total to 100 due to third party votes.
2 Lost the popular vote.

euphoric bubble burst. On January 20, 2010, Gallup released a poll and poll analysis asserting:

> President Barack Obama begins his second year as president with 50 percent of Americans approving and 44 percent disapproving of his overall job performance... Obama's initial approval rating in his second year as president is among the lowest for elected presidents since Dwight Eisenhower. Only Ronald Reagan—who, like Obama, took office during challenging economic times—began his second year in office with a lower approval score.[2]

What happened? How does a president go from the most popular on Election Day to among the least popular in only one year? Was it simply the bad economy, as Gallup suggests? Initially, scholars believed time spent in office was enough to cause presidential approval to decline. The longer presidents spent in office, the bigger the "coalition of minorities" became.[3] The coalition of minorities represents those individuals who did not get what they wanted on the issues confronted by the president during his tenure. A study of 65 years and 12 presidents reveals that, "approval typically falls 5 points in a president's second year. Only two of the last eight presidents have avoided a second-year slump in approval rating."[4] However, Obama's approval declined more significantly than the ratings of most of his predecessors.

As a variable, time in office lacked specificity, as it did not reflect context. Scholarly analysis revealed that events and conditions, like recessions, failed treaty talks, or losing on an agenda item, could specifically detract from presidential approval.[5] However, the economy is a peculiar drag on presidential approval as John Mueller noted, "an economy in slump harms a president's popularity but an economy that is improving does not seem to help his rating."[6] As Obama took office in the midst of the worst economic period in American history since the Great Depression, his approval rating should have been influenced by his approach to the economy. However, the economy cannot be the only variable to influence approval, as George W. Bush ended his presidency amid the same dire economic period and his approval rating averaged 20 points lower.

In addition to the economy, other domestic and foreign events influence attitudes about presidential performance.[7] The president's handling of foreign events or foreign and domestic crises typically produces the strongest increase to a president's approval rating. Scholars call the rise in approval the "rally around the flag effect."[8] A Gallup poll taken September 7–10, 2001 gave George W. Bush a 51 percent approval rating. A poll on September 14–15, 2001 marked the President's approval at 86 percent. Bush's stratospheric rise in approval culminated on September 21–22, 2001 at 90 percent. A horrific, catastrophic and deadly event does not seem to suggest great job performance; yet, whenever a challenging event or crisis faces the nation, the American public typically responds by signaling support the only way they can, via the approval rating.

Media coverage also significantly influences the public's response to the president. Richard Brody considered public opinion a two-step process: Opinion elites classify and categorize events and then the media transmit those interpretations to the mass public.[9] The approval rating, as an evaluation of the president, stems from events, but is also driven by elite interpretations of those events. For recent presidents, the media influence on approval ratings is not good news. The relationship between the media and presidents used to be one of mutual dependency: Presidents needed to disseminate information and media organizations needed information to disseminate. In the twenty-first century, media organizations are no longer friendly, nor are they dependent. Instead, media coverage reflects increased negativity and cynicism.[10]

External events and intermediating institutions are not the only factors affecting the public's appraisal of the president. An individual's own attitudes also help determine presidential approval. Partisanship, gender, race, and all manner of socioeconomic factors influence performance evaluations of the president. Differences in evaluation by individuals stem from two different sources: experience and the importance of the experience. Blacks and Whites may experience a down economy differently, while men and women might weigh the importance of having a family leave policy differently. In elections, individual factors produce effects like the gender gap. Since 1980, women voted more frequently and differently than did men. A gendered vote emerged in response to Reagan's presidential campaign and the distinction of voting for "guns" versus "butter." Since 1980, both scholars and candidates noted that women were more likely to vote Democratic. The gap traditionally hovers around 7 percent; it reached a high of 11 percent in both 1996 and 2016, and hit 10 percent in 2000 and 2012. In 2008, Obama received approximately eight million more votes from women than men, a 7 percent difference.[11] In office, his approval rating reflected a similar gap. Gallup found a "six-point average weekly gender gap" with a high of an "11-point difference between the genders."[12] In 2016, Hillary Clinton won among all women voters, though lost to Trump among White women voters; the "gender gap widened ... for the same reason Trump took the White House: men, especially White men, surged right."[13] Once in office, Trump's gender gap shrunk over his first 100 days as he lost support from White men, although his core support did not decline.[14]

Obama and Trump's approval rating declines reflect the hyperpartisanship of the last 20 years. In March 2010, Obama earned a 12 percent approval rating from Republicans. Eighty-eight percent of Democrats in the same poll approved of the president's performance, while 44 percent of Independents approved of Obama. The Democratic National Committee tried to mitigate this enormous difference in political evaluation in an email to reporters by suggesting "Only 20 percent of Americans admit to being Republicans."[15] In March of his second year, still buoyed by the unifying effect of September 11th, Bush had an approval rating of 80 percent. Within that 80 percent, the differential stemming from partisanship was muted: Bush's popularity was 31 percent lower from Democrats and 17 percent lower from Independents than from Republicans. However, in September 2008, partisan differences sharpened, producing an overall approval rating of 27 percent for Bush. Among Democrats, Bush's approval rating was 3 percent, 61 points lower than Republican views. Independents were slightly more approving at 22 percent, but still 42 percent less than Republicans.[16] Trump's partisan gap is even wider than his predecessors, as Democrats view Trump much less favorably than Democrats viewed George W. Bush or Republicans viewed Obama.[17]

Presidential Power and Job Approval

The approval rating provides an explicit weekly critique of presidential performance based on the public's view of events, experienced through the media and an individual's own attitudes. The question for students of the presidency is: Does it matter that this evaluation is out there? Is it significant that by asking questions of 1,500–3,000 individuals there exists a measure of the president? What meaning does the measurement have within the political system?

There are two distinct views of the public as a source of presidential power. The first originates with Richard Neustadt's view.[18] Neustadt considers the public a secondary source of power, a means to soften up the true avenues to presidential power. Neustadt argues that mass opinion is important only because elites pay attention to it; the public's view of the president matters because elites anticipate public reaction to the president. It is this anticipation that factors into presidential efforts to persuade elites, and persuasion, for Neustadt, is presidential power. The second avenue is the dominant view; it begins with Elmer Cornwell, and culminates in Samuel Kernell's view of leadership discussed in *Going Public*.

In *Presidential Leadership of Public Opinion*, Cornwell argues that with few constitutional tools to influence the course of policy and events, "the President can and does and probably should shape popular attitudes, and not just respond to them passively."[19] For Neustadt, public evaluations of the president simply exist, and therefore influence the mood surrounding institutional bargaining. Cornwell implicitly rejects the idea that approval of the president is an independent evaluation of the president, tangentially related to the system.

Brace and Hinckley contend that presidents, as strategic actors, do not accept a passive role in public evaluations of their efforts. In fact, they argue that the ability to measure approval ratings produced a dependence on the polls.[20] Brace and Hinckley term this dependence a follower presidency, as presidents respond with action to the fluctuations in their ratings. The preeminent presidential goal then is not reelection, a legacy, or good public policy, but rather to achieve high approval ratings, because the ratings influence everything else.[21] The response to these external cues (approval ratings) drives presidential behavior.

Presidents universally reject followership as the principle factor guiding their behavior. In an interview with Martha Raddatz, on ABC News, Vice President Dick Cheney summed up what most presidents and their staff believe:

RADDATZ: Two-third of Americans say it's [the War in Iraq] not worth fighting.
CHENEY: So?
RADDATZ: So? You don't care what the American people think?
CHENEY: No. I think you cannot be blown off course by the fluctuations in the public opinion polls. There has, in fact, been fundamental change and transformation and improvement for the better. That's a huge accomplishment.[22]

The press and blogosphere universally mimicked Raddatz's reaction, implicitly arguing that in a representative democracy, the White House should care what the public thinks. Cheney's comment, while politically insensitive, reflects the constitutional design that allows elected officials to ignore public opinion between election cycles. Yet, Brace and Hinckley insist that all presidents must accept tradeoffs and act without regard for public opinion, and the approval rating suffers.[23] In particular, Brandice Canes-Wrone argues that presidents chose their policy positions and strategies focused on policies already consistent with mass opinion.[24]

The approval rating appeared most significant as a resource or source of power for the president to achieve his legislative program, what Kernell termed "going public." When going public, presidents present their policy desires to the public to influence Congress.[25] Neustadt claimed public opinion influenced the environment for bargaining, as a popular president will have more leverage to bargain with members of Congress. In contrast, Kernell argues that public support preempts bargaining and forces congressional compliance.[26] Kernell contends that the need for members of Congress to be reelected forces acceptance of a popular president's desires. Thus, the popularity rating is a source of significant power, or pressure, to achieve legislative success. A popular president, in Kernell's theory, will more likely be a successful president.

Analysis of going public as a strategic mechanism for achieving legislative success challenges the idea of the approval rating as a source of presidential power. For the presidential approval rating to reflect a source of power, the president needs to able to influence the rating. To influence presidential approval, the president needs to communicate his desires directly or indirectly. The public needs to be receptive, or at least attentive to the president. George C. Edwards argues that the president may be speaking to the nation, but the nation was not listening to the president and was certainly not acting on any presidential requests.[27]

Although President Obama took office with a 67 percent approval rating and ended his eight years in office with a 59 percent rating, for most of his tenure, Obama's approval ratings averaged around 50 percent. A 50 percent approval rating appears to be a weak tool to provide pressure. If 50 percent approve, then 50 percent disapprove, and neither side represents a ringing endorsement for a member of Congress to support a presidential policy. However, the public approved of Obama, Trump, and George W. Bush by a much wider margin than they do Congress. Congress' approval ratings have not been higher than 40 percent since 2009, and have not been above 50 percent since the aftermath of 9/11.[28] In fact, Trump's ratings look extraordinary at 43 percent approval, in comparison to Congress, who hit a high of 28 percent approval in February 2017. Thus, if presidential popularity is a predictor of retrospective voting, then the popularity ratings suggest a mild amount of protection for beleaguered members of Congress, at least from the 15 percent who approve of Trump but do not approve of Congress.

But even above 50 percent, if presidential approval is the key weapon in a president's arsenal to pressure Congress, then the president is in trouble. Congress is only mildly responsive to these ratings.[29] Edwards finds that presidential popularity influences congressional voting only "at the margins," meaning more traditional congressional explanations for voting behavior dominate decisions (e.g., constituency demands, leadership demands, party demands). Mark Peterson even finds that high levels of approval reduces the likelihood of a president achieving a particular policy item.[30] Congress is attentive to the president's agenda as a list of priorities, but not as specific calls to action.[31] The president's approval rating does have an effect on congressional elections; low ratings of the president generally signal poor reelection rates for members of his party. However, for voting decisions, the threat from the presidential approval rating appears to dissipate. The approval rating is a national measure, and as a result is of lesser meaning to an individual member of Congress, particularly while voting on policy.[32] Party line voting on the bulk of the presidential agenda in recent years suggests how partisanship matters equally as much, if not more, to members of Congress.

Presidential Power and Public Opinion

Up to this point, the public's voice appears represented only by the approval rating. Although the approval rating is a virtually continuous measure of the public's opinion, the question itself is an extremely flawed and limited picture of what the public thinks. The approval rating question asks the public, "Do you approve of the job the president is doing?" The answer to that question is along a three- or five-point scale: approve, disapprove, don't know; or strongly approve, approve, disapprove, strongly disapprove, or don't know. Moreover, the question is relatively ambiguous, as it means different things to different people and different things across presidencies. Does approving of the president refer to personal approval or job approval? Bill Clinton received relatively positive approval ratings, including a rating of 63 percent during the height of the Monica Lewinsky scandal in 1998. The public approved of the job the President was doing, despite rejecting his personal behavior. For a respondent who answers, "don't know," what exactly does the individual not know? If he/she approves or disapproves or does not know enough to answer the question? The answer to that single question does not explicitly explain for the president or anyone else *why* the respondent approves or disapproves.

For presidents to use public opinion strategically and to gain an advantage from public opinion, they need to know something about it that no one else knows, or they need to know how to benefit from the information. For this reason, presidents created a White House polling operation.[33] Presidents, through their party organizations, paid significant sums of money to design the questions asked of the public.[34]

The White House Polling Operation

Prior to the presidency of FDR (1933–1945), the parties controlled political information, particularly what voters wanted from government. The party organizations coordinated attitudes and funneled wants and needs from the local ward to Congress and the president. Robert Eisinger and Jeremy Brown argued that the interest in and attention to public opinion polling stemmed from a desire to achieve political autonomy from the party: "Emil Hurja's polls for the [Democratic National Committee] and Hadley Cantril's polling for FDR signified the birth of presidential polling."[35] Initially, it was too expensive and polling was too difficult to provide more than infrequent glimpses into public attitudes. Moreover, the fear of perception shrouded FDR's efforts to gather public opinion from the public and the media; a president who polled might look lacking in leadership.

Polling did not become an institutional feature of the presidency until the Richard Nixon administration.[36] The Harry Truman and Dwight Eisenhower administrations polled the public rarely. The John F. Kennedy and Lyndon Johnson administrations polled more frequently, primarily for elections, but also for governing.[37] In stark contrast, the administrations that followed, from Nixon through Obama, all devoted substantial time, money, and attention to a White House public opinion apparatus.[38]

The rise of the presidential polling operation mirrored the change in approach to presidential campaigning, from party centered to candidate centered. Candidate centered behavior reflected an individual focus rather than a party focus; "vote for me because I am me," rather than, "vote for me as the party's choice." The domination of an individually centered approach requires the candidate's campaign to employ a means to ascertain "why me" over other candidates.

As candidate centered behavior led to victory, individually centered rather than party-centered governing emerged at the White House. Scholars and pundits tracked the shift from party to individual and termed the change, "campaigning to govern" or "the permanent campaign."[39] Party-centered governing employs the party's agenda as the focal point of legislative efforts; president centered governing places the individual president's needs at the fore. An individual president seeks reelection and a legacy, both of which are separate from party goals and needs. However, it was not simply the change in attitude that suggested to presidency watchers that a new approach to leadership existed; it was the change in behavior.

Since 1968, presidents no longer abandon their campaign staff and campaign tools when they take the oath of office. Campaign staff, particularly pollsters and consultants, began working for the president as part of the White House staff in large numbers. Moreover, these former campaign staffers directed their campaign expertise to White House decision making. All presidents since 1968, including Nixon, Gerald Ford, Jimmy Carter, Reagan, George H.W. Bush, Clinton and George W. Bush, directed their top staff to be attentive to public opinion.[40] Interestingly, the staffers who did not straddle the political and policy line, like the cabinet secretaries and other purely policy driven offices like the Council of Economic Advisors, did not employ public opinion data.[41] The perception problem regarding the exercise of leadership, which presidents as early as FDR were aware of, makes determining the use of polls by a sitting president difficult to specify. However, it is possible to compare what is known about the Obama White House employment of polls with the patterns of past White Houses.

Previous presidents were reluctant to admit to poll usage, fearing the appearance of followership.[42] Obama's rhetoric is interestingly illustrative of poll usage and simultaneously dismissive of it. In the first year and a half of his administration, Obama mentioned public opinion polls 35 times. Mentioning polling twice a month seems quite open, particularly in comparison to the previous presidential views. However, Obama spoke and/or issued a statement over 887 times. Obama mentioned polling in 0.03 percent of his public utterances. Despite the infrequency, the mentions of public opinion polling are significant and reflective of the employment of polls at the White House. Obama specifically, albeit humorously, acknowledged the presence of the polling apparatus. For example, this is what Obama said during remarks at a Democratic National Committee Fundraiser at a question-and-answer session on February 4, 2010:

> Now, I—you heard me at the State of the Union—I didn't take this on because it was good politics. I love how the pundits on these cable shows, they all announce, "Oh, boy, this was really tough politically for the President." Well, I've got my own pollsters; I know—[*laughter*]—I knew this was hard. I knew seven Presidents had failed. I knew seven Congresses hadn't gotten it done. You don't think I got warnings, "Don't try to take this on"? [Laughter] I got those back in December of last year.[43]

The Obama White House polling operation looked very much like the Obama campaign operation, as is typical in most White Houses.[44] Moreover, the Obama polling operation maintained the same political relationship as the previous White Houses, controlled by the administration, but staffed and paid for by the national party committee of the president.[45]

According to Ben Smith of *Politico*, Obama's polling operation combined "elements of the Clinton and Bush models. He is polling more than Bush—a bit less than once a week."[46] The frequency of polling and the money spent on polling has long been of interest to scholars,[47] but the findings reveal little about usage. Comparatively speaking, determining that one president purchased more polling data than another and determining when polls are employed reveals White House intent and belief about the role of public opinion. However, to determine how and more importantly if public opinion influences presidential decision making requires a means to get inside the "black box" of White House decision making. Investigations into that "black box" reveal that the White House uses public opinion polls to track and monitor their constituency support between election and reelection; to design rhetorical outreach and "craft" appeals to the public; and to focus the agenda but not to make specific policy choices.[48]

While it is currently impossible to use the same scholarly techniques (coding of internal White House documents) to determine Obama White House polling usage, there have been media discussions of the employment of White House polling. The press consideration of the polling operation, plus the President's own references to the polls, provides a clear, if not complete, picture of the apparatus.

As an outgrowth of political campaigns, the White House primarily employs polls in relation to constituency and reelection. In January 2010, Obama's former campaign manager, David Plouffe, one of the few top campaign staffers not employed in the White House, returned to work for Obama. Plouffe's new responsibilities included management of the political message, management of the 2010 midterm elections, and the White House polling operation.[49] Plouffe returned to the Obama fold in the wake of the loss of Independents in the 2009 New Jersey, Virginia, and Massachusetts special elections. In addition, Obama himself talked about the constituency monitoring that the polling operations perform in a daylong meeting between Democrats and Republicans at the White House on health care reform on February 25, 2010:

> And as I said, I hear from constituents in every one of your districts and every one of your States. And what's interesting is, actually, when you poll people about the individual elements in each of these bills, they're all for them. So you ask them, do you want to prohibit preex-isting conditions? Yes, I'm for that. Do you want to make sure that ev-erybody can get basic coverage that's affordable? Yes, I'm for that. Do you want to make sure that insurance companies can't take advantage of you and that you've got the ability, as Ron said, to fire an insurance company that's not doing a good job and hire one that is—but also, that you've got some basic consumer protections? Yes, we like that.

The more significant and potentially concerning use of public opinion by the president is the use of polls to determine how to get the public behind the president's preferred policy positions. If, as Kernell argues, the public's pressure on Congress for the president's choice is the exertion of presidential leadership, then the president needs to get the public on board. However, in contrast to Kernell's argument, presidents do not rely on the approval rating as the source of pressure; presidents want support for the specific policy choice and use the polls to attempt to achieve it.[50]

The Reagan White House famously changed the name of their satellite weapons protection system from the Strategic Defense Initiative (SDI) to Star Wars after the polling apparatus demonstrated quite clearly that the public did not support the project when termed SDI but did support it when termed Star Wars.[51] The lesson learned for all subsequent White Houses: terminology matters. Press reports find evidence of similar behavior from the Obama administration:

> Elements of Obama's approach bear the hallmarks of message test-ing, like the introduction of the words "recovery" and "reinvest-ment" to rebrand the "stimulus" package, and aides said the polling has focused almost entirely on selling policy, not on measuring the president's personal appeal. A source familiar with the data said a central insight of more recent polling had been that Americans see no distinction between the budget and the popular spending mea-sures that preceded it, and that the key to selling the budget has been to portray it as part of the "recovery" measures.[52]

However, in language eerily similar to previous White House officials, Press Secretary Robert Gibbs argued, "Not unlike news organizations, we poll public attitudes about where the economy is…. We're not polling to see what should be in an economic-recovery plan."[53]

Other Ways to Connect with the Public

Presidents have primarily relied on public opinion polling for two reasons: Polling was the main currency employed by all political actors in the media and during campaigns to determine political attitudes, and, it was the least anecdotal tool for collecting opinion. Presidents and their staffs today use polls, and their small group counterpart—focus groups—as well as the twenty-first-century additions of Internet polling and social media.

Where polls are mechanisms to gather data from 1,500 to 3,000 individuals in order to statistically represent a much larger population, focus groups are small gatherings of ten to 20 individuals who are paid a nominal fee to discuss the questions posed by the coordinator. Commercial enterprises (such as: What is the preferred brand of soap?) as well as political actors (How is the president doing on health care?) all use focus groups. Focus groups allow pollsters and consultants to understand what is behind the multiple-choice answers of public opinion polls. Few poll questions allow the public to provide the scope of the answer, beyond the fill-in-the-blank question: What do you think is the most important problem (MIP) facing the country? Focus groups, with their open-ended opportunities to answer questions, have a dialogue with other participants that provide depth and breadth to attitudes and responses. By definition, focus groups provide data that does not extrapolate directly to non-participants as polls do. Working in tandem with public opinion poll data, focus groups provide the White House with the means to understand and use poll data to design public relations campaigns for the president's agenda.[54]

In addition to polls and focus groups, the twenty-first century president also has a wealth of social media to gather opinion from the public directly. The Trump White House has a wealth of online tools with which to track and connect with the public. Obama set the bar high for how the White House webpage and social media accounts could enable engagement with the public and gather public opinion.[55] Starting in 2009, the White House website offered what was at the time a state-of-the-art means to connect, from email to RSS feeds. They created regular features on the White House webpage and on YouTube and invited feedback.[56] By the time Obama left office, the president's website, "whitehouse.gov" sought public engagement in myriad ways. Visitors could see Obama's daily schedule, the photo of the day, and could click on different ways to get in touch with the President and the White House via email. The

"Engage and Connect" page offered many social media links to Twitter, Facebook, YouTube, Scribd, Flickr, SlideShare, Google+, GitHub, LinkedIn, and Foursquare, and included the opportunity to participate in White House petitions.

The Trump White House version of "whitehouse.gov" retains many of the features from the Obama White House webpage. Interested individuals can sign up for updates by providing their email address. The "participate" page provides links to Twitter, Facebook, Instagram, and YouTube. The "share your thoughts" section includes the White House petition page. The Trump White House is clearly not censoring this open forum as the petitions with the most signatures were "Immediately release Donald Trump's full tax returns, with all information needed to verify emoluments clause compliance" with over one million signatures and "Divest or put in a blind trust all of the President's business and financial assets" with over 350,000 signatures.[57]

Social media and the White House webpage offer the White House the opportunity to hear directly from the people, but also provide a mechanism to get around the criticism inherent in the media marketplace. Trump's extensive use of his private Twitter account demonstrates the costs and benefits of direct interaction with the public, but also the cost and benefits of the president rather than the presidency directly interacting with the public on a regular basis.

Conclusion

The Constitution provides a limited mandate for public involvement in the presidency. The public only indirectly votes for the president via the Electoral College. The modern creation of the means to measure public attitudes of all players and processes in American politics seemingly provides a more direct role for the public in the political sphere. On the surface, the presidential approval ratings provide a meaningful measure of public support for the presidency and his policy, a temperature rating of the president—Is he hot or not? A president with high approval seemingly owns the political process; he will be reelected, and he will get what he wants from Congress.

Unfortunately for the president, the public is often harshly judgmental, moved by factors outside the president's control and determinedly resistant to persuasion. The public represents potential power to be harnessed as well as a dangerous threat to be feared. A popular president is not always legislatively successful and an unpopular president is not always doomed to legislative failure. After all, as Obama watched his approval rating plummet from an all-time high of 69 percent to a low of 45 percent, he managed to achieve arguably the single most significant piece of domestic legislation in 75 years: health care reform.

Notes

1 Only Gerald Ford had a higher popularity rating, 71 percent, as the nation responded positively to Richard Nixon's resignation in August 1974.
2 Lydia Saad, "Obama Starts 2010 with 50% Approval," *Gallup*, January 6, 2010, www.gallup.com/poll/124949/Approval-Obama-Starts-2010-Shaky-Spot.aspx.
3 See John E. Mueller, "Presidential Popularity from Truman to Johnson," *American Political Science Review* 64 (1970): 18–34; and John E. Mueller, *War, Presidents and Public Opinion* (New York: John Wiley, 1973).
4 Jeffrey M. Jones, "Approval Typically Falls 5 Points in a President's Second Year," *Gallup*, January 20, 2010, www.gallup.com/poll/125294/Approval-Typically-Falls-Points-President-Second-Year.aspx.
5 Samuel Kernell, "Explaining Presidential Popularity," *American Political Science Review* 72 (1978): 506–522.
6 Mueller, *War, Presidents, and Public Opinion*, 215.
7 Paul Gronke and Brian Newman, "FDR to Clinton: Mueller to?: A Field Essay on Presidential Approval," *Political Research Quarterly* 56 (2003): 501–512.
8 Mueller first used the term in 1973, and now it is conventional wisdom.
9 See Richard Brody, *Assessing the President: The Media, Elite Opinion and Public Support* (Stanford, CA: Stanford University Press, 1991).
10 See Jeffrey E. Cohen, *The Presidency in the Era of 24-Hour News* (Princeton, NJ: Princeton University Press, 2008).
11 "The Gender Gap: Voting Choices in Presidential Elections," Center for American Women and Politics, Eagleton Institute of Politics, Rutgers University, www.cawp.rutgers.edu/sites/default/files/resources/ggpresvote.pdf.
12 Frank Newport, "Obama Weekly Job Approval Average at 48%, Tied for Lowest," *Gallup*, March 15, 2010, www.gallup.com/poll/126701/Obama-Weekly-Job-Approval-Average-Tied-Lowest.aspx.
13 Danielle Paquette, "The Unexpected Voters behind the Widest Gender Gap in Recorded Election History," *Washington Post*, November 9, 2016, www.washingtonpost.com/news/wonk/wp/2016/11/09/men-handed-trump-the-election/?utm_term=.59ca039fff24.
14 Jeffrey M. Jones, "Gender Gap Shrinks as Trump Loses Support among Men," *Gallup*, March 28, 2017, www.gallup.com/poll/207497/gender-gap-shrinks-trump-loses-support-among-men.aspx.
15 Ian Jannetta, "Democrats Claim Only 20 Percent of Americans Call Themselves Republicans," *Politifact*, October 16, 2009, www.politifact.com/truth-o-meter/statements/2009/oct/16/democratic-national-committee/democrats-claim-only-20-percent-americans-call-the/.
16 "Presidential Job Approval Center," *Gallup*, www.gallup.com/poll/124922/Presidential-Job-Approval-Center.aspx.
17 "Partisan Gap in Trump Approval Ratings Much Wider than for Recent Presidents," *Pew Research Center*, April 17, 2017, www.people-press.org/2017/04/17/public-dissatisfaction-with-washington-weighs-on-the-gop/0_2-7/.
18 See Richard E. Neustadt, *Presidential Power and the Modern Presidents: The Politics of Leadership from Roosevelt to Reagan* (New York: Free Press, 1990).
19 Elmer E. Cornwell, Jr., *Presidential Leadership of Public Opinion* (Bloomington, IN: Indiana University Press, 1965), 6.
20 See Paul Brace and Barbara Hinckley, *Follow the Leader: Opinion Polls and Modern Presidents* (New York: Basic Books, 1992).
21 Ibid.

22 "ABC News Full Interview: Vice President Dick Cheney," March 19, 2008, http://abcnews.go.com/WN/Vote2008/story?id=4481568&page=1.

23 See Brace and Hinckley, *Follow the Leader.*

24 See Brandice Canes-Wrone, *Who Leads Whom? Presidents, Policy, and the Public* (Chicago, IL: University of Chicago Press, 2006).

25 See Samuel Kernell, *Going Public: New Strategies of Presidential Leadership,* 4th ed. (Washington, DC: CQ Press, 2007).

26 Ibid.

27 See George C. Edwards III, *On Deaf Ears: The Limits of the Bully Pulpit* (New Haven, CT: Yale Univesity Press, 2003).

28 "Congress and the Public," *Gallup,* www.gallup.com/poll/1600/congress-public.aspx.

29 See Jon R. Bond and Richard Fleisher, *The President in the Legislative Arena* (Chicago, IL: University of Chicago Press, 1990); George C. Edwards III, *At The Margins: Presidential Leadership of Congress* (New Haven, CT: Yale University Press, 1989); and George C. Edwards III, "Aligning Tests with Theory: Presidential Influence as a Source of Influence in Congress," *Congress & the Presidency* 24 (1997): 113–130.

30 See Mark A. Peterson, *Legislating Together: The White House and Capitol Hill from Eisenhower to Reagan* (Cambridge, MA: Harvard University Press, 1990).

31 See Jeffrey E. Cohen, *Presidential Responsiveness and Public-Policy Making* (Ann Arbor, MI: University of Michigan Press, 1997); and Jeffrey E. Cohen, "Presidential Rhetoric and the Public Agenda," *American Journal of Political Science* 39 (1995): 87–107.

32 Stephen A. Borrelli and Grace L. Simmons, "Congressional Responsiveness to Presidential Popularity: The Electoral Context," *Political Behavior* 15 (1993): 93–112.

33 See Lawrence R. Jacobs and Robert Y. Shapiro, "The Rise of Presidential Polling: The Nixon White House in Historical Perspective," *Public Opinion Quarterly* 59 (1995): 163–195; Lawrence R. Jacobs and Robert Y. Shapiro, *Politicians Don't Pander: Political Manipulation and the Loss of Democratic Responsiveness* (Chicago, IL: University of Chicago Press, 2000); Robert Eisinger, *The Evolution of Presidential Polling* (New York: Cambridge University Press, 2003); Diane J. Heith, *Polling to Govern: Public Opinion and Presidential Leadership* (Stanford, CA: Stanford University Press, 2004); and Kathryn Dunn Tenpas, *Presidents as Candidates: Inside the White House for the Presidential Campaign* (New York: Garland, 1997).

34 See Heith, *Polling to Govern.*

35 Robert Eisinger and Jeremy Brown, "Polling as a Means toward Presidential Autonomy: Emil Hurja, Hadley Cantril and the Roosevelt Administration," *International Journal of Public Opinion Research* 10 (1998): 237–256.

36 See Heith, *Polling to Govern.*

37 See Jacobs and Shapiro, "The Rise of Presidential Polling."

38 See Heith, *Polling to Govern*; and Eisinger, *The Evolution of Presidential Polling,* for a discussion of the evolution of the polling apparatus.

39 See Hugh Heclo, "Campaigning and Governing: A Conspectus," in *The Permanent Campaign and Its Future,* eds. Norman Ornstein and Thomas Mann (Washington, DC: Brookings, 2000); and Sidney Blumenthal, *The Permanent Campaign: Inside the World of Elite Political Operatives* (Boston, MA: Beacon Press, 1980).

40 See Heith, *Polling to Govern,* and Kathryn Dunn Tenpas and Jay McCann, "Testing the Permanence of the Permanent Campaign: An Analysis of

Presidential Polling Expenditures, 1977–2002," *Public Opinion Quarterly* 71 (2007): 349–366.

41 See Heith, *Polling to Govern*.

42 Ibid; see also Eisinger, *The Evolution of Presidential Polling.*

43 Barack Obama, "Remarks at a Democratic National Committee Fundraiser and a Question-and-Answer Session," February 4, 2010, www.presidency. ucsb.edu/ws/index.php?pid=87499.

44 The George H. W. Bush White House is an exception; they spent less money and employed fewer consultants and staffers than other administrations. See Heith, *Polling to Govern*.

45 See Heith, *Polling to Govern*, and Kathryn Dunn Tenpas, "Campaigning to Govern: Presidents Seeking Reelection," *PS: Political Science and Politics* 36 (2003): 199–202.

46 Ben Smith, "Meet Obama's Pollsters," *Politico*, April 3, 2009, www.politico. com/news/stories/0409/20852.html.

47 Kathleen Shoon Murray and Peter Howard, "Variation in White House Polling Operations: Carter to Clinton," *Public Opinion Quarterly* 66 (2000): 527–558.

48 See Heith, *Polling to Govern*; and Jacobs and Shapiro, *Politicians Don't Pander.*

49 Chris Cillizza, "Former Obama Campaign Manager to be White House Adviser," *Washington Post*, January 24, 2010, p. A8.

50 See Heith, *Polling to Govern*; and Jacobs and Shapiro, *Politicians Don't Pander.*

51 See Heith, *Polling to Govern*.

52 Smith, "Meet Obama's Pollsters."

53 Mark Blumenthal, "New Flash: Obama Using Polling Data," *Pollster.com*, January 9, 2009, www.pollster.com/blogs/news_flash_obama_using_polling. php.

54 See Heith, *Polling to Govern*.

55 Diane Heith, "Obama and the Public Presidency: What Got You Here Won't Get You There," in *The Obama Presidency: Appraisals and Prospects*, eds. Bert A. Rockman, Andrew Rudalevige, and Colin Campbell (Washington, DC: CQ Press, 2012).

56 Ibid.

57 "We the People: Your Voice in the White House," https://petitions.whitehouse. gov.

7 Presidents and Congress

Brandon Rottinghaus

Many scholars studying the policy-making institutions in the United States have genuflected on Edwin Corwin's infamous explanation of shared constitutional powers as "an invitation to struggle." In perhaps no other venue is the interconnectedness of the Constitution on display than in matters involving joint executive-legislative policy making. The shared power to create and implement policy is at the center of the relationship between the authorities vested in Articles I and II of the Constitution. Article I (governing legislative actions) gives the legislature specific powers to regulate finances, provide for defense, and, generally, "make all laws" necessary for carrying out the execution of their powers. Article II (governing executive actions) is vaguer but provides that "executive powers" are "vested" in the president, allows control of executive departments, the ability to make recess appointments, and, with the advice and consent of the Senate, make appointments. Similarly, on foreign affairs, Article I provides Congress the ability to regulate commerce with foreign nations while Article II provides the executive branch with the ability to negotiate treaties (concurrent with Senate approval) and the sole power to be "commander-in-chief."

This focus on the formal aspects of the congressional-executive relationship has been fruitful. However, several works have treated the president as the geometric center of the legislative system. But, recent theoretical research on the presidency has suggested that scholars should move away from thinking of the president as an "input" in the system, and should instead develop the idea that lawmaking is a "two-way street"[1]; that is, the president is influenced by Congress in pursuing his agenda in a range of situations. In particular, Jones views the relationship between the president and Congress as "diffused responsibility" with the policy success and failure of the American political system inextricably linked.[2] Mark Peterson also argues "treating the president and Congress as a decision-making 'system', furthermore, opens up new opportunities for understanding their collective decisions."[3] Such an analysis could more fully develop Richard Neustadt's concept of the president and the legislature as "separated institutions sharing powers."[4] Indeed, scholars have noted that presidents who introduce policy initiatives that are mutually beneficial need not engage in rhetorical appeals or quid pro quo bargaining with great frequency.[5]

The shared powers drawn in the Constitution builds in elements of intentional friction to invigorate debate, ensure careful deliberation, and check institutional powers. This relationship is reexamined in this chapter with an eye toward understanding contemporary trends in executive-legislative relations as a shared "struggle." In particular, I explore general trends in executive-legislative relations, the shared power of making political appointments, the joint powers to create and carry out foreign policy and national security, and "shared" presidential unilateral powers (executive orders, proclamations and executive memoranda). Yet, consistent with the scope of this volume, this chapter will draw heavily on more recent academic literature to summarize "what we know" in the context of recent debates and will draw on examples from the Barack Obama and Donald J. Trump administrations to illustrate key points.

Presidential Relations with Congress

Generally, the farther apart, ideologically, the president and Congress (or the president's and Congress' parties), the less likely we are to see political agreement. Certain variables, such as a partisan majority in one or both branches of Congress or more members of the president's party in Congress, are generally associated with greater fluidity in the president's agenda passing.[6] Presidential support from party loyalists in both chambers is often the determining factor predicting presidential success in Congress, even considering other potentially important factors like leadership skills and presidential popularity.[7] Similarly, the margin of the president's party in Congress is shown to be a factor in predicting the (usually fewer) number of veto challenges issued by the president.[8] Even in instances where separate parties control the executive and legislative branches ("divided government"), greater unity of party is associated with a more easy translation of bills into law, while less party unity is associated with a more cumbersome process.[9] Presidents are likely to veto legislation, not necessarily simply because of divided government, but rather pursuant to objectionable legislation from Congress.[10] Ironically, presidential attempts to lead the public or Congress may itself exacerbate political polarization.[11] Polarization and close elections also incentivize members of Congress to sharpen distinctions between themselves and the other party, minimizing the promise of bipartisan legislation and withering the president's ability to negotiate across the partisan aisle.[12]

Related to this point, divided government *could* cause more friction in policy making. Many analysts have commonly associated this relationship with legislative gridlock. The growth of political partisanship has made legislating in modern times more difficult.[13] The impact of divided government has recently been challenged, however, in that some scholars argue that divided government is commonly associated with inefficient and irresponsible government, while others argue that this institutional phenomenon has no effect on legislative outcomes.[14] Edwards et al. find that presidents oppose significant legislation more often under divided government, and that much more important legislation fails to pass under divided government than under unified government. "Lame duck" presidents also find less success in Congress as coalition formation becomes "more erratic and costly" as a term ends.[15] Thus, there is evidence that, at the least, conflict reigns in legislative-executive battles where the parties are split, especially as partisanship has taken firm root in Washington.[16]

Yet, conflict resulting from divided government may be overstated. Other evidence contradicts the hypothesis that "gridlock" results from divided government. For example, Peterson looks more closely at how Congress responds to presidential initiatives (with conflict, cooperation, or compromise), and argues that outright conflict over the president's programs is found to be less prevalent than previous case studies have suggested, occurring on about one third of the president's initiatives. Consensus and compromise were more frequent outcomes. Peterson reports that over 54 percent of the president's domestic policy proposals received positive treatment.[17] Yet, congruent with other studies, the more negative "contexts" challenges the president's ability to work with Congress (such as decentralization of committees or the state of the economy). And, not surprisingly, if the president's party has a majority in a chamber, the amount of conflict was reduced. Similarly, when policies are passed, they are usually passed as a result of a large and bipartisan coalition.[18]

As noted, recent scholarship has argued researchers should include additional variables when studying this relationship, including,

> the importance of reciprocity between the president and members of Congress, the dynamic nature of political trade-offs between the two branches, and the impact of the kind of policy being considered in the strategy used by the White House and the Hill.[19]

Recent evidence suggests that presidents adapt their strategies to accommodate concerns over congressional makeup. Presidents are able to use their executive policy expertise to influence committee stages, but only for issues that are technical or relatively noncontroversial.[20] Presidents are also shown to develop their yearly domestic policy agenda in anticipation of the policy's success or failure in Congress, specifically congressional political makeup and the federal budget deficit.[21] Other research has suggested that the formal powers of the president, such as the veto power, may be influenced by anticipating the actions of Congress.[22] Support of the president in Congress as registered through higher approval is endogenously related to presidential success—that is, these affect each other.[23] These results show that understanding how the branches work together is more useful than understanding how they battle each other.

Trump

Like Obama, Trump came into office with favorable but not overwhelming majorities in both houses of Congress. Table 7.1 shows the percentages of majority party control of each chamber for a president's first year in office (shaded regions are when the president's party controls the chamber)—this shows that his party holds almost 54 percent of the seats in both houses (54 percent in the House and 52 percent in the Senate). Controlling the House presented the outspoken president with opportunities to legislate, but less than 60 supportive Republican votes in the Senate complicated his ability to pursue an agenda without Democratic support. Although more co-partisans in Congress (ostensibly) support a president's research agenda, Jimmy Carter and Bill Clinton, both with unified government, found out that keeping a fragile coalition together was as challenging as battling the opposing party. Both Carter and Clinton had dissension within their own party on their economic and energy policies, causing consternation for their first years in office and their key legislative programs. Scholars have found that approval of the president's base is important in predicting legislative success, possibly suggesting tumultuous waters ahead for the Trump administration.[24]

Clearly, majorities in both houses of Congress should give Trump a general advantage in pursuing his agenda. But, although beneficial to pursuing his legislative agenda, united opposition by the Democrats and threats of dissension by moderate Republicans make the White House's job require finesse in the bargaining process. Highlighting how party unity is critical to presidential success, Trump had difficulty lining up Republican support (especially conservative members of the Freedom Caucus) for "repeal and replace" legislation for the Affordable Care Act

Table 7.1 Percentage of Majority Party Seats in Congress in Presidents' First Year in Office, 1969–2017

President	Percentage of Seats	
	House (%)	*Senate (%)*
Nixon	56	58
Ford	56	56
Carter	67[1]	61
Reagan	56	53
George H. W. Bush	55	60
Clinton	51	50
George W. Bush	51	50
Obama	51	50[2]
Trump	55	52

Source: Data compiled by the author.

1 Shaded boxes are when president's party had a majority.

2 Two Independents caucused with the Democrats (Senators Lieberman and Sanders) thus being counted in the majority.

(Obamacare). Conservatives were concerned that the Republicans' preferred health care legislation was too costly and did not go far enough to roll back federal health insurance mandates. Even moderate Republicans balked as estimates from the Congressional Budget Office suggested that the Republican health reform bill may result in millions of Americans losing health insurance.[25] Pushing the negotiations to the brink, the President warned House Republicans that he would leave Obama's health care plan in place if the House did not approve legislation to repeal and replace it. The Trump White House implicitly declared that "it's now or never" in his ultimatum.[26] The vote was scheduled, but the inability of Speaker Paul Ryan (R-WI) and the White House to secure the needed Republican votes forced them to pull the bill and retreat with no action.

Appointment Process

Most scholars argue that the White House largely controls the appointment process. These arguments are in line with a "presidency-centered" model of presidential-legislative power sharing. As described above, this "presidency-centered" viewpoint emphasizes the president's primary (and often determinative) role in the legislative process. Although the *Federalist Papers* describe the value of Senate compliance in appointments, *Federalist* 76 notes:

> The sole and undivided responsibility of one man will naturally beget a livelier sense of duty and a more exact regard to reputation. He will, on this account, feel himself under stronger obligations, and more interested to investigate with care the qualities requisite to the stations to be filled, and to prefer with impartiality the persons who may have the fairest pretensions to them.

Indeed, the Constitution provides the president a "presumption of confirmation," allowing the president to have an advantage in the nomination process.[27] In extending this normative argument to the "administrative presidency," Nathan argues "it is appropriate—in fact, desirable—for political chief executives to exert greater managerial influence over the bureaucracy."[28] Juxtaposed with the other branches of government, "the chief executive is in a much better position than a large group of people in a legislative body or the courts to give cohesive policy direction and guidance to the work of large public bureaucracies."[29] Public perceptions of competency matter too—public perceptions of appointee competence is positively associated with policy importance.[30] Responding to this, presidents, including Obama, are more likely to place appointees selected for non-policy reasons in agencies less associated with his agenda.[31]

Empirically, as a result of these trends, scholars have found support for this "presidency-centered" theory, especially as it relates to presidential success in getting their nominees confirmed. G. Calvin Mackenzie finds that "nominations to federal offices are almost always approved. In an average year, approximately 97 percent of all nominations will be confirmed," and incidents of rejection of "major nominations are exceedingly rare."[32] Others find that the higher up the position (labeled "first tier" for cabinet positions and agency heads), the more quickly the president's nominee was confirmed, suggesting congressional deference. The Senate is found to consistently defer to the president on most types of confirmation decisions, adding weight to the idea that presidents prevail in appointments.[33] The same scenario is largely accurate for judicial nominees, especially the Supreme Court, where a vast majority of the president's appointments are confirmed.[34] This pattern of deference suggests considerable presidential autonomy in getting their nominees confirmed.

This theory has been tested extensively in relation to presidential appointment and Senate confirmation of District, Circuit, and Supreme Court nominations. Much of this literature assumes that the president's nominees are of his own design, often by ideology or personal connection to the president.[35] Other works utilize data concerning the length of time nominee-designates wait to be confirmed by the Senate with the presumption that these individuals are largely picked by the president.[36] The focus in the literature on the Senate's right to first refusal ("senatorial courtesy") further presumes that they play a reactive role as a veto player rather than the role of agenda setter.[37] Christine Nemacheck conducts an interesting analysis of congressional endorsements of Supreme Court nominees from Herbert Hoover to George W. Bush, although she only focuses on judicial offices at the highest level. Still, other works anecdotally argue that members of Congress submit their own pressure for patronage after a transition to a new president but do not empirically test these claims.[38]

But, on the other hand, the legislature has a clear interest in and resources to assist the White House in making political appointments. Judith Michaels argues that "from the beginning of the Republic, presidents, having few alternate sources and limited time and staff resources, relied on political allies close to them, such as members of Congress, personal acquaintances, or party leaders for suggestions for appointments."[39] In addition, members of Congress (especially the Senate who confirm many nominees) have particular political preferences that presidents take into account when evaluating whether or not to confirm an individual to an agency.[40] This phenomenon is not only relegated to the members of the Senate, however; those in the House of Representatives also have "a direct interest in appointments to individual offices."[41] Indeed, the White House may also find the process of staffing so many positions daunting and may rely on help from Congress. Richard Waterman notes that, with many positions to fill, "presidents may rely on members of Congress to help them select individuals for important positions."[42] The sheer volume of presidential commissions, executive committees, boards of directors, advisory councils, and hundreds of other smaller offices makes it difficult for the White House to staff all of these offices without the help of Congress. This is especially true during the presidential transition and when Congress creates new boards, councils, or commissions during the legislative term.[43]

Congress' role (especially the Senate) in the appointment and confirmation process has been growing as a result of the centralization attempted by presidents and political factors that engender political polarization.[44] Christopher Deering argues that the Senate's attention to presidential nominations has been rising, and the time spent evaluating nominees has increased because "a period of divided party government, political scandals, increases in committee and personal staff, and evolutionary changes in the Senate's mode of operation have combined to foster greater concern for its confirmation responsibility."[45] Congress has also been shown to have a significant influence in the appointment-nomination process.[46] This comports with recent scholarship that suggests that Congress and the president work together on nominations so as to not test the public's patience for delay.[47] Indeed, delays may result in less competent nominees.[48] Therefore, to avoid complications, the president must work with Congress in this process. Indeed, when the process has been politicized, it has produced somewhat routine (but primarily high profile) delays in the process.[49] Ideological divergence between the president and the Senate filibuster delays nominations, but only under divided government.[50]

It is clear that Congress shares the political power of appointment and confirmation, yet, we still know little about the role that members of Congress play in shaping the pre-appointment phase of the appointment process. For instance, when presidents pay heed to those appointment or nomination requests from members of Congress, do they do so based upon party affiliation (which signals efforts to appease the president's allies), ideology (which signals proximity to presidential preferences), or other factors such as electoral connections or legislator resources? Or, do presidents ignore Congress and their party to staff according to their own agenda? In two recent works, I explain the important role members of Congress play in the appointment process. Examining requests by members of Congress during the Eisenhower and Ford administrations, for all appointments, legislator resources, Senate membership, and those closer ideologically to the president are related both to the number of requests made and the number of successful appointment related requests granted.[51] In explaining who is nominated to federal courts, the characteristics of the nominee matter more than the characteristics of the nominator, with the party affiliation of a nominee being the strongest predictive factor. Institutional characteristics are more prevalent at the confirmation stage, where the Senate relies more heavily on its members and the judicial experience of nominees than do presidents in nominating them.[52] These results imply that presidents tend to pursue their own interests when staffing the executive branch, except for judicial posts where they tend to heed Congress' will.

Obama

Where did the balance of executive-legislative power with regards to nominations fall during the Obama administration? Perhaps no better evidence is found that Congress (and the media) has an important say in the appointment and confirmation process than in Obama's first 100 days in office. At seven months into his presidency, fewer than half of his top appointees were in place—43 percent of 500 senior policy-making positions requiring Senate confirmation were filled.[53] The length of the vetting process and the growing delays in Congress reflecting political battles has increased the length of vacancies. Part of the delay is also the political process—after several failed nominations, including high profile positions for Secretary of Commerce, Secretary of Health and Human Services, and Chief Performance Officer of the Office of Management and Budget, the White House tightened the vetting process and created more strict criteria that would let its nominees pass congressional muster.

Although a minority in the House and Senate during the first two years of the Obama administration, Republican lawmakers attempted to retain some say in the appointment and nomination and confirmation process.[54] For example, early in his term, all 41 Republican Senators signed a letter to Obama urging him to consult with them about whom to nominate and that he re-nominate certain individuals nominated by George W. Bush who were not given the chance for confirmation.[55] The Obama administration was also criticized by Republicans in Congress for its use of "policy czars" to advance his agenda. These individuals are "special advisers"—technically chairs of White House advisory boards, special envoy and cabinet agency deputies who are asked by the president to guide high-priority initiatives.[56] For instance, on domestic policy, the "faith-based czar" heads the White House's Office of Faith-Based and Neighborhood Partnerships, and, on foreign policy, Richard Holbrooke served as the special envoy for Afghanistan and Pakistan (called the "intelligence czar"). Critics claimed that the White House used these appointments to circumvent the normal appointment process, while the White House argued that these positions have existed for (in some cases) decades and that the president has the power to appoint individuals who are tasked with helping him govern the executive branch.[57] Such inter-branch skirmishes led the Obama administration in March 2010 to use their recess appointment power, over the objections of Republicans in the Senate, to temporarily appoint individuals whom the Senate failed or refused to confirm.[58]

Trump

Trump's pace of appointing and getting nominees confirmed was slower than all recent predecessors, with less than 30 of the almost 700 executive department appointments done on the day before his inauguration.[59] In several high-profile withdrawals, the White House nominee for Labor Secretary, National Security Adviser, and Navy Secretary, all vacated their positions before hearings because of past controversial statements, inability to resolve conflicts of interest, or personal issues. Filling a full cabinet can take time—the Obama administration did not get a full cabinet until April 28, 2009.[60] Yet, the internal dysfunction of the Trump transition team (removing and replacing transition directors) and the fragmented nature of the President's contentious primary victory, which split many members of the Republican Party, contributed to the difficulty in staffing the White House. These troubles undercut the opportunity Trump had to reshape the federal judiciary through appointment. Because of the median age of judges on the federal judiciary, the number of senior seats, and current vacant seats, Trump is expected to have the chance to replace 38 percent of the judiciary due to vacancies, more than any other president since Richard Nixon.[61]

Shared Foreign Policy Powers

There has been qualified support for the "two presidencies" thesis, first proffered by Aaron Wildavsky in 1961, whereby presidents are suggested to succeed more on congressional votes on foreign policy than domestic policy.[62] This concept is predicated on the assumption that the president is primarily in charge of decision making on foreign policy. Less public attention to most matters of foreign policy may also allow presidents to be less responsive to public opinion in that area.[63] Foreign policy, international crises, or military events may often seem removed, complicated, or arcane to the public, causing the public to trust the president on foreign or military matters more than on domestic policy matters (when policies are generally more contested). Further, political participants understand that the White House has more institutional power and knowledge on matters of foreign policy, allowing them to appear authoritative.[64] Perceptions of White House competency have a positive effect on legislative success, linking the foreign policy and domestic policy realms.[65] The "wartime effect" rallies co-partisans and out-partisans to the president's camp on foreign policy matters during war.[66] Yet, scholars find that as partisan support for presidents declines, and when presidents seek to divert Congress from passing economic legislation, presidents use force abroad in response to inflation or unemployment.[67]

As noted above, however, scholars have begun to view the relationship between the executive and legislative branches as cooperative rather than conflicting. This approach has proven fruitful for understanding the inter-branch relationship, even in areas generally presidency-dominated such as foreign policy,[68] and these theories can help us to explain the political changes after a dramatic event like 9/11. Indeed, several prominent policy studies in the aftermath of the tragedies of 9/11 requested additional congressional oversight in matters of domestic surveillance, the conduct of international conflicts, and the trajectory of foreign policy.[69] Others have shown that, although Congress generally leaves military policy to the executive branch, it injects itself into the policy-making process when political incentives are greater (divided government, protracted conflicts, or souring public opinion).[70] Congress has also recently played a more significant role in financing international commitments and in resisting presidential nominees.[71] In practice, consultation between the branches also produces the best political outcomes.[72]

Indeed, recent scholarship has documented the essential contribution of the role of the legislative branch in the making of foreign policy throughout time. Not surprisingly, this relationship is reshaped during moments of foreign conflict or challenges to the sovereignty of the United States. When present, the resurgent power of Congress historically appears to be driven by a retrenchment of an unfavorable policy and the will of individual members of Congress to challenge the status quo. In particular, three historical peaks in the twentieth century characterize the ebb and flow of the dynamic relationship, including the "isolationists" in the aftermath of World War I, the "revisionists" during the height of the Cold War, and the "new institutionalists" during the Vietnam War.[73] The "isolationists" in Congress were powerful (and savvy) enough to block Woodrow Wilson's proposed League of Nations and force the administration to withdraw troops from revolutionary Russia.[74] During the origin of the Cold War, congressional power again enlarged, with congressional "revisionists" as "players on virtually every key issue of the day, in a bipartisan foreign policy where formal and informal powers seamlessly intersected."[75] Because of strong sentiments from the Republican leadership (and a relatively ineffectual Democratic leadership), several factions of the Republican Party were permitted to continue their ideological goals to limit the spread of Communism, both at home and abroad.

Riding in the wake of the "imperial presidency," Congress sought to significantly reassert itself again in the mid-1970s.[76] The "new institutionalists" challenged presidential supremacy during the Vietnam War, coalescing years earlier as critics of foreign aid policies that supported anti-Communist regimes in the 1960s.[77] Stalwart Senators, including Stuart Symington (D-MO), Edward Kennedy (D-MA), John Tunney (D-CA), Dick Clark (D-IA), Frank Church (D-ID), and members of the "Watergate Class of 1974," led the charge with legislation limiting covert assistance, convening hearings on human rights abuses, and cutting off aid to governments deemed reckless with power.[78] These idealistic changes prompted many to argue for more transparency in national security affairs and the justification of American international actions to the public, culminating in the War Powers Act of 1973 that ostensibly limited formal presidential war-making power.[79]

The most dramatic of these post-Watergate moments was Senator Frank Church's investigation of the United States' intelligence community (including the FBI, CIA, and other intelligence agencies) from 1975 to 1976 through the Senate Select Committee to Investigate the Intelligence Agencies of the United States. The "Church Committee" (as it came to be known) investigated some of the many abuses of the United States during this time, including assassination plots against foreign leaders and the overthrow of democratically elected governments in Latin America.[80] Out of these proceedings emerged significant legislation restricting presidential power in covert operations by requiring court-granted warrants for international surveillance (called the Foreign Intelligence Surveillance Act).[81] The Ford White House largely viewed the committee as resultant from the power shift during Watergate, suggesting emerging political energy (even if temporary) in the legislative branch on foreign policy.[82]

As is clear from these examples, this power-sharing relationship between the branches is not static. And, as we have seen in the past, this dynamic relationship bends and reforms as function of the political will expended by the political actors involved and as international events unfold. Even in recent events, the pendulum of power sharing continues to sway back and forth on contemporary issues, primarily the "War on Terror." In advance of the 2006 elections, the White House and Congress, after key congressional Republicans questioned the White House's blanket authority to detain prisoners, negotiated a compromise on rules for trials for "enemy combatants." Under new rules, detainees have some expanded rights to fair trials where the president is able establish military tribunals without potential review from federal courts.[83] In addition, while these legislative determinations give the executive more power to classify military detainees, the Congress, even members of the president's party, have been periodically willing to challenge this executive authority. Senator Arlen Specter (R-PA) went so far as to initiate Judiciary Committee hearings to investigate Bush's use of signing statements to interpret laws or statutes as he signs them into law, particularly on the president's ability to interpret Article 3 (regarding "cruel treatment and torture") of the Geneva Convention.[84]

Obama

These power-sharing themes are continuous and integral to the discussion of the American political system in the post-9/11 world. Indeed, these are the lasting lessons of the Church Committee—balancing executive authority with legislative oversight and public disclosure. Congress has played a big role in national security and foreign policy issues, with minimal politics injected into the process (to date). This has come from both parties. Congress, led by Democrats, promoted a compromise package of additional resources for the conflict in Afghanistan that would emphasize training for Afghan security forces but deny additional combat troops requested by the White House to regain the initiative against the Taliban insurgency.[85] Congress has also played an active role in shaping presidential policy. For instance, in May 2009, after Obama requested $80 million for the closing of Guantanamo Bay, the Senate rejected Obama's request for funding and "vowed to withhold federal dollars until the president decides the fate of the facility's 240 detainees."[86] Although the President signed an executive order ordering the closing (see below), Congress' position as organizer and funder of national security and military issues gives them a potent say in the fate of the controversial facility.

Democrats, especially, have attempted to make their voices heard on foreign policy matters. Frustration with the wars in Afghanistan and Iraq were significant factors in the substantial Democratic gains in 2006 and 2008, and, as a result, party activists and leaders sought to make their positions known to the White House. For instance, in May 2009, the House passed legislation approving an additional $96 million in funding for the wars in Afghanistan and Iraq through September 30th, requested by Obama. But, 51 Democrats opposed it, claiming that, like Bush before him, the White House was escalating a conflict with no exit strategy.[87] The bill passed 368 to 60, with 200 Democrats and all but nine Republicans supporting it; but cracks in the Democratic Party began to widen. The same legislation in the Senate required Obama "to intervene repeatedly to lobby members of his own party for his foreign policy vision."[88] Part of the hang up was that this legislation was labeled "emergency spending," allowing it to be considered independent of the budget (and with less scrutiny). The "Out of Iraq" Caucus (70 Members opposed to U.S. troop presence in Iraq) hounded the Obama White House.[89]

Although Republicans have been largely supportive of the Obama administration's foreign policy objectives and actions, fissures developed. Several commentators argued,

> As he embraces direct talks with Iran and weighs his strategy in Afghanistan President Obama is facing a new political threat from Republicans: Be hawkish on foreign policy or risk letting your party be painted as weak in next year's midterm elections.[90]

Similarly,

> GOP strategists are honing in on Obama's recent policy shift on missile defense, in which the administration decided to cancel a radar

installation in the Czech Republic and ground-based interceptors in Poland that had been proposed by Bush to protect Europe from Iranian long-range missiles.[91]

The conflicts in Iraq and Afghanistan, as well as other potentially troubling relations, required the White House and opposition in Congress to work together to fund present and future conflicts, even at a time where there are differences of opinion about the future of international relations.

Obama's penchant for diplomacy over conflict, multi-nationalism over unilateralism, and negotiations over friction have found favor with most Democratic leaders, although the appeal of this approach may not last beyond his term as a new Republican administration takes power.[92] Republican opposition to Obama's nuclear deal with Iran and opposition to the White House's opening the door to ease sanctions on Cuba were prominent signals of the breakdown of bipartisanship over foreign affairs. Obama's attempt to seek approval from Congress for the use of force (via military strike) against the Syrian government in 2013 put him at the mercy of conservative House Republicans and led to him being the first president to lose a vote on the use of force in modern times.[93] Trump responded early in his presidency in 2017 to a chemical weapons attack by the Assad government with a missile strike for which he did not seek congressional approval. A Republican-controlled Congress generally backed the President's actions, although some were critical. But the episode opens up questions about executive-legislative power sharing on foreign policy as a White House justifies that muscular actions is in the interest of the United States, and does so without obtaining congressional approval or without a larger geopolitical strategy.[94]

Unilateral Presidential Powers

Recent academic discussion on the importance of the unilateral presidency has expanded Neustadt's edict that presidential power is partly "command-based."[95] These unilateral powers come in a variety of forms. Executive orders are

> directives issued by the president to officers of the executive branch, requiring them to take an action, stop a certain type of activity, alter policy, change management practices, or accept a delegation of authority under which they will henceforth be responsible for the implementation of law.[96]

Presidential proclamations allow the president to make a political determination about a particular fact and are usually directed (unlike executive orders) at someone outside of government.[97] Presidential memoranda, similar to executive orders, are pronouncements by the chief executive directed at executive branch officials and often the White House staff, but "without fitting into" legal requirements.[98] These edicts typically rely on statutory authority, presumed statutory authority, or presidential constitutional prerogatives. Interestingly, many of these directives grew out of the president's ambiguous powers as outlined in Article II. Although each has been sanctioned by the Supreme Court in various ways, there is still potential for abuse of power, or the overcoming of the separation of powers, because presidents have the authority to make policy-based decisions without input from Congress.[99]

These works provide evidence that a president's ability to shape and act without the consent of Congress, the courts, and (often) the public is largely unchecked by traditional institutional arrangements.[100] These works have also examined executive orders in relation to the development of the institutional presidency,[101] in detaining "enemy combatants"[102] and in examining the shifting balance of powers between the executive and legislative branches.[103]

Politics does play a role in these unilateral policy actions, as many scholars have found the ability of presidents to act is enhanced or limited by political circumstances. The relative ambiguity of constitutionally-granted powers provides incentives for presidents to attempt to use unilateral action to send policy signals to other political actors and to expand their own formal powers.[104] Presidents are found to use these tactics (especially executive orders) at the ends of their terms, when running for reelection, when Congress is weak or of the same party, and when lagging in public opinion polls.[105] These powers are also more prevalent during times of national crisis, concurrent to moments where presidential power is at its highest.[106] These actions are often covert presidential actions that receive little or no support from Congress and may be done to actively circumvent Congress.[107]

Yet, even while these actions are unilateral, others have found that presidents often only use these actions when the action is not likely to be overturned in Congress,[108] or where there is already some prior agreement between the executive and legislative branches.[109] The authority cited in most executive orders is statutory, indicating some coordination between the executive and legislative branches.[110] Presidential power in unilateral actions is used to show that presidents exercise their dual executive functions in ways that allow them to dictate policy or share power.[111] As an administrator, a president acts together with Congress keeping the wheels of government oiled as a means to carry out executive functions. Presidents are more demure about using their executive authority when Congress has a stronger hand politically. As an independent, a president fulfills the expectation to advance his or her own policy objectives even if it is *against* Congress. Presidents are more likely to forge ahead with greater independence when the issue is on their agenda, and they are less able to bargain with Congress. In fact, in policy issues related to the establishment of national monuments, or on trade policy (increasing or decreasing the Generalized System of Preferences which governs tariff rates between the United States and other nations), Congress provides the president the statutory authority to operate within a specific boundary.[112] Attempts by the president to conduct unilateral authority outside these prearranged boundaries would be illegal. Likewise, executive orders are rarely overturned, but, if these presidential directives run afoul of the Constitution, the courts can step in to halt the action. This minimizes (but does not erase) the potential for presidents to overstep the constitutionally proscribed separation of powers. Indeed, scholars find presidents significantly constrained in employing unilateral tools for these reasons, especially in exercising discretion within those rules.[113]

Obama

The use of these powers are not new. As shown in Figure 7.1, in their first 100 days in office, presidents have routinely issued dozens of executive orders, proclamations, and executive memoranda. Although the number of executive orders issued in the first 100 days of an administration has been declining since the Carter administration, the number of proclamations is consistently high for recent presidents (Clinton to Obama), and the number of executive memoranda has been steady from the Clinton

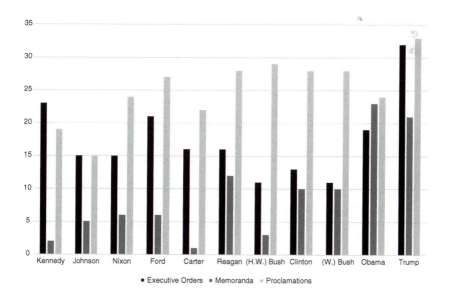

Figure 7.1 Executive Orders, Memoranda, and Proclamations

administration (13), to the Bush administration (11), to the Obama administration (19), to the Trump administration (21). The growth in interest groups and political organizations covetous of an official proclamation from the White House has contributed to historic highs in the number of presidential proclamations in the recent few decades. The Obama and Trump administrations had more orders than prior presidents since Ford, in part as a means to undo the administrative state set by their predecessors.[114] Likewise, the growth of government, especially executive agencies, boards, and commissions, hastens the increase in the number of executive memoranda, allowing the president to exercise more control over his own bureaucracy. Interestingly, all four recent presidents in Figure 7.1 entered office with unified government, suggesting presidents are using their unilateral powers when Congress is potentially most acceptant of their leadership.

Obama used these unilateral powers, like other presidents, to advance his policy agenda. For instance, Obama issued a ban for federal workers (including contractors) from using the text message function of their phones while driving:

> A Federal Government-wide prohibition on the use of text messaging while driving on official business or while using Government-supplied equipment will help save lives, reduce injuries, and set an example for State and local governments, private employers, and individual drivers.[115]

Obama issued a proclamation on "Pay Equity Day" and shortly thereafter signed legislation making it easier for individuals to sue employers for pay discrimination.[116] Such executive actions are also used by presidents to manage emerging conflicts. In response to air bombings by Israel in Gaza, Obama issued a memoranda offering monetary aid to refugees because

> it is important to the national interest to furnish assistance under the Act in an amount not to exceed $20.3 million from the United States Emergency Refugee and Migration Assistance Fund for the purpose of meeting unexpected and urgent refugee and migration needs.[117]

This again implies a coordination of inter-branch efforts.

Congress has pushed back against executive power. Opposition politicians chastised Obama for aggressive assertions of executive discretion and accuse him of "arrogance and sidestepping the political process" after he issued directives on gun control, health care, and immigration.[118] For instance, in 2014 when the Supreme Court took the case of whether or not Obama's unilaterally issued regulations on greenhouse gas emissions exceeded his authority, a frustrated Congress pounced. In a brief filed with the Supreme Court, Republican lawmakers challenged the President's specific and general use of unilateral orders and

> pressed that theme, one that hewed closely to criticism of the administration's delays in carrying out the Affordable Care Act, its decision not to defend the Defense of Marriage Act in court, and its tolerance of state marijuana laws in Colorado and Washington.[119]

A brief from Representative Michele Bachmann (R-MN) and other House Republicans argued:

> The regulations under challenge were "an intolerable invasion of Congress's domain that threatens to obliterate the line dividing executive from legislative power." The brief added that the regulations were "perhaps the most audacious seizure of pure legislative power over domestic economic matters attempted by the executive branch" since President Harry S. Truman tried to take control of the nation's steel mills during the Korean War.[120]

In response to executive action to defer deportation for young immigrants who entered the United States illegally, Representative Steve King (R-IA) noted: "Americans should be outraged that President Obama is planning to usurp the Constitutional authority of the United States Congress and grant amnesty by edict to 1 million illegal aliens," and "President Obama, an ex-constitutional law professor, whose favorite word is audacity, is prepared to violate the principles of Constitutional Law that he taught."[121]

Obama, often chastened for acting on his own, has used both his bargaining leverage and his unilateral authority, often in the same instance. The Obama administration's pronouncement that the administration planned to use either the pen (unilateral powers) or the phone (persuasion) underscores the idea that the president might either sign "executive orders or use[s] the bully pulpit of the White House as convening power to make progress on issues ranging from the economy to the environment."[122] In early 2013, the White House issued 23 new unilateral rules on gun control in the wake of a school shooting tragedy in Connecticut, including steps to strengthen background checks, promote research on gun violence, and provide additional training. By pursuing an overhaul of the nation's gun laws, the President "is wagering that public opinion has evolved enough after a string of mass shootings to force passage of politically contentious measures that Congress has long stymied."[123] Simultaneous with these unilateral actions, the President "hosted groups of Republican senators for dinner, and his Chief of Staff, Denis McDonough, tried to repair relations with several key senators." This meeting achieved no specific significant legislative breakthroughs, although both parties, led by Senator

Patty Murray (D-WA) and Representative Paul Ryan (R-WI), arrived at a budget deal later in the year.[124] While presidents possess multiple tools to make policy, both endogenous and exogenous factors (including mutual influence) affect unilateral action.

Trump

Promising quick action on his agenda, the White House shocked Washington by immediately issuing several controversial orders in his first week in office. For instance, on his first day in office, the President signed orders to declare his intention to repeal the Affordable Care Act and direct agencies to slow the implementation of some regulations, and establish a hiring and regulatory action freeze. Days later, the White House followed up with an order stating the United States' intent to withdraw from the Trans Pacific Partnership (TPP), a trade deal he criticized on the campaign trail, and reinstated the "Mexico City Policy," a global "gag rule" that bans American non-governmental organizations from discussing abortion (and a policy that has been established and undone by the presidents of opposition parties since Ronald Reagan).[125] These actions, except the withdrawal from TPP, were welcomed by congressional Republicans. The furor over these orders led many to make comparisons to Obama who also issued a flurry of orders in his first 100 days, many revoking orders from previous administrations. Trump actually issued more orders in his first 100 days than any president since Kennedy.

Several orders were immediately impactful because of the controversy they generated. Following his long-running promise, the Trump administration signed an executive order to take a step toward constructing a wall along the U.S. border with Mexico by identifying costs and potential funds. The President also signed three memoranda to expand oil pipelines in the United States, specifically directing agencies to approve construction of the Dakota Access Pipeline and Keystone XL Pipeline in addition to requirements that the construction materials be made in the United States. On the regulatory side of the executive's responsibilities, the White House issued an order that caps spending on new regulations at $0 and requires for every regulation the executive branch proposes, two must be identified to be eliminated. To accomplish this, the administration issued an order that may tear up many of the regulations on the financial industry that Congress put in place after the 2008 financial crisis, worrying opponents that the roll backs could increase risk in financial systems but cheered by proponents who aimed to reduce government oversight of Wall Street to encourage competition. Another order directed federal agencies to revise the Clean Water Rule, a major regulation established by the Obama White House that clarified what waterways were protected under the Clean Water Act.[126] Other orders called on agencies to look for ways to reduce regulations for U.S.-based manufacturing.

The most impactful and controversial order in the Trump administration's first 100 days was the travel ban on immigrants from certain
Muslim majority countries. The White House's order implicitly followed
through on Trump's promise to have "extreme vetting" and issued an
order banning people from seven Muslim-majority countries for 90 days
and blocked all refugees seeking asylum for 120 days. The first iteration
of the order was held up by federal court rulings claiming it was discrim-
inatory, while the second order was issued a month later with revisions
that included provisions that existing visa holders would not be subjected
to the ban, and Iraq was removed from the list of countries (from the
seven countries identified in the first order). Corollary orders, in the
form of a memoranda, instructed the Departments of State, Justice, and
Homeland Security on how to implement the travel ban. Specifically, the
order directs the agency heads to enhance the vetting of visa applicants
and submit a report to the White House concerning the long-term costs
of the program. The order has been blocked by a federal judge and as of
this writing is still in litigation. The legal outcome aside, the ban split
many in the Republican Party who believed the ban to be "overly broad,"
tantamount to a "religious test" for entry to the United States, and dam-
aging to the country's ability to recruit allies in global security efforts.[127]

Some of the President's orders, especially proclamations, however,
were common and uncontroversial—the sort most presidents issue either
at the behest of Congress or in undertaking routine assessments of the
executive branch. The White House proclaimed March 19 to March 25 as
National Poison Prevention Week to encourage Americans to safeguard
their homes and protect children from accidentally ingesting poisonous
materials. The Trump administration also proclaimed March 5 to March
11 as National Consumer Protection Week to remind Americans of the
risk of identify theft and cyber scams and to monitor their privacy both
online and off line. Trump also issued an executive order with his gath-
ered cabinet flanking him to improve the efficiency of the federal government, which would "eliminate or reorganize unnecessary or redundant
federal agencies after a 180 day review."[128] The Office of Management
and Budget and the budget director is to review plans submitted by each
agency head to reorganize or shrink their departments and submit a plan
to streamline their agency to the White House.

Conclusion

Alexander Hamilton's edict for "energy" in the executive can creatively
contradict the constitutional authority given to the legislative branch.
A visible and powerful president necessarily detracts from a legislature
whose job it is (at least on paper) to be the engine of legislative ingenu-
ity. The Constitution sought to "buttress 'parchment barriers' by pitting
ambition against ambition; and the principle means of doing that was

the election of public officials at different times, by different people and for somewhat different reasons."[129] Although the powers of the president have grown immeasurably beyond what the framers envisioned, and have surpassed Congress in terms of the ability to lead in the American system, the function of shared powers continues to shape the political process in America.

To consider this relationship a *pendulum* (an analogy some have used[130] to suggest the power balance swings from one branch to another) may overstate the zero-sum game of Washington politics—the truth is that legislative powers are shared, even if certain powers are exercised at certain times by specific institutions that perhaps encroach on the power of another branch. A pendulum analogy implies that the power shifts between the branches (potentially at regular, predictable intervals). This arrangement is false because, even during times where one branch appears to have more power than another, the truth is that the branches still rely on one another for shared policy making power. In reality, the executive-legislative relationship is more like a *rubber band*, where it retains a fundamental shape, but can be stretched to change as legislative and executive tools change and political events occur. So, for instance, in utilizing unilateral powers, presidents can stretch that part of the rubber band, even while Congress asserts themselves on matters of foreign policy or the appointments process. In legislating, most presidents enter office popular and enjoy a "honeymoon" effect, a phenomenon that fades after 100 days of executive-legislative interaction.[131]

Indeed, following the rubber band analogy, jointly understanding presidency-centered and Congress-centered variables is also shown to better account for variations in policy making.[132] For instance, recent evidence suggests a resurgent Congress in the creation of foreign policy, a fact that seems at odds with the two presidencies thesis[133] or other literature that claims that Congress always defers to the president in foreign policy matters.[134] Public opinion as seen through the lens of congressional action may restrain presidential executive action on foreign policy.[135] This supports the literature that Congress may not be involved in the formal aspects of foreign policy making, but does play a role in the informal aspects.[136] The evidence presented here also reveals that Congress has more say on when and how the president uses his unilateral powers and whom the president recommends for nomination and confirmation than previously assumed. If the president pushes too far, especially in divided government or when the legislature is less able to legislate, Congress may ramp up investigations of the White House.[137]

Of course, this does not suggest that presidents are not critical to the process—in fact, in the case of foreign policy, presidents' intent on using their powers are rarely stopped by Congress.[138] Presidents, as "first movers" in foreign policy, can set a stable agenda and chart a course for policy action that is difficult to undo. As a result, because Congress often has less information than the White House, Congress has an incentive to delegate foreign policy powers to the president.[139] Similarly, on issues like agency design, where the executive and legislative branches jointly construct a regulatory agency like the National Biological Service or the National Nuclear Security Agency, the executive often has the upper hand since the legislature may have a short term view of the bureaucracy and the president can create agencies by executive order.[140] But, on the other hand, to claim that Congress' lawmaking powers have been co-opted by the executive would also be overstating the case. Yet, as recent evidence reveals, Congress' role in the political process remains important. Fisher argues that "very few operations of Congress and the presidency are genuinely independent and autonomous."[141] Even presidential "unilateral" actions, which can be undertaken by the president often without prior consent of Congress, are often done on behalf of Congress or with Congress' implicit consent. That such concurrent powers and the politics that guide them exist cannot be overlooked.

All told, a rubber band analogy seems most appropriate to demonstrate the executive-legislative political arrangement. A pendulum swings on a plane and rarely deviates, while a rubber band can be stretched in many directions at once. The evidence from this chapter shows that power sharing is conducted in different patterns, with different branches holding an advantage at different times and in unique tools. The primary aspiration of the actors in this inter-branch relationship should be to stretch the rubber band without breaking it.

Notes

1 See Gary Andres and Patrick J. Griffin, "Successful Influence: Managing Legislative Affairs in the Twenty-first Century," in *Rivals for Power: Presidential-Congressional Relations*, ed. James A. Thurber (New York: Rowman and Littlefield, 2002); Mark A. Peterson, *Legislating Together: The White House and Capitol Hill from Eisenhower to Reagan* (Cambridge, MA: Harvard University Press, 1990); and Brad Lockerbie, Stephen Borrelli and Scott Hedger, "An Integrative Approach to Modeling Presidential Success in Congress," *Political Research Quarterly* 51 (1998): 155–172.
2 Charles O. Jones, *The Presidency in a Separated System* (Washington, DC: Brookings, 1994), 24.
3 Peterson, *Legislating Together*, 79.
4 Richard E. Neustadt, *Presidential Power and the Modern Presidents: The Politics of Leadership from Roosevelt to Reagan* (New York: Free Press, 1990), 372.
5 Jeffrey Burnham, "The President and the Environment: A Reinterpretation of Neustadt's Theory of Presidential Leadership," *Congress & the Presidency* 37 (2010): 302–322.
6 Barbara Sinclair, "Legislative Cohesion and Presidential Policy Success," *Journal of Legislative Studies* 9 (2003): 41–56.
7 See Jon R. Bond and Richard Fleisher, *The President in the Legislative Arena* (Chicago, IL: University of Chicago Press, 1990); and Jon R. Bond,

Richard Fleisher and B. Dan Wood, "The Marginal and Time-Varying Effect of Public Approval on Presidential Success in Congress," *Journal of Politics* 65 (2003): 92–110. However, public approval of the president has been shown to be effective when the issue is salient or when the issue is complex. See Brandice Canes-Wrone and Scott de Marchi, "Presidential Approval and Legislative Success," *Journal of Politics* 64 (2002): 491–509.

8 Manabu Saeki, "Override Propensity in the U.S. Congress: Veto Challenge and Override Vote by the Two Chambers," *Journal of Legislative Studies* 10 (2004): 70–83.

9 Richard S. Conley, "Divided Government and Democratic Presidents: Truman and Clinton Compared," *Presidential Studies Quarterly* 30 (2000): 222–244.

10 John B. Gilmour, "Institutional and Individual Influences on the President's Veto," *The Journal of Politics* 64 (2002): 198–218.

11 Frances E. Lee, "Dividers Not Uniters: Presidential Leadership and Senate Partisanship 1981–2004," *The Journal of Politics* 70 (2008): 914–928.

12 See Frances E. Lee, *Insecure Majorities: Congress and the Perpetual Campaign* (Chicago, IL: University of Chicago Press, 2016).

13 Barbara Sinclair, "Hostile Partners: The President, Congress and Lawmaking in the Partisan 1990s," in *Polarized Politics*, eds. Jon R. Bond and Richard Fleisher (Washington, DC: CQ Press, 2000).

14 On the former point, see Morris Fiorina, *Divided Government* (New York: Macmillan, 1992); and James L. Sundquist, *Constitutional Reform and Effective Government* (Washington, DC: Brookings, 1986); on the latter point, see David R. Mayhew, "Divided Party Control: Does It Make a Difference?" *PS: Political Science and Politics* 24 (1991): 637–640.

15 Terry Sullivan and Scott de Marchi, "Congressional Bargaining in Presidential Time: Give and Take, Anticipation, and the Constitutional Rationalization of Dead Ducks," *Journal of Politics* 73 (2011): 748–763.

16 George C. Edwards III, Andrew Barrett and Jeffrey Peake, "The Legislative Impact of Divided Government," *American Journal of Political Science* 41 (1997): 545–563; Daniel P. Franklin and Michael P. Fix, "The Best of Times and the Worst of Times: Polarization and Presidential Success in Congress," *Congress & the Presidency* 43 (2016): 377–394.

17 See Peterson, *Legislating Together.*

18 See Keith Krehbiel, *Pivotal Politics: A Theory of U.S. Lawmaking* (Chicago, IL: University of Chicago Press, 1998).

19 Gary Andres, Patrick Griffin and James Thurber, "Managing White House-Congressional Relations: Observations from Inside the Process," *Presidential Studies Quarterly* 30 (2004): 553–563.

20 See Roger T. LaRocca, *The Presidential Agenda: Sources of Executive Influence in Congress* (Columbus, OH: Ohio State University Press, 2002).

21 Matthew Eshbaugh-Soha, "The Politics of Presidential Agendas," *Political Research Quarterly* 58 (2005): 257–268.

22 See Charles M. Cameron, *Veto Bargaining: Presidents and the Politics of Negative Power* (New York: Cambridge University Press, 2000).

23 Jeffrey E. Cohen, "Everybody Loves a Winner: On the Mutual Causality of Presidential Approval and Success in Congress," *Congress & the Presidency* 40 (2013): 285–307.

24 Matthew J. Lebo and Andrew J. O'Green, "The President's Role in the Partisan Congressional Arena," *Journal of Politics* 73 (2011): 718–734.

25 Maureen Groppe, "CBO Says Latest GOP Health Care Bill Would Cost More, Not Expand Coverage," *USA Today*, March 23, 2017, www.usatoday. com/story/news/politics/2017/03/23/cbo-says-latest-gop-health-care-bill-would-cost-more-not-expand-coverage/99553348/.

26 Julie Hirschfeld Davis, Robert Pear and Thomas Kaplan, "Trump Tells G.O.P. It's Now or Never, Demanding House Vote on Health Bill," *New York Times*, March 23, 2017, www.nytimes.com/2017/03/23/us/politics/health-republicans-vote.html?_r=0.

27 See Michael J. Gerhardt, *The Federal Appointment Process: A Constitutional and Historical Analysis* (Durham, NC: Duke University Press, 2003).

28 Richard P. Nathan, *The Administrative Presidency* (New York: John Wiley, 1983), 1.

29 Ibid., 10.

30 Gary E. Hollibaugh, Jr. "Presidential Appointments and Policy Priorities," *Social Science Quarterly* 98 (2017): 162–184.

31 Gary E. Hollibaugh, Jr., Gabriel Horton and David E. Lewis, "Presidents and Patronage," *American Journal of Political Science* 58 (2014): 1024–1042.

32 See G. Calvin Mackenzie, *The Politics of Presidential Appointments* (New York: Free Press, 1981).

33 See Judith E. Michaels, *The President's Call: Executive Leadership From FDR to George Bush* (Pittsburgh, PA: University of Pittsburgh Press, 1997); Nolan McCarty and Rose Razaghian, "Advice and Consent: Senate Responses to Executive Branch Nominations, 1885–1996," *American Journal of Political Science* 43 (1999): 1122–1143; and Timothy P. Nokken and Brian R. Sala, "Confirmation Dynamics: A Model of Presidential Appointments to Independent Agencies," *Journal of Theoretical Politics* 12 (2000): 91–112.

34 See Christine L. Nemacheck, *Strategic Selection: Presidential Nomination of Supreme Court Justices from Herbert Hoover through George W. Bush* (Charlottesville, VA: University of Virginia Press, 2007).

35 See Glendon Schubert, *The Judicial Mind* (New York: Free Press, 1965); David W. Rhode and Harold J. Spaeth, *Supreme Court Decision Making* (San Francisco, CA: Freeman, 1976); Jeffery A. Segal and Harold J. Spaeth, *The Supreme Court and the Attitudinal Model Revised* (New York: Cambridge University Press, 2002); and David M. O'Brien, *Storm Center: The Supreme Court in American Politics*, 6th ed. (New York: Norton, 2003).

36 McCarty and Razaghian, "Advice and Consent."

37 Sarah A. Binder, "The Senate as a Black Hole? Lessons Learned from the Judicial Appointments Experience," in *Innocent Until Nominated: The Breakdown of the Presidential Appointments Process*, ed. Calvin Mackenzie (Washington, DC: Brookings, 2001).

38 See Nemacheck, *Strategic Selection*; and James P. Pfiffner, *The Strategic Presidency: Hitting the Ground Running* (Lawrence, KS: University of Kansas Press, 1996), 70.

39 See Michaels, *The President's Call*.

40 Thomas H. Hammond and Jeffery S. Hill, "Deference of Preference? Explaining Senate Confirmation of Presidential Nominees to Administrative Agencies," *Journal of Theoretical Politics* 5 (1993): 23–59.

41 Mackenzie, *The Politics of Presidential Appointments*, xvii.

42 Richard Waterman, *Presidential Influence and the Administrative State* (Knoxville, TN: University of Tennessee Press, 1989), 29.

43 See Pfiffner, *The Strategic Presidency*.

44 G. Calvin Mackenzie, "The State of Presidential Appointments," in *Innocent Until Nominated: The Breakdown of the Presidential Appointments Process*, ed. Calvin G. Mackenzie (Washington, DC: Brookings, 2001).

45 Christopher J. Deering, "Damned If You Do and Damned If You Don't," in *The In-And-Outers: Presidential Appointees and Transient Government in Washington*, ed. G. Calvin Mackenzie (Baltimore, MD: Johns Hopkins University Press, 1987), 100.

46 Susan K. Snyder and Berry R. Weingast, "The American System of Shared Powers: The President, Congress and the NLRB," *Journal of Law Economics & Organization* 16 (2000): 269–305; Nolan McCarty, "The Appointments Dilemma," *American Journal of Political Science* 48 (2004): 413–428; and Berry R. Weingast, "Caught in the Middle: The President, Congress, and the Political-Bureaucratic System," in *The Executive Branch*, eds. Joel D. Aberbach and Mark A. Peterson (New York: Oxford University Press, 2006).

47 See Michael Sollenberger, *The President Shall Nominate: How Congress Trumps Executive Power* (Lawrence, KS: University of Kansas Press, 2008).

48 Gary E. Hollibaugh, Jr., "Vacancies, Vetting, and Votes: A Unified Dynamic Model of the Appointments Process," *Journal of Theoretical Politics* 27 (2015): 206–236.

49 See Norman Vieira and Leonard Gross, *Supreme Court Appointments: Judge Bork and the Politicization of Senate Confirmations* (Carbondale, IL: Southern Illinois University Press, 1998); and Burdett Loomis, "The Senate: An "Obstacle Course" for Executive Appointments?" in *Innocent Until Nominated: The Breakdown of the Presidential Appointments Process*, ed. Calvin Mackenzie (Washington, DC: Brookings, 2001).

50 Gary E. Hollibaugh, Jr. and Lawrence S. Rosenberg, "The When and Why of Nominations: Determinants of Presidential Appointments," *American Politics Research* 45 (2017): 280–303.

51 Brandon Rottinghaus and Daniel E. Bergan, "The Politics of Requesting Appointments: Congressional Requests in the Appointment and Nomination Process," *Political Research Quarterly* 64 (2011): 31–44.

52 Brandon Rottinghaus and Chris Nicholson, "Counting Congress In: Patterns of Success in Judicial Nomination Requests by Members of Congress to the President," *American Politics Research* 38 (2010): 691–717.

53 Peter Baker, "Obama's Team Is Lacking Most of Its Top Players," *New York Times*, August 24, 2009, http://query.nytimes.com/gst/fullpage. html?res=9E0DE7DA103EF937A1575BC0A96F9C8B63.

54 Jonathan Weisman, "Delays in Cabinet Nominations Demonstrate GOP Resolve," *Wall Street Journal*, January 24, 2009, www.wsj.com/articles/ SB123275672929711875.

55 See Joseph A. Pika and John Anthony Maltese, *The Politics of the Presidency*, 7th ed. (Washington, DC: CQ Press, 2009).

56 Michael A. Fletcher and Brady Dennis, "Obama's Many Policy 'Czars' Draw Ire from Conservatives," *The Washington Post*, September 16, 2009, www. washingtonpost.com/wp-dyn/content/article/2009/09/15/AR2009091501424. html.

57 David B. Rivkin Jr. and Lee A. Casey, "Misplaced Fears About the 'Czars,'" *Washington Post*, September 19, 2009.

58 Sheryl Gay Stolberg, "Obama Bypasses Senate Process, Filling 15 Posts," *New York Times*, March 28, 2010, www.nytimes.com/2010/03/28/us/politics/ 28recess.html.

59 Maggie Haberman and Glenn Thrush, "A Trump Administration, With Obama Staff Members Filling in the Gaps," *New York Times*, January 19, 2017, www.nytimes.com/2017/01/19/us/trump-cabinet-picks-inauguration.html.

60 Ben Casselman, Harry Enten, Kathryn Casteel and Maggie Koerth-Baker, "TrumpBeat: Return of the Facts," *FiveThirtyEight*, March 17, 2017, https:// fivethirtyeight.com/features/trumpbeat-return-of-the-facts/?ex_cid= 538twitter.

61 Josh Katz, "Older Judges and Vacant Seats Give Trump Huge Power to Shape American Courts," *New York Times*, February 14, 2017, www.nytimes.com/

interactive/2017/02/14/upshot/trump-poised-to-transform-american-courts. html.

62 Aaron Wildavsky, "The Two Presidencies," *Trans-Action* 4 (1961): 7–14; see also Bond and Fleisher, *The President in the Legislative Arena.*

63 See Benjamin I. Page and Jason Barabas, "Foreign Policy Gaps Between Citizens and Leaders," *International Studies Quarterly* 44 (2000): 339–364; and Richard Sobel, *The Impact of Public Opinion on U.S. Foreign Policy Since Vietnam* (New York: Oxford University Press, 2001).

64 See Graham Allison and Philip Zelikow, *Essence of Decision: Explaining the Cuban Missile Crisis* (New York: Addison-Wesley, 1999); and Robert Scigliano, "The War Powers Resolution and the War Powers Act," in *The Presidency and the Constitutional Order*, eds. Joseph M. Bessette and Jeffrey K. Tulis (Baton Rouge, LA: Louisiana State University Press, 1981).

65 Christopher Gelpi and Joseph Grieco, "Competency Costs in Foreign Affairs: Presidential Performance in International Conflicts and Domestic Legislative Success, 1953–2001," *American Journal of Political Science* 58 (2015): 440–456.

66 William G. Howell and Jon C. Rogowski, "War, the Presidency, and Legislative Voting Behavior," *American Journal of Political Science* 57 (2013): 150–166.

67 David J. Brule and Wonjae Hwang, "Diverting Legislature: Executive-Legislative Relations, the Economy, and US Uses of Force," *International Studies Quarterly* 54 (2010): 361–379.

68 D. Roderick Kiewiet and Matthew D. McCubbins, "Appropriations Decisions as a Bilateral Bargaining Game Between President and Congress," *Legislative Studies Quarterly* 10 (1985): 181–210; Bert A. Rockman, "Reinventing What for Whom? President and Congress in the Making of Foreign Policy," *Presidential Studies Quarterly* 30 (2000): 133–156; and Lee H. Hamilton and Jordan Tama, *A Creative Tension: The Foreign Policy Roles of the President and Congress* (Princeton, NJ: Woodrow Wilson Center Press, 2002).

69 The 9/11 Commission Report: Final Report of the National Commission on Terrorist Attacks Upon the United States (Washington, DC: Government Printing Office, 2002), 419–423.

70 James Meernik, "Congress, the President and the Commitment of the U.S. Military," *Legislative Studies Quarterly* 20 (1995): 377–392.

71 See Rockman, *Reinventing What for Whom?* and Randall B. Ripley and James M. Lindsay, *Congress Resurgent: Foreign and Defense Policy on Capitol Hill* (Ann Arbor, MI: University of Michigan Press, 1993).

72 See Hamilton and Tama, *A Creative Tension.*

73 Robert David Johnson, *Congress and the Cold War* (New York: Cambridge University Press, 2006), xiv.

74 See Lloyd Ambrosius, *Woodrow Wilson and the American Diplomatic Tradition: The Treaty Fight in Perspective* (New York: Cambridge University Press, 1987). Congress used the "power of the purse" to threaten to not fund the presence of military personnel in Russia, thereby forcing the White House to suspend troop allocations to Russia.

75 Johnson, *Congress and the Cold War*, xvi.

76 Arthur M. Schlesinger, Jr., *The Imperial Presidency* (New York: Houghton Mifflin, 1973), 252.

77 See Louis Fisher, *Presidential War Power* (Lawrence, KS: University of Kansas Press, 1995b).

78 Johnson, *Congress and the Cold War*, xx–xxi. Others have deemed this period of congressional presidential relations (from 1974 to 1976) as the "era

of skepticism." See Loch K. Johnson, *A Season of Inquiry: Congress and Intelligence* (Chicago, IL: Dorsey Press, 1988), 253.

79 See Gary Hart, *The Shield and the Cloak* (New York: Oxford University Press, 2006). Senator Hart was an original member of the Church Committee that investigated these themes.

80 See Johnson, *A Season of Inquiry*.

81 David Cohen and John Wells, *American National Security and Civil Liberties in an Era of Terrorism* (New York: Palgrave Macmillan, 2004), 24.

82 Leroy Ashby and Rod Gramer, *Fighting the Odds: The Life of Senator Frank Church* (Pullman, WA: Washington State University Press, 1994), 472.

83 Charles Babington, "House OKs Bush-Backed Bill on Detainees," *Washington Post*, September 28, 2006, A1; and Charles Babington and Jonathan Weisman, "Senate Passes Detainee Bill," *Washington Post*, September 29, 2006, A1. By a 51 to 48 vote in the Senate, the body rejected legislation that would allow for review of these decisions by federal courts. See David G. Savage and Richard Simon, "Legal Battle Over Detainee Bill Is Likely," *Los Angeles Times*, September 29, 2006, A1.

84 Charlie Savage, "Senators Renew Calls for Hearings on Signing Statements," *Boston Globe*, June 16, 2006, A4. Senator Arlen Specter also challenged the Bush administration's interference with the hearings on domestic wiretapping, accusing the administration (and Vice President Dick Cheney) of persuading other Republican members of the Judiciary Committee to not issue subpoenas requiring phone company executives to testify about the sharing of phone records. See Michael A. Fletcher, "Cheney Downplays Dispute with Specter," *Washington Post*, June 9, 2006, A4.

85 Scott Wilson, "On War, Obama Could Turn to GOP," *Washington Post*, October 1, 2009, www.washingtonpost.com/wp-dyn/content/article/2009/09/30/AR2009093005114.html.

86 Shailagh Murray, "Senate Demands Plan for Detainees; Democrats Scrap Funding to Close Guantanamo Bay," *Washington Post*, May 20, 2009, www.washingtonpost.com/wp-dyn/content/article/2009/05/19/AR2009051903615.html.

87 Perry Bacon Jr., "House Passes War Funds as 51 Democrats Dissent," *Washington Post*, May 15, 2009, www.washingtonpost.com/wp-dyn/content/article/2009/05/14/AR2009051403480.html.

88 Perry Bacon Jr., "Senate Approves War Funding Bill After Obama Presses Democrats," *Washington Post*, June 19, 2009, www.washingtonpost.com/wp-dyn/content/article/2009/06/18/AR2009061804094.html.

89 Ross K. Baker, "Obama's Left Flank; Anti-War Democrats Make President Vulnerable on National Security," *USA Today*, July 1, 2009, p. 13A.

90 Peter Wallsten, "GOP Targets Obama's Foreign Policy," *Los Angeles Times*, October 2, 2009, http://articles.latimes.com/2009/oct/02/nation/na-iran-politics2.

91 Ibid.

92 Bruce Miroff, "Barack Obama's Legacy in American Foreign Policy," *The Presidency and Executive Politics Report*, Spring 2017.

93 Peter Baker and Jonathan Weisman, "Obama Seeks Approval by Congress for Strike in Syria," *New York Times*, August 31, 2013, www.nytimes.com/2013/09/01/world/middleeast/syria.html.

94 Jennifer Steinhauer, "GOP Lawmakers, Once Skeptical of Obama Plan to Hit Syria, Back Trump," *New York Times*, April 7, 2017, www.nytimes.com/2017/04/07/us/politics/syria-bombing-republicans-trump.html?_r=0.

95 See Neustadt, *Presidential Power*.

96 Phillip J. Cooper, *By Order of the President: The Use and Abuse of Executive Direction Action* (Lawrence, KS: University of Kansas Press, 2002), 16.

97 Brandon Rottinghaus and Jason Meier, "The Power of Decree: Presidential Use of Executive Proclamations, 1977–2005," *Political Research Quarterly* 60 (2007): 338–343.

98 Phillip J. Cooper, "George W. Bush, Edgar Allan Poe, and the Use and Abuse of Presidential Signing Statements," *Presidential Studies Quarterly* 35 (2005): 515–532; and Kenneth Lowande, "After the Orders: Presidential Memoranda & Unilateral Action," *Presidential Studies Quarterly* 44 (2014): 724–741.

99 See Louis Fisher, *The Politics of Shared Power: Congress and the Executive* (College Station, TX: Texas A&M University Press, 1998).

100 William G. Howell, "Unilateral Powers: A Brief Overview," *Presidential Studies Quarterly* 35 (2005): 417–439; Kenneth R. Mayer, *With the Stroke of a Pen: Executive Orders and Presidential Power* (Princeton, NJ: Princeton University Press, 2001); Cooper, *By Order of the President*; and William G. Howell, *Power without Persuasion: The Politics of Direct Presidential Action* (Princeton, NJ: Princeton University Press, 2003).

101 George A. Krause and Jeffrey E. Cohen, "Opportunity, Constraints and the Development of the Institutional Presidency: The Issuance of Executive Orders, 1939–1996," *Journal of Politics* 62 (2000): 88–114.

102 Jennifer K. Elsea, "Presidential Authority to Detain 'Enemy Combatants,'" *Presidential Studies Quarterly* 33 (2003): 568–601.

103 Cristopher J. Deering and Forrest Maltzman, "The Politics of Executive Orders: Legislative Constraints on Presidential Power," *Political Research Quarterly* 52 (1999): 767–783.

104 Terry M. Moe and William G. Howell, "Unilateral Action and Presidential Power: A Theory," *Presidential Studies Quarterly* 29 (1999): 850–873.

105 See Kenneth R. Mayer, "Executive Orders and Presidential Power," *Journal of Politics* 61 (1999): 445–466; and Howell, *Power without Persuasion*.

106 William G. Howell and Jon Pevehouse, "Presidents, Congress and the Use of Force," *International Organization* 59 (2003): 209–232.

107 Cooper, *George W. Bush, Edgar Allan Poe.*

108 Deering and Maltzman, *The Politics of Executive Orders.*

109 Brandon Rottinghaus and Elvin Lim, "Proclaiming Trade Policy: Presidential Unilateral Enactment of Trade Policy," *American Politics Research* 37 (2009): 1003–1023; Matthew J. Dickinson and Jesse Gubb, "The Limits to Power without Persuasion," *Presidential Studies Quarterly* 46 (2016): 48–72.

110 See Adam L. Warber, *Executive Orders and the Modern Presidency: Legislating from the Oval Office* (Boulder, CO: Lynne Rienner, 2006).

111 See Michelle Belco and Brandon Rottinghaus, *The Dual Executive* (Stanford, CA: Stanford University Press, 2017).

112 Michelle Belco and Brandon Rottinghaus, "Proclamation 6920: Using Executive Power to Set a New Direction for the Management of National Monuments," *Presidential Studies Quarterly* 39 (2009): 605–618.

113 See Fang-Yi Chiou and Lawrence S. Rothenberg, *The Enigma of Presidential Power: Parties, Policies, and Strategic Uses of Unilateral Action* (New York: Cambridge University Press, 2017).

114 Julia Azari, "A President's First 100 Days Really Do Matter," *FiveThirty Eight*, January 17, 2017, https://fivethirtyeight.com/features/a-presidents-first-100-days-really-do-matter/.

115 Executive Order 13513, Federal Leadership on Reducing Text Messaging While Driving, October 1, 2009, https://obamawhitehouse.archives.gov/

the-press-office/executive-order-federal-leadership-reducing-text-messaging-while-driving.

116　David Jackson, "President Touts Equal-Pay Bill at First Signing," *USA Today*, January 30, 2009, p. 4A.

117　Executive Memoranda. "Unexpected Urgent Refugee and Migration Needs Related to Gaza," January 27, 2009, https://obamawhitehouse.archives.gov/the-press-office/unexpected-urgent-refugee-and-migration-needs-related-gaza.

118　Jeff Mason, "Republicans Decry Obama Plans to Bypass Congress to Advance Agenda," *Chicago Tribune*, January 26, 2014, http://articles.chicagotribune.com/2014-01-26/news/sns-rt-usa-obamaspeech-republicans-20140123_1_immigration-reform-republican-leaders-congress; Andrew Rudalevige, *The New Imperial Presidency: Renewing Presidential Power after Watergate* (Ann Arbor, MI: University of Michigan Press, 2005).

119　Adam Liptak, "As Obama Vows to Act on Climate Change, Justices Weigh His Approach," *New York Times*, February 19, 2014, www.nytimes.com/2014/02/20/us/politics/in-emissions-case-supreme-court-to-consider-the-limits-of-obamas-authority.html?_r=0.

120　Ibid.

121　Frank James, "With DREAM Order, Obama Did What Presidents Do: Act Without Congress," *NPR*, June 15, 2012, www.npr.org/sections/itsallpolitics/2012/06/15/155106744/with-dream-order-obama-did-what-presidents-do-act-without-congress.

122　Philip Rucker, "Obama's 7 State of the Union Talking Points. No. 6: 'The Pen and Phone' Strategy," *Washington Post*, January 27, 2014, www.washingtonpost.com/blogs/the-fix/wp/2014/01/27/obamas-7-state-of-the-union-talking-points-no-6-the-pen-and-phone-strategy/.

123　Philip Rucker and Ed O'Keefe, "Obama's Far-Reaching Gun-Proposals Face Uncertain Fate in Divided Congress," *Washington Post*, January 16, 2013, www.washingtonpost.com/politics/obama-unveils-gun-control-proposals/2013/01/16/58cd70ce-5fed-11e2-9940-6fc488f3fecd_story.html?utm_term=.dc55a4224758.

124　Rucker, *Obama's 7 State of the Union Talking Points.*

125　Aidan Quigley, "All of Trump's Executive Actions So Far," *Politico*, March 8, 2017, www.politico.com/agenda/story/2017/01/all-trump-executive-actions-000288.

126　Rebecca Harrington, "Trump Signed 90 Executive Actions in His First 100 Days—Here's What Each One Does," *Business Insider*, May 3, 2017, www.businessinsider.com/trump-executive-orders-memorandum-proclamations-presidential-action-guide-2017-1/#executive-order-march-13-reorganizing-the-executive-branch-3.

127　Aaron Blake, "Whip County: Here's Where Republicans Stand on Trump's Controversial Travel Ban," *Washington Post*, January 31, 2017, www.washingtonpost.com/news/the-fix/wp/2017/01/29/heres-where-republicans-stand-on-president-trumps-controversial-travel-ban/?utm_term=.d323b2c62072; Nicholas Fandos, "Growing Number of G.O.P. Lawmakers Criticize Trump's Refugee Policy," *New York Times*, January 29, 2017.

128　Harrington, *Trump Signed 90 Executive Actions in His First 100 Days.*

129　Morris Fiorina, *Divided Government* (New York: Longman, 1992), 410.

130　See Schlesinger, *The Imperial Presidency.*

131　Casey Byrne Knudsen Dominguez, "Is It a Honeymoon? An Empirical Investigation of the President's First Hundred Days," *Congress & the Presidency* 32 (2010): 63–78.

132 Cary R. Covington, J. Mark Wrighton and Rhonda Kinney, "A 'Presidency-Augmented' Model of Presidential Success on House Roll Call Votes," *American Journal of Political Science* 39 (1995): 1001–1024.

133 See Wildavsky, *The Two Presidencies.*

134 See Barbara Hinckley, *Less Than Meets the Eye: Foreign Policy Making and the Myth of the Assertive Congress* (Chicago, IL: University of Chicago Press, 1994).

135 Andrew Reeves and Jon C. Rogowski, "Unilateral Powers, Public Opinion, and the Presidency," *Journal of Politics* 78 (2016): 137–151; Dino P. Christenson and Douglas L. Kriner, "Political Constraints on Unilateral Executive Action," *Case Western Reserve Law Review* 65 (2015): 897–931.

136 See Rebecca K.C. Hersman, *Friends and Foes: How Congress and the President Really Make Foreign Policy* (Washington, DC: Brookings, 2000).

137 See Douglas L. Kriner and Eric Schickler, *Investigating the President: Congressional Check on Presidential Power* (Princeton, NJ: Princeton University Press, 2016).

138 Bert A. Rockman, *Reinventing What For Whom?*

139 Brandice Canes-Wrone, William G. Howell and David E. Lewis, "Toward a Broader Understanding of Presidential Power: A Reevaluation of the Two Presidencies Thesis," *Journal of Politics* 70 (2008): 1–16.

140 See David E. Lewis, *Presidents and the Politics of Agency Design* (Stanford, CA: Stanford University Press, 2003).

141 Fisher, *The Politics of Shared Power,* xi.

8 Presidents and the Courts

Nancy Kassop

Ask anyone to name episodes in history that illustrate the far-reaching significance of the relationship between the presidency and the courts, and most likely, the answer will be, first, Franklin D. Roosevelt's unsuccessful effort in 1936 to persuade Congress to pass legislation that would allow him to "pack" the Supreme Court by increasing the number of justices relative to those over 70 years of age, and second, the 5-4 Supreme Court decision in *Bush v. Gore* in December 2000 that halted the recount in Florida of that state's popular vote in the 2000 presidential election. Both were spectacular historical events that marked the outer limits of that inter-branch relationship. If Congress had granted FDR's request to provide him with authority to nominate additional justices beyond the existing nine-member Court under the specific circumstances at that time, it would have collaborated in a blatant presidential attempt to change the direction of Supreme Court decisions on the fate of FDR's New Deal legislation, and, thus, undermined the independence of the federal judiciary.[1] Similarly, permitting the outcome of a presidential election to rest solely in the hands of nine Supreme Court justices is an extraordinary leap of faith for a nation, straining the democratic, self-governing principles upon which our system was founded.[2]

These examples are, perhaps, the most extreme incidents of what scholars describe as "politicizing" the Supreme Court, when a president uses the courts to try to gain political advantage rather than take his chances in the more routine political processes. Between 1934 and 1936, the Court invalidated, by either 5–4 or 6–3 votes, 13 laws that formed the basis of FDR's New Deal to promote economic recovery from the Great Depression; thus, the President proposed a plan that would maximize his chances to replace or to counteract those justices who opposed this legislation with Court appointees who would be more supportive of his legislative agenda.[3] In November 2000, candidate George W. Bush asked the Supreme Court to hear an appeal from a decision of the Florida Supreme Court that, if left uncontested, would have permitted the manual vote recount in that state to continue until a final election result was reached. Bush's lawyers challenged the Florida court decision, and asked the U.S. Supreme Court to halt the Florida recount at the point where Bush was leading Al Gore by 537 votes.

Thus, in both cases, a president turned to the Supreme Court in what were nothing less than transparent efforts to manipulate it for specific political advantage. FDR "lost" the battle but "won" the war, in the larger sense, in that Congress rejected his specific Court-packing proposal in 1937, and, yet, he managed to get the opportunity within two and a half years to appoint five new justices, as an eventual result of what has been termed "the switch in time that saved nine." This phrase describes the pivotal vote switch of Justice Owen Roberts and Chief Justice Charles Evan Hughes in *West Coast Hotel v. Parrish* (1937), upholding the federal government's authority under the commerce clause to require states to adhere to minimum wage legislation, thus paving the way for federal regulation of the economy, the cornerstone of FDR's New Deal. The Court's decision was soon followed by the resignation of a sufficient number of economically conservative justices to permit FDR to replace them with appointees of his choosing, who then voted, 5–4, to uphold his New Deal policies in subsequent cases. George W. Bush succeeded in winning a 5–4 decision from the Supreme Court in December 2000 that halted the recount in Florida, thrusting the Court into the unusual and controversial position of effectively "deciding" a presidential election.

The most current example of "hardball" judicial politics between the president and the Court that will go down in history as equivalent to these two earlier episodes begins with the response by the Republican majority in the Senate in February 2016 to Barack Obama's nomination of D.C. Circuit Court of Appeals Chief Judge Merrick Garland to fill the Supreme Court vacancy left by the sudden death of Justice Antonin Scalia. Senate Majority Leader Mitch McConnell (R-KY) vowed unequivocally to refuse to consider any nomination until after the 2016 presidential election. He said, "The American people should have a voice in the selection of their next Supreme Court Justice. Therefore, this vacancy should not be filled until we have a new president."[4] Senate Judiciary Committee Chair Chuck Grassley (R-IA) chimed in,

> This president, above all others, has made no bones about his goal to use the courts to circumvent Congress and push through his own agenda. It only makes sense that we defer to the American people who will elect a new president to select the next Supreme Court Justice.[5]

Thus began the unprecedented showdown between the president and the Senate over filling a Supreme Court seat as the latest and, perhaps, the most virulent entry in the judicial confirmation "wars," only to end in the extraordinary act by the Senate in April 2017 to use the "nuclear option" to jettison the filibuster for Supreme Court confirmations. This smoothed the way to confirm the nomination by Donald J. Trump of Judge Neil Gorsuch on a 54–45 party-line vote. Eliminating the 60-vote requirement for cloture on Supreme Court confirmations was the most politically charged way that Republicans could counter the Democratic opposition to the Gorsuch nomination; Democrats felt wholly aggrieved by the obstinate Republican refusal to hold a hearing and vote for Garland, and expressed that frustration by mounting a filibuster to Gorsuch, with full cognizance that the Republicans would call their bluff by voting to eliminate the filibuster for this and all future Supreme Court confirmations. It was a gamble that Senate Democrats were willing to take, and Republicans took the bait and ratcheted up the level of conflict to its highest possible extreme, changing the long-standing rules of the Senate by a simple majority vote to produce a politically favorable outcome for their party and for their new president, feeling relatively secure in the likelihood that they had solidified a conservative vote on the Court.

Although these three incidents were at the far edges of presidential-judicial interactions, the strategic and "political" nature of the relationship between these two institutions was certainly not new, and was evident at the very start of the nation's history. Chief Justice John Marshall's decision in *Marbury v. Madison* (1803) was the culmination of efforts by outgoing President John Adams to "pack" the federal judiciary with Federalist Party supporters as the last bastion of his defeated party to counteract the influence of the incoming Jefferson administration and its Democratic-Republican Party control of both Congress and the presidency. Marshall had been Secretary of State in the Adams administration and had played a defining role in signing the commissions of the "midnight judges" appointed by Adams the night before Jefferson took office; Marbury was one of those appointees whose commission, signed by then-Secretary of State Marshall, somehow went astray and was not delivered by the time Jefferson took the oath of office the next morning.

Under modern norms, Marshall's primary role in the events that led to the Supreme Court case of *Marbury v. Madison*, along with the fact that the appointment of Marshall as chief justice was, itself, one of Adams' final acts before stepping down from office, would be strong reasons supporting his recusal, or non-participation, in the case, due to an obvious conflict of interest in its outcome. And yet, undaunted, Marshall, as the new chief justice, proceeded to rule on this matter, producing the momentous decision that established the principle of judicial review of the actions of the legislative and executive branches.

Alexander Hamilton, in *Federalist* 78, characterized the judiciary as "having no influence over either the sword or the purse... It may truly be said to have neither FORCE nor WILL but merely judgment" and that "the judiciary is beyond comparison the weakest of the three departments of power."[6] References to Congress and the president as the "political branches" suggest that, by deduction, the judiciary is somehow, "non-political" or to be excluded, or protected, from the practice of politics. But the story of *Marbury v. Madison* makes clear that from the beginning, such a characterization was never true.

Today, "judicial politics," in all its ferocity and divisiveness, is evident to even the most casual observer.[7] Every Supreme Court retirement is an invitation to the inevitable partisan and ideological combat that is certain to follow, and such pitched battles are reflected in the nomination and appointment process for the lower federal courts as well.[8] The appointment process for federal judges, at all levels, is viewed by incumbent presidents as an opportunity to secure their legacy by installing persons of their own choosing in lifetime positions, since any federal judge's tenure will long outlast that of the president who appointed him or her. In the especially hyper-partisan and polarized environment fueled by fierce interest group pressures that now characterize this process, each side views every new vacancy as a coveted chance to affect the outcome of Court decisions for years to come. Scholars—and history—have shown, however, that taking for granted the voting choices of any newly appointed judge or justice is a tricky business, indeed, and presidents can be disappointed in the performance of their appointees to the Court. George H.W. Bush's appointment of David Souter to the Court in 1990, on advice from Chief of Staff John Sununu that Souter would be a reliably conservative justice, proved incorrect (and embarrassing to the administration), and served as a cautionary tale to later presidents about expectations from their appointees.[9]

Intersections between the Presidency and the Courts

We see, then, that the relationship between presidents and the federal courts is manifested in a variety of ways. First and foremost is the president's Article II constitutional authority to nominate and, "by and with the advice and consent of the Senate," to appoint all federal judges. This is a formidable power, of which presidents are well aware, giving them the opportunity to shape the direction of courts for decades to come. The closely divided nature of the justices on recent Supreme Courts has intensified this competition between political parties and ideological opponents to use the judicial appointments process as a proxy for policy battles. The threat by Republicans in 2005 to employ the "nuclear option" against the Democratic-led Senate filibuster of Republican judicial nominees on the lower federal courts was indicative of the depth of ill will and the high stakes with which both sides viewed this process, described by Sarah A. Binder and Forrest Maltzman as "acrimonious and dysfunctional."[10] The nuclear option was averted in 2005, when a compromise was reached by a bipartisan "Gang of 14" senators who agreed not to support efforts to invoke the filibuster for the rest of 2005 and 2006 except in "extraordinary circumstances."[11]

That threat then materialized, full-blown, eight years later in November 2013 when the Senate, led by Majority Leader Harry Reid (D-NV), voted to eliminate the 60-vote requirement to close filibusters on all nominations to the executive branch and to the lower federal courts, leaving only nominations to the Supreme Court unscathed—at that point. By April 2017, as noted above, the Supreme Court, also, fell victim to the rule change, this time, engineered by Republicans under Majority Leader McConnell, to advantage the majority party in the Senate.

Second, the reason why judicial appointments are approached with such intensity by all the players involved is the common assumption that there is a direct connection between a president's selection of judicial nominees and judicial decision making (i.e., the outcome of cases). Presidents have good reason to be as strategic as possible in their judicial appointment choices, since cases challenging presidential uses of power or contesting key policies of a president's agenda inevitably find their way into the courts. On its face, it would seem reasonable for a president to assume that his or her "interests" would be best construed by judges or justices of his or her choice. However, history has shown that such assumptions can be naïve and unfounded, as presidents have lost at the Supreme Court, just as any other disappointed litigant,[12] even when the Court contains members selected by the incumbent president.

The most recent example of a justice voting contrary to expectations was Chief Justice John Roberts' central role in upholding the constitutionality of the Affordable Care Act, the signature legislative accomplishment of the Obama administration, in *NFIB v. Sebelius* (2012). He not only provided the fifth and decisive vote but also wrote the majority opinion, ruling that the individual mandate provision, the heart of the law, was constitutional under Congress' tax and spend power. Conservatives who had railed against the law since its passage were shocked and incensed, hurling cries of "traitor" at Roberts for his betrayal of conservative values that they had come to expect from him.[13]

In fact, this episode may say more about the institutional role of chief justice than about Roberts personally. This case was suffused with politics, and the Court was thrust into its midst. However the Court ruled, the June 2012 decision would play a pivotal role in the impending national elections that fall. Roberts had to have understood the intense pressure on the Court, and, as many chief justices before him, recognized that a decision that would throw millions of people off the health care that they had only recently acquired under the historic new law would put the Court, at least temporarily, on the wrong side of history. He acted, thus, with an understanding of the delicate role of the Court in especially charged cases of national significance.[14]

Finally, presidents have one other link to the judiciary, one that operates less visibly than the appointment or decision processes, but one that is just as integral to governmental operations. That link is epitomized in the work of the office of the solicitor general, the third-ranking official in the Department of Justice. The solicitor general is nominated by the president and confirmed by the Senate, and is a key executive branch player whose duties bring him or her into the most direct contact with the courts. Those duties are: (1) serving as the attorney for the U.S. government in cases before the federal and state courts where the United States is a party, representing the government through briefs and oral arguments; (2) authorizing civil cases, where the United States is a party, to be appealed from district courts to circuit courts; (3) determining which cases to appeal to the U.S. Supreme Court, when the federal government is the losing party; and (4) operating as an advisor to the Supreme Court, when that court asks for what is known as "CVSG" or "calls for the views of the solicitor general." That last duty, as a "bridge" between the executive and judicial branches, has earned the solicitor general the nickname "the Tenth Justice," and is symbolized, physically, by the fact that the solicitor general maintains an office in the Supreme Court building as well as in the Department of Justice.[15]

Common to all three of these presidential-judicial interactions (presidential appointment of all federal judges; judicial decision making in cases where the president has an interest; and presidential appointment of the solicitor general as the person who decides how to represent the interests of the federal government in court cases) is the fact that they all represent points where presidential politics intersects with the law. As such, they offer avenues to a president where the choices he or she makes can impact his or her administration's agenda in the short term, and the institution of the presidency in the longer term.

Politics in Recent Executive-Judicial Relations

Political considerations, then, have always figured prominently in executive-judicial relations; recent administrations, including the Obama administration, provide rich examples of just how fraught with tension and high drama these relationships can be. We will explore some of these in each of the three categories, and will suggest the controversies that bring these conflicts to life.

The Judicial Selection Process

There may be nothing else upon which all participants in this process agree except that it is "broken" in its current state, and no one has yet found a way to "fix" it. Many would identify the origins of this painful debate in the failed confirmation process for Robert Bork in 1987,[16] where the Senate, by a vote of 42-58, rejected his nomination for being "out of the mainstream" in his jurisprudential thinking. Those confirmation hearings focused on judicial philosophy and on methods of constitutional interpretation. Both topics now figure prominently in every Supreme Court confirmation hearing and in questioning of lower federal court nominees, as well, and both lay bare the divide between two opposite visions of the role of judging.

Binder and Maltzman cite the Bork debacle as the event that some scholars identify as the "breaking point" that ushered in a "sea change in appointment politics" where the traditional norms of deference and restraint no longer applied—they label this the "big bang" theory of judicial selection.[17] Other scholars provide an alternative view that there is "nothing new under the sun" when it comes to judicial appointments— they have always been political, so the current jockeying for political advantage through judicial selection simply continues an entrenched tradition.[18]

Judicial philosophy refers to differing views of the appropriate role of a judge—whether one sees that role as expansive or limited. The traditional understanding has been that judges "interpret" the law, not "make" it, but that simple statement is fraught with complexity. The controversy arises from the fact that the act of "interpreting" is, itself, variable and subjective: Each judge may have his or her own view of how to implement the interpretive function. At opposite ends are two models, or ideal types, of judicial philosophy: activism vs. restraint. The characteristics associated with one are, thus, completely opposite in the other. These characteristics include: (a) constitutional interpretation—broad vs. narrow, (b) adherence to precedent—rigid vs. flexible on whether to overturn, c) deference to the actions of the political branches—willingness vs. refusal to strike down democratically based judgments as unconstitutional, and d) interpretation of individual liberties—willingness vs. refusal to judicially recognize ("create") new rights not explicit in the text of the Constitution or amendments.

Critics of judicial activism allege that proponents of that model (a) interpret the Constitution too broadly, (b) are too willing to overturn precedent, (c) are too willing to declare unconstitutional actions of the political branches, and (d) are too willing to "create" new rights beyond those in the text of the Constitution. Conversely, critics of judicial restraint allege that proponents of that model (a) interpret the Constitution too narrowly, despite the passage of more than 200 years of national development, (b) are too willing to adhere to precedent, even in the face of changed circumstances, (c) are too willing to defer uncritically to the judgments of the political branches, even where the democratic will of the people may impose unequal or dubious burdens, and (d) refuse to acknowledge that judges may "find" new rights that the framers could not have anticipated but that are consistent with the fundamental values that guided the framers.

Incorporated within these dichotomies is the larger, more encompassing, interpretive debate between "original intent" and "the living Constitution." Judges who interpret the Constitution in the "original intent" mode maintain that the meaning of the document was fixed in 1787, and future generations should be faithful to the enduring intent of those who wrote it. Originalists, such as Antonin Scalia, believe that these meanings are sufficient to apply to contemporary times, and they are critical of any efforts (by "activists") to graft onto the document's "modern" understandings of its phrases and provisions. Such adaptations, they assert, would be unduly subjective, leaving the meaning of this fundamental charter up for grabs, vulnerable to individual tastes, and based on the whim of any five justices who happen to agree at any one time. In essence, originalists maintain that permitting such varying and constantly changing interpretations would amount to "law-making" by judges, an activity that is the province of legislatures, not judges.

The classic example of invalid judicial "law-making" is the "finding," through the approach of substantive due process, of a right to privacy in the Due Process Clause of the Fourteenth Amendment, as enunciated first in *Griswold v. Connecticut* (1965) and as further established in *Roe v. Wade* (1973) to apply specifically to a woman's right to choose whether to bear a pregnancy to term. These two decisions represent for originalists an unacceptable expansion of the judicial role into a realm uniquely intended for legislatures and for policy determination by democratic majorities, not unelected judges. The guiding principle is that the framers of the Fourteenth Amendment could not have intended in 1868 for "liberty" to encompass a right to personal privacy as to matters of childbearing. Rather, if such a "right" was to be created, its legitimacy needed to come from the people directly through the constitutional amendment process. Alternatively, the public *policy* of permitting a woman to choose to terminate a pregnancy could be established by an act of the legislature. As history has demonstrated, the exact opposite has occurred, and, instead, state legislatures have enacted laws *prohibiting* such conduct, and women and their legal advocates have looked to the Constitution and its amendments to find guarantees to protect their freedom of action against such restrictive state laws.

Conversely, judges who espouse "the living Constitution" approach, such as Justice William Brennan, proceed from a more expansive and more dynamic vision of the judicial role. They deem it not only perfectly acceptable but necessary for judges to interpret the Constitution with an understanding of and sensitivity to the vast changes the nation has experienced in the 230 years since the document was written. The touchstone to the framers lies in the *fundamental values*, rather than the precise words, that undergird the Constitution's provisions, values such as liberty and due process, that permit of adaptation to contemporary conditions. For example, the framers could not have anticipated the vast scope of modern communications in all their electronic complexity. However, the *fundamental value* underlying the First Amendment's freedom of the press—protection against unwarranted governmental restriction of publication and dissemination of information—can surely be extrapolated to apply to our contemporary understanding of whatever constitutes the "press" today.

Further complicating this interpretive debate, and in a way that the general public (as opposed to constitutional scholars) often misunderstands, is the fact that *both* activism and restraint can be employed to serve *both* liberal and conservative ends. A typical misperception is that "activism" is the exclusive province of judges perceived to be politically liberal, and that "restraint" is practiced only by those judges perceived to be politically conservative. But this conflation of activism with liberal judges and restraint with conservative judges is incorrect—and incomplete. It is just as possible for judges with a reputation as political *conservatives* to "actively" promote *conservative* constitutional values, such as protecting the rights of gun owners or property owners against governmental regulation; and, equally, it is possible for judges believed to be political *liberals* to be "restrained" by deferring to the political branches and upholding laws that promote *liberal* constitutional values, such as the Civil Rights Act of 1964 or the Voting Rights Act of 1965.

Thus, efforts to simplify this debate between judicial activism and judicial restraint flounders upon closer analysis; trying to portray this complexity to the public during politically charged judicial confirmation hearings is a challenge, even during the best of times. Hearings over the last three decades have been especially contentious, as partisans have calculated the enormity of the stakes involved in the selection of each new Supreme Court justice, as well as judges on the lower federal bench.

Binder and Maltzman identify three sets of factors that have contributed toward increased politicization of the judicial appointments process for the lower federal courts, but the same forces apply to nominations to the Supreme Court: the convergence of ideological and partisan forces in the Senate (i.e., liberalism with Democrats and conservatism with Republicans), heightened under repeated bouts of divided government; institutional forces (i.e., the exploitation by partisans of the long-standing rules and practices of the Senate in the confirmation process); and the electoral context in which judicial nominations are made (i.e., "vacancy hoarding" in presidential election years, for which the treatment by Republicans of Judge Garland in 2016 was Exhibit A of that practice).[19] They conclude that, despite the presence of politics throughout the history of the judicial appointment process, there is, indeed, "something new under the sun" here. What is "new" is the intense lobbying role played by outside groups on both sides of the political divide, and the recognition that courts are a major source of policymaking (thus, there is a keen, strategic interest in their composition).[20] On the other end, they have also offered that the result of intense political combat on the Senate floor, along with delays in nominations by presidents, has been prolonged vacancies, at least on the lower federal bench, leading to case delays, and thus, more fundamentally, prompting a decline in public trust of the courts.[21] Slotnick, Goldman, and Schiavoni have constructed an "Index of Obstruction and Delay" to measure the percentage of a president's nominees left unconfirmed at the end of a congressional session (obstruction) or the percentage of nominees whose time from nomination to confirmation exceeded 180 days (delay): The 112th and 113th Congresses (2011–2012 and 2013–2014) during the Obama administration reached historically high levels of 0.87 and 0.64 on a score from 0.0000 to 1.0, with the latter representing complete obstruction and/or delay. Thus, even the "improved" score of the 113th Congress still represented almost two-thirds of the nominations that were treated with these obstructive tactics.[22]

Appointments to the Supreme Court during the Bush and Obama Administrations

With the glaring exception of the Garland nomination, Bush and Obama were successful in the two appointments that each made to the Supreme Court. Bush stumbled in his effort to fill the vacancy left by Justice Sandra Day O'Connor's surprise announcement of her retirement in 2005. Initially, Bush had nominated D.C. Circuit Judge John Roberts, whose sterling credentials within the Washington legal community made him a "safe" and respected choice. However, in the period between O'Connor's retirement and Bush's tapping of Roberts as her replacement, Chief Justice William Rehnquist passed away, and the White House was suddenly faced with the enviable task of filling two Supreme Court vacancies. Bush then "switched" Roberts' nomination to fill the chief justice position, and Roberts easily gained confirmation by a vote of 78-22.

To fill the O'Connor vacancy, Bush then nominated his friend and then-White House counsel, Harriet Miers. However, Miers withdrew her name three weeks later, amid wide-scale concern by conservative interest groups that she was insufficiently conservative and also because of a gnawing realization that she was not sufficiently well informed on the kinds of constitutional questions she would be asked by senators, and was likely to perform poorly at her Senate confirmation hearing. Bush next nominated Third Circuit Judge Samuel Alito to fill O'Connor's seat. His Senate confirmation hearing was far rougher than Roberts' had been, but he was ultimately confirmed in 2006 by a 58-42 vote.

Obama had two Supreme Court vacancies within the first two years of his administration, when Justice David Souter resigned in 2009 and when Justice John Paul Stevens resigned in 2010. Obama made history in his appointment of the first Latina justice, elevating Second Circuit Judge Sonia Sotomayor to the high court to fill Souter's seat, and next, appointed then-Solicitor General Elena Kagan to the Court a year later as the replacement for Stevens. Both were confirmed, 68-31 and 63-37, respectively.

Commentators could not resist noting that these four recent Supreme Court confirmation votes were of a vastly different nature—and number—from those of their most immediate predecessors, even when acknowledging the unabashedly intense ideological positions held by these earlier nominees. In 1986, Ronald Reagan's nominee Antonin Scalia was confirmed, 98-0, and in 1993, Bill Clinton's nominee Ruth Bader Ginsburg was confirmed, 96-3.[23] Comparing those lopsided—and highly *bipartisan*—votes to the much closer margins and more contested character of the Bush and Obama confirmation votes presents a stark contrast and a vivid illustration of how much partisanship has seeped into this process. The 54-45 vote on Gorsuch's confirmation is the latest manifestation of how poisoned the process has become.

Appointments to the Lower Federal Courts during the Bush and Obama Administrations

Although Bush and Obama suffered some "rough" spots in the appointment of their Supreme Court nominees, they were mostly successful in the end. Other than the miscalculation about Miers and the unprecedented treatment of Garland by Senate Republicans, Bush and Obama succeeded in placing their two nominees apiece on the Court.

The story at the level of the lower federal courts was a far more contentious and complex one. By the time of the Obama administration, a legacy of bad blood from the confirmation conflicts during the Clinton and George W. Bush administrations—conflicts that included lengthy, multi-year delays in Senate votes on lower court nominees and opposition party filibusters on the Senate floor that ended with an outright failure to vote by the end of a Senate session—was deeply ingrained amid mistrust and resentment on both sides. Senate Republicans were in no mood to forget the Democratic filibuster in 2003 of Bush's nomination of Miguel Estrada to the D.C. Circuit and the subsequent withdrawal of that nomination after two years of delays, and were only too eager to deliver payback to their Senate colleagues when nominations were coming from a Democratic president. They had opportunities to do so, when Obama nominated Goodwin Liu to the Ninth Circuit in 2011 and Caitlin Halligan to the D.C. Circuit in 2013; after lengthy, bruising battles, both withdrew their nominations after Republicans successfully filibustered them.[24]

The lower federal courts have become the prime battleground in the judicial wars, as the public increasingly realizes the stark fact that the caseload in these courts far exceeds that of the U.S. Supreme Court; thus, more "law" is made in these lower courts than at the high court. The 2016 caseload for the 12 regional courts of appeals was approximately 50,000 cases, while the caseload for the 94 federal district courts was approximately 350,000 cases, compared to the 75–80 cases decided per year by the Supreme Court.[25] Each federal court judgeship is a lifetime appointment, and thus presents an incomparable opportunity for presidents to leave a lasting legacy on the law. Since presidents make hundreds of appointments to the lower courts, and only a handful, at best, to the Supreme Court, the strategic significance of lower court appointments becomes obvious.

In a series of articles over a five-year span of time, Goldman, Slotnick, and Schiavoni have produced a wealth of statistics and close analysis of Obama's lower federal court appointments. Russell Wheeler at Brookings Institution also provides useful information on the Obama judiciary, and with the advent of the Trump administration in January 2017, the time was ripe for a retrospective look at the impact of Obama's appointments to the lower federal courts.[26]

His legacy begins with the marked increase in diversity of lower federal court judges: Slotnick, Schiavoni, and Goldman state that, by the spring of 2016, 65 percent of Obama's lower court appointments were nontraditional, meaning other than straight white males. Thirty-two percent of his appointments were women, while 32 percent of the 127 female judges he appointed were women of color; almost 20 percent of all judges were African American; 11 percent were Hispanic; 7 percent were Asian American/Pacific Islander; and almost 4 percent were openly gay. These percentages surpassed those of Clinton, who was the president best known previously for a commitment to—and good success in—appointing diverse judges.[27]

Beyond the historic increase in the diversity of the federal bench, Obama's judicial legacy can be best understood as the (equally) historic change in the partisan makeup of the circuit courts. The significance of the "flips" from majority Republican to majority Democratic courts cannot be over-emphasized. When Obama took office in January 2009, one of the 13 courts of appeals had a majority of Democratic judges. By the time he left office in January 2017, nine of those courts now had a majority of Democratic appointees, including the two most consequential circuit courts, the D.C Circuit and the Fourth Circuit.[28]

The Fourth Circuit went from a court with a 7-5 Republican majority in 2009 to a 10-5 Democratic majority by 2017. The "flip" of the D.C. Circuit was the most important of all, as it is the court that hears the largest number of appeals in cases challenging federal laws and regulations. "Flipping" this court did not come easily, and required use of the "nuclear option" by Democratic Majority Leader Harry Reid (D-NV) in November 2013 to change the rules of the Senate.[29] By that action, Obama was able to "turn" the D.C. Circuit from a 6-3 Republican majority (with two vacancies) in 2009 to a 7-4 Democratic majority in 2014. Reid took a calculated risk, knowing that the elimination of the filibuster for lower court nominations could come back to haunt his party if the Senate and the White House turned Republican in future elections. That is exactly what happened in 2016, and is what motivated Republicans to "return the favor" and extend the elimination of the filibuster to Supreme Court nominees during the Gorsuch confirmation process.[30] However,

Reid believed that the short-term gain of control of the D.C. Circuit was worth the potential longer-term costs of removing the filibuster.

In total, Obama appointed 331 lower federal court judges over his two terms: 270 district court judges and 49 circuit court judges (and six judges to the Federal Circuit and four to the Court of International Trade). Those numbers were comparable to judicial appointments from the George W. Bush and Clinton administrations. Viewed another way, of the approximately 800 judges on lower federal courts, 437 are Democratic appointees and 314 are Republican appointees.[31] That 4-3 ratio means that there is an increased chance that Democratic judges will hear proportionately more cases at the district court level and, even more importantly, that there is a strong likelihood that at least one if not more judges appointed by Democratic presidents will sit in three-judge panels at the circuit court level. Those predictions suggest considerable odds for decisions favoring Democratic/liberal outcomes at both levels.

The practical impact of these odds became apparent in decisions toward the end of the Obama administration and during the early days of the Trump administration. For example, the Fourth Circuit decision in July 2016 that struck down a North Carolina strict voter ID law came from a three-judge panel with two Obama judges and one Clinton judge, and the panel decision from that same circuit that ruled in favor of a transgender student in Virginia in April 2016 had a 2-1 Democratic majority (the two were Obama judges).[32] Similarly, nearly all of the decisions at the district and circuit court levels in cases challenging Trump's early executive orders (imposing a travel ban on Muslims and on blocking federal funding to "sanctuary" jurisdictions) came from Democratic trial judges or Democratic majorities on three-judge circuit court panels. All decisions, as of May 2017, except one in Boston on the travel ban, enjoined both executive orders from going into effect.

But there is a darker side to the Obama legacy, as it goes forward, with the potential to substantially undermine that legacy. Obama left office with a record number of vacancies in the lower federal courts (129) waiting to be filled by Trump.[33] If Trump manages to successfully appoint all of these (and this figure does not account for anticipated future vacancies from retirements that will occur over the next four years), the number of federal judges appointed by each party would amount to a virtual 50/50 split. Thus, the partisan divide that permeates the contemporary political environment is already burrowing down into the federal judiciary, and all signs indicate that there is little chance of it abating any time soon.[34]

It is useful to remember, though, that the appointment process, even under the best of circumstances (which the current environment is decidedly not), is long, intricate, layered, and, prior to reaching the level of a presidential decision, involves coordination, vetting and approvals from officials in the Department of Justice, the White House Counsel's office, and home state senators of nominees. The Trump administration, as of

May 2017, has already been somewhat slower than expected in naming its first batch of lower court nominees, announcing ten nominees on May 8, 2017 (and one previously announced nominee on March 21, 2017).[35] A dose of reality was expressed by Sara Schiavoni: "There is not going to be an instantaneous impact on the lower courts. It is going to be years before they can even make a dent in the vacancies."[36]

Cases Involving Matters of Interest to Presidents and the Presidency

Inevitably, during each president's administration, cases will come to the Supreme Court or the lower federal courts that either (a) challenge the president's use of constitutional powers, or (b) contest legislation or administrative regulations that are key to a president's policy agenda. Thus, presidents have an obvious, vested interest in the selection of federal judges, even beyond the ultimate reason that these choices contribute significantly toward their presidential legacy beyond their four or eight years in office. Presidents seek nominees to the courts whose jurisprudential philosophy and political ideology are most compatible with their own. It is naïve folly to automatically assume that a president's appointee will agree 100 percent of the time with the appointing president's legal positions, but, alternatively, it is, at least, reasonable to presume that there will be some consistency between the appointing president and the voting behavior of his or her judicial appointees. Such a presumption guides presidents in the judicial appointment process.

Recent presidents have had their share of Supreme Court cases that address questions of constitutional authority and interpretation of statutes and regulations that promote their agenda, as well as cases where appointees have not ruled in ways fully sympathetic to the appointing president. Notable examples of such cases from the Nixon, Reagan, Clinton, and George W. Bush administrations are: *U.S. v. Nixon* (1974); *Morrison v. Olson* (1988); *Clinton v. Jones* (1997); and *Hamdan v. Rumsfeld* (2006).[37]

Chief Justice Warren Burger, appointed to the Court in 1969 by Nixon, rejected the interpretation of executive privilege advanced by Nixon's lawyers in *U.S. v. Nixon* (1974) that would have shielded the President from having to turn over the Watergate tapes to Special Prosecutor Leon Jaworski. Burger may have mitigated the severity of the ruling's applicability to future presidents by recognizing, for the first time, a constitutional basis for executive privilege, and one that permitted a narrow opening for presidents to claim it in matters of national security. But this exception was of no help to Nixon, who faced the 8-0 ruling (William Rehnquist, not participating) that his generalized claim of absolute privilege would not prevail against the more compelling need for evidence in a criminal proceeding.

Chief Justice William Rehnquist delivered the blow to Reagan's efforts in *Morrison v. Olson* (1988) to declare unconstitutional the office of independent counsel that Congress had created in the Ethics in Government Act of 1978. The act provided a series of procedural steps creating the office and authorizing investigations and prosecution of executive branch officials alleged to have engaged in wrongdoing. Reagan challenged the law's constitutionality on multiple grounds: as an infringement on Article II appointment power, "executive power," and "take care" authority; as an invasion of Article III judicial power; and as a violation of separation of powers. Rehnquist's opinion for the Court rejected these claims, and ruled that inter-branch appointments of inferior officers and the removal provisions in the 1978 act do not violate Article II, Article III, or the separation of powers by "imped(ing) the President's ability to perform his constitutional duty." Rehnquist had been elevated to chief justice by Reagan in 1986, and he was joined on the opinion by Sandra Day O'Connor, a 1981 Reagan appointee. Antonin Scalia, a 1986 Reagan appointee, was the lone dissenter in the case.

Clinton's claims in *Clinton v. Jones* (1997) for temporary immunity from civil liability in a sexual harassment suit involving his unofficial conduct were soundly rejected, 9-0, by a Court that included two of his appointees, Justices Stephen Breyer and Ruth Bader Ginsburg. The wisdom of the Court's judgment that the district court could "manage" any potential interference with a president's official duties that might arise from subjecting him to civil liability during his term of office proved overly optimistic, as his testimony in the Paula Jones case ultimately led to further legal difficulties that set the path toward his impeachment in January 1999. The larger significance here is that the ruling established that sitting presidents may be sued while in office for unofficial conduct (that, in Clinton's case, occurred prior to taking office), thus, rejecting any presidential immunity in such civil suits.

George W. Bush's presidency was dominated by a focus on antiterrorism policy and the scope of the president's constitutional authority to address that issue. It did not take long for challenges to his authority to materialize in the federal courts, and four such cases made their way to the Supreme Court. The role of Bush's appointees, Roberts and Alito, however, differed from the above examples. First, they were seated on the Court for only the last two of these antiterrorism cases (*Hamdan* and *Boumediene*): both sided with the position of the President in *Boumediene v. Bush* (2008), and dissented from the majority opinion that rejected Bush's arguments. Alito also dissented in *Hamdan* (2006) (again, agreeing with the President's position that was rejected by the majority), but Roberts recused himself, due to his earlier participation in the case when he was a judge on the D.C. Circuit Court. All four cases— *Hamdi*, *Rasul*, *Hamdan*, and *Boumediene*—resulted in rulings largely unfavorable to the president (*Hamdi* was a mixed bag, in that the Court agreed that the president had authority from the 2001 Authorization to Use Military Force to detain terrorist suspects on the battlefield, even if

American citizens, but it held also that suspects are entitled to challenge their detention through a "fair opportunity to rebut the Government's factual assertions before a neutral decisionmaker").

As often tends to happen, and as is true, for the most part, for the cases mentioned here for all four presidents, when the president's power is challenged in court, decisions are more likely to reject the executive branch claims or to interpret the president's powers relatively narrowly. There are exceptions, certainly (e.g., *U.S. v. Curtiss-Wright* [1936] and others), but the majority of Supreme Court cases that have addressed presidential power throughout most of history have rejected broad executive branch claims, and the examples described in this section are typical of that pattern.

Important legal disputes involving matters of interest to the president and the presidency found their way to the U.S. Supreme Court during Obama's time in office. Some were issues that did not involve presidential power directly but implicated policies that had relevance for the administration, either because they were key issues on his political agenda, such as the state challenges to health care legislation, or because they were thorny, high-profile, legal matters that were sure to draw a response from the administration.

Obama's major legislative accomplishment, passage of the Affordable Care Act (2010), was challenged repeatedly in federal court, and produced three Supreme Court decisions (and one "non-decision"), largely upholding the law and supporting the administration's interpretation of it. The Court (1) upheld the constitutionality of the statute in *NFIB v. Sebelius* (2012), resting on the taxing and spending power, rather than the commerce clause, as had been commonly expected; (2) dealt a blow to the administration in *Burwell v. Hobby Lobby* (2014) when it ruled that the Religious Freedom Restoration Act permitted for-profit businesses to deny contraceptive coverage to their employees, where companies had a religious objection; (3) interpreted the language, "exchanges established by the state," in the context of the statute as a whole to reach the broad intent of Congress to provide health insurance coverage to as many qualified people as possible (*King v. Burwell*, 2015); and (4) in a per curiam decision in May 2016 in *Zubik v. Burwell*, remanded the case to the lower courts with guidance for the parties to try to reach agreement on a way to accommodate First Amendment concerns of religious non-profits and educational institutions who objected to complying with the ACA's mandate to include contraceptive coverage in employer health plans.

A president's constitutional power was directly at issue in *NLRB v. Noel Canning* (2014), where the Court declared unconstitutional Obama's intra-session recess appointments to the National Labor Relations Board during a "pro forma" session of the Senate, while permitting a president, under specific, limited circumstances, to continue to make recess appointments during intra-session recesses; and in *Zivotofsky v. Kerry*

(2015), which represented a big "win" for a president's foreign affairs power. Here, the Court interpreted a president's power to "recognize" foreign governments as one that rested exclusively with the president where Congress may not interfere.

Some Supreme Court cases in which the Obama administration had a *policy* interest included *Shelby County v. Holder* (2013), *Obergefell v. Hodges* (2015), and *Whole Woman's Health v. Hellerstedt* (2016). *Shelby County* was a painful "loss," while *Obergefell* was an historic "win," and *Whole Woman's Health* signified an important reaffirmation of the constitutional protection of a woman's right to choose whether to carry a pregnancy to term. The Court in *Shelby County* held Section 4 of the Voting Rights Act of 1965 unconstitutional as a basis for requiring pre-clearance of any election law changes for "covered jurisdictions." This decision removed restrictions on states and other governmental units with a history of racial discrimination in elections when making any changes in their election laws. It opened the floodgates to new state laws requiring strict voter ID and to other laws imposing previously impermissible burdens on voting (e.g., the decision now permitted new laws that disallowed early voting).

The Obama administration notched a big "win" in the culmination of earlier cases on marriage equality in which it participated (*U.S. v. Windsor* [2013], where the Court struck down part of the Defense of Marriage Act of 1996, and this decision prompted a flurry of action in states to provide legal paths for same-sex marriage), leading up to *Obergefell v. Hodges*, where the Court provided a definitive ruling that there is a constitutional right for same-sex couples to marry, and that all states must permit such marriages and must recognize such marriages from other states. In a 5-3 decision, the Court in *Whole Woman's Health v. Hellerstedt* concluded that a state's asserted interest in imposing restrictions on clinic access imposed a "substantial burden" on a woman's choice to obtain an abortion, and constituted impermissible and arbitrary requirements that did not advance the state's interest in protecting women's health.

Perhaps the most dynamic issue to energize president-Court interactions was Obama's public aim at the *Citizens United v. FEC* (2010) decision, which struck down as unconstitutional the Bipartisan Campaign Reform Act of 2002 ban on corporate political spending in election campaigns as an infringement of the First Amendment freedom of speech of corporations. He issued a statement on the day of the decision, saying that:

> With its ruling today, the Supreme Court has given a green light to a new stampede of special interest money in our politics. It is a major victory for big oil, Wall Street banks, health insurance companies and the other powerful interests that marshal their power every day in Washington to drown out the voices of everyday Americans. This ruling gives the special interests and their lobbyists even more

power in Washington—while undermining the influence of average Americans who make small contributions to support their preferred candidates. That's why I am instructing my Administration to get to work immediately with Congress on this issue. We are going to talk with bipartisan Congressional leaders to develop a forceful response to this decision. The public interest requires nothing less.[38]

A week later, Obama continued his pointed criticism of the Court's decision in his State of the Union address, comments that drew an unusual, publicly visible reaction from Justice Alito, who appeared, while sitting in the House chamber at the address, to shake his head and mouth the words "not true" in immediate response to the President's following remarks:[39]

> With all due deference to separation of powers, last week the Supreme Court reversed a century of law that I believe will open the floodgates for special interests – including foreign corporations-to spend without limit in our elections (Applause.) I don't think American elections should be bankrolled by America's most powerful interests, or worse, by foreign entities (Applause.) They should be decided by the American people. And I'd urge Democrats and Republicans to pass a bill that helps to correct some of these problems.[40]

The press had a field day with this "open warfare" between the President and the Court, and the journalistic coverage alternated between noting that previous presidents (but not many) had criticized the Supreme Court in public addresses versus finding this public disagreement between two institutions uncomfortable to witness, at the very least, and, for some, inappropriate conduct on the part of such high-profile officials.[41]

Presidents and Solicitors General: The Agenda Connection

Although the importance to a president of the selection of the person who will serve in the position of solicitor general may not be a concept that readily comes to mind, there is good reason to recognize that this Senate-confirmed appointment of the third-ranking official in the Department of Justice is even more influential than the attorney general when it comes to advancing the president's political agenda in the courts, and thus is the most direct link between the president and the judiciary. The solicitor general is the lawyer for the federal government; essentially, this means that this official is the legal representative of the administration in court cases. As such, the judgment and choices of the solicitor general as to which cases to appeal to higher courts and as to the substantive, legal arguments of the government in cases (and, to a somewhat lesser degree, the choice to enter as amicus curiae in any case where the solicitor general believes there is a federal government "interest," even though the government is not a party to the case) matter greatly. It will fall to the solicitor general to craft legal arguments in briefs and oral arguments that accurately reflect the political and policy agenda of the administration, when these positions can be supported by law. Conversely, as noted earlier, the solicitor general has dual responsibilities in that he or she is also an advisor to the Court, owing to the 1870 statute that requires that the solicitor general be "learned in the law" and in the practice known as "CVSG"—when the solicitor general receives a request from the Supreme Court for a "call for the views of the Solicitor General." The justices look to the solicitor general to guide them when in need of clarity in the law, and they rely on the integrity and "independence" that the office of solicitor general has come to embody.[42]

"Independence" is the key—and the dilemma—here. Traditionally, this was the essence of the role of the solicitor general's office. But, maintaining that independence in the face of administration expectations, especially in times of excessively polarized politics, can be a daunting challenge. There is a constant tension over whether this position is to be independent of political pressure as a servant of the law or, alternatively, a policy advocate for the administration.[43] Three factors play a role in how each solicitor general operates in the job: (a) the specific political context and environment at the time; (b) the perspective of the president who appoints the solicitor general; and (c) the relationship between the solicitor general and the attorney general. The choice of the solicitor general by a president will be a cue as to how "political" the office may be. The president will obviously choose someone who shares his political and policy views, although the specific emphasis on professional credentials, along with the special relationship as advisor to the Supreme Court, gives this position a different and unique cast to it.

Scholars note that the increased "political" nature of the office began during the Reagan administration, exemplified in the handling of the *Bob Jones University vs. U.S.* (1983) case, where Deputy Solicitor General Lawrence Wallace, as the author of the brief, appended a footnote to it that registered his personal disagreement with the legal position of the Justice Department in the brief.[44] Political scientist Lawrence Baum also explains that "the political side of the solicitor general's work has become more prominent," as the connections between that office and the administration have become stronger, and he also traces the origin of that development to the Reagan presidency.[45]

Primarily, the influence of the solicitor general comes in the high success rate at both stages of Supreme Court review. At the level of reviewing certiorari petitions, the solicitor general's petitions are granted about 75 percent of the time. At the merits stage (the outcome of the substantive Court decision—win vs. loss), the solicitor general wins about 70 percent of the time.[46] Explanations for these high success rates include: (1)

the solicitor general is usually chosen simply because he or she is a superb legal professional, with recognized expertise (although it is interesting that Elena Kagan, appointed in 2009 as solicitor general by Obama, had no litigating experience and had never argued a case before the Supreme Court, when she was nominated). Because of the esteem with which the justices view the solicitor general, they rely on him or her as a "gate-keeper" for the Court. The justices expect that the solicitor general will appeal to the Court only those cases most worthy of review. Therefore, if the solicitor general "screens" cases carefully when determining which ones to appeal, the high rates of success at the cert petition and merits stages become more understandable;[47] and (2) the solicitor general is a "repeat player"—someone who appears before the Supreme Court more than any other single lawyer, and thus someone who accumulates more experience and more knowledge than any other peer in the legal profession at that time of how to appeal strategically to the justices.[48]

Recent solicitor generals, such as Drew Days, Walter Dellinger, and Seth Waxman in the Clinton administration, Theodore Olson and Paul Clement in the George W. Bush administration, and Elena Kagan and Donald Verrilli in the Obama administration, recognized the tenuous balance they needed to maintain between their role as an advocate for their client—essentially, the federal government, but with a keen awareness that they operated as representatives of the president who appointed them—and the office's traditional posture of its unique relationship to and with the Court. All had to navigate tricky waters.

Days, Dellinger and Waxman worked on key federalism cases (*Seminole Tribe of Florida* [1996], *Printz v. U.S.* [1997], *Alden v. Maine* [1999], and *Kimel v. Florida Board of Regents* [2000]), First Amendment religion (*Rosenberger v. University of Virginia* [1995], *Boerne v. Flores* [1997], and *Agostini v. Felton* [1997]), redistricting (*Shaw v. Reno*, 1993), line-item veto (*Clinton v. City of New York*, 1998), a partial-birth abortion ban (*Stenberg v. Carhart*, 2000), commerce clause (*U.S. v. Lopez*, 1995 and *U.S. v. Morrison*, 2000), physician-assisted suicide (*Washington v. Glucksberg*, 1997), hate crime (*Wisconsin v. Mitchell*, 1993), affirmative action (*Adarand Constructors v. Pena*, 1995), a challenge to Miranda (*Dickerson v. U.S.,* 2000), and sex discrimination (*U.S. v. Virginia*, 1996) cases.

Olson, in addition to *Bush v. Gore* (argued and decided in December 2000, prior to his confirmation as solicitor general), worked on redistricting (*Hunt v. Cromartie*, 2001), election law (*FEC v. Colorado Republican Campaign Committee*, 2001) death penalty (*Atkins v. Virginia*, 2002), homosexual rights (*Lawrence v. Texas*, 2003), affirmative action (*Gratz v. Bollinger* and *Grutter v. Bollinger*, 2003), and First Amendment religion cases (*Zelman v. Simmons-Harris*, 2002), while Clement had four cases in which he defended unsuccessfully the Bush antiterrorism policies (*Rasul v. Bush* [2004], *Hamdi v. Rumsfeld* [2004], *Hamdan v. Rumsfeld* [2006], and *Boumediene v. Bush* [2008]), along with cases on campaign finance reform

(*McConnell v. FEC*, 2003), eminent domain/property rights (*Kelo v. City of New London*, 2005), Second Amendment gun rights (*D.C. v. Heller*, 2008), and First Amendment expression related to conditioning federal funds on university policies on military recruiting (*Rumsfeld v. Forum for Academic and Institutional Rights, Inc., [FAIR]*, 2006).

Two important cases were argued by the solicitor general's office in 2009, prior to Elena Kagan's confirmation: Title VII disparate impact discrimination (*Ricci v. DiStefano*, 2009) and a Voting Rights Act case (*Northwest Austin Municipal Utility District Number One v. Holder*, 2009). Kagan's first Supreme Court argument as solicitor general was the high-profile, First Amendment political expression/campaign finance reform case, *Citizens United v. FEC* (2010). As there is no longer any question that the Supreme Court has developed into a key policymaker, the discretion that solicitors general exercise in their case selection process has greater consequences today than ever before.

Upon Kagan's appointment as a justice to the Supreme Court in 2010, Obama selected Donald Verrilli as her replacement as solicitor general for the remaining six years of that administration. Reflections (or a "report card") on Verrilli's tenure as solicitor general illustrate just how influential and consequential this official can be—and how an effective solicitor general can be extraordinarily significant to the president he or she serves. Verrilli had major "wins" for the administration, both in cases where the administration was a party and in cases where he participated as an amicus, because of a federal government interest in the case. He was responsible for arguing all four Affordable Care Act cases (winning two, losing one, and reaching a "draw" on the fourth); for arguing *Zivotofsky*; and for participating as an amicus in *Obergefell* and *Whole Woman's Health v. Hellerstedt* (2016). Verrilli did not prevail for the administration in *Shelby County* and received a mixed ruling from the Court in *NLRB v. Noel Canning* by preserving a limited power for the president to make recess appointments but dealing a defeat to Obama's specific use of it in this case.[49]

Conclusion

The relationship between the presidency and the courts is one that may seem less visible than that between the presidency and Congress, but it is no less consequential and every bit as intriguing for scholars to study. The public sees this relationship most vividly at the time of a Supreme Court nomination or, perhaps, when the Court issues a decision in a highly anticipated case with national policy implications. But scholars follow the executive-judicial relationship, in all its manifestations, on an ongoing basis, and are acutely aware of its dynamic quality and constant tensions. The fact that the courts are now a major player in government policymaking is the most significant change from their earlier reputation as a mostly passive institution that could only react incrementally to the controversies brought before it.

Today, we see how the three dimensions of this inter-branch relationship that were outlined in this chapter continue to spur debate and controversy. The judicial appointment process, judicial cases of interest to a president and to the institution of the presidency, and the work of the solicitor general's office are all government operations which either depend upon or promote interactions between the president and the federal judiciary. All are woven into the fabric of relationships that support the governmental process in all its complexity. There will always be issues that animate these relationships, although they are especially vibrant at this time, as a consequence of the highly charged, contemporary political environment. Thus, the executive-judicial relationship is a rich one that merits our attention, as its outputs can produce policy effects for years to come.

Notes

1 William E. Leuchtenberg, *Franklin D. Roosevelt and the New Deal: 1932–1940* (New York: Harper and Row, 1963), 231–238; and Jeff Shesol, *Supreme Power: Franklin Roosevelt vs. The Supreme Court* (New York: W.W. Norton, 2010).
2 See Howard Gillman, *The Votes that Counted: How the Court Decided the 2000 Presidential Election* (Chicago, IL: University of Chicago Press, 2001).
3 Henry J. Abraham, *Justices, Presidents and Senators: A History of the U.S. Supreme Court Appointments from Washington to Clinton* (Lanham, MD: Rowman & Littlefield, 1999), 157–160.
4 Burgess Everett, "McConnell Throws Down the Gauntlet: No Scalia Replacement Under Obama," *Politico*, February 13, 2016, www.politico.com/story/2016/02/mitch-mcconnell-antonin-scalia-supreme-court-nomination-219248.
5 Ibid.
6 Alexander Hamilton, James Madison, and John Jay, *The Federalist Papers* (New York: New American Library, 1961), 465–466 (emphasis in original).
7 See David A. Yalof, *Pursuit of Justices: Presidential Politics and the Selection of Supreme Court Nominees* (Chicago, IL: University of Chicago Press, 1999); Jan Crawford Greenburg, *Supreme Conflict: The Inside Story of the Struggle for Control of the United States Supreme Court* (New York: Penguin Press, 2007); David M. O'Brien, *Storm Center: The Supreme Court in American Politics*, 8th ed. (New York: W.W. Norton, 2008); and Jeffrey Toobin, *The Nine: Inside the Secret World of the Supreme Court* (New York: Doubleday, 2007).
8 Sheldon Goldman, Elliot Slotnick, and Sara Schiavoni, "Obama's Judiciary at Midterm: The Confirmation Drama Continues," *Judicature* 94 (2011): 262–301; Sheldon Goldman, Elliot Slotnick, and Sara Schiavoni, "Obama's First Term Judiciary: Picking Judges in the Minefield of Obstructionism," *Judicature* 97 (2013): 7–47; Elliot Slotnick, Sheldon Goldman, and Sara Schiavoni, "Writing the Book of Judges, Part I: Obama's Judicial Appointments Record After Six Years," *Journal of Law and Courts* 3 (2015): 331–367; Elliot Slotnick, Sara Schiavoni, and Sheldon Goldman, "Writing the Book of Judges, Part II: Confirmation Politics in the 113th Congress," *Journal of Law and Courts* 4 (2016): 187–242; and Sheldon Goldman, *Picking Federal Judges: Lower Court Selection from Roosevelt Through Reagan* (New Haven, CT: Yale University Press, 1997).

9 Sununu assured conservatives that Souter would be "a home run" for them. See Toobin, *The Nine*, 20–21.

10 Sarah A. Binder and Forrest Maltzman, "New Wars of Advice and Consent: Judicial Selection in the Obama Years," *Judicature* 97 (2013): 49.

11 Sarah A. Binder and Forrest Maltzman, *Advice and Dissent: The Struggle to Shape the Federal Judiciary* (Washington, DC: Brookings, 2009), 100.

12 See, for example, *Youngstown Sheet and Tube Co, v. Sawyer* (1952); *U.S. v. Nixon*, 418 U.S. 683 (1974); *Morrison v. Olson*, 487 U.S. 654 (1988); *Clinton v. Jones*, 520 U.S. 681(1997); and *Hamdan v. Rumsfeld*, 548 U.S. 557 (2006).

13 Ken Connor, "Conservatives Should Tone Down Criticism of Roberts," *Townhall*, July 4, 2012, https://townhall.com/columnists/kenconnor/2012/07/04/conservatives-should-tone-down-criticism-of-roberts-n838520;TomMcCarthy, "John Roberts: The Conservative Chief Justice Who Saved the Day for Liberals," *The Guardian*, June 28, 2012, www.theguardian.com/law/2012/jun/28/john-roberts-conservative-chief-justice.

14 Adam Winkler, "The Roberts Court is Born," *SCOTUSblog*, June 28, 2012, www.scotusblog.com/2012/06/the-roberts-court-is-born/.

15 See Lincoln Caplan, *The Tenth Justice: The Solicitor General and the Rule of Law* (New York: Random House, 1987); and Rebecca Mae Salokar, "Politics, Law and the Office of the Solicitor General," in *Government Lawyers: The Federal Legal Bureaucracy and Presidential Politics*, ed. Cornell Clayton (Lawrence, KS: University Press of Kansas, 1995).

16 See John Anthony Maltese, "Anatomy of a Confirmation Mess: Recent Trends in the Federal Judicial Selection Process," *JURIST* Online Symposium (University of Pittsburgh School of Law, April 15, 2004) http://jurist.law.pitt.edu/forum/Symposium-jc/Maltese.php#2; and Stephen L. Carter, *The Confirmation Mess: Cleaning Up the Federal Appointments Process* (New York: Basic Books, 1995).

17 Binder and Maltzman, "New Wars of Advice and Consent," citing Wendy L. Martinek, Mark Kemper, and Steven H. Van Winkle, "To Advise and Consent: The Senate and Lower Federal Court Nominations, 1997–1998," *Journal of Politics* 64 (2002).

18 Binder and Maltzman, "New Wars of Advice and Consent," at 50, citing Lee Epstein and Jeffrey Segal, *Advice and Consent: The Politics of Judicial Appointments* (New York: Oxford University Press, 2005), 4.

19 Binder and Maltzman, "New Wars of Advice and Consent," 52–54.

20 Ibid., 55–56.

21 Ibid., 50–52.

22 Slotnick, Goldman, and Schiavoni, "Writing the Book of Judges, Part I," 339–340.

23 Darla Cameron, "Confirmations for the Sitting Supreme Court Justices Were Not Nearly as Partisan as Judge Gorsuch's," *Washington Post*, April 7, 2017, www.washingtonpost.com/graphics/politics/scotus-confirmation-votes/?utm_term=.dcb0396063f8.

24 James Oliphant, "Obama Court Nominee Goodwin Liu Withdraws After Filibuster," *Los Angeles Times*, May 25, 2011, http://articles.latimes.com/2011/may/25/nation/la-na-0526-goodwin-liu-20110526; Rachel Weiner, "White House Withdraws Caitlin Halligan Nomination," *Washington Post*, March 22, 2013, www.washingtonpost.com/news/post-politics/wp/2013/03/22/whitehouse-withdraws-caitlin-halligan-nomination/?utm_term=.e7d2ad6d25e1.

25 "Federal Judicial Caseload Statistics 2016," *United States Courts*, March 31, 2016, www.uscourts.gov/statistics-reports/federal-judicial-caseload-statistics-2016.

26 Goldman, Slotnick, and Schiavoni, "Obama's Judiciary at Midterm;" Goldman, Slotnick, and Schiavoni, "Obama's First Term Judiciary;" Slotnick, Goldman, and Schiavoni, "Writing the Book of Judges, Part I;" and Slotnick, Schiavoni, and Goldman, "Writing the Book of Judges, Part II." See also Russell Wheeler, "No Further Obama Impact on the Make-up of Courts of Appeals," www.brookings.edu/blog/fixgov/2015/12/16/no-further-obama-impact-on-the-make-up-of-courts-of-appeals/; Lawrence Hurley, "Obama's Judges Leave Liberal Imprint on the Law," *Reuters*, August 26, 2016, www.reuters.com/article/us-usa-court-obama-idUSKCN1110BC; and Jennifer Bendery, "How Barack Obama Transformed the Nation's Courts," *Huffington Post*, January 12, 2017, www.huffingtonpost.com/entry/barack-obama-judicial-legacy_us_586c1944e4b0de3a08f9eb1f.

27 Slotnick, Schiavoni, and Goldman, "Writing the Book of Judges, Part II," 226–234.

28 Hurley, "Obama's Judges Leave Liberal Imprint on the Law."

29 Paul Kane, "Reid, Democrats Trigger 'Nuclear' Option: Eliminate Most Filibusters on Nominees," *Washington Post*, November 21, 2013, www.washingtonpost.com/politics/senate-poised-to-limit-filibusters-in-party-line-vote-that-would-alter-centuries-of-precedent/2013/11/21/d065cfe8-52b6-11e3-9fe0-fd2ca728e67c_story.html?utm_term=.c54fb14303c7.

30 Matt Flegenheimer, "Senate Republicans Deploy 'Nuclear Option' to Clear Path for Gorsuch," *New York Times*, April 6, 2017, www.nytimes.com/2017/04/06/us/politics/neil-gorsuch-supreme-court-senate.html?_r=0.

31 Hurley, "Obama's Judges Leave Liberal Imprint on the Law."

32 Ibid.

33 "Judicial Vacancies," *United States Courts*, May 2017, www.uscourts.gov/judges-judgeships/judicial-vacancies.

34 Kim Soffen, "Trump's Judicial Influence Could Go Far Beyond Putting Gorsuch on the Supreme Court," *Washington Post*, February 1, 2017, https://www.washingtonpost.com/graphics/politics/judge-appointments/; Jonathan Adler, "How President Trump Will Shape the Federal Courts," *Washington Post*, January 20, 2017, www.washingtonpost.com/news/volokh-conspiracy/wp/2017/01/20/how-president-trump-will-shape-the-federal-courts/?utm_term=.7965cff8bd86; Russell Wheeler, "How Trump Could Reshape the Lower Federal Courts," *Brookings Institution*, November 17, 2016, www.brookings.edu/blog/fixgov/2016/11/17/trump-lower-courts/; and Joe Palazzolo, "Donald Trump Looks to Put His Stamp on Federal Courts," *Wall Street Journal*, November 11, 2016, www.wsj.com/articles/donald-trump-looks-to-put-his-stamp-on-federal-courts-1478892603; and "The Trump Administration on Federal Courts," https://ballotpedia.org/The_Trump_administration_on_federal_courts#Trump.27s_nominations_to_lower_federal_courts.2C_2017.

35 "President Donald J. Trump Announces Judicial Candidate Nominations," www.whitehouse.gov/the-press-office/2017/05/08/president-donald-j-trump-announces-judicial-candidate-nominations; and "President Donald J. Trump Announces Intent to Nominate Judge Amul R. Thapar for the U.S. Court of Appeals for the Sixth Circuit," www.whitehouse.gov/the-press-office/2017/03/21/president-donald-j-trump-announces-intent-nominate-judge-amul-r-tha.

36 Palazzolo, "Donald Trump Looks to Put His Stamp on Federal Courts."

37 *U.S. v. Nixon*, 418 U.S. 683 (1974); *Morrison v. Olson*, 487 U.S. 654 (1988); *Clinton v. Jones*, 520 U.S. 681(1997); and *Hamdan v. Rumsfeld*, 548 U.S. 557 (2006).

38 "Statement from the President on Today's Supreme Court Decision," January 21, 2010, www.whitehouse.gov/the-press-office/statement-president-todays-supreme-court-decision-0.

39 "Obama: Supreme Court Opened the Floodgates for Special Interests," *The BLT: The Blog of Legal Times*, January 27, 2010, http://legaltimes.typepad. com/blt/2010/01/obama-supreme-court-opened-the-floodgates-for-special-interests.html.

40 "Remarks by the President in State of the Union Address," January 27, 2010, www.whitehouse.gov/the-press-office/remarks-president-state-union-address.

41 Robert Barnes, "Reactions Split on Obama's Remark, Alito's Response at State of the Union," *Washington Post*, January 28, 2010, www. washingtonpost.com/wp-dyn/content/article/2010/01/28/AR2010012802893. html; Jan Crawford, "Obama Skewers Court—and Signals Change Ahead," *CBS News*, January 28, 2010, www.cbsnews.com/8301-504564_162-6150742-504564.html?tag=contentMain%3bcontentBody; Jeffrey Toobin, "Alito's Reaction to Obama was Fair," *CNN*, January 28, 2010, www.cnn.com/2010/OPINION/01/28/toobin.obama.alito/; and Andy Barr, "Orrin Hatch: Obama 'Rude' to Court," *Politico*, January 28, 2010, www.politico.com/news/stories/0110/32163.html.

42 For extended analysis of the Office of Solicitor General, see Richard L. Pacelle, Jr., *Between Law and Politics: The Solicitor General and the Structuring of Race, Gender and Reproductive Rights Litigation* (College Station, TX: Texas A&M University Press, 2003), especially, Chapters 1 and 2; Caplan, *The Tenth Justice*; and Rebecca Mae Salokar, "Politics, Law and the Office of the Solicitor General."

43 See Lawrence Baum, *The Supreme Court* (Washington, DC: CQ Press, 2007), 83–84; Pacelle, *Between Law and Politics*, 10–12, 22, 30–32.

44 Salokar, "Politics, Law and the Office of the Solicitor General," 64.

45 Baum, *The Supreme Court*, 85–86.

46 Salokar, "Politics, Law and the Office of the Solicitor General," 68–70; Rebecca Mae Salokar, *The Solicitor General: The Politics of Law* (Philadelphia, PA: Temple University Press, 1992); Baum, *The Supreme Court*, 84, 95; Doris Marie Provine, *Case Selection in the United States Supreme Court* (Chicago, IL: University of Chicago Press, 1980), 82; and Lee Epstein and Jack Knight, *The Choices Justices Make* (Washington, DC: CQ Press, 1998), 87.

47 Baum, *The Supreme Court*, 95.

48 Marc Galanter, "Why the 'Haves' Come Out Ahead: Speculations on the Limits of Legal Change," *Law and Society Review* 9 (1974): 98.

49 David A. Graham, "The Solicitor General Rests," *The Atlantic*, June 2, 2016, www.theatlantic.com/politics/archive/2016/06/donald-verrilli-solicitor-general-resign/485270/; Richard Wolf, "Solicitor General Donald Verrilli Departing After Historic Run at Supreme Court," *USA Today*, June 2, 2016, www.usatoday.com/story/news/politics/2016/06/02/solicitor-general-donald-verrilli-retiring-obamacare-gay-marriage/85289966/; and Matt Zapotosky and Robert Barnes, "U.S. Solicitor General is Stepping Down," *Washington Post*, June 2, 2016, www.washingtonpost.com/news/post-nation/wp/2016/06/02/u-s-solicitor-general-is-stepping-down/?utm_term=.60bd10433a5a.

9   Presidents, the White House, and the Executive Branch

Matthew J. Dickinson

On April 20, 2010, an explosion rocked the BP-leased Deepwater Horizon oil-drilling platform located 41 miles off the coast of Louisiana, killing 11 workers and injuring dozens more. The explosion, caused when methane gas leaking from an underwater well ignited, destroyed the drilling platform and fractured the wellhead pipe located a mile below the water's surface. The heavily pressurized oil began spewing from the break into the Gulf of Mexico at a rate eventually estimated at some 35,000 to 60,000 barrels a day.[1] In the next days and weeks, as BP engineers tried first to cap and then to contain the spill, the leaking oil formed a surface slick that eventually expanded to cover 2,500 square miles of Gulf water, endangering coastal wetlands, recreation areas, and fisheries. Additional oil plumes of indeterminate size lingered underwater, threatening to wreak further environmental damage. By July 15, when the well was finally capped 87 days after the explosion, the leak had spewed an estimated 4.9 million barrels of oil into the Gulf, making it the largest oil spill in U.S. history, and one of the nation's worst environmental disasters, one whose adverse consequences continue to impact the Gulf region more than seven years after the explosion, and which may continue to do so for years—if not decades—to come.[2]

As it became clear that BP had no workable contingency plan to handle a spill of this magnitude a mile below the surface, critics wondered how the company had been allowed to drill at that depth. That question focused attention on a heretofore little-known government agency—the Mineral Management Service (MMS; since renamed the Bureau of Ocean Energy Management). Established in 1982 by an administrative directive issued by then-Interior Department Secretary James Watt, the MMS was a 1,700-person agency charged with overseeing the leasing of federal property for mineral extraction by private firms.[3] Toward this end, the MMS was charged with both collecting royalty payments from the private firms leasing federal property and regulating how they did so. This included issuing permits allowing oil companies to drill in U.S. waters and inspecting the drilling rigs.

In April 2009, the MMS authorized BP to drill at the Deepwater Horizon site. They did so, evidently, with only a cursory review of the assumptions built into BP's application, including its faulty estimates regarding the likelihood, and subsequent consequences, of a well blow-out a mile down in Gulf waters.[4] As it turned out, such a lax permitting process seemed more the norm than the exception for the MMS; reports issued by the Government Accountability Office (GAO) and hearings by congressional oversight committees paint a picture of an understaffed agency engaged in a cozy relationship with the same oil companies it was supposed to regulate.[5] Witnesses told a House energy subcommittee investigating the oil spill that the MMS lacked the knowledge and man-power to adequately verify oil-drilling permit requests, and thus often relied on these companies to, in effect, write their own permits.[6] Mean-while, news accounts, some citing previous government investigations, recounted instances of MMS members accepting gifts and other ameni-ties from energy companies—a relationship nurtured by a revolving door through which former MMS employees went on to work in the industry the agency ostensibly regulated.[7]

The revelations regarding the MMS' dysfunctional history only added to the political troubles the Gulf spill caused for President Barack Obama. Already on the defensive against charges that his administration had moved too slowly to contain the spill, Obama now found himself pushed to explain what had gone wrong in the permitting process, particularly since less than a month before the April 20th Deepwater explosion he had proposed expanding off-shore oil drilling to areas along the eastern Gulf of Mexico and the north coast of Alaska.[8] He did so while praising "new technologies that reduce the impact of oil exploration" and vowed to "pro-tect areas that are vital to tourism, the environment, and our national security."[9] Two days after proposing expanded drilling, he issued an even more sweeping assurance: "It turns out, by the way, that oil rigs today generally don't cause spills.... They are technologically very advanced."[10]

With those words now thrown back against him, and under mounting pressure to demonstrate his leadership in response to the spill, Obama held a rare televised press conference on May 27 (his first in more than 300 days) to highlight the actions his administration had taken to date, but also to address the MMS' role in the debacle. In his opening state-ment he acknowledged the "scandalously close relationship between oil companies and the agency [the MMS] that regulates them," and con-ceded that his administration had moved too slowly when first taking office to sever that relationship. But he also touted the steps taken af-ter the spill by Interior Secretary Ken Salazar to reform the MMS and promised more to come.[11] Those steps included Salazar's May 19th issu-ance of an administrative order dividing the MMS internally into three entities—the Bureau of Ocean Energy Management, the Bureau of Safety and Environmental Enforcement, and the Office of Natural Resource Revenue—so as to separate the agency's leasing-for-pay process from its regulatory and research functions.[12] Moreover, on the day Obama gave his press conference, Salazar accepted the resignation of MMS Director Elizabeth Birnbaum, who Obama had appointed at the start of his administration to head that agency. (She was eventually replaced by former Justice Department Inspector General Michael Bromwich.) And, to drive home the point of organizational change, on June 18th Salazar issued a directive changing the agency's name from the Minerals Management Service to the Bureau of Ocean Energy Management, Regulation, and Enforcement.[13]

It would take another three years, however, to complete the primary cleanup of the spill—a process that at its peak involved more than 48,000 people, most under BP's supervision, and that (as described more fully below) was hampered by jurisdictional disputes between BP, federal, state, and local authorities.[14] In total, BP paid out more than $61 billion in penalties, legal settlements, and for the extensive restoration effort toward plant and wildlife habitats damaged by the spill.[15] That total includes a $20.8 billion settlement with the U.S. government, negotiated by Obama's Justice Department. [16] And, in a sign of the political significance of the Deepwater Horizon event, as one of his last acts as president, Obama issued a directive banning drilling in millions of acres in the Artic and Atlantic oceans. Obama's directive was promptly reversed by Donald J. Trump as one of his first acts as president in early 2017.[17]

Lessons from the Spill

The Gulf oil spill may be, in many respects, unprecedented, but the lessons it teaches about the executive branch are by no means new. First, it is a reminder that although the press and the public often focus attention on the more visible side of national politics—elections and the words and deeds of elected officials, particularly the president and Congress—it is the less visible actions of the executive branch departments and agencies, such as the MMS, that often determine whether these officials succeed. Second, when the public focus does shift to the executive branch, it is almost always in response to a perceived bureaucratic failure. Government agencies are rarely rewarded for success. Third, and most critically, when a government agency fails to carry out its mission, it is the president more than any other elected official who is held responsible.

Obama was but the latest president to be reminded of these lessons— reminders that he experienced more than once. In October 2013, the planned unveiling of the Obamacare website Healthcare.gov was plagued by a series of glitches attributed to faulty planning and oversight by the government's Centers for Medicare and Medicaid Services (CMS). Ultimately, as with the Gulf spill, it was Obama who suffered the political backlash for the botched rollout of his most significant domestic achievement.[18]

Obama's immediate predecessor, George W. Bush, learned these lessons as well. Bush embroiled the nation in a costly war in Iraq based in part on the Central Intelligence Agency's (CIA) faulty intelligence estimates regarding whether Iraq possessed chemical or biological weapons of mass destruction—estimates whose uncertainty Bush evidently never fully grasped. He also suffered politically for the highly criticized response by the Federal Emergency Management Agency (FEMA) in the hours and days after Hurricane Katrina struck the Gulf Coast in 2005. Some critics even hold Bush responsible for failing to prevent the September 11, 2001 terrorist attacks on the World Trade Center and Pentagon—a failure that occurred in part because the Federal Bureau of Investigation (FBI) and CIA did not share information regarding the Al Qaeda hijackers.[19]

Why are presidents so often held responsible for the perceived failures of the executive branch? Primarily because under the Constitution, as Alexander Hamilton first pointed out in the *Federalist Papers*, no one else appears so well situated to coordinate the executive branch as a whole nor has as strong an incentive to do so. In *Federalist* 70, Hamilton links "bad government" to weak administration by a "feeble" president: "A feeble Executive implies a feeble execution of government. A feeble execution is but another phrase for bad execution; and a government ill-executed ... must be, in practice, a bad government."[20] In *Federalist* 72, he reiterated the primacy of the president's administrative role: "The administration of government ... in its most precise signification ... is limited to executive details and falls peculiarly within the province of the executive department."

For Hamilton, then, an effective government requires presidential leadership of the executive branch. Hamilton's ideas have resonated with most presidents. But when pursuing their constitutional charge to "take Care that the Laws be faithfully executed,"[21] presidents invariably confront a countervailing reality: The same Constitution that compels them to seek control precludes them from completely fulfilling this aspiration. As Hugh Heclo reminds us, the Constitution binds executive branch agencies to an independent legislature. Moreover, presidents must exercise managerial control through political appointees who often find that their influence depends on adopting the agency's perspective rather than the president's.[22] This means that presidential efforts to control the executive branch are often resisted by Congress and even by their own political appointees, to say nothing of the permanent bureaucracy. The courts, too, can limit a president's administrative influence, as shown when a federal judge struck down Obama's effort shortly after the Deepwater Horizon explosion to impose a six-month moratorium on offshore drilling.[23] And, as Trump's reversal of Obama's drilling ban illustrates, a president's administrative legacy can be undone by his successor.

The Constitution, then, creates a political dynamic in which presidents feel compelled to manage the executive branch, but lack the means to completely do so. That dynamic, moreover, has gradually taken on greater significance to presidents as the executive branch has grown, acquired new responsibilities, and become an important influence on policy. In response, presidents have sought more powerful management tools by which to overcome resistance to their exercise of administrative control. Those efforts have not completely overcome the constitutionally derived impediments to presidential leadership, but over time they have made the executive branch's organizational structure and processes more amenable to presidential influence. The result, as Dan Carpenter notes, is that "The executive nature of the U.S. administrative state remains its most enduring and telling feature."[24]

But there is a potential downside to that "enduring and telling feature": Management strategies designed to enhance a president's administrative control can come at the cost of executive branch organizations' competence. If that loss of competence leads to bureaucratic failure, the consequences may weaken—not strengthen—presidential leadership. Presidents thus face a challenge: How can they make the agencies and departments in the executive branch more responsive to presidential control without eroding their ability to perform effectively? When does the desire for responsiveness undermine executive branch competence? The search by presidents to find the appropriate balance between loyalty and responsiveness has been the primary factor affecting presidential-executive branch relations since the nation's inception. That search has been complicated, however, by the changing and complex nature of the executive branch itself.

The Executive Branch: A Many Splintered Thing

What is "the executive branch"? A succinct answer is that it consists of the major government departments and agencies responsible for carrying out the nation's laws under the president's direction. These governmental organizations generally perform some combination of three functions: carrying out essential government duties, such as defending the nation against attack or conducting international diplomacy; regulating the private sector; and transferring federal dollars to third parties. This description, however, does not begin to hint at the variegated nature of the histories, cultures, and functions of these organizations. Consider the most familiar part of the executive branch: the 15 major departments that comprise the traditional presidential "cabinet."[25] As Table 9.1 indicates, these cabinet departments vary widely in size, from the Department of Defense (DoD), which employs more than 700,000 civilians, to the much smaller Department of Education, with a little more than 4,000 employees, and in budgets, with the Department of Treasury's budget authority more than 50 times that of the Department of Commerce.

Most importantly, of course, their missions differ. At the risk of oversimplification, some departments, like Defense, State, Justice,

Table 9.1 Executive Branch Employment Figures

Department	Created	2013 Employees	2013 Budget Authority (in millions)	2013 Total Outlays (in millions)	2013 Discretionary Budget (in millions)
State	1789	41,768	31,608	31,888	30,729
Treasury	1789	1,12,461	5,19,490	5,43,322	13,242
Interior	1849	71,543	11,357	13,345	11,374
Justice	1870	1,15,616	30,023	36,517	17,919
Agriculture	1889	95,223	1,54,667	1,54,502	22,957
Commerce	1903	45,035	9,239	8,990	7,990
Labor	1913	17,187	88,993	1,01,693	11,975
Defense	1947	7,28,823	6,20,259	6,72,879	6,13,916
Health and Human Services	1953	72,703	9,21,605	9,40,832	71,977
Housing and Urban Development	1965	8,136	44,010	46,283	35,347
Transportation	1966	55,288	74,280	98,523	13,755
Energy	1977	15,213	32,300	33,272	27,155
Education	1979	4,166	55,685	71,906	69,837
Veterans Affairs	1989	3,23,208	1,37,381	1,39,742	61,012
Homeland Security	2002	1,92,073	45,109	55,345	44,939

Sources: Office of Management & Budget, *Budget of the U.S. Government, Historical Tables: Budget Authority*, Government Printing Office, *www.gpoaccess.gov;* U.S. Office of Personnel Management, *Employment and Trends, Federal Civilian Workforce Statistics*, bimonthly release, *www.opm.gov.*

Treasury, and Homeland Security, are responsible for handling essential national functions. Others, such as Agriculture, Commerce, Labor, Interior, Education, and Veterans Affairs, primarily provide information, subsidies, and other services to influential client groups. Finally, a third subset—Health and Human Services, Transportation, Housing and Urban Development, and Energy—use federal dollars to promote research and development in particular issue areas.

This broad-stroke tripartite categorization should not be taken to suggest that each department is a unified organization with a single mission. In fact, most cabinet departments contain smaller agencies that often operate with relative autonomy in the pursuit of their own specific missions. Thus, although the MMS was part of Interior, it conducted its permitting process with little oversight from Interior's political leadership. Indeed, Salazar's much vaunted reforms at the outset of the Obama administration apparently had almost no effect on MMS operations.

The existence of these semi-autonomous agencies is a reminder that most of the cabinet departments, and even some of the agencies within them, are typically cobbled together from existing government bureaus and offices rather than created out of whole cloth with a single mission in mind. For example, Interior was established in 1849 by combining the Patent Office, Pension Office, and the General Land Office, among others.[26] Similarly, the most recent cabinet addition, the Department of Homeland

Security (DHS), was created by Congress in the aftermath of the 9/11 terrorist attacks by merging portions of 24 existing government organizations. When George W. Bush signed the authorizing legislation into law, the DHS instantly became the third largest cabinet department in terms of employees, but one that continues to struggle more than a decade after its creation to assimilate its constituent parts into a cohesive whole.[27]

Nor did all 15 departments originate with "cabinet" distinction. Agriculture was created in 1862 but did not receive cabinet status until 1889. The Bureau of Labor was first established within the Interior Department in 1888 and did not achieve cabinet designation until 1913. Education was initially part of the Federal Security Agency and then folded into the cabinet-level Health Education and Welfare (HEW) Department at HEW's creation in 1953 before being hived off to form a separate Education cabinet department in 1979.[28]

Cabinet designation, then, is no guarantee that a department is a unified entity with a single mission. The façade of cabinet designation may conceal the existence of several agencies or bureaus, each operating with relative autonomy in pursuit of missions that are unrelated, or even in tension, with one another. If we are to understand what a cabinet department does, then, we must look more closely at the organizational history of its constituent elements. The MMS, for example, was established in 1982 within Interior by combining elements of the U.S. Geological Survey, the Bureau of Land Management, and the Bureau of Indian Affairs that dealt with the leasing of federal lands to private parties. For the most part, these agencies focused on the surveying and leasing of government lands—not on environmental issues. Knowing the MMS' origins, it is perhaps less surprising that its permitting process centered primarily on revenue generation rather than on concern for the environment.

Moreover, some of the nation's most prominent agencies, such as the CIA, the Environmental Protection Agency (EPA), and the Army Corps of Engineers, are not located within the major cabinet departments at all. Some of these agencies, such as the EPA or the General Services Administration (GSA), employ more people and spend more money than do some of the cabinet departments. The 2016 *U.S. Government Manual* lists 59 such independent government organizations, in addition to several, such as the Smithsonian Institute, that have quasi-governmental status.[29] Finding a way to neatly categorize these agencies is not easy; they differ in terms of the composition of the directing authority,[30] the process by which officers are appointed and removed,[31] the officers' qualifications for appointment,[32] and the methods by which they are financed.[33] Harold Seidman and Robert Gilmour suggest that the most telling indicator of their significance may be the personnel pay rates of top-level executives as established by the Executive Schedule. The secretaries heading the 15 cabinet departments are paid at Executive Level I, the highest rate. Major agencies within the Executive Office of the President (EOP), such as the head of the Office of Management and Budget (OMB), are often paid at

Level II, while the heads of the various independent agencies may fall anywhere from Level II down to Level V, depending on the agency's status. Beyond this, however, there is often no clear reason why one agency has cabinet rank and another does not. As Seidman and Gilmour conclude, "The differences have their roots in custom and tradition and cannot be discovered in law books."[34] More importantly, despite differences in status, there is no clear distinction in power or authority between cabinet departments and independent agencies.

Government by Proxy?

At this point, the reader may be tempted to conclude that there is no useful way to generalize about the executive branch. That conclusion would be premature. If we step back from looking at differences between individual agencies, and consider instead aggregate trends in government employment (total and civilian) and budgets since 1940, a clearer picture emerges (see Figure 9.1).

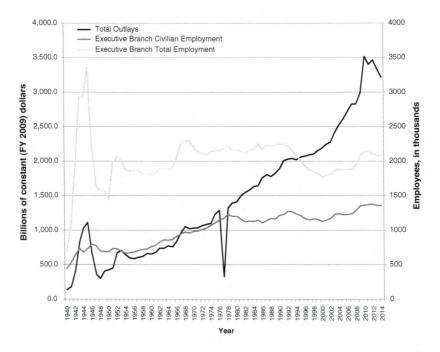

Figure 9.1 Growth in Federal Outlays and Executive Branch Employment, 1940–2016

Sources: U.S. Office of Personnel Management, *Historical Federal Workforce Tables: Executive Branch Civilian Employment*, www.opm.gov; Office of Management & Budget, *Budget of the U.S. Government, Historical Tables: Overview of Federal Government Finances*, U.S. Government Printing Office, *www.gpoaccess.gov.*

Not surprisingly, both budgets and employees have increased during the last seven decades. However, when we chart the relative growth of the two in terms of percentage changes, we see that outlays are growing much more rapidly than is federal employment (see Figure 9.2).

As of 2016, the federal government employed more than 1.3 million civilians, almost three times the number of employees it had in 1940. In that same period, however, government outlays, as measured in constant dollars, grew 26 times larger: from \$117 billion to \$3.1 trillion by the end of the 2016 fiscal year. By far the greatest portion of that increase in spending is due to nondefense related activities (see Figure 9.3).

In other words, the ratio of what the federal government does, as measured by the money it spends, versus how many it takes to do it, as measured by federal employees, has steadily increased since 1940 (see Figure 9.4).

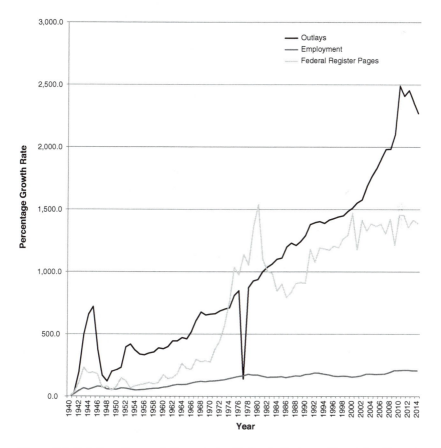

Figure 9.2 Relative Rate of Growth in Federal Outlays, Executive Branch Civilian Employment, and Number of Pages in the *Federal Register*, 1940–2014

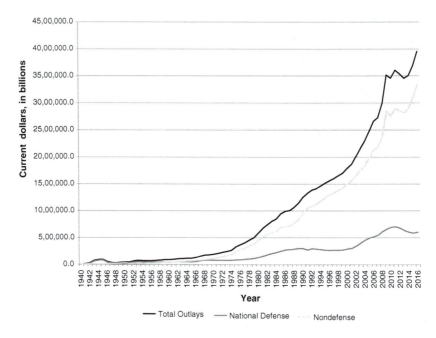

Figure 9.3 Growth of Federal Outlays, 1940–2016

This trend hints at two developments that have tended to complicate presidential efforts to manage the executive branch. First, a growing proportion of what government does is disburse checks for entitlement programs including Social Security, Medicare and Medicaid, Children's Health Insurance, and subsidies for the Affordable Care Act. Almost half of the current federal budget goes toward spending by these programs. Because they are entitlement programs that are not funded, for the most part, through the annual budgetary process, they are less amenable to presidential administrative control. Instead, expenditures for these programs are determined by how many people qualify to receive benefits, rather than by how much Congress or the president decides to spend each year.

Second, an increasing number of government programs are funded by federal monies, but administered by third parties, particularly state and local governments but also by private organizations. After leveling off in the Reagan-Bush years (1981–1993), federal outlays to state and local governments resumed their climb, reaching more than $440 billion (constant 2005 dollars) today (see Figure 9.5).

Although budgetary estimates of the money spent on contracting to private groups is only available for recent years, they were trending upward until 2009, when they peaked at approximately $538 billion paid by the federal government to private companies. In 2016, the amount was

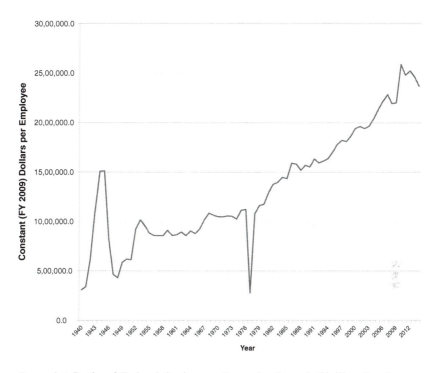

Figure 9.4 Ratio of Federal Outlays to Executive Branch Civilian Employees, 1940–2016

Sources: U.S. Office of Personnel Management, *Historical Federal Workforce Tables: Executive Branch Civilian Employment*, www.opm.gov; Office of Management & Budget, *Budget of the U.S. Government, Historical Tables: Overview of Federal Government Finances*, U.S. Government Printing Office, *www.gpoaccess.gov.*

$472 billion, still more than double what it paid in 2000 and more than what it pays out to state and local governments (see Figure 9.6).

The overall impact of these trends is to, in Heclo's phrase, "promote the idea of government by remote control."[35] That is, the great growth in government is not in programs administered at the national level, but rather in those programs that are outsourced to third parties, either at the state and local level or in the private sphere.

To retain some semblance of control over this government by proxy, federal officials have typically attached rules and regulations stipulating how this federal money can be spent. Figure 9.2 lists the percentage change in the annual number of pages in the Federal Register, a simple but telling measure of the growth of administrative rules and regulations. Note that its rate of growth is comparable to that of budget outlays.

The aggregate data, then, suggests that the outsourcing of government functions first highlighted by Heclo in the 1970s continues unabated.

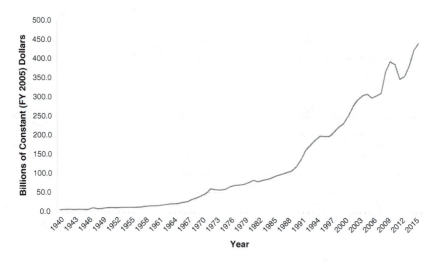

Figure 9.5 Growth of Total Outlays for Grants to State and Local Governments, 1940–2016

Source: Office of Management & Budget, *Budget of the U.S. Government, Historical Tables: Federal Grants To State and Local Governments* (Washington, DC: U.S. Government Printing Office).

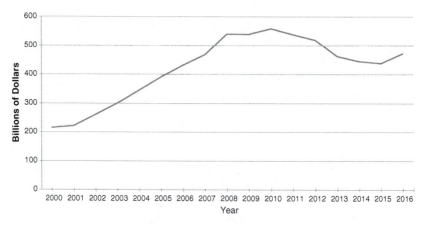

Figure 9.6 Growth in Federal Contracts, 2000–2016

Source: Federal Spending Trends, *www.usaspending.gov.*

Now, one can argue that in the post-New Deal era of structural budget deficits and increasing public distrust of government solutions to social and economic problems, a policy of government by proxy makes eminent sense. First, it allows government to expand its policy reach without establishing a massive federal bureaucracy. By relying on third parties with special expertise or competencies, moreover, government can do more and do it more effectively. And devolving some functions to state and local governments that are, in theory, more responsive to the public, may strengthen federalism. Of course, as Paul Light points out, this strategy has the additional political benefit of helping to hide the true size and cost of government.[36]

But the outsourcing of government functions carries significant risks as well. First, it opens the possibility that the third party will implement a government program in a way that does not comport with presidential and congressional intent. This is particularly problematic when private organizations expropriate public authority for their own ends. To illustrate, consider the MMS' relationship with the oil industry. Not surprisingly, given its limited resources in staffing and money, the MMS relied on the oil industry to provide technology and expertise to locate drilling areas in federal waters and assess their potential market value before putting them up for auction for leasing rights.[37] It is true that the money from these leases made the MMS the second highest source of revenue for the federal government (after the IRS).[38] But Congress repeatedly questioned whether the MMS was charging enough for these leases, with members suggesting that the MMS' reliance on oil industry expertise may have led it to accept less than full value. Moreover, because the MMS had limited resources for inspecting these sites once the drilling commenced, they again had to rely on oil industry assurances regarding drilling safety and contingency plans to deal with deep water spills.[39]

The issuance of rules and regulations, of course, is meant to prevent third parties from contravening presidential and congressional intent. But this strategy carries its own risk. For one, it is hard to know from a distance if these administrative directives are being followed. In the MMS case, it appears they were not, at least not diligently. Adding still more rules, however, risks inundating third parties with red tape, thus undercutting the benefits of government by proxy by stifling bureaucratic initiative at the point of program implementation.

There is an additional problem with government by proxy. Contracting out for services, or even privatizing them, can erode a government agency's core competency at carrying out its central mission. Strictly speaking, of course, the MMS was not formally outsourcing its function to private industry for a fee. But the practical effect was much the same. Over time, critics contend, the MMS' concern, prodded by congressional inquiries, to maximize revenue came at the cost of its regulatory effectiveness; by relying on the oil industry to carry out key functions, the MMS lost a core competence (if it ever possessed it) that was central to its mission. That erosion of regulatory competence was the primary justification for Salazar's decision, in reorganizing the MMS, to separate its revenue collecting function from its regulatory duties.

If this argument is correct—if elected officials continue to invest in a strategy of government by proxy—it poses potentially ominous implications for presidents' ability to fulfill their Hamiltonian expectation to lead the executive branch. The outsourcing of functions may pay political dividends for members of Congress who wish to provide government services without appearing to increase the size of government, but it is the president, more than any other official, who bears the consequences when this strategy backfires.

Government by Proxy: How New?

If we assume that the MMS' dependence on private groups to carry out its mission is not an isolated incident, and instead reflects a more pervasive reliance on government by proxy, as suggested by the trends in government spending, employment, and rules and regulations, we might still ask: Is this really new? After all, political scientists writing in the 1950s and 1960s documented the existence of "iron triangles"— enduring alliances between private groups, congressional oversight, or appropriations committees and the relevant executive branch agencies— that appeared to control policymaking across a range of policy sectors, from agricultural commodities to public works to military contracting.[40] At first glance, the process that led to the Deepwater Horizon incident seems to be another classic illustration of policymaking controlled by an iron triangle, this one composed of oil companies and related industries, members of Congress representing regions highly dependent on the oil industry, and the MMS itself. If so, how much more difficult is the president's managerial task in the current context?

The evidence suggests it is much more difficult. To begin, as Heclo suggested nearly three decades ago, the iron triangle model was "not so much wrong as it was dangerously incomplete."[41] Several trends in the last half-century, including greater policy complexity and congestion, more transparency in government operations, combined with a diffusion of political control have, if anything, made that model even less relevant today.

Those trends are clearly visible in the aftermath of the Deepwater Horizon platform explosion. To begin, the complexity of the issues commonly addressed by government today cuts across existing bureaucratic jurisdictions, complicating decision making and rendering it difficult to determine accountability. The Gulf spill is a perfect illustration: The Coast Guard ostensibly took charge of clean up operations, but that required close consultation and coordination with the Army Corps of Engineers, the Interior department (including the MMS), the National Guard, and the EPA, as well as state and local authorities. The high number of agencies involved, some with different missions, confused and lengthened the chain-of-command and led to jurisdictional disputes.[42] For example, when a Florida county sought to prevent oil from reaching the county coastline by placing several floating barges, installing a submerged oil-catching curtain, and projecting a wall of air from an underwater pipe, it waited two months for approval from state and federal officials.

Second, the complexity of the issues related to the spill which Obama and his officials had to address—calculating the rate of oil flow and its likely dispersion pattern, estimating the possible environmental impacts of the various control and containment possibilities and, not least, figuring out how to stem the leak—taxed the administration's technical capabilities and knowledge. Ultimately, executive branch agencies were forced to reach out to specialists, including engineers, biologists, hydrologists, and geologists working in the private sector, at universities and in think tanks for assistance. For example, the Army Corps of Engineers, in rejecting a Louisiana state plan to dump large rocks to create a barrier preventing oil from reaching the coast, based its decision in part on consultations with scientists working in other government bureaucracies but also with private environmental interest groups who said the rock berm would damage existing barrier islands.[43]

The Obama administration's reliance on a wide range of specialists to deal with the oil spill perfectly illustrates a broader trend first highlighted by Heclo three decades ago, when he identified the growing influence of knowledge-based "issue networks" composed of "technopols" who move seamlessly between appointed positions in government bureaucracies and private organizations. These networks did not supersede the system of iron triangles so much as they were overlaid on it, further complicating the president's managerial task.

The number of participants in these issue networks has exploded in recent years, driven in part by the supply of policy experts churned out by think tanks, policy schools, and public interest organizations. As government programs increase in scope and complexity, these technopols grow more influential, either by serving as consultants to government or by occupying executive branch positions themselves. In contrast to participants in the traditional iron triangles, however, issue activists are motivated less by material goods than by ideas and ideals regarding what makes "good policy." This has both positive and negative consequences for the president's ability to manage the executive branch.

On the positive side, policy specialists provide a ready source of expertise with which to tackle problems. It was specialists in the private sector who first alerted the Obama administration to the fact that BP was underestimating the amount of oil spilling into the Gulf. On the other hand, as Obama and his aides discovered, because issue experts tend to view problems from their own relatively narrow specialty, their increased participation in policy debates can make it much harder to come to a consensus regarding how to solve the problem. For instance, when BP began applying chemical dispersants to help dissipate the oil in the water, the EPA—prodded by environmental groups—objected, arguing that the dispersants BP chose were potentially toxic when used on the scale BP had proposed. Cleaning the oil from the water in an environmentally sensitive manner proved more difficult than simply choosing the quickest removal method.

Both the growth in the number of issues that cut across traditional bureaucratic jurisdictions and the proliferation of issue specialists willing to participate in addressing those issues have not happened in isolation. Instead, these developments have taken place within an increasingly open and contentious political climate. Consider the changes to the media during the last several decades. Four decades ago, live television broadcasts of breaking events were rare and most people received their news from one of the three major networks' nightly newscasts. Today, as the Gulf story illustrated, live news coverage is far more common, and news outlets have proliferated. Viewers could access scenes from the Gulf, even including video of the spill itself, in real time on television and computer screens. Partisan-leaning cable news shows posted graphics indicating how many days since the oil spill began. Bloggers catering to specialized and often opinionated audiences debated Obama's handling of the crisis. The immediacy and the pervasiveness of this "narrowcasting," in which media coverage is fractured into smaller but more ideologically slanted outlets on both cable television and in the Internet-based blogosphere made it far more difficult for Obama to shape the public narrative of the spill.

Congress, too, has changed considerably from how it was described in the iron triangle literature. Committee and subcommittee hearings are now open to the public. This provides an opportunity for issue activists—most of who hold views more ideologically extreme relative to those held by the general public and who are far less amenable to compromise—to push members of Congress to adopt these less mainstream views and to punish those who do not fall in line.[44] This pressure often comes by channeling campaign donations and other electoral resources to the more extreme candidates in a congressional race, particularly during the primaries in which issue activists form a greater proportion of the electorate. The result is a Congress with a shrinking moderate middle, something Trump experienced early in his presidency when his efforts to repeal Obamacare were initially thwarted by a combination of Democrats and the House Freedom Caucus consisting of conservative Republicans.

The polarization of Congress, moreover, has occurred simultaneously with a process of party sorting that has purified both parties by eliminating members whose views were often closer to those of the opposition. This process began during the 1960s when a combination of residential migration patterns and technological innovations helped transform the once solidly Democrat South into a Republican stronghold. As the Democrat Party shed its southern conservative congressional wing and liberal Republicans in Congress lost their seats in the northeast, both congressional parties became both more internally homogenous and farther apart from one another, ideologically.[45]

The upshot of this has been the nationalization of congressional elections and of political discourse more generally, as members in each party see their political fortunes ebb and flow in unison.[46] This means, as Frances Lee demonstrates, that both the majority and minority party believe its political fate is more closely linked to the president's. This gives both sides a stronger incentive to make the president's performance, including his administrative effectiveness, the focal point of political debate. With one side pushing for the president to "win" the debate and the other equally vested in seeing him "lose," policy compromise is that much less likely.[47]

What does all this mean for the president's ability to manage the executive branch? The growth of policy specialists and single-issue groups in the context of a more nationalized and polarized political setting has had two effects: It has tended to open policy debate to wider participation and scrutiny, and it has infused that debate with new and often contradictory perspectives, making it that much harder to achieve policy solutions and political consensus. The collective impact has been to increase pressure on the president to strengthen his control over the executive branch to bring coherence to policy debate and achieve political closure. At the same time, however, it has made exercising that administrative control far more difficult. It is a situation the framers could hardly have envisioned when they considered how much administrative power to allocate to the president.

The Politics of Executive Branch Design

Even as the political context has made managing the executive branch more difficult for presidents, the stakes for doing so have grown greater as the executive branch takes on new functions and responsibilities. That process started slowly but accelerated in the post-Civil War era and continued more-or-less steadily thereafter. The overall long-term trend is clear—more bureaucracies employing more civilians and spending more money across a growing array of policy areas. Although there are no clean demarcation points delineating specific periods or patterns of growth, Dan Carpenter presents a useful historical framework that divides the evolution of the executive branch into three historical phases: the initial founding in 1789 through the end of Reconstruction in 1876; a second phase lasting to the end of World War II, and the modern era, dating from 1947 to the present.[48] In that latter period alone, at least through 1997, David Lewis counts 182 government agencies created by statute and another 248 established by administrative action, such as reorganization authority granted to the president.[49] To be sure, not all these agencies were created de novo; they often resulted from the recombination of existing agencies. Nor are they of equal significance; more than half of the agencies created by administrative directive do not even warrant a separate line item in the federal budget. Lewis notes, moreover, that 57 percent of the agencies created in this period were eventually terminated, although their functions were often absorbed by other government bureaucracies.[50]

This aggregate data, however, masks tremendous variation in the process by which individual agencies are created, grow, and, in some cases, terminated. It is impossible in a book chapter to do full justice to the myriad ways this process unfolded. At best, we can outline the fundamental structural dynamics that govern it. The growth of the executive branch, as described below, was dictated by the interplay of partisan and institutional factors against the backdrop of a constitutional system that compels presidents to seek managerial control, but prevents them from fully achieving it.

The first mover in this process is undoubtedly the U.S. Constitution. To be sure, it provides little specific reference to an executive branch beyond a few oblique references to "executive departments" and departmental "officers." Article II gives the president the power to appoint, with Senate consent, ambassadors, ministers and consuls, justices, and "all other Officers of the United States." and authorizes him to "require the opinion, in writing, of the principal officer in each of the executive departments…" However, in a reminder that presidents must compete for influence over the executive branch, the Constitution provides that Congress decides where to vest control of the "appointment of inferior officers"—in the courts of law or in the heads of departments.[51]

That constitutional mandated system of shared administrative powers at the national level, overlaid on the existing system of state governments, largely determined the general thrust of executive branch development during the next two centuries, even if it did not determine particulars. It did so by setting out the incentives—both institutional and, eventually, partisan—that shapes the interaction of the president and Congress during the ongoing 228-year process of building the executive branch. Generally speaking, presidents sought to mold that developmental process in ways that maximized their managerial control. Congress, depending on its partisan composition and how strongly it focused on its institutional interests, sometimes found itself allied with the president's managerial goals, but at other times it resisted them.

The framers, of course, understood that the newly established government would need executive departments to perform essential government functions. They were familiar with the major ministries of the British crown and had established, under the short-lived Articles of Confederation (1781–1789), three executive departments responsible for finance, the military, and foreign affairs. Accordingly, after the Constitution was ratified, one of Congress' first acts in 1789 was to reestablish those departments in the form of Treasury, War, and State, as well as creating an Office of Attorney General. Along with the Post Office Department (it did not achieve cabinet status until 1872) and a Navy department that split off from War in 1798, these constituted the major departments of the executive branch for the next half-century.

Initially, the partisan and institutional struggle between the president and Congress regarding executive branch control was somewhat muted. This was because, as James Q. Wilson documents, there was not much to fight over; the executive branch was small in both size and scope of activities. At its inception, the State Department had nine employees, not counting the secretary. The War Department numbered only 80 civilians a decade after its creation, with an army of only several thousand soldiers. The Treasury Department was perhaps the most powerful department because it collected taxes, ran the national bank, and managed the public debt, but this was in the context of a still tiny national government.

From the citizen's perspective, the most important department was probably the Post Office. During the period 1816 to 1861, the executive branch grew, as measured by the number of employees, from 4,837 to more than 36,000, but almost all of that was driven by an expansion in the number of post offices, itself the result of a growing population and commercial sector.[52] Beyond providing military protection to the frontier, delivering the mail, and occasionally subsidizing internal improvements such as building canals, the executive branch was not much of a presence in most people's lives. It was not until 1849, 60 years after the Constitution's ratification, that another new executive branch department— Interior—was added.[53]

That slow rate of growth began to change after the Civil War and the end of Reconstruction due to the expansion and diversification of the nation's economy in the second half of the nineteenth century. Between the start of the war in 1861 through 1900, the executive branch added 200,000 civilian employees. Although both the Civil War and the Spanish-American War occurred during this period, less than a quarter of that growth in employment was defense related. About half consisted of additional postal workers.[54] The rest came about through the creation of new government departments formed specifically to cater to the interests of those working in emerging economic sectors, including farmers, manufacturers, and laborers. In 1862, the Department of Agriculture was established, followed by the Bureau of Labor in 1888.[55] In 1903, Labor expanded to become the Department of Commerce and Labor, but it was split into two separate departments ten years later at labor unions' insistence.

In contrast to the first wave of executive departments established at the nation's founding, which oversaw essential government functions, such as diplomacy, defense, and finances, this second wave of new departments more directly catered to groups with growing political clout. They did so by serving as repositories of statistical information, expertise and advice, and eventually by working through Congress to provide more tangible group-based benefits, such as agricultural subsidies and veterans' pensions.

The development of these client-oriented departments was an explicit response not just to the development of groups with shared economic interests, such as labor unions and sector-specific manufacturing and industrial groups, but also to emerging professional classes. These new groups influenced executive branch growth on the supply side as well by providing new sources of government recruitment. Up to this time, hiring in executive branch agencies (with the partial exception of the military) had been based on political patronage—the winning political party rewarded its followers with government jobs. Because national politics in the period from the founding through the 1820s was dominated by the Northeast-based Federalist Party and then the Virginia-centered Democrat-Republicans, most federal jobs in this period went to a social network composed of "eastern elites." That changed with Andrew Jackson's election in 1828; under the direction of his chief political operative and eventual presidential successor Martin Van Buren, Jackson expanded the "spoils" system to encompass his more rural, western-based constituency. The principle underlying the spoils system, however, did not change: When a new party gained a majority, there was wholesale turnover in federal employment. This meant, for example, that when the Democrats replaced the Whigs in power, Whig-appointed postal workers were all replaced by Democrat-sponsored ones.

The great virtue of the spoils system is that it ensured that executive branch employees were responsive to elected officials. In fact, federal workers were expected to contribute a portion of their salaries to the party in control or risk termination. However, a hiring process based on who one knew was no guarantee of competence—an increasingly problematic issue as government tasks expanded beyond simple clerical work to embrace more technically demanding responsibilities. The dismal performance of a partially patronage-based system of military leadership at the outset of the Civil War served as an early warning sign regarding the dangers of the spoils system. By the 1880s, a reform movement, galvanized in part due to President James Garfield's assassination by a disappointed office seeker, spurred the adoption of legislation to end the spoils system. The Pendleton Act, passed in 1883, was the first of a series of legislation that, in addition to creating a three-person bipartisan

Civil Service Commission (CSC)[56] to oversee federal personnel policies, also outlawed direct payment by federal employees to parties, instituted competitive examinations for hiring and promotion and prevented the removal of employees for reasons other than inefficiency. Although civil service protection expanded slowly, by the end of World War II more than 80 percent of federal workers were protected by the merit system. Since then, however, many departments have opted to establish their own personnel system outside of the civil service system, so today only about half of the nation's roughly 2.1 million civilian employees are under traditional civil service protection.[57] Nonetheless, many of these separate personnel systems have adopted the basic tenets of the civil service system.

If the second wave of client-oriented cabinet departments differed in function from the first wave, they shared a similar organizational form at the upper level—all were headed by a single executive appointed by the president with the Senate's consent. Seidman and Gilmour argue that the single-secretary, department-based executive branch that was the norm through the end of the nineteenth century comported with the framer's belief that multiheaded organizations were to be avoided because they weakened accountability. Moreover, presidential control over the executive branch was strengthened by placing administrative functions within departments led by a presidential appointee.[58]

In 1887, however, a new type of administrative agency appeared with the creation of the Interstate Commerce Commission (ICC). The ICC's job was to regulate the emerging railroad industry, and it was the first sign of Congress' willingness to move away from the traditional single secretary, department-based organizational approach to executive organization.[59] This new bureaucratic structure, in which agencies were headed by a multimember and often bipartisan leadership directorate whose members served fixed terms, was inspired in part by the Progressive Movement, which hoped to insulate these regulatory agencies from both the influence of private economic interests and from purely partisan control. The practical effect, however, was to make commissions less amenable to presidential influence; a point driven home by the Supreme Court's 1935 decision in the case of *Humphrey's Executor v. United States.* The case centered on Franklin D. Roosevelt's efforts to fire William Humphrey from the Federal Trade Commission (FTC), a regulatory agency established in 1913 to limit market collusion and monopolies by corporations. The Court ruled that because the FTC was a quasi-legislative body that exercised some judicial functions, the president could not fire an FTC member solely for political reasons. That decision distinguished regulatory agencies from the more traditional executive branch departments and agencies headed by a single secretary that did not perform "quasi-judicial" functions. In its previous 1926 ruling in *Myers v. United States*, the Court had affirmed the president's unilateral power to remove any executive officer appointed by him, with the advice and consent of the Senate, to head these traditional departments.

The creation of the ICC signaled an increased willingness for Congress (sometimes even with presidential support) to establish executive agencies with new regulatory powers and structures outside the traditional departmental functions and format. Wilson suggests that these regulatory agencies tended to be formed in waves coinciding with periods dominated by progressive or liberal presidents supported by strong congressional majorities.[60] Examples include the Security and Exchange Commission (SEC, created in 1934) and the National Labor Relations Board (NRLB, created in 1938), both established by FDR when Democrats had large majorities in both chambers of Congress. These commissions exercised powers ranging from the ability to set the rates industry could charge customers, to establishing standards for products or services, to even bringing criminal charges against companies that violated those standards.

But not all commission-style bodies were created to limit free enterprise. Some, such as the Civil Aeronautics Authority (created in 1938 and later renamed the Civil Aeronautics Board), the Federal Communications Commission (FCC; created in 1933), and the Maritime Commission (created in 1936) were deliberately intended to nurture fledgling industries, often by establishing rules restricting entry or regulating competition between firms. Again, many of these grew out of existing bureaus that were often located in cabinet departments. For example, the FCC's origins date back to the Navy Department's bureau of marine radio regulation.

The third phase of bureaucratic development beginning in the post-World War II era saw the creation of several more cabinet departments—Health and Human Services (formerly HEW), Veteran's Affairs, Education, and Homeland Security—again typically by upgrading the status of or combining existing bureaus and agencies. Regulatory commissions, such as the Consumer Product Safety Commission (CPSC, created in 1973), and the Occupational Safety and Health Administration (OSHA, created in 1970, although officially located within the Labor Department) continued to be established. But the post-war period also saw a proliferation of a third type of executive branch agency—the so-called "independent" agencies—independent in the sense that they were not part of the traditional cabinet departments. Typically, they were established to undertake a single primary task or function. For example, the National Aeronautics and Space Administration (NASA) was created in 1958 in the aftermath of the Soviet launch of Sputnik, the first manmade satellite. Its mission is to oversee the nation's manned space program. The EPA, created in 1970, enforces the nation's environmental regulations. In contrast to regulatory commissions, these agencies are typically headed by a single individual nominated by the president with the advice and consent of the Senate. As noted earlier, they are usually (but not always) smaller than the major departments and lack cabinet status as reflected in the lower pay scales for those heading independent agencies.[61] In terms of authority, however, independent agencies do not differ from cabinet departments.

We see, then, that the growth of the executive branch has been accompanied by a proliferation of organizational forms. But what explains the variation in the structural characteristics of these agencies? Carpenter warns of the scholarly "hubris ... that a simple set of generalizations can explain behavior and operations across diverse agencies or over centuries of time."[62] But in the modern era, it appears that organizational structures, at least in part, reflects the institutional and partisan dynamics governing presidential-congressional relations in a system of shared powers. Lewis shows that of the 182 agencies created by statute during the 1947–1997 period, 64 percent have at least one of four characteristics that make them less amenable to presidential control.[63] Twenty-nine (16 percent) of these agencies possess all four characteristics. The likelihood that an agency will be structured in a way that makes it more insulated from presidential control goes up under conditions of divided government, when a president from one party confronts a Congress controlled by a strong majority of the opposing party. In contrast, when the government is unified, with strong majority partisan support for the president, Congress will be less likely to insulate a newly created agency from the president's managerial control. Not surprisingly, agencies created administratively by the president, or his subordinates, tend to have fewer characteristics insulating them from presidential control.[64]

Lewis' study addresses only the post-World War II modern era, of course. But his findings remind us that presidents are not passive bystanders when Congress creates executive branch agencies. Instead they will actively intervene to try and structure those agencies in ways that meet their policy and administrative preferences. Their ability to do so, however, is constrained by partisan and institutional factors playing out within a system of shared powers.

Managing the Executive Branch: The Perils of Politicization

Most scholars date the advent of the modern presidency to FDR's presidential tenure. Not surprisingly, the characteristics associated with modernization can all be linked in some way to FDR's struggle to manage the executive branch, which had vastly expanded in size and importance as a result of his New Deal. His effectiveness as president, he realized, was tied directly to his ability to manage this administrative state—something he acknowledged when an aide asked him how the Republican presidential candidate Alf Landon might have defeated him in 1936. Roosevelt replied, "I would say 'I am for social security, work relief, etc., but the Democrats cannot be entrusted with the administration of these fine ideals.'"[65]

As the first modern president, it is not surprising that FDR made the most concerted effort to restructure the executive branch of any president to date, through his establishment of the three-person Brownlow Committee, headed by public administration expert Louis Brownlow, in 1936. FDR charged the Brownlow Committee with conducting a thorough study of the executive branch, with an eye toward making his administrative authority more commensurate with his responsibilities. Previous presidents, dating back to Theodore Roosevelt's creation of the Keep Commission in 1905, had commissioned studies of the executive branch. Typically, these early efforts were characterized by presidents as efforts to achieve economy and efficiency in government by eliminating waste and red tape and generally putting government operations on a more business-like footing.[66] Although the Brownlow Committee Report, released in 1937, couched its findings in the neutral-sounding language of "administrative science," it was clear to anyone who read it that this was more than simply another plan to save money. The broader purpose was to strengthen FDR's managerial capacities. Toward that end, the Committee recommended: (1) Creating two new cabinet departments for public works and social welfare; (2) Replacing all independent boards and commissions with single directors that reported to the president; (3) Bringing government corporations within the jurisdiction of the cabinet departments (4) Placing the administrative functions of all independent regulatory commissions within existing cabinet departments, with their heads appointed by the president, with senatorial consent; and (5) Granting the president continuous authority to reorganize the executive branch.[67]

Congress, not surprisingly, saw the Report in part as an effort to weaken its own ties to the executive branch, and it responded accordingly. In what was to be a preview of reorganization efforts to come, Congress granted FDR limited reorganization authority, subject to Congress' exercise of its legislative veto. It stipulated that FDR could not use his reorganization authority to revamp the Civil Service Commission, which oversaw executive branch hiring policies. FDR was also prohibited from changing the name or number of any of the existing ten cabinet departments and from reorganizing any of 21 other agencies specifically listed by Congress.[68]

Congress proved more willing, however, to let FDR expand his own staff support—something Brownlow had also proposed. In 1939, FDR used his reorganization authority to formally create the EOP, into which he moved the Bureau of the Budget (BoB). He also received authorization to expand his White House staff by up to six more aides within a formal White House Office (WHO), to add an assistant to handle personnel policy, and to create a policy planning office within the EOP.

FDR's failure to restructure the executive branch, even while beginning to broaden his staff support, points out the management strategies his successors would adopt. They proved no more successful than he at using their limited reorganization authority to bring some administrative coherence to the executive branch, and eventually even this power lapsed permanently in 1984, its demise hastened by a 1983 Supreme Court decision that ruled the legislative veto—which had given Congress the means to disapprove reorganizations plans—unconstitutional.[69]

On the other hand, presidents have been much more successful in expanding their staff capacity, particularly within the WHO, albeit in a more politicized fashion and to a far greater extent than FDR likely would have countenanced (see Figure 9.7). Whereas FDR's White House staff consisted of only a handful of generalists reporting directly to him, by Richard Nixon's presidency, the White House Office had evolved into a large (numbering close to 600 budgeted members and many more detailed from other agencies) bureaucracy, functionally specialized and hierarchically arranged (an organizational prototype that has remained in place, more or less, for the ensuing four decades).

At the top half of the modern White House Office, encompassing roughly half of its budgeted staff, are the commissioned staff—those whose titles include "to the President" indicating that they work directly for the president. They are typically organized in three layers: the top-level assistants, deputy assistants, and special assistants. Below the commissioned aides, and reporting to them, are the non-commissioned staff who generally handle purely administrative tasks.

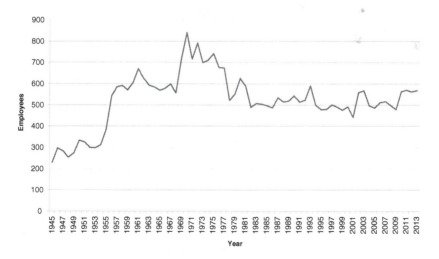

Figure 9.7 "Real" White House Staff Growth, 1945–2013

Note: Combines WHO, NSC, OPD, Special Projects and Detailed Employees. Data on detailed employees not available for 2001, 2004–2005, and 2008–2013.

Among the most important commissioned staff is the chief of staff, a position first created by President Dwight Eisenhower who recognized that with the expansion in staff size and specialization, presidents could no longer be expected to personally manage their White House aides. Beginning with Nixon, every president, with short-lived exceptions, has followed suit.

Although the senior-level assistants in recent presidencies have numbered a dozen or more, they are not all equal in stature or influence. Under Trump, for example, there appears to be three primary senior-level aides, supported by deputies, who are vying for his ear. As of early 2017, the first, responsible for running the White House on Trump's behalf, was Chief of Staff Reince Priebus (he was replaced by Gen. John Kelly in July 2017). Steven Bannon, the former Breitbart News chairman, oversees a second locus of power as Trump's chief strategist and senior counselor. Trump's son-in-law, Jared Kushner, oversees a third power center in his roles as senior White House adviser. Although it is early in Trump's presidency, history suggests that managing a White House with competing power centers can be quite difficult, and it is often the case that one aide will acquire primary power.

Functionally, the White House staff performs three primary roles: the administrative care and feeding of the president, outreach to key political actors and constituencies, and as a source of policy development and implementation. To accomplish the latter function, the presidency has evolved an elaborate system of White House staff-controlled policy councils, consisting of White House advisers working with the secretaries and their aides from the relevant cabinet departments and agencies. Under Trump, as has been the case for most recent presidencies, there are three such policy staffs: the national security staff headed by National Security Advisor H. R. McMaster;[70] the Domestic Council under the leadership of White House aide Andrew Bromberg; and the National Economic Council led by former Goldman Sachs executive Gary Cohn. In theory, these councils allow the president, and his key White House aides, to exercise some influence over the major executive branch departments during the policymaking process.

From the president's perspective, the White House is an ideal locus for building administrative support because it can be done without the need for Senate acquiescence (although the White House Office budget must be approved by Congress). A larger and more specialized White House staff provides presidents, in theory at least, with enhanced control over fundamental administrative processes affecting the executive branch, including budgeting, policy and regulatory planning and development, and personnel hiring.[71] In practice, however, this pursuit of "salvation by staff" has not always enhanced the president's administrative control. There are several reasons for this.

To begin, as staffs have grown larger they have also tended to suck once peripheral tasks into the White House orbit, raising the expectations regarding what issues a president is expected to address. The tendency is reflected by recent presidents' decisions to appoint what the media has dubbed "White House czars" charged with coordinating the handling of a policy area, often one that has recently risen in public prominence.[72] The difficulty, however, is that the czar often lacks the budgetary and administrative control necessary to address the problem. It was Tom Ridge's lack of budget authority as George W. Bush's White House homeland security "czar" that in part prompted Congress' creation of the Department of Homeland Security.

In a related vein, because White House aides are often selected for their demonstrated loyalty to the president on the campaign trail, they often take office lacking the understanding or expertise to govern. As a result, they can act in ways that undercut a president's influence, something Trump discovered early in his presidency when he allowed Bannon and his assistant Stephen Miller to draft an executive order putting a temporary hold on immigration from seven predominantly Muslim nations.[73] That order was drafted without input from the relevant legal experts, or from DHS, and was subsequently overruled by federal judges.[74]

More generally, as the White House staff has grown, there are more and more aides acting in the president's name but without his direct knowledge or control over what they are doing. The prime example, cited by Richard Neustadt, is the Iran-Contra Affair, in which Lieutenant Colonel Oliver North, a Marine detailed to Ronald Reagan's national security staff, ran an intelligence operation that involved selling arms to Iranians for the release of American hostages, despite Reagan's public declaration that he would not negotiate with terrorists, and then used the residuals from those sales to support the Nicaraguan Contras at a time when such aid was banned by Congress, and apparently without Reagan's knowledge.[75]

It is also much more difficult, as Trump discovered with former National Security Adviser Michael Flynn, for presidents to disavow the actions of an administration official who is a handpicked member of the president's White House team. Flynn, Trump's first choice to serve as national security adviser, was fired less than a month into Trump's presidency for concealing his business dealings with the Russian government prior to joining the Trump administration. Despite Trump's effort to severe ties with Flynn, however, the subsequent investigation into Flynn's business dealings threatened to embroil Trump in continuing controversy. Not surprisingly, media reports indicated that scarcely six months into his presidency Trump was already contemplating a major White House overhaul.[76] If so, he would not be the first president to revamp his staff within a year of taking office.[77] Bill Clinton undertook a similar housecleaning and for similar reasons related to his campaign aides' inability to adjust to governing. More generally, those features that make the White House a superficially appealing tool by which to manage the bureaucracy—the ability to appoint proven loyalists who respond primarily to the president—also makes it less than ideal at achieving that goal in practice.

But there is a second administrative control strategy presidents have pursued in tandem with expanding the White House—politicizing the executive branch. One method for doing so is to increase the number of upper-level positions that can be filled with political appointees and to use the enhanced White House personnel capability to nominate individuals to these positions who are loyal to the president and supportive of his policies. As Paul Light shows, this is precisely what has happened during the post World War II era. According to his calculations, the total number of senior executives and presidential positions in executive Levels I-IV—the top management levels in executive branch agencies—grew by 430 percent from 1960 to 1992, from 451 to 2,393.[78]

These positions are staffed primarily by Senate-confirmed presidential nominees (PAS) and political appointees (as well as careerists) serving in the Senior Executive Service (SES).[79] Although the pace of political thickening began slowing after Jimmy Carter's presidency, it remains the case, as Tables 9.2 and 9.3 indicate, that cabinet departments and major independent agencies continue to be layered with political appointees at the upper echelons.[80] Subsequent studies show that midway through George W. Bush's presidency, the layering of political appointees was still on the rise, albeit at a slower pace.[81]

All told presidents are responsible for placing some 550–600 Senate-confirmed PAS nominees in executive branch departments and agencies. An additional 10 percent of the roughly 7,000 SES officials in the upper management positions are also political appointees selected by the

Table 9.2 Executive Branch Positions (Cabinet)

Department	PAS	SES Career	SES Noncareer	SES Total
State	265	133	40	173
Treasury	31	114	39	153
Interior	17	151	38	189
Justice	209	68	62	130
Agriculture	14	103	50	153
Commerce	21	58	46	104
Labor	16	33	26	59
Defense	52	327	93	420
Health and Human Services	18	299	83	382
Housing and Urban Development	13	40	28	68
Transportation	22	138	33	171
Energy	21	183	34	217
Education	15	63	21	84
Veterans Affairs	11	337	13	350
Homeland Security	17	63	56	119

Source: The United States Government Policy and Supporting Positions (Plum Book) 2016 edition, *www.gpoaccess.gov.*

Table 9.3 Executive Branch Positions (Non-Cabinet)

Agency	PAS	SES Career	SES Noncareer	SES Total
Army Corps of Engineers	0	2	0	2
Social Security Administration	3	148	12	160
National Science Foundation	2	75	10	85
Small Business Administration	4	37	14	51
National Aeronautics and Space Administration	3	29	4	33
Environmental Protection Agency	13	94	26	120
Corporation for National and Community Service	17	3	0	3

Source: The United States Government Policy and Supporting Positions (Plum Book) 2016 edition, *www.gpoaccess.gov.*

president or his aides. However, this thickening of political appointments at the top of the executive branch represents only the most visible portion of politicization. Presidents also control appointments to some 1,600 so-called Schedule C positions. These are positions within the executive branch designated as confidential or of a policy determining, as opposed to a primarily clerical, nature.[82]

Presidents, then, are directly or indirectly responsible for filling some 3,000 appointed positions (some requiring Senate approval) throughout the executive branch. Not all this thickening is driven by successive presidents' attempts to strengthen their managerial control, of course. Light argues that much of it is caused by a simple increase in bureaucratic responsibilities. Moreover, the degree of thickening, as Tables 9.2 and 9.3 indicate, varies by department. Lewis suggests that presidents aggressively politicize those departments whose policy preferences are farthest from their own.[83] They will be less likely to do so, however, in agencies whose missions require substantial technical knowledge.

Lewis' finding points to a potential downside to presidential efforts to expand administrative control via saturation of the executive branch with political loyalists. As I have argued elsewhere, the strategy can produce what I describe as the paradox of politicization; as executive branch agencies become more responsive to the president, they may also become less competent.[84] The reason is that the layering of political appointees can insulate decision makers, including the president, from input by careerists who possess critical expertise for understanding and carrying out an agency's tasks. The lack of input, in turn, can demoralize civil servants, leading to higher turnover and less commitment to the agency. The net result, through time, is to erode an agency's capacity to carry out its mission. For example, Lewis provides evidence that the greater the degree to which FEMA was politicized, as measured by the number of high-ranking and Schedule C political appointees in its employee structure, the more poorly it performed in the period from its inception in 1978 through its transfer to DHS in 2002.[85] Lewis links the poor response by FEMA during Hurricane Katrina to the politicization of the agency after its absorption by the DHS. FEMA's poor performance was laid at George W. Bush's feet and directly contributed to the Democratic takeover of Congress in 2006.

Conclusion

Hugh Heclo, in his seminal study of American administrative politics *A Government of Strangers*, described the struggle by presidents, his appointees, and high-ranking bureaucrats to control the executive branch as "usually a leap into the dark."[86] This chapter has sought, by drawing on existing research, to shed some light on that leap. It is one that every president, and his subordinates, must make, for reasons first described by Hamilton in the Federalist Papers—reasons that have taken on *greater* importance, however, particularly since the New Deal and the emergence of the modern administrative state.

As Obama discovered with the MMS and Gulf oil spill, no two leaps are alike, and one can never be sure how, or where, one will land. It is almost certainly true that Obama had at best a nodding acquaintance, if that, with the MMS when he took office in January 2009. And yet, scarcely a year into his presidency, he found his political future unexpectedly yoked to the failings of this relatively minor government agency.

Of course, all presidents understand from the moment they assume office the need to take charge of the executive branch. Typically, they respond to this challenge in two ways—by using the White House-centered presidential staff system to control key administrative processes (budgeting, personnel hiring, regulatory and policy development) that affect how the executive branch operates and by saturating the executive branch with political appointees loyal to the president and his policies. These strategies possess a superficial logic. In the short run, they may make agencies more responsive to presidential directive. They have the added benefit of providing a means to place loyal supporters in government jobs—the modern-day equivalent of the "spoils" system. And in an era of "government by proxy," in which government programs are increasingly outsourced to state and local agencies, and to private contractors, the need for presidents to control administrative processes, particularly budgeting and the development of rules and regulations, is more crucial than ever.

But there are risks to an administrative approach that emphasizes political responsiveness. Evidence suggests that, through time, excessive politicization can weaken bureaucratic effectiveness. That, in turn, can undercut a president's political standing. In this regard, the Gulf oil spill is an important reminder of the stakes involved in presidential efforts to control the bureaucracy. In an era of increasing policy congestion, a more open political process, the growth of new issue-oriented political groups, the development of a 24-hour, seven-days-a-week news cycle, the repercussions from a president's failure, real or perceived, to "take care" that the laws are faithfully executed is greater than ever. The MMS and the Gulf oil spill is just one illustration of this. And yet the failure of the MMS to properly assess BP's oil permit request, or to inspect the Deepwater Horizon rig, was not because it lacked political responsiveness to the president. It was because it lacked competence to carry out its regulatory mission. Whether due to a too-cozy relationship with the oil industry, a lack of resources, or a combination of both, the MMS failed its bureaucratic mission, and Obama paid the political consequence. Gulf state residents paid a price as well in the form of polluted waters, contaminated wetlands and beaches, and economic devastation.

As with his predecessors, Trump will undoubtedly confront incidents that will highlight the crucial link between presidential power and executive branch effectiveness. Indeed, he has already found himself in political hot water for his decision to remove FBI Director James Comey who was overseeing an investigation into allegations that members of Trump's campaign team colluded with Russians trying to influence the 2016 presidential campaign.[87] The political firestorm erupting after Comey's firing is a reminder that while Trump possesses the formal authority to remove political appointees with whom he has grown disenchanted, it is not always in his political interest to exercise this power. The reaction to the Comey firing is a reminder that managing the executive branch is a far different task than serving as the CEO of a private business. This is a distinction that Trump early in his presidency may not have yet fully grasped. Whether he eventually does will go a long way toward determining how effective a president he will be. To date, however, Trump's administrative actions seem primarily predicted on ensuring that those working for him demonstrate the requisite political and personal loyalty, or risk removal. As we have seen, a concern with loyalty among appointees is not unique to Trump, although he may be emphasizing this requirement to a greater degree than his predecessors. However, in judging appointees primarily by their personality fealty, Trump would do well to remember what Hamilton wrote two centuries ago, in *Federalist* 68: "[T]he true test of a good government is its aptitude and tendency to produce good administration." Trump, like all presidents, must decide when balancing personal loyalty and administrative competence, where "good administration" resides.

Acknowledgments

I thank Martina Berger for research assistance on this chapter.

Notes

1 Estimates of the amount of oil spilled differ depending on assumptions regarding not just the rate of flow but also the relative mix of oil, natural gas, and other elements in the flow. See Joel Achenbach and David Fahrenthold, "Oil-Spill Flow Rate Estimate Surges to 35,000 to 60,000 Barrels a Day," *Washington Post*, June 15, 2010, www.washingtonpost.com/wp-dyn/content/article/2010/06/15/AR2010061504267.html.

2 In comparison, the 1990 Exxon Valdez accident dumped about 275,000 barrels of oil into waters off Alaska. For a discussion of the environmental impact of the Gulf spill, see David A. Fahrenthold, "Determining Oil Spill's Environmental Damage is Difficult," *Washington Post*, July 5, 2010, www.washingtonpost.com/wp-dyn/content/article/2010/07/04/AR2010070403990_2.html?hpid=topnews&sid=ST2010070404378.

3 Watt's administrative directive, issued January 19, 1982, consolidated mineral management functions previously exercised by the U.S. Geological Survey, the Bureau of Land Management and the Bureau of Indian Affairs.

4 For example, BP's regional response plan, submitted as part of the Deepwater drilling application, lists cold-water marine mammals including walruses, sea otters, sea lions and seals as "sensitive biological resources." None of those animals live anywhere near the Gulf. It also asserted that because the drilling rig was located so far offshore, no oil was likely to reach the Gulf coast in case of an oil spill. See Tim Dickinson, "The Spill, the Scandal and the President," *Rolling Stone*, June 8, 2010, http://news.yahoo.com/s/ap/20100609/ap_on_bi_ge/us_gulf_oil_spill_sketchy_plans.

5 To be sure, these inquiries focused less on the environmental aspects of the permitting process and more on the fees the MMS charged oil companies for drilling; the GAO issued a series of reports alleging that the MMS was undercharging oil companies for the right to drill in U.S. waters. See, for example, Mark Gaffagan, "Royalties Collection: Ongoing Problems with Interior's Efforts to Ensure a Fair Return for Taxpayers Require Attention," U.S. Government Accountability Office, March 28, 2007, www.gao.gov/new.items/d07682t.pdf. For an assessment of the MMS from a member of its advisory committee, see Tyler Priest, "The Ties That Bind MMS and Big Oil," *Politico*, June 9, 2010, www.politico.com/news/stories/0610/38270_Page2.html.

6 See generally the June hearings of the House Natural Resources subcommittee, televised on C-Span at http://cspan.org/Watch/Media/2010/06/17/HP/A/34368/House+Natural+Resources+Subcmte+Hearing+on+Gulf+Coast+Oil+Spill+MMS+Operations.aspx.

7 Ian Urbina, "Inspector General's Inquiry Faults Regulators, *New York Times*, May 24, 2010, www.nytimes.com/2010/05/25/us/25mms.html.

8 John M. Broder, "Obama to Open Offshore Areas to Oil Drilling for First Time," *New York Times*, March 31, 2010, www.nytimes.com/2010/03/31/science/earth/31energy.html.

9 Obama's remarks can be found at https://obamawhitehouse.archives.gov/the-press-office/remarks-president-energy-security-andrews-air-force-base-3312010.

10 "Flashback: Obama Says 'Oil Rigs Today Don't Generally Cause Spills'," *RealClearPolitics*, April 29, 2010, www.realclearpolitics.com/video/2010/04/29/flashback_obama_says_oil_rigs_today_dont_generally_cause_spills.html.

Obama later defended himself by saying he had been misled regarding the safety of offshore drilling.

11 See the transcript at https://obamawhitehouse.archives.gov/the-press-office/remarks-president-gulf-oil-spill.

12 Administrative Order 3299, May 19, 2010; see https://fas.org/sgp/crs/misc/R42599.pdf.

13 Critics were quick to point out that the acronym for the newly titled agency was pronounced "bummer." Administrative Order 3302, June 18, 2010; see https://fas.org/sgp/crs/misc/R42599.pdf. The agency name was shortened to Bureau of Ocean Energy Management in October 2011.

14 See, for example, the dispute between federal and state officials regarding whether to construct coastal barriers to block the oil from washing ashore; John Collins Rudolf, "Louisiana and Scientists Spar over How to Stop Oil," *New York Times*, July 6, 2010, www.nytimes.com/2010/07/07/science/earth/07rocks.html?_r=1&hp; For a summary of the overall cleanup effort, see Jessica Hartogs, "Three Years after BP Oil Spill, Active Clean-Up Ends in Three States," *CBS News*, June 10, 2013, www.cbsnews.com/news/three-years-after-bp-oil-spill-active-clean-up-ends-in-three-states/.

15 Nathan Bomey, "BP's Deepwater Horizon Costs Total $62B," *USA Today*, July 14, 2016, www.usatoday.com/story/money/2016/07/14/bp-deepwater-horizon-costs/87087056/.

16 Devlin Barrett, "U.S., BP Finalize $20.8 Billion Deepwater Oil Spill Settlement," *Wall Street Journal*, October 5, 2015, www.wsj.com/articles/u-s-says-20-8-billion-bp-spill-settlement-finalized-1444058619.

17 Dan Merica and Elizabeth Landers, "Trump Signs Order Looking to Reverse Obama's Ban on Off-Shore Drilling," *CNN*, April 28, 2017, www.cnn.com/2017/04/28/politics/trump-obama-off-shore-drilling/.

18 Sheryl Gay Stolberg and Michael D. Shear, "Inside the Race to Rescue a Health Care Site, and Obama," *New York Times*, November 30, 2013, www.nytimes.com/2013/12/01/us/politics/inside-the-race-to-rescue-a-health-site-and-obama.html?pagewanted=all&_r=0.

19 For a discussion of these incidents, see Don Kettl, *System Under Stress: Homeland Security and American Politics*, 3rd ed. (Washington, DC: CQ Press, 2014).

20 Hamilton, *Federalist* 70.

21 The U.S. Constitution, Article II, section 3.

22 Hugh Heclo "One Executive Branch or Many?," in *Both Ends of the Avenue*, ed. Anthony Kind (Washington, DC: American Enterprise Institute, 1983), 26–27.

23 Charlie Savage, "Drill Ban Blocked; U.S. Will Issue New Order," *New York Times*, June 22, 2010, www.nytimes.com/2010/06/23/us/23drill.html?_r=0.

24 Dan Carpenter, "The Evolution of the National Bureaucracy in the United States," in *The Executive Branch*, eds. Joel D. Aberbach and Mark Peterson (New York: Oxford University Press, 2005), 66.

25 Although Article II, Section 2 of the Constitution references the "Principal officers in each of the executive Departments," the president's "cabinet" has no formal status. Instead the term traditionally is used to refer to those principal officers—the secretaries heading the major executive branch departments. They are designated as holding cabinet-level status, which qualifies them for Executive Level I rank on the government pay scale. Other officials, however, such as the vice president or White House chief of staff, may be given cabinet rank by the president. According to the White House website, Trump's "cabinet" currently includes 24 individuals. See www.whitehouse.gov/administration/cabinet.

26 Carpenter, "Evolution," 51.

27 See Kettl, *System Under Stress*, chapter 3, 46–71.

28 Note that the Navy Department was split off from War in 1798 before be-
    ing folded into the newly created Defense Department in 1947. The Postal
    Department was created in 1792, and its head, the Postmaster General, was
    invited to sit in the president's cabinet in 1829, but the department did not
    achieve cabinet designation until 1872.

29 See "United States Government Manual," www.usgovernmentmanual.
    gov/?AspxAutoDetectCookieSupport=1.

30 Some are headed by a single director, while others have a multi-member
    board or commission.

31 Do they require Senate confirmation? Do they serve fixed terms, or can they
    be removed at will by the President?

32 Is there a requirement for bipartisan membership, for example?

33 Some government agencies, such as the Tennessee Valley Authority or
    Federal Reserve Board, must generate a portion of their own operating reve-
    nues, acting much like private corporations.

34 Harold Seidman and Robert Gilmour, *Politics, Position and Power*, 4th ed.
    (New York: Oxford University Press, 1986), 259–64.

35 Hugh Heclo "The Executive Establishment," in *The New American Political
    System*, ed. Anthony King (Washington, DC: American Enterprise Institute,
    1978), 92.

36 Paul Light, *True Size of Government* (Washington, DC: Brookings, 1999).

37 See "G&G Data Acquisition and Analysis," Bureau of Ocean Energy Manage-
    ment, www.boem.gov/Oil-and-Gas-Energy-Program/Resource-Evaluation/
    Geological-and-Geophysical-Data-Acquisition/GGData-Geophysical-
    Surveys.aspx.

38 See "Fair Market Value," Bureau of Ocean Energy Management, www.
    boem.gov/Oil-and-Gas-Energy-Program/Energy-Economics/Fair-Market-
    Value/econFMV.aspx.

39 According to testimony before a House subcommittee, the MMS had only
    60 inspectors to oversee nearly 4,000 drilling facilities in the Gulf of Mexico,
    while on the Pacific Coast ten inspectors cover only 23 facilities. Jackie
    Calmes and Helene Cooper, "BP Chief to Express Contrition in Remarks
    to Panel," *New York Times*, June 16, 2010, www.nytimes.com/2010/06/17/us/
    politics/17obama.html.

40 See, for example, Grant McConnell, *Private Power and American Democracy*
    (New York: Alfred Knopf, 1966); and Douglas Cater, *Power in Washington*
    (New York: Vintage, 1954). Progressive historians leveled similar charges
    in their studies of the first attempts by government to regulate industry
    during the Progressive era at the start of the twentieth century. See, for ex-
    ample, Gabriel Kolko's *The Triumph of Conservatism: A Reinterpretation of
    American History, 1900–1916* (New York: Free Press of Glencoe, 1963).

41 Heclo, "The Executive Establishment," 88.

42 Ryan Tracy, "Florida, Bureaucracy, and the Oil-Spill Cleanup, *Newsweek*,
    July 6, 2010, www.newsweek.com/2010/07/01/the-mire-next-time.html.

43 Rudolf, "Louisiana and Scientists Spar."

44 See Morris Fiorina, *Disconnect: The Breakdown of Representation in
    American Politics* (Norman, OK: University of Oklahoma Press, 2009).

45 Nelson Polsby provides a detailed description of this process, including how
    the introduction of air conditioning influenced residential migration pat-
    terns. See Polsby, *How Congress Evolves: Social Bases of Institutional Change*
    (New York: Oxford University Press, 2004).

46 Matthew J. Dickinson "The President and Congress," in *The Presidency and the Political System*, 10th ed., ed. Michael Nelson (Washington, DC: CQ Press, 2014), 406–47.

47 Frances Lee, *Beyond Ideology: Politics, Principles and Partisanship in the U.S. Senate* (Chicago, IL: University of Chicago Press, 2009).

48 Carpenter, "The Evolution of the National Bureaucracy in the United States," 49–50.

49 Examples of important agencies created by administrative directive include the National Security Agency (NSA) and the Peace Corps.

50 Peak periods of legislative creation of bureaucracies occurred in the immediate aftermath of the war during Truman's administration, and again during Johnson's and, perhaps surprisingly, Nixon's presidencies. See David Lewis, *Presidents and the Politics of Agency Design* (Stanford, CA: Stanford University Press, 2003), 42–44.

51 U.S. Constitution, Article II, section 2.

52 James Q. Wilson, "The Rise of the Bureaucratic State," *The Public Interest* 41 (1975): 77–79.

53 Carpenter, "The Evolution of the National Bureaucracy in the United States," 51.

54 Wilson, "The Rise of the Bureaucratic State," 87–88.

55 Initially these departments were headed by commissioners, not secretaries. Agriculture did not become a cabinet-level department until 1889, and Labor achieved this status only after expanding with the addition of Commerce in 1903. See Seidman and Gilmour, *Politics, Position and Power*, 252.

56 The CSC was replaced by the Office of Personnel Management in 1978.

57 For example, Congress has granted both the DoD and the DHS the authority to create their own personnel systems. See David Lewis, *The Politics of Presidential Appointments: Political Control and Bureaucratic Performance* (Princeton, NJ: Princeton University Press, 2008), 18–20.

58 Seidman and Gilmour, *Politics, Position and Power*, 249–51.

59 As Seidman and Gilmour point out, however, the ICC was initially established under the Secretary of the Interior's nominal control, and did not become a truly independent agency until 1889. See *Politics, Position and Power*, 251.

60 Wilson, "The Rise of the Bureaucratic State," 96–97.

61 Due to space constraints, I do not describe other types of executive branch entities, such as government corporations and foundations. Corporations gained prominence as early as World War I, although they did not achieve full legitimacy until the New Deal era. Examples include the Tennessee Valley Authority (TVA), and the Federal Deposit Insurance Corporation (FDIC). Typically, corporations are chartered under state law, but supervised by a federal board of directors or in some cases a cabinet secretary. They usually are responsible for generating their own operating revenue. These corporations are, by design, meant to be almost entirely immune to political control and instead function much like private entities. Seidman and Gilmour provide a useful overview of corporations and of government "foundations" such as the National Science Foundation, in their work *Politics, Positions, and Power*, 254–55.

62 Carpenter, "Evolution," 65.

63 Those characteristics include: being created outside a cabinet department; being led by a multi-member board; having directors with fixed terms of appointment; or stipulating a specific set of qualifications for agency administrators.

64 Lewis, *Presidency and the Politics of Agency Design*, 88–95.

65 Matthew J. Dickinson, *Bitter Harvest: FDR, Presidential Power and the Growth of the Presidential Branch* (New York: Cambridge University Press, 1996), 82, footnote 136.

66 The best survey of these managerial studies is Peri Arnold's *Making the Managerial Presidency: Comprehensive Reorganization Planning, 1905–96*, 2nd ed. (Lawrence, KS: University Press of Kansas, 1998).

67 FDR's predecessor, Herbert Hoover, had been granted permanent reorganization authority by Congress through the 1932 Economy Act, but Congress rescinded that grant nine months later. Thereafter presidents were given reorganization authority of limited duration, subject to a legislative veto.

68 Dickinson, *Bitter Harvest*, 86–113.

69 See *Immigration and Naturalization Service v. Chadha* (1983). For an argument for resurrecting the president's reorganization authority, see Paul Light's 2005 testimony before a subcommittee of the House's Governmental Reform Committee, http://wagner.nyu.edu/files/performance/RESTORING%20 THE%20PRESIDENT%27S%20REORGANIZATION%20AUTHORITY. pdf.

70 Under the 1947 National Security Act, which established the National Security Council, there is little mention of a national security staff. However, through the years, the staff to the NSC, under the direction of the national security adviser, has become the primary source of national security advice to the president.

71 I describe this process in some detail in my essay "The Executive Office of the President: The Paradox of Politicization," in *The Executive Branch*, eds. Joel D. Aberbach and Mark Peterson (New York: Oxford University Press, 2005), 135–73.

72 See, for example, Randy James, "A Brief History of White House Czars," *Time*, September 22, 2009, http://time.com/3516927/history-of-white-house-czars/. More generally, see Justin Vaughan and Jose Villalobos, *Czars in the White House* (Ann Arbor, MI: University of Michigan Press, 2015).

73 "Bannon Driving Force behind Trump's Hardline Immigration Ban, Officials Say," *Newsweek*, January 30, 2017, www.newsweek.com/donald-trump-steve-bannon-immigration-ban-immigration-muslim-550415.

74 Alexander Burns, "2 Federal Judges Rule against Trump's Latest Travel Ban," *New York Times*, March 15, 2017, www.nytimes.com/2017/03/15/us/politics/trump-travel-ban.html?_r=0.

75 Richard Neustadt, *Presidential Power and the Modern Presidents: The Politics of Leadership from Roosevelt to Reagan* (New York: Free Press, 1990), 279–94.

76 Jason Silverstein and Leonard Greene, "President Trump Eyes White House Staff Shakeup for Damage Control after Jared Kushner-Russia Bombshell," *New York Daily News*, May 28, 2017, www.nydailynews.com/news/politics/frustrated-trump-eyes-white-house-overhaul-russia-scandal-article-1.3201926.

77 Matthew J. Dickinson and Kathryn D. Tenpas, "The Revolving Door at the White House: Explaining Increasing Turnover Rates Among Presidential Advisers, 1929–1997," *Journal of Politics* 64 (2002): 434–48.

78 Paul Light, *Thickening Government: Federal Hierarchy and the Diffusion of Accountability* (Washington, DC: Brookings, 1995), 12.

79 The SES was created by Jimmy Carter in 1978, when he revamped the civil service system to make it more amenable to presidential influence. It consists of some 7,000 senior bureaucrats, of which about ten percent are political appointees, with the rest drawn from career civil servants. The Office of Personnel Management (OPM) allocates a fixed number of SES positions to each department, and presidents (or their appointees) decide whether to fill these

with political appointees or careerists. By law, political appointees cannot exceed ten percent of the entire SES nor 25 percent of the SES positions within a department. See Lewis, *The Politics of Presidential Appointments*, 21–24.

80 Because departments and agencies differ in size, of course, one cannot measure the depth of politicization by raw numbers alone.

81 See Paul C. Light, "Fact Sheet on the Continued Thickening of Government," *Brookings*, July 23, 2004, www.brookings.edu/research/fact-sheet-on-the-continued-thickening-of-government/.

82 Schedule C positions were initially created by Dwight Eisenhower in 1953, and at one point included upper management positions as well. Most of these were converted into SES positions in 1978.

83 In making this claim, Lewis distinguishes between political "policy" appointments, and purely "patronage" appointments. The latter, he argues, will increase in agencies that share a president's policy views.

84 See Dickinson, "The Executive Office of the President: The Paradox of Politicization."

85 Lewis, *The Politics of Presidential Appointments*, 141–71. Lewis backs up the findings from this case study with more systematic evidence based on an analysis of the performances of multiple executive branch agencies during George W. Bush's presidency.

86 Hugh Heclo, *A Government of Strangers* (Washington, DC: Brookings, 1977), 1.

87 Michael D. Shear and Matt Apuzzo, "F.B.I. Director James Comey Is Fired by Trump," *New York Times*, May 9, 2017, www.nytimes.com/2017/05/09/us/politics/james-comey-fired-fbi.html.

10 Presidents and Domestic Policy

Jeremy L. Strickler

Today, the presidency is recognized as the center of domestic policymaking. Much is expected of the president, with those in the public frequently tallying his policy successes or failures as a measurement of his political leadership and greatness. The recent tenure of President Barack Obama is instructive in this regard. Above all, Obama's most visible policy legacy is that of health care reform, an initiative that has become synonymous with the president's name. Of course, "Obamacare" was not a policy single-handedly designed and established by the President. From the decades-long push by the Democratic Party to bring health care reform to the national agenda, to the byzantine procedures of congressional lawmaking, the passage of the Affordable Care Act reflects the complex nature of policymaking in the United States, of which Obama was just one participating actor. This case, then, raises several questions about the broader dynamic between presidents and domestic policy. How has the institution of the presidency come to assume such increased expectations for policy leadership? What resources do presidents use in their capacity as policymakers? What opportunities and constraints do presidents face as they navigate the policymaking process? How might we compare and contrast presidential domestic policy leadership across modern American political history?

This chapter will explore these questions in four sections. It begins with an examination of the development of modern presidential policymaking to better appreciate both the changing resources of the institution and the increasing expectations for policy leadership. The next section traces the president's role in the policymaking process. In particular, we will survey what scholars know about how presidents attempt to realize their domestic policy agenda amid a constrained political environment. The third section introduces an alternative approach to studying the relationship between presidents and domestic policy that calls attention to the varying contextual factors that shape policymaking opportunities and constraints over time. As we will see, such a perspective takes seriously issues of historical change and presidential agency. The final section brings the various insights of the chapter together through a brief review of presidential efforts to reform health care.

The Development of Presidential Domestic Policymaking

The president's role in domestic policymaking has been anything but static through the course of American history, with the institution becoming increasingly involved in public policy over time. Writing in 1898, Henry Jones Ford observed that the framers' vision of a restrained republican executive had become "a master force in shaping public policy."[1] Ford's recognition of the agency of the office presaged aspects of what scholars have come to call "the modern presidency." While the Madisonian system may have been designed as "a government of separated institutions sharing powers,"[2] as notably described by Richard Neustadt, political and institutional developments have led to the emergence of presidency-centered government since the tenure of Franklin D. Roosevelt. This historical trend associated with the modern presidency has two implications of importance for presidential policymaking: (1) the evolving resources for the presidency to make policy and (2) the heightened expectations for the executive to pursue bold policy leadership. The origins of this modern governing reality are best illustrated by three interrelated dynamics: the rise of rhetorical presidential leadership, the changing nature of presidential-congressional relations, and the development of the institutional presidency.[3] Although not mutually exclusive, these developments can be traced in turn.

We begin with the "rhetorical presidency."[4] Consider, for a moment, why the president discusses public policy issues at all, especially politically controversial ones like abortion or gun control. Such a thought undoubtedly strikes a contemporary citizen as odd, but the founders were quite wary about the executive making direct policy appeals to the people. Moreover, many founders held deep suspicions of popular leadership, fearing it could lead to demagoguery—the act of influencing popular passions. The president, they argued, should rise above the perceived partisanship of domestic policy concerns and focus on the broader constitutional interests of the nation. However, through the pull of electoral politics, the presidency came to develop a direct relationship with the American public. As early as Thomas Jefferson and Andrew Jackson, presidents have cast themselves as the "tribune of the people" and have increasingly sought to frame their campaign victories as mandates to enact specific partisan policy agendas. In this manner, says the president, the people have expressed their desire for a course of action. Relatedly, using his "bully pulpit"—in the words of Theodore Roosevelt—the president can "go public" to promote his policy agenda, effectively bypassing intermediary actors such as Congress and political parties.[5] The contours of the "rhetorical presidency" have thus emerged alongside advances in technology, mass media, and transportation. Where FDR perfected the use of radio via his famed "fireside chats," and Kennedy connected to the public through the television airwaves, Trump now tweets directly to his supporters on a smartphone. Regardless of the method of communication, the people demand to hear the president's point of view across a range of domestic (and international) concerns.

Of course, Americans expect that presidents will not simply pay lip service to a given policy problem, but will take the lead in pursuing legislative action and countering objectionable bills. This speaks to the second important hallmark of modern presidential leadership, the "legislative presidency."[6] How did the president's legislative expectations come to be? As with the emergence of the rhetorical presidency, we can look to past precedents and institutional innovations. Constitutionally, the president is only afforded two roles in the legislative process: the veto power and the duty to provide "to the Congress Information of the State of the Union, and recommend to their Consideration such Measures as he shall judge necessary and expedient." Traditionally, use of the former was rare, with the power of the veto being utilized in cases where the president deemed the legislation to be unconstitutional. However, echoing Andrew Jackson's defense of the veto power, modern presidents often justify its use in striking down legislation solely on policy grounds. For example, Obama unsurprisingly vetoed Republican-passed legislation aimed at repealing the Affordable Care Act, his signature policy achievement.

A more significant change for presidential-congressional relations is found in the practice of proposing a legislative policy agenda.[7] In this regard, the president's constitutional obligation to report on the State of the Union has developed dramatically over the years into a highly-anticipated vision of the nation's future direction. This expectation began in earnest during the administration of Woodrow Wilson, as he saw the potential in utilizing the presidency's rhetorical authority. The former political scientist, and student of legislative affairs, argued that the president should act as a de facto prime minister by engaging with Congress to enact his policy preferences into law.[8] The progressive precedent set by Wilson came to full fruition in the presidency during the tenure of FDR and his vaunted "One Hundred Days." As Andrew Rudalevige notes, "by the time Harry Truman took office, the president's involvement in the legislative process had become a given."[9] With the benchmark set, each Congress anxiously awaits the reception of specific legislative proposals directed from the White House.

This brings us to the "institutional presidency." Due in part to the increased demands brought about through the presidency's rhetorical and legislative leadership, the institution has grown tremendously in size and form over time. The foundation of the "institutional presidency"[10] came with the establishment of the Executive Office of the President (EOP) during the FDR administration, as a result of the Reorganization Act of 1939 and the Brownlow Committee's claim that "the president needs help." Prior to this "watershed event," as John Burke describes it, the president's "help" amounted to little more than a handful of personal secretaries and clerks.[11] Today, in contrast, there are roughly 2,000 aides and associates helping the president with policymaking throughout the broader EOP and, more directly, as part of the White House staff. Along with the various units of the White House Office—such as the Domestic Policy Council, the Office of Communications, and the Office of Legislative Affairs—the EOP includes agencies such as the Council of Economic Advisors, the National Security Council, and the Office of Management and Budget. As we will see in the following section, this institutionalization "serve[s] as a springboard for the president to take on greater responsibility and involvement in leading the policy making process."[12]

Presidents and the Policy Process

Since the publication of Richard Neustadt's notable book, *Presidential Power*, scholars have continually grappled with what Hugh Heclo calls "The Big Question."[13] That is, "how do and how can presidents try to get their way in governing?" For our purposes, let us restate this into a set of questions about presidential policymaking. How successful are modern presidents in meeting their increased domestic policy expectations? What policymaking constraints do presidents confront? Under what conditions are presidents likely to achieve policy victories? To better appreciate how political scientists approach and answer such questions, this section will trace the president's leadership role in the policymaking process.[14] The concept of "the president's policy agenda" provides us an analytical lens through which to view this process. Generally, as Jeffrey Cohen defines it, "the president's policy agenda [is] the list of problems, issues, and policies to which the president has committed some attention and resources."[15] With an eye toward *domestic* policy in particular, we turn now to a look at the behaviors, strategies, and resources utilized by presidents as they seek to build and push their agenda, from the initial stage of their campaign promises to the final enactment of their policy initiatives.

Agenda-Setting

As the most visible political actor, the president has potential influence at the front end of the policy process to set the national agenda.[16] Put differently, through the media exposure gained by the rhetorical presidency, it has been found that the executive may draw attention to particular issues just by discussing them in public.[17] Unsurprisingly, the agenda-setting process often begins during the presidential campaign when the then-candidate raises policy topics while out on the hustings. As an example, consider Donald J. Trump's repeated pledges during the 2016 election to repeal the Affordable Care Act and to build a wall along the Mexican border. The specific issues a president (and candidate) chooses to promote can reflect a range of factors, including personal preference, partisan motivation, ideological commitment, and/or considerations of their historical legacy. The objective for the president, then, is to make good on his word by developing campaign pledges into a coherent domestic policy agenda. In this way, says Andrew Busch, "[t]he campaign serves as a crucial place to lay policy groundwork, and what is said (or not said) at that time sets the parameters for much of the president's subsequent domestic policymaking."[18]

While campaign promises may establish the initial "parameters" of policymaking, the president's domestic agenda encounters many obstacles on its path toward enactment. First, with an eye always on reelection for themselves and/or their party, presidents are keenly aware of how policy initiatives will be met by members (or potential members) of their electoral coalitions.[19] Additionally, as we will see below, Congress— specifically when highly polarized—poses a difficult challenge to the president's agenda. This is due in part to the fact that members of Congress often have their own agenda priorities that may not line up with those of the White House. What is more, the clock is always ticking down the days left in a president's administration and he must pick his policy priorities wisely. Finally, a president may inherit an already existing and full policy agenda.[20] Of significance are those foreign policy crises and economic calamities that come to preoccupy the time, energy, and resources of newly elected presidents. In this instance, Obama entered the presidency saddled with two wars in the Middle East and a volatile economy.

Managing Policy Development

While the president attempts to set the national agenda, he must manage the development of his administration's domestic policy initiatives. It is at this stage of the policy process that a president's domestic agenda begins to take shape and strategies for its enactment are plotted. While individual presidents bring their own unique managerial skills and leadership styles to the Oval Office,[21] the emergence of the institutional presidency poses an enduring challenge for the direction of domestic policy formulation.[22] Although modern presidents have created various structures and processes for developing policy over time, the general trend has been for policymaking to be centered in the White House staff instead of the broader executive branch. The creation and evolution of the president's Domestic Policy Council since the Richard Nixon administration illustrates this theme.[23]

Scholars point to an underlying logic and rationale for the rise of White House-centered policymaking. Terry Moe has argued that the disparity between the president's increased public expectations and the institution's limited formal authority leads presidents to centralize control of policy, to reflect the interests of the president and not those of the wider executive departments and agencies.[24] But, as Rudalevige has found in his analysis of presidential policy formulation, the trend of centralization has been "contingent" rather than linear. That is, presidents are likely to use centralization as an instrument of policy management under certain conditions, including if a policy proposal cuts across a range of various departmental jurisdictions, involves executive reorganization or personnel management, is a new issue on the president's agenda, or was proposed suddenly as a response to a crisis event.[25] Building on this notion of variation in centralization, Daniel Ponder suggests that as presidents' "leverage" increases—measured using indicators of presidential approval and public trust in the government—they are "less likely to centralize, more likely to procure innovative and complex policies, and perhaps more likely to enjoy congressional success."[26] It is to this latter issue, presidential success in Congress, that our examination of the policy process now turns.

Advancing the Legislative Policy Agenda

Naturally, a central focus in the study of presidential policymaking is to understand the dynamic between the president's agenda and Congress.[27] Research in this area asks two related questions: (1) How does the congressional context impact presidential agenda building, and (2) what skills and strategies do presidents employ to successfully achieve policy initiatives on their legislative agenda? Regarding the first perspective, scholars assess how the processes of building and formulating the president's agenda are influenced by the setting in Congress.[28] Matthew Eshbaugh-Soha, for instance, argues that the types of policies that presidents pursue reflect their surrounding political environment. He finds that a "more liberal" makeup of Congress is likely to encourage the president to advocate for a "major" policy.[29] More significantly, in a systematic examination of presidential agenda building from 1789 to 2002, Jeffrey Cohen posits that "presidents take into account the congressional environment when deciding which proposals to submit to Congress: That is, they calculate the likelihood that Congress will enact a proposal." According to this theory of "congressional anticipations," because no president wants to see their agenda suffer defeat in the legislative realm, he may deliberately modify a given proposal to increase the chances of its final passage.[30]

The claim that presidents engage in strategic behavior as they interact with Congress to pass their policy priorities speaks directly to the second, and much more robust, avenue of research on presidential-congressional relations and domestic policymaking. The overriding premise is that the president governs in a "separated system" where policymaking responsibility is shared with Congress, and limitations to exercise policy leadership are many.[31] Where political scientists once looked to the character and skill of individual presidents to assess their potential in influencing congressional lawmakers through sheer persuasion,[32] a different trajectory of scholarship emphasizes the "strategy" involved in recognizing and exploiting legislative opportunities amid various constraints.[33] As noted, several means of strategic influence, albeit somewhat limited, are the president's ability to promote his policy priorities and set the legislative agenda.[34] Moreover, presidents also attempt to sway legislators through lobbying efforts aimed at building supportive coalitions in Congress. In his study on the effects of presidential lobbying, Matthew Beckmann contends that presidents have two main strategies before them during the legislative process: one at the "endgame" of voting, the other at the "earlygame" of agenda setting. Rather than "engage in knock-down, drag-out floor fights" for the final necessary votes on his preferred bill, the president

> can rally leading allies' support and strike a 'deal' with opposing leaders in the legislative earlygame, ... [and] actually sign into law a bill more to his liking than would have been possible by just waging an endgame offensive for aye votes.

The use of this lobbying strategy was on display during the early months of the George W. Bush administration as the President and his associates sought to build a congressional coalition for their 2001 tax cut legislation.[35] While the example of Bush's 2001 tax cut illustrates the presidential desire to "win" in Congress, the institution of the presidency provides alternative routes for the realization of domestic policy.

Implementing the President's Policy Agenda

Even as a president begins the formidable task of developing his legislative strategy, he enters the office on day one with the constitutional power and administrative resources to implement his domestic agenda through other means.[36] As the nation's executive, the president is responsible for directing the implementation and administration of existing public policy, which includes considerable tools such as regulatory enforcement and rulemaking. So, of course, some of the first decisions that newly elected presidents need to make are those regarding personnel and appointments of policy positions throughout the bureaucracy.[37] Although a president may select his appointees for a number of reasons, such as patronage, expertise, and professional reputation, there is a modern tendency within the institution to "politicize" the executive branch by placing individuals loyal to the president's preferred policy objectives in key positions.[38] Ronald Reagan notably tasked his director of the Office of Personnel Management with educating "incoming cabinet members and other political leaders on the new political theory of administration" embraced by the President.[39] Scholars note, however, that choosing presidential loyalists over more "neutral" careerist bureaucrats may ultimately be counterproductive and stymie the successful implementation of the president's agenda.[40]

Beyond the appointment power, presidents also rely on the use of "unilateral power" to further their domestic policy aims.[41] Through unilateral action, presidential policymaking can occur in the form of presidential directives, memoranda, signing statements, and executive orders. Regardless of the method chosen, such policy instruments allow presidents to effectively make law, especially if confronted with a hostile legislative environment. Although, research on the use of executive orders during divided government, in particular, suggests variation in both the type of policy order issued[42] and the president's inclination toward unilateral action over time.[43] Scholars also note, however, the limitations of these tools of the presidency. First, rather than establishing new laws through unilateral means, presidents must justify their use according to existing constitutional or statutory law. For example, Obama, facing an opposition Congress and a Democratic base pushing for action on the minimum wage, issued an executive order in 2014 directed at increasing the wage for federal contractors to a minimum of $10.10 an hour. While his critics accused him of executive overreach, the President claimed the authority to take such action through current law—the Federal Property and Administrative Services Act.[44] Second, as Rudalevige observes, during both the formulation and implementation stage of executive orders, presidents must "persuade" executive branch actors to follow their policy directives instead of "commanding" that they do so. More specifically, by focusing on the implementation process—the "aftermath"—of a president's issuance of an executive order, we become attuned to the "realities of intrabranch policy making."[45] Notwithstanding these constraints, a president may ultimately come to use unilateral action as they enter "the last one hundred days" of their administration and attempt to either assist or hinder their successor's policy prospects while also solidifying their own domestic policy legacy.[46]

Historical Patterns and Variations in Presidential Domestic Policy Leadership

As we have seen, much has been gained by analyzing the general strategic behavior of presidents and their use of institutional resources in their attempts to realize a domestic policy agenda amid a highly constrained political setting. But when we broaden our analytical perspective we come to recognize that individual presidents have confronted different policymaking environments over the course of American political history, and these environments affect presidential policy leadership. A historical approach to understanding the president's role in policymaking emphasizes the ways in which presidential action at the various stages of the policymaking process are influenced by a variety of contextual factors over time. In this way, the nature of presidential policy success "is shaped in disparate fields of action by the contours of each ground upon which presidents must maneuver."[47] In other words, the dynamic of presidential policymaking neither follows the linear process that scholars have often used to evaluate presidential success nor does it occur in a uniform context across administrations. From the disruptions of the Great Depression and the War on Terror, to the partisan makeup of the 80th Congress and the enduring appeal of conservative ideology, the surrounding political structure through which presidents pursue domestic policy objectives has changed dramatically. Yet, even among the seemingly chaotic nature of history, key historical patterns and variations in the dynamic between presidents, policymaking, and the American political system have been identified.

One way to analyze the effect of the policymaking environment is by considering how amenable it is to a president's efforts. Traditionally, scholars have singled out presidents who were afforded greater, or broader, opportunities than their peers for the prospects of policymaking. Such "high-opportunity" presidents as FDR, Lyndon Johnson, and Reagan shared similar conditions regarding the public mood, their approval rating, the legislative setting, the amount of promising issues on the agenda, and influences in the economic, budgetary, and international arena. Of course, on the other end of the spectrum are those narrow, or "low-opportunity," presidents like Richard Nixon, Jimmy Carter, George H.W. Bush, and Bill Clinton.[48] As Daniel Tichenor notes, whether a president encounters a "broad or narrow" opportunity to assert policy leadership can significantly affect their relationship with organized interest groups. Productive relations with such groups can lead to increased fundraising and expanded support for the president's agenda. Strained relations, on the other hand, can be a constant source of policy resistance. For example, while FDR and Reagan were successful at relegating the domestic agendas of rival interest groups to the political sidelines, Carter and Clinton had no such luck. As we will see in greater detail in the section below, Clinton's attempt at health care reform was scuttled in large part by the extremely organized campaigns of opponents in the insurance industry and the conservative grassroots. According to Tichenor, Clinton's experience is a case in point of the potential pitfalls awaiting presidents with narrow capacity in the policy realm: "When presidents do not dominate the policymaking process, oppositional groups will play a significant role in helping to set the public agenda and shape new policy initiatives."[49]

Despite the environmental factors faced by presidents, their ability to realize their objectives is not simply determined from without. Presidential agency can respond to a given context more or less effectively. Lest one think that modern executives, and their policymaking possibilities, are ultimately captive to the surrounding political environment, recent scholarship has sought to probe the underlying dynamics of the president's "opportunity structure," revealing the complex interplay between presidential agency and its external constraints.[50] Research in this vein has produced two interrelated insights relevant to the study of presidential policymaking over time: (1) the reality of change, and (2) the efficacy of presidential leadership. First, because there are many factors that comprise the context in which a president governs, the overall opportunity structure is constantly in flux throughout one's time in office. In other words, the policymaking environment is never static. In this regard, presidents should understand their political terrain as a "river," says Andrew Polsky. "Though from a distance it appears to follow the same course, those who navigate it realize that it is always changing and thus always requiring adjustments to avoid new hazards."[51] A president may come to office with the clearest of objectives but, inevitably, political events and crises emerge, bringing with them potential shifts in policy direction. Emotional policy problems come to the fore, like drug abuse under Reagan or mass gun violence under Obama. Elections are held, and partisan control of Congress swings across the aisle. Economic recessions take hold and budgets became strained. And, most significantly, international conflicts and wars arise. To this latter point, Polsky elsewhere has argued that when the domestic problems of war become too great "any president, liberal or conservative, will find policy victories scarce for the remainder of his term."[52] Yet, even then, a president with policy ambition may not cease in their quest for reform but strategize how to "link" their domestic and foreign policy commitments on the national agenda.[53] Regardless of the way the "river" flows, presidents must be ready to fight the current.

This leads to the second insight into the relationship between the president's opportunity structure and public policymaking. Presidential leadership plays a significant role in navigating through the challenges that arise during the policymaking process, and it also can have an impact on the policy environment itself. In contrast to viewing "presidential acts or fates [as] predetermined," taking stock of the pressures, limitations, and various other contextual factors with which a president must contend "is a prerequisite to assessing the intentions, strategies, and records of presidents" as they navigate the policy realm.[54] In this way, scholars have discerned specific patterns and variations in presidential behavior, particularly concerning policy choice and policy leadership. For starters, Daniel Galvin has examined how the context of electoral competition, at times, shapes the domestic policy approach of the president.[55] The variation in policy choice depends on the "competitive standing" of the president's party. That is, does the president view his party as being in the national minority or majority, and thus, electorally weak or strong, respectively? As Galvin argues, minority-party presidents are motivated, among other things, to "design policies that expand their party's appeal."

In contrast, the charge of majority-party presidents is to "exploit their party's electoral advantages and translate its basic commitments into public policies." George W. Bush's pursuit of education reform early on in his administration illustrates the "policy accommodation" approach of the former dynamic, while his push for Social Security reform after his 2004 reelection captures the "combative" position of the latter. This shift in Bush's perception of his "competitive political environment" from his first term to his second term further demonstrates the ebb and flow of a president's opportunity structure, as discussed above.[56]

Unfortunately, for most contemporary presidents, Bush's failed attempt to reform Social Security represents the norm, rather than the exception, when bold policy change is attempted. (There's a reason, after all, why Social Security is referred to as the "third rail" of American politics.) Given the preponderance of failed policy initiatives, an examination of the occasions where presidents have been successful in attaining landmark legislative victories is instructive. As Bruce Miroff wisely observes,

> [n]ot all of these victories, however, have similar origins, dynamics, or ultimate satisfactions for presidents. It is important to distinguish policy victories where presidents deserve full credit as entrepreneurial innovators from victories where the lion's share of credit belongs to other political actors or groups...[57]

Along these lines, Miroff classifies three patterns of presidential leadership in domestic policymaking: entrepreneurial initiation, policy responsiveness, and credit claiming.[58] A brief look at these three patterns is in order.

FDR's passage of the Social Security Act and George W. Bush's success with the No Child Left Behind (NCLB) education reform typify the first pattern identified by Miroff. In this regard, policymaking through entrepreneurial initiation is marked by the president's personal and stated preference in pursuing the policy in question, his committed involvement in both the policy development and policy promotion stages, and his willingness to reach compromises to ensure the legislation's final approval. Alternatively, the pattern of policy responsiveness is reflected in the examples of FDR and the National Labor Relations Act and John F. Kennedy and the Civil Rights Act. Through this type of leadership, the president's role in policy development is one of reaction, as he responds to the increasing demands of his party's coalitional members. While the president may express some rhetorical interest in the stated policy change, his initial legislative approach is one of general reservation. In the end, the president comes to support a more robust piece of legislation, in large part to quell the growing political distraction.

The third type of policy leadership, credit claiming, is a purely strategic tactic employed by presidents in their struggle against political opponents. Nixon's environmental legislation and Clinton's crime bill are two cases in point. In this pattern of domestic policymaking, the president's past record does not indicate strong support for the issue at hand. Moreover, the policy concern "may be peripheral to the president's agenda, perhaps reflecting personal ambivalence or even distaste."[59] Still, in an attempt to co-opt his rivals' objectives, and reap potential electoral benefits in the process, the president shifts his support to "score the win" on landmark legislation. As we will see below, the pursuit of health care reform—the pinnacle of landmark legislation—has bedeviled presidents for a generation. A brief glimpse at the politics behind this domestic policy illuminates continuities and changes in presidential policymaking.

Presidents and the Politics of Health Care Reform

To better appreciate patterns and variations in presidential policymaking over time, we can look at how different executives approached health care policy. Since the 1930s, every president, to some degree, has entertained the idea of reforming health care in the United States. Of course, many more presidents have experienced failure rather than success, and each episode of reform has been fraught with political tensions and blowups. Because of its ever-present presidential attention, health policy is a fitting "lens" through which to view both the skills of individual presidents and the political dynamics of presidential domestic policy leadership.[60] This section briefly examines the reform efforts of Democrats Harry Truman, Bill Clinton, and Barack Obama, asking a set of interrelated questions: (1) How did health care emerge on the political agenda and how significant was the issue for the president's domestic agenda? (2) How did the president manage the development and promotion of his administration's legislative proposal? (3) What impact did the broader political environment have on the end result of the health care initiative?

Truman and National Health Insurance

While FDR never publicly endorsed health insurance as a plank of his New Deal domestic reform agenda, he did hope to pursue the issue once World War II came to an end. In asserting what is often referred to as the "Second Bill of Rights" in his January 1944 Message to Congress, FDR recognized as "self-evident ... the right to adequate medical care and the opportunity to achieve and enjoy good health."[61] Only a few months after the death of FDR, Truman would directly quote this line from his predecessor when he made history, sending a special message to Congress calling for a comprehensive health program, including prepayment of medical costs through compulsory insurance. Although legislation for national health insurance had first been introduced by a group of congressmen in 1943, Truman's efforts, while limited, represent the origins of subsequent presidential commitments to health policy reform in modern American politics.

Not long after Truman's initial call for national health insurance, the Republicans took control of Congress in the 1946 midterm elections and refused to hold hearings on the existing legislation. In an attempt to show his continued commitment to reform, Truman sent another special message to Congress in May 1947, specifically on the topic of "health and disability insurance," proclaiming that a health program was "crucial to our national welfare." Without compulsory health insurance as "a part of our national fabric, we shall be wasting our most precious national resource and shall be perpetuating unnecessary misery and human suffering."[62] Again, there was little movement on the legislative front. However, in the 1948 presidential campaign, Truman would make health insurance a key theme. With his upset victory over Thomas E. Dewey in that campaign, Truman once more renewed his call for a comprehensive health program. While it was met with a legislative firewall erected by congressional conservatives, the plan also faced unprecedented resistance by the American Medical Association (AMA).[63] In fact, the medical lobby hired a public relations firm and spent over $1 million vigorously opposing Truman's objective, framing it as "socialized medicine"—a charge that carried much more weight as the Korean War began in the fall of 1950. Confronted with such obstacles, Truman's request for Congress to take up a program of national health insurance was a nonstarter. Reflecting on his effort, Truman wrote that he never could quite "understand all the fuss some people make about government wanting to do something to improve and protect the health of the people."[64]

Clinton and the Health Security Act

When Bill Clinton announced his presidential candidacy in Little Rock, Arkansas in October 1991, he pledged that if elected he would "present a plan to Congress and the American people to provide affordable, quality health care for all Americans."[65] Throughout the ensuing election, Clinton proceeded to make health care a signature issue of his campaign agenda and would interpret his victory as a mandate from the people to pursue reform. Although only elected with 43 percent of the vote, Clinton entered the White House with Democratic majorities in both houses of Congress—60 percent in the House and 57 percent in the Senate—creating initial optimism for legislative success. However, from the beginning, missteps were made that ultimately doomed the prospects for policy reform.

First, and most crucially, the Clinton administration dragged its feet during a heavily centralized, and seemingly secretive, policy formulation process. The president placed his wife, Hillary Rodham Clinton, and friend, Ira Magaziner, in charge of a controversial task force that operated in private, failing to appropriately include members of Congress and concerned interest groups in their deliberations. Over 250 days after the process began, the task force revealed their plan for "managed competition." Titled the American Health Security Act, the legislation called for private insurance companies to compete for customers in a highly regulated market, while also requiring employer mandates for coverage. While the delay in sending the proposal to Congress would prove costly, mounting resistance to the plan intensified its reception in the public, with the media bemoaning the lack of transparency and inefficiency of the task force.[66]

More importantly, as mentioned above, there was an intense opposition campaign from the beginning led by the healthcare industry and the health insurance industry, both with substantial ties to conservative grassroots constituencies. Notably, the Health Insurance Association of America (HIAA) funded television ads touting the bill's flaws, while the "Christian Coalition, anti-tax groups, and a variety of other conservative interest groups [invested] ... new resources into the effort to kill health care reform."[67] Attempting to counter the narrative, Clinton tried to sell the Health Security Act to the American people by "going public" through a series of television town hall forums, to no avail.[68] Facing budgetary constraints and other items on the agenda, such as free trade, tax credits, and medical leave, and combined with the organized resistance, Clinton's health care plan was officially pronounced dead by the Senate leadership in the middle of 1994. That fall, riding the wave of opposition, Republicans would take back control of Congress, foreclosing any chance of the bill's revival.

Obama and the Affordable Care Act

Although Obama had slowly warmed to the issue of health care reform through the months-long process of the 2008 Democratic primary, by the time his presidency began, he was prepared to push for the domestic policy objective that had escaped presidents for a generation. Determined not to squander the opportunity to usher in the "hope and change" he had campaigned on—validated in his eyes through the 53 percent of the vote won during the election—Obama pressed ahead with health care, adding it to a list of commitments that included winding down two wars in the Middle East and economic recovery. As the centerpiece of the president's domestic agenda, the challenge was to develop legislation that addressed two dramatic problems with the nation's health care: a staggering 46 million uninsured and the rising costs of coverage.[69]

With Clinton's experience of the Health Security Act squarely in mind, the Obama administration employed two strategies at the outset. First, the President set out to bring potential opposition groups into the fold. This included holding private initial meetings with lobbyists and executives from the pharmaceutical industry regarding drug prices and striking a deal with the hospital industry on revenue limits. Moreover, both the AMA and the American Health Insurance Plans (AHIP) withheld their opposition, favoring instead the prospect of increased revenues.[70] While the bargain stuck between the administration and the drug companies did not sit well with the Democratic Party's liberal base, the President pushed forward with another strategy aimed at increasing the chances of legislative success.

Besides reaching out to interest groups, Obama also deviated from Clinton's attempt at health care reform by not sending up White House-formulated legislation to Congress, rather letting the House and Senate take charge of devising a bill. Yet, divisions soon emerged over the proposal to add a public insurance option, with the two chambers passing competing bills. Compounding this problem was the surprising loss of a special Senate election in Massachusetts, which foreclosed the potential for a filibuster-proof majority in the Senate, leading the Obama administration and congressional leaders to regroup in winter, 2010. Finally, through the use of a legislative procedure called reconciliation, the House and Senate passed legislation without any Republican support that, although lacked the "public option," mandated insurance coverage for all Americans, created health insurance exchanges, expanded access to Medicaid, and prevented the denial of coverage based on pre-existing health conditions. The passage of the Affordable Care Act was a significant policy victory for Obama and the Democratic Party. But as we have seen in recent years, and in recent months, the future prospects of this legislation, and Obama's domestic policy legacy, are yet to be determined.[71]

Conclusion

As way of concluding our look at presidential policymaking, let us briefly consider the domestic policy leadership of Trump's young administration, with an understanding that doing so at such an early stage offers us only provisional insights. Throughout the 2016 campaign, Trump stressed that repealing the Affordable Care Act would be one of his top priorities upon taking office. Thus far, however, the President has found it difficult to do so, resulting in a slow start to advancing his broader domestic agenda. Trump's failure to realize any significant legislative victories in his first 100 days in office reflects, in part, the constraints of the surrounding policymaking environment. First, Trump won the presidency without securing a majority of the popular vote and entered the White House amid a highly polarized country. Moreover, even though Republicans control the levers of power in Congress, the party remains internally divided, thus creating a challenge for the President in his attempts to build a legislative coalition. While Democrats are also divided, there has emerged a strong grassroots opposition to Trump's agenda. Compounding these problems, Trump and his administration have been slow to fill many key vacancies throughout the executive branch and have faced controversies regarding staffing decisions.

However, despite these constraints—or because of them—Trump has utilized the presidency's institutional resources to act on his agenda through alternative means. Like his recent predecessors, he has relied heavily on unilateral action and the administrative presidency to strike out on his own early on and to begin rolling back policies put in place under Obama. While Trump's opportunity for bold policy leadership may seem limited at the moment, as we learned above, the contours of the policymaking context are ever changing. Consider, for instance, how the 2018 midterm elections, a resurgent economy, or a sudden crisis event might impact his domestic agenda prospects. What is more, congressional Republicans may come to pass their alternative to Obamacare, building the foundation for Trump to establish his own domestic policy legacy.

Notes

1 Richard Ellis, *The Development of the American Presidency* (New York: Routledge, 2012), xx.
2 Richard Neustadt, *Presidential Power and the Modern Presidents: The Politics of Leadership from Roosevelt to Reagan* (New York: Free Press, 1990), 372.
3 For an in-depth account of these historical developments see Ellis, *Development of the American Presidency*. Relatedly, Andrew Rudalevige briefly describes these "research areas" in presidential studies. See Rudalevige, "Presidential Authority in a Separated System of Governance," in *New Directions in American Politics*, ed. Raymond J. La Raja (New York: Routledge, 2013), 64–68.
4 Often the "rhetorical presidency" and "public presidency" are used interchangeably. On the origins of the "rhetorical presidency" see Jeffrey Tulis, *The Rhetorical Presidency* (Princeton, NJ: Princeton University Press, 1987); and Richard Ellis, ed., *Speaking to the People: The Rhetorical Presidency in Historical Perspective* (Amherst, MA: University of Massachusetts Press, 1998). For the "public presidency" and "plebiscitary presidency" see Samuel Kernell, *Going Public: New Strategies of Presidential Leadership*, 4th ed. (Washington, DC: CQ Press, 2007); Theodore Lowi, *The Personal Presidency: Power Invested, Promise Unfulfilled* (Ithaca, NY: Cornell University Press, 1987); and Barbara Hinckley, *The Symbolic Presidency: How Presidents Portray Themselves* (New York: Routledge, 1990).
5 Kernell, *Going Public*.
6 See Stephen J. Wayne, *The Legislative Presidency* (New York: Harper & Row, 1978).
7 See Jeffrey E. Cohen, *The President's Legislative Policy Agenda, 1789–2002* (New York: Cambridge University Press, 2012).
8 See Ellis, *Development of the American Presidency*, 183–186.
9 Andrew Rudalevige, *Managing the President's Program: Presidential Leadership and Legislative Policy Formulation* (Princeton, NJ: Princeton University Press, 2002), 43.
10 See John P. Burke, *The Institutional Presidency*, 2nd ed. (Baltimore, MD: Johns Hopkins University Press, 2000).

11 Burke, *Institutional Presidency*, 3.
12 Justin S. Vaughn and Jose D. Villalobos, "White House Staff," in *New Directions in the American Presidency*, ed. Lori Cox Han (New York: Routledge, 2011), 123.
13 Hugh Heclo, "Whose Presidency Is It Anyway?" in *The Oxford Handbook of the American Presidency*, eds. George C. Edwards and William G. Howell (New York: Oxford University Press, 2011), 774.
14 For examples of books using the policymaking process as lens for studying presidential leadership see Steven A. Shull, ed. *Presidential Policymaking: An End-Of-Century Assessment* (Armonk, NY: M.E. Sharpe, 1999); and Erwin C. Hargrove and Michael Nelson, *Presidents, Politics, and Policy* (New York: Knopf, 1984).
15 Cohen, *President's Legislative Policy Agenda*, 20–21. See also Paul C. Light, *The President's Agenda: Domestic Policy Choice from Kennedy to Carter* (Baltimore, MD: Johns Hopkins University Press, 1982); and Rudalevige, *Managing the President's Program*.
16 See John W. Kingdon, *Agendas, Alternatives, and Public Policies*, 2nd ed. (Boston, MA: Longman, 2011); Frank R. Baumgartner and Bryan D. Jones, *Agendas and Instability in American Politics*, 2nd ed., (Chicago, IL: University of Chicago Press, 2009); and Roger W. Cobb and Charles D. Elder, *Participation in American Politics: The Dynamics of Agenda-Building* (Boston, MA: Allyn and Bacon, 1972).
17 See Jeffrey E. Cohen, *Presidential Responsiveness and Public Policymaking: The Public and the Policies that Presidents Choose* (Ann Arbor, MI: University of Michigan Press, 1997); and George C. Edwards III, *On Deaf Ears: The Limits of the Bully Pulpit* (New Haven, CT: Yale University Press, 2003).
18 Andrew E. Busch, "Domestic Policy from Campaigning to Governing," in *Governing at Home: The White House and Domestic Policymaking*, eds. Michael Nelson and Russell Riley (Lawrence, KS: University Press of Kansas, 2011), 28.
19 See Martin A. Levin, Daniel DiSalvo, and Martin M. Shapiro, eds., *Building Coalitions, Making Policy: The Politics of the Clinton, Bush, and Obama Presidencies* (Baltimore, MD: Johns Hopkins University Press, 2012).
20 See Charles O. Jones, *The Presidency in a Separated System* (Washington, DC: Brookings, 1994); Light, *President's Agenda*.
21 For a perspective on individual leadership styles see Fred Greenstein, *The Presidential Difference: Leadership Style from FDR to Barack Obama*, 3rd ed. (Princeton, NJ: Princeton University Press, 2009).
22 Shirley Anne Warshaw, *The Domestic Presidency: Policy Making in the White House* (Boston, MA: Allyn and Bacon, 1997).
23 See Warshaw; Richard P. Nathan, *The Plot That Failed: Nixon and the Administrative Presidency* (New York: John Wiley, 1975); and Karen M. Hult and Charles E. Walcott, "Domestic Policy Development in the White House," in *Governing at Home: The White House and Domestic Policymaking*, eds. Michael Nelson and Russell Riley (Lawrence, KS: University Press of Kansas, 2004).
24 Terry Moe, "The Politicized Presidency," in *The New Direction in American Politics*, eds. John E. Chubb and Paul E. Peterson (Washington, DC: Brookings, 1985).
25 Rudalevige, *Managing the President's Program*, 87.
26 Daniel E. Ponder, "Presidential Leverage and the Politics of Policy Formulation," *Presidential Studies Quarterly* 42 (2012): 300–323, 301.
27 For an overview of this literature see Cohen, *President's Legislative Policy Agenda*; and Matthew N. Beckmann, *Pushing the Agenda: Presidential*

Leadership in U.S. Lawmaking, 1953–2004 (New York: Cambridge University Press, 2010).

28 See Cohen, *President's Legislative Policy Agenda*; Light, *President's Agenda*; and Jeremy Gelman, Gilad Wilkenfeld, and E. Scott Adler, "The Opportunistic President: How U.S. Presidents Determine Their Legislative Programs," *Legislative Studies Quarterly* 40 (2015): 363–390.

29 Matthew Eshbaugh-Soha, "The Politics of Presidential Agendas," *Political Research Quarterly* 58 (2005): 257–268; 260, 266. Eshbaugh-Soha defines a "major" policy as initiatives that "were slated to be active for more than four years and when applicable, had substantial allocation of funds."

30 Cohen, *President's Legislative Policy Agenda*, 4.

31 Jones, *Presidency in a Separated System*. See also Mark A. Peterson, *Legislating Together: The White House and Capitol Hill from Eisenhower to Reagan* (Cambridge, MA: Harvard University Press, 1990).

32 Neustadt, *Presidential Power*.

33 See George C. Edwards III, *At the Margins: Presidential Leadership of Congress* (New Haven, CT: Yale University Press, 1989).

34 See George C. Edwards III and Andrew Barrett, "Presidential Agenda Setting Congress," in *Polarized Politics: Congress and the President in a Partisan Era*, eds. Jon R. Bond and Richard Fleisher (Washington, DC: CQ Press, 2000); Andrew W. Barrett and Matthew Eshbaugh-Soha, "Presidential Success on the Substance of Legislation," *Political Research Quarterly* 60 (2007): 195–222; Peterson, *Legislating Together*.

35 Beckmann, *Pushing the Agenda*, 66–67.

36 Steven A. Shull, *Policy by Other Means: Alternative Adoption by Presidents* (College Station, TX: Texas A&M University Press, 2006).

37 See James Pfiffner, *The Strategic Presidency: Hitting the Ground Running*, 2nd ed. (Lawrence, KS: University Press of Kansas, 1996).

38 Moe, "The Politicized Presidency." Also, see Richard P. Nathan, *The Administrative Presidency* (New York: John Wiley, 1983); and Nathan, *The Plot That Failed*.

39 Quote found in Busch, "Domestic Policy from Campaigning to Governing," 34.

40 See William G. Resh, *Rethinking the Administrative Presidency: Trust, Intellectual Capital, and Appointee-Careerist Relations in the George W. Bush Administration* (Baltimore, MD: Johns Hopkins University Press, 2015).

41 See William G. Howell, *Power without Persuasion* (Princeton, NJ: Princeton University Press, 2003); Kenneth Mayer, *With the Stroke of a Pen* (Princeton, NJ: Princeton University Press, 2001); Phillip Cooper, *By Order of the President: The Use and Abuse of Executive Direct Action* (Lawrence, KS: University Press of Kansas, 2002).

42 Jeffrey A. Fine and Adam L. Warber, "Circumventing Adversity: Executive Orders and Divided Government," *Presidential Studies Quarterly* 42 (2012): 256–274.

43 Alexander Bolton and Sharece Thrower, "Legislative Capacity and Executive Unilateralism," *American Journal of Political Science* 60 (2016): 649–663.

44 Ellis, *Development of the American Presidency*, 280–283.

45 Andrew Rudalevige, "Executive Orders and Presidential Unilateralism," *Presidential Studies Quarterly* 42 (2012): 138–160; 157.

46 William G. Howell and Kenneth Mayer, "The Last One Hundred Days," *Presidential Studies Quarterly* 35 (2005): 533–553.

47 Bruce Miroff, *Presidents on Political Ground: Leaders in Action and What They Face* (Lawrence, KS: University Press of Kansas, 2016), 162.

48 For variations on this theme see William Lammers and Michael Genovese, *The Presidency and Domestic Policy* (Washington, DC: CQ Press, 2000); and Hargrove and Nelson, *Presidents, Politics, and Policy*.

49 Daniel J. Tichenor, "The Presidency and Interest Groups: Allies, Adversaries, and Policy Leadership," in *The Presidency and the Political System*, 10th ed., ed. Michael Nelson (Washington, DC: CQ Press, 2014), 279.

50 See Stephen Skowronek's groundbreaking work on this concept. Skowronek, *The Politics Presidents Make: Leadership from John Adams to Bill Clinton* (Cambridge, MA: Belknap Press, 1997); and *Presidential Leadership in Political Time: Reprise and Reappraisal*, 2nd ed. (Lawrence, KS: University Press of Kansas, 2011). Also, for an elaboration on the concept see Andrew J. Polsky, "Shifting Currents: Dwight Eisenhower and the Dynamic of Presidential Opportunity Structure," *Presidential Studies Quarterly* 45 (2015): 91–109.

51 Polsky, "Shifting Currents," 92.

52 Polsky, *Elusive Victories: The American Presidency at War* (New York: Oxford University Press, 2012).

53 Jeremy Strickler, "Visions of National Strength: The Modern Presidency and the Politics of Linkage," Paper presented at the annual meeting of the American Political Science Association, Philadelphia, PA, September 1–4, 2016.

54 Miroff, *Presidents on Political Ground*, 6.

55 Daniel Galvin, "The Dynamics of Presidential Policy Choice and Promotion," in *Building Coalitions, Making Policy: The Politics of the Clinton, Bush, and Obama Presidencies*, eds. Martin A. Levin, Daniel DiSalvo, and Martin M. Shapiro (Baltimore, MD: Johns Hopkins University Press, 2012), 312.

56 Galvin, "The Dynamics of Presidential Policy Choice and Promotion," 312, 321–324.

57 Miroff, *Presidents on Political Ground*, 160.

58 Ibid., 99–125.

59 Ibid., 123.

60 David Blumenthal and James A. Morone, *The Heart of Power: Health and Politics in the Oval Office* (Berkeley, CA: University of California Press, 2009), 3.

61 Franklin D. Roosevelt, "State of the Union Message to Congress, January 11, 1944," The American Presidency Project, www.presidency.ucsb.edu/ws/?pid=16518.

62 Harry S. Truman, "Special Message to the Congress on Health and Disability Insurance, May 19, 1947," The American Presidency Project, www.presidency.ucsb.edu/ws/?pid=12892.

63 See Monte Poen, *Harry S. Truman versus the Medical Lobby* (Columbia, MO: University of Missouri Press, 1979).

64 Harry S. Truman, *Memoirs, Volume Two: Years of Trial and Hope* (Garden City, NY: Doubleday, 1956), 17.

65 Bill Clinton, "Announcement Speech from Little Rock, AR, October 3, 1991," www.4president.org/speeches/1992/billclinton1992announcement.htm.

66 Carol S. Weissert and William G. Weissert, *Governing Health: The Politics of Health Policy* (Baltimore, MD: Johns Hopkins University Press, 1996), 93–95.

67 Tichenor, "The Presidency and Interest Groups," 290.

68 Weissert and Weissert, *Governing Health*, 66.

69 Barack Obama, "Why We Need Health Care Reform," *New York Times*, August 15, 2009, www.nytimes.com/2009/08/16/opinion/16obama.html.

70 Tichenor, "The Presidency and Interest Groups," 294–295.

71 Barbara Sinclair, "Doing Big Things: Obama and the 111th Congress," in *The Obama Presidency: Appraisals and Prospects*, eds. Bert A. Rockman, Andrew Rudalevige, and Colin Campbell (Washington, DC: CQ Press, 2012).

11 Presidents and Foreign Policy

Meena Bose

"The Constitution ... is an invitation to struggle for the privilege of directing American foreign policy."[1] This fundamental insight about American foreign policy making from Edward S. Corwin is as relevant in the twenty-first century as it was when the framers of the Constitution drafted the document in 1787. The Constitution of the United States grants shared power to the legislative and executive branches to make foreign policy—for example, Congress has the power to declare war, but the president is Commander in Chief of the armed forces; the president may negotiate treaties with foreign powers, but they require approval from two-thirds of the Senate for ratification; the president appoints Ambassadors to represent the United States abroad, but they require confirmation by the Senate with a majority vote. The two branches must cooperate to define and pursue American foreign-policy interests, even though their perspectives sometimes come into conflict with each other.

While the U.S. system of separation of powers and checks and balances gives both Congress and the presidency a voice in foreign policy, the chief executive bears the primary responsibility for shaping, negotiating, and conveying U.S. priorities abroad. The many constitutional roles granted to the president mandate leadership in foreign affairs. As Clinton Rossiter writes, the president serves as Chief of State, Chief Executive, Chief Diplomat, Commander in Chief, and Chief Legislator.[2] Each role demands executive initiative to represent the United States abroad and guide domestic agencies and institutions, including Congress, in deciding how to address other nations' interests and expectations of the United States.

The constitutional preeminence of the president in foreign policy has become more pronounced with the rise of the United States as a global superpower. After World War II, the United States did not shift its focus inward as it did after World War I. Instead, the United States played a highly significant role in rebuilding Western Europe with the Marshall Plan, in protecting its allies from the advance of communism through the creation of the North Atlantic Treaty Organization (NATO), and in assisting developing countries through the creation of such organizations as the World Bank and International Monetary Fund. When Richard E. Neustadt first published his classic analysis of the workings of presidential power in 1960, he included "abroad" as one of the president's constituencies, along with executive officials, party members, Congress, and the public at large.[3] Neustadt did not explain who comprised "abroad," leaders of other nations or foreign publics, or both, but his recognition of the importance of foreign constituencies for presidential power indicated the chief executive's leadership in foreign policy.

In addition to the constitutional responsibilities that the president and Congress have in foreign policy, other agencies and actors participate in the process as well. Cabinet officials, such as the secretaries of State and Defense (originally War), serve as the president's top advisers in international affairs. The National Security Act of 1947 created the modern-day Department of Defense, the National Security Council, the Central Intelligence Agency, and the Joint Chiefs of Staff to assist the chief executive in the development of national security policy.[4] The creation a few years later of the special assistant to the president in national security affairs position, popularly known today as the national security adviser, centralized the foreign policy-making process in the White House. How presidents manage the diverse advisory and political resources at their disposal will significantly influence their prospects for achieving their policy goals.

This chapter evaluates the evolution of the presidency in foreign policy making and the consequences for twenty-first-century governance. It begins by examining the constitutional debates about executive and legislative responsibilities in foreign affairs. (The judiciary plays an important role in modern American politics in defining the boundaries of institutional power in foreign affairs, and its contributions are discussed later in the chapter.) Next, the chapter traces the development of American foreign policy interests as defined by presidents, from George Washington into the twentieth century.

The chapter then examines changing presidential priorities in foreign affairs from the Cold War through the post-Cold War era, focusing particularly on consequences of the Korean and Vietnam Wars. It next turns to the expansion of executive initiative in foreign affairs in the post-9/11 world, with case studies of the George W. Bush and Barack Obama presidencies, and a brief look at the early months of the Donald J. Trump presidency. The chapter concludes by assessing the prospects for and challenges of continued presidential preeminence in foreign affairs in the twenty-first century.

Constitutional Framework for Foreign Policy

When the framers drafted the Constitution, they made Congress the first branch of government because it would represent the people most closely through districts in the House and states in the Senate. The president and vice president would be the only nationally elected leaders, and the executive branch would follow legislative direction in policy making. At the same time, by creating separate institutions, the framers ensured that the president would have the platform as well as the authority to define the national interest and represent U.S. interests to other nations. As Neustadt famously wrote, the Constitution "created a government of separated institutions *sharing* powers."[5]

The constitutional foreign-policy power that has sparked the most debate over executive-legislative authority is the power to declare war. In Article I, Section 8, the Constitution clearly states that "The Congress shall have Power to ... declare War."[6] Initially, the Constitution had stated that Congress would have the power to "make war," but the framers decided that the president should be able to act quickly to protect the country in times of national emergency—as James Madison and Elbridge Gerry explained, "to repel sudden attacks."[7] Granting the legislative branch the war power marked a break with the British form of government, in which all powers for war making and foreign affairs rested with the monarch. Giving Congress this power ensured that the president would not serve as a king.[8]

At the same time, the Constitution also states in Article II, Section 2, that "The President shall be Commander in Chief of the Army and Navy of the United States, and of the Militia of the several States, when called into the actual Service of the United States."[9] Because Congress has the authority to create and maintain the armed forces (originally an Army and Navy, as described in Article I, Section 8 of the Constitution), and to call state militias into national service, it determines the opportunities for the president to fulfill these responsibilities. Louis Fisher writes that the framers wanted the president to have the title of Commander in Chief to "preserv[e] civilian supremacy over the military."[10] In *Federalist* 69, Alexander Hamilton wrote that the Commander in Chief would mean "nothing more than the supreme command and direction of the military and naval forces,"[11] but Fisher points out that Hamilton understated the importance of those actions, which "can be powerful forces in determining the scope and duration of war."[12]

With appointments and treaties, the framers granted the power of initiation to the president and approval to the Senate. The Constitution states that the president "shall have Power, by and with the Advice and Consent of the Senate, to make Treaties,"[13] with a two-thirds vote required for ratification. The president also may nominate ambassadors and other diplomatic representatives of the United States, along with executive-branch officials in foreign affairs, with a majority vote in the Senate required for appointment. As the Constitutional Convention neared conclusion in the summer of 1787, the framers decided "to extend even further the president's role"[14] in both appointments and treaties, recognizing the necessity and importance of executive leadership in each area.

The constitutional sharing of power in foreign policy between Congress and the president, then, did not mean equal participation from idea to implementation. As Louis Henkin writes:

> In foreign affairs the president represents the United States, and the people of the United States, to the world. Congress represents the people at home, the sum of different groups, constituencies, interests (general and special). The president leads; Congress legislates. The president represents needs for expertise, secrecy, speed, efficiency. Congress provides wider, soberer, more deliberate, more cautious, longer-term values and judgments.[15]

Henkin suggests that while the president directs foreign policy on a daily basis, Congress ultimately determines American priorities and interests. This delineation of responsibility is consistent with the framers' concerns about balancing the need for executive leadership with representative democracy. In practice, the president's influence on day-to-day decisions has become highly consequential in shaping, and sometimes constraining, long-term choices.

Evolution of Presidential Power in Foreign Policy

In the early decades of the United States, presidential power in foreign policy focused primarily on protecting the boundaries of the new republic. Presidential statements about the extent of American interests abroad served as doctrines that guided foreign policy through the nineteenth century. Those interests expanded with the Spanish-American War in 1898, when the United States acquired control over overseas territories in the Atlantic and Pacific. In the early decades of the twentieth century, presidents gradually expanded U.S. leadership abroad but did not establish sustained international leadership. This changed after World War II, with the rise of the United States as a global superpower and the onset of the Cold War. The expansion of American responsibilities abroad was matched by the expansion of presidential power to determine and execute those responsibilities.

When George Washington took office as the nation's first president, he gave practical meaning to the powers outlined in Article II of the Constitution through his decisions and policies. Washington and Treasury Secretary Alexander Hamilton asserted the president's right to issue executive orders independently of Congress through the Neutrality Proclamation of 1793, which ensured that the United States would not become involved in the war between Great Britain and France. The proclamation was issued over the objections of Secretary of State Thomas Jefferson. In a famous written debate with Hamilton under the pen name "Helvidius," Madison stated that the legislative branch needed to participate in making such decisions. Hamilton, using the pen name "Pacificus," declared that "The Legislative Department is not the *organ* of intercourse between the U[nited] States and foreign Nations."[16]

Apart from this debate over executive-legislative power, Washington is best known in foreign affairs for asserting a limited role for the United States abroad. In his Farewell Address to the nation, published in newspapers around the country in 1796, Washington encouraged diplomatic and economic ties with other nations, while cautioning against "permanent alliances."[17] As he explained, "Our detached and distant situation invites and enables us to pursue a different course."[18] James Monroe expanded slightly on this statement in his 1823 message to Congress, in which he declared that the United States would object to any attempts by European nations to colonize western North America, or to assert control over newly independent countries in South America. The Monroe Doctrine established U.S. authority over the western hemisphere, and became policy through presidential decree, without legislative input.[19]

U.S. engagement in foreign affairs expanded permanently after the Spanish-American War of 1898, with the acquisition of Cuba and Puerto Rico in the Atlantic, and Guam and Puerto Rico in the Pacific. As the United States assumed political control in overseas territories, its interest in those countries' internal political debates grew as well. In December 1904, Theodore Roosevelt famously extended the reach of the Monroe Doctrine from defensive protection of states in the western hemisphere to the possibility of intervention in those countries if needed to ensure political stability. As Roosevelt stated in his message to Congress:

> Chronic wrongdoing, or an impotence which results in a general loosening of the ties of civilized society, may in America, as elsewhere, ultimately require intervention by some civilized nation, and in the Western Hemisphere the adherence of the United States to the Monroe Doctrine may force the United States, however, reluctantly, in flagrant cases of such wrongdoing or impotence, to the exercise of an international police power.[20]

The Roosevelt Corollary to the Monroe Doctrine made the case for U.S. intervention in the western hemisphere in the early 1900s. The president presented the doctrine to Congress in his annual written report, and he did not seek legislative input in the decision-making process, nor did Congress pursue such participation.

Less than a decade after Roosevelt left office, Woodrow Wilson brought the nation into its first global conflict with World War I, for which Congress issued a declaration of war in 1917 (three years after the war began in Europe). Wilson envisioned a postwar world in which diplomacy would supersede conflict between states, and he led the negotiations after the war ended to draft the Treaty of Versailles and propose a League of

Nations to prevent future wars. But Wilson refused to address congressional concerns about restrictions that the League might impose on state sovereignty and, consequently, the Senate failed to ratify the treaty, leaving the United States out of the new international organization.[21]

Learning from the problems that Wilson faced after World War I, Franklin D. Roosevelt was much more attentive in World War II at including members of Congress in the planning for postwar international agencies. The International Monetary Fund, World Bank, and United Nations were all established in the 1940s through presidential initiative and congressional approval.[22] And Congress had of course endorsed U.S. involvement in World War II after the bombing of Pearl Harbor on December 7, 1941.[23] While presidents thus presented U.S. doctrine without congressional involvement in the nineteenth and early twentieth centuries, they still, for the most part, worked with the legislative branch to create international organizations that would be instrumental in American foreign policy. This balance of power between the executive and legislative branches began to change after the onset of the Cold War.

Presidential Leadership of Foreign Policy from the Cold War to the Post-Cold War Era

Presidential initiative in foreign affairs expanded with the rise of the United States as a global superpower after World War II. The president defined and communicated U.S. national security interests, and Congress assisted the White House in this process through establishing institutions and organizations to develop those policies. But executive decisions to send American troops abroad into extended military conflicts in Korea and Vietnam without congressional declarations of war sparked a backlash against presidential foreign policy making. Consequently, Congress attempted to reassert its authority in foreign affairs, albeit with limited success.

The Harry Truman administration conceptualized the national security strategy that would guide American foreign policy during the Cold War, namely, the "containment" doctrine. George F. Kennan developed the doctrine as director of policy planning in the State Department in 1947, and it provided the basis for policy choices until the fall of the Berlin Wall in 1989. Congress approved many of the specific policies that resulted from the containment doctrine such as the Marshall Plan for foreign assistance to rebuild Western Europe and the creation of the North Atlantic Treaty Organization (NATO) to provide collective security to participating countries against the spread of communism. But the development of the containment strategy, and its many variations from 1947 to 1989, took place in the executive branch, under White House direction.[24]

Congress facilitated this process with the passage of the National Security Act of 1947, which created the modern infrastructure for defense planning and policy making. The law created the Department of Defense (to replace the Department of War), the National Security Council (NSC), the Central Intelligence Agency (CIA), and the Joint Chiefs of Staff (JCS). These agencies are in the executive branch, and while their agency heads typically require Senate confirmation, they are part of the president's advisory circle, and they represent the president's agenda. Thus, since the onset of the Cold War, the president has had more advisory resources to develop foreign and national security policy, thereby increasing executive leadership opportunities in both areas.[25]

As the president's advisory resources in foreign affairs have expanded, organizing those resources to create a systematic decision-making process is a continuing challenge. Early studies of presidential decision making in foreign affairs concentrated on the differences between formally structured and more loosely organized, or informal, decision-making systems. More recent scholarship, drawing on the archival record in the modern presidency, presents more nuanced explanations of strengths and weaknesses in decision-making procedures, depending on the president's personality, the issue at hand, time constraints, and other variables.[26] Alexander George's case for "multiple advocacy" in presidential foreign policy making blends the positive features of formal and informal decision-making models to develop a carefully structured process that maximizes informed debate over policy options with the president's active participation.[27] Given the importance of presidential policy communication, as well as policy doctrine in the modern era, "multiple advocacy" has relevance to the development of a president's public speeches as well, to ensure that signals to other nations are not misinterpreted.[28]

In waging the Cold War, presidents managed their expanded advisory processes in different ways. The declassified record reveals that Dwight D. Eisenhower employed what later became known as multiple advocacy through weekly NSC meetings, in which advisers systematically debated policy options, and the President was fully involved in the process.[29] Eisenhower created the post of special assistant to national security affairs to ensure that someone would be responsible for managing meeting preparation, debate, and follow-up actions. His successor, John F. Kennedy, initially rejected the extensive bureaucratic structure that accompanied Eisenhower's weekly NSC meetings. After the failure of the Bay of Pigs invasion in April 1961, however, Kennedy adapted his decision-making procedures to incorporate some more formal organizational features, and his deliberations during the Cuban missile crisis in October 1962 are viewed as a textbook model of weighing options carefully before making a decision.[30] Also under Kennedy, the special assistant for national security affairs became a policy advocate rather than only a policy manager, and the position has been known informally since then as national security adviser.[31]

White House leadership of national security decision making after World War II seemed a logical outgrowth of the United States' role in the world. More controversial, however, were executive decisions to wage two extended conflicts without seeking a congressional declaration of war. In 1950, Truman decided to combat the North Korean invasion of South Korea under the auspices of a United Nations Security Council resolution authorizing the use of force to repel the invasion. Truman did not seek congressional authorization, and while he did not face significant criticism at the time, his failure to secure legislative support became more significant as the war settled into a stalemate.[32]

In 1964, Lyndon B. Johnson requested an open-ended commitment to aid the U.S. ally South Vietnam against communist insurgents, and Congress wholeheartedly endorsed this action by passing the Gulf of Tonkin Resolution.[33] The resolution became the basis for ultimately sending more than half a million U.S. troops to fight the Vietnam War. By the early 1970s, criticism of each president's decision not to seek a congressional declaration of war was aptly illustrated by historian Arthur M. Schlesinger's famous description of the White House as an "imperial presidency."[34]

Congress responded to what it viewed as presidential usurpation of its constitutional war powers by passing the War Powers Resolution (WPR) of 1973 over Richard Nixon's veto. The WPR specified deadlines for the president to inform Congress of sending troops abroad and for securing congressional approval; if Congress did not authorize the use of force or ordered the president to bring troops home, then the president would have to comply. No president, however, has viewed the WPR as constitutional, and Congress to date has not pressed the president into a showdown over following it; in fact, Congress has used joint resolutions to support presidential decisions to send troops abroad.[35]

While the WPR illustrated congressional frustration with what legislators viewed as executive overreach in foreign affairs, those concerns became less pressing, for the most part, as the Cold War came to closure in the 1980s. Ronald Reagan went from describing the Soviet Union as an "evil empire" in his first term to having four summit meetings in his second term with Soviet leader Mikhail Gorbachev. The meetings resulted in the signing of the Intermediate-Range Nuclear Forces (INF) Treaty, in which the two superpowers agreed for the first time to reduce their respective nuclear arsenals.[36] Two years later, one of the most visible symbols of the Cold War, the Berlin Wall, came down, and the 40-plus year conflict ended without confrontation between the two superpowers.[37]

Reagan's legacy in foreign affairs was tarnished by the Iran-Contra scandal, in which his National Security Council sold arms to Iran and diverted profits to the Contra rebels in Nicaragua, in violation of congressional prohibitions of such assistance.[38] The Iran-Contra hearings in Congress in the summer of 1987 raised anew questions about executive arrogance in foreign affairs. The Reagan administration deflected some of those questions by removing officials involved in the covert program and quickly establishing a special commission to investigate the matter.[39] Because the news was revealed halfway through Reagan's second term, many members of Congress were not keen to seek major structural reforms to restrict an outgoing president's hand in foreign affairs.

In the post-Cold War era, presidents worked closely with Congress in foreign affairs, and while the executive agenda still guided U.S. actions, Congress supported presidential leadership, and at times shaped presidential actions significantly. In the 1991 Persian Gulf War, George H.W. Bush secured approval from the United Nations Security Council to use military force to repel Iraq's invasion of Kuwait. Although he maintained that he did not need congressional approval to send U.S. forces abroad, he ultimately secured a joint congressional resolution authorizing military action a few days before the war began.[40] Bill Clinton worked closely with a Republican-led Congress in the late 1990s to resolve payment of outstanding U.S. dues to the United Nations. While Clinton's political opponents were sharply critical of the international organization, Congress ultimately agreed to reduce U.S. arrears, provided that the percentage of U.S. financial contributions to the U.N. would be reduced as well.[41]

Presidential Leadership of Foreign Policy in the Post-9/11 World

Presidential preeminence in foreign affairs returned after the terrorist attacks of September 11, 2001, when the American public as well as Congress looked to the White House for leadership. This expansion of executive leadership in the post-9/11 era is viewed by some as constitutional and necessary for national security and by others as unconstitutional and dangerous to American principles of separation of powers and checks and balances. While Congress has endorsed many executive decisions, and played a major role in establishing new offices and institutions to combat terrorism, the new infrastructure is part of the executive branch and thus falls under presidential direction. A key question to consider in evaluating post-9/11 presidential leadership is whether conflict between the White House and Congress stems from specific individuals and institutions or whether it represents more endemic challenges in U.S. foreign policy making.

George W. Bush

The George W. Bush administration worked to combat terrorism through numerous means, including military action, interrogation and surveillance of suspected terrorists, development of new agencies to pursue coordination and collaboration among existing entities within the executive branch, and more. One week after the 9/11 attacks, Congress approved the "Authorization for Use of Military Force Against Terrorists" (AUMF), which gave the President power "to use all necessary and appropriate force" against nations, groups, or people who were involved in the attacks or assisted the terrorists.[42] This legislation provided the basis for the U.S. war in Afghanistan to destroy terrorist networks in the country.

The Bush administration's 2002 National Security Strategy declared that the United States reserved the right to wage preemptive warfare to halt threats to American national security before they turned into attacks.[43] Asserting the right to wage preemptive war—"even if uncertainty remains as to the time and place of the enemy's attack"[44]—clearly implied that such determination would be made by executive initiative, with no mention of congressional input.[45] Nevertheless, the White House did seek congressional support to authorize military action against Iraq, which the Bush administration declared was necessary to destroy weapons of mass destruction (WMD) that could harm the United States and its allies, and the U.S.-led military attack against Iraq started in the spring of 2003.[46] Both Congress and the American public initially supported the wars in Afghanistan and Iraq, but the failure to find WMD in Iraq led to sharp critiques of the war and questions about whether it distracted from the ongoing conflict in Afghanistan.[47] By the end of the Bush administration, the Iraq War had become a highly divisive and politically polarizing conflict in American politics.

Apart from military action, the George W. Bush administration asserted executive power to combat terrorism in other ways as well. The administration suspended the writ of habeas corpus for what it termed "enemy combatants" and declared that they could be tried in military tribunals; issued memoranda granting broad latitude in interrogation of detainees; permitted surveillance of suspected terrorists without warrants; and greatly expanded the use of signing statements to declare that the president was not bound by parts of the legislation that conflicted with his authority.[48] Supporters of the Bush White House's expansion of executive power used the concept of a "unitary executive" to justify such actions, declaring that the president's control of the executive branch granted autonomy in these areas and that the other branches of government may not constitutionally infringe upon such autonomy.[49] The office of the vice presidency was instrumental in endorsing and promoting this expansion, raising the question of whether the President or Vice President was directing executive decisions in combating terrorism.[50]

In response to the Bush administration's actions, Congress and the Supreme Court attempted to restore a balance of power with the executive branch in combating terrorism. Congress passed legislation prohibiting torture of detainees, authorizing the creation of military commissions, and permitting wiretapping of suspected terrorists without warrants. The Supreme Court held that Congress had to authorize the creation of military commissions (which it did) and that while suspected terrorists could be detained, they could not be held indefinitely without cause—they could not be denied the *writ of habeas corpus*. Nevertheless, the executive branch in the post-9/11 era still clearly retained the initiative in deciding how the United States would thwart terrorist attacks.[51]

Congress did play a larger role in establishing new executive agencies that would centralize programs to protect the United States from future threats and coordinate intelligence gathering to anticipate and prevent such disasters. Two weeks after the September 11, 2001 terrorist attacks Bush announced that the White House would create an Office of Homeland Security, whose director would have Cabinet status and report directly to the president.[52] Members of Congress advocated for the creation of a cabinet-level department, and the White House eventually endorsed this proposal, with Bush signing the Homeland Security Act in November 2002 to establish the Department of Homeland Security (DHS). Twenty-two federal agencies were placed under the direction of DHS in the largest reorganization of the government since the National Security Act of 1947.[53] To oversee and coordinate intelligence gathering among separate federal intelligence agencies, Congress and the President created the position of Director of National Intelligence (DNI) to serve as the president's primary adviser for national security-related intelligence.[54]

Barack Obama

In response to the Bush presidency, Obama's 2008 presidential campaign slogan of "change we can believe in" referred as much to the practice of politics as to policy choices. As a relative newcomer to Washington, first elected to national office in 2004 when he won the U.S. Senate race in Illinois, Obama made a credible case that he would govern differently than Bush or other more experienced presidential candidates, with more openness and engagement with the American public. He also pledged significant policy changes, which in foreign affairs included reducing the U.S. presence in Iraq, as well as pursuing diplomacy with nations that posed threats to American interests such as Iran and North Korea.

In his first year in office, Obama was awarded the Nobel Peace Prize largely because of his public communication about the importance of diplomacy in foreign affairs. As the award committee stated, Obama demonstrated "extraordinary efforts to strengthen international diplomacy and cooperation between peoples."[55] In his inaugural address, Obama had obliquely criticized the previous administration's policies by stating "we reject as false the choice between our safety and our ideals," alluding to such controversies as treatment of detainees and surveillance of suspected terrorists.[56] The President spoke directly to the Muslim world calling for "a new way forward, based on mutual interest and mutual respect," and he emphasized the importance of diplomacy, promising corrupt or illegitimate leaders that "we will extend a hand if you are willing to unclench your fist."[57] During his first six months in office,

Obama made trips to both large and small countries, including Russia and Ghana as well as four Middle Eastern states: Egypt, Iraq, Saudi Arabia, and Turkey. In Egypt, Obama gave a widely publicized speech at Cairo University in which he called for a "new beginning between the United States and Muslims around the world."[58]

Despite his focus on communication and diplomacy, Obama's foreign-policy activity largely centered on military action. In December 2009, he announced that the United States would send an additional 30,000 troops to Afghanistan for 18 months to provide security and stability to the war-torn country.[59] Although Obama had planned to bring most U.S. forces home before leaving office, the ongoing conflict resulted in about 8,400 U.S. troops still in Afghanistan in early 2017.[60] In 2011, U.S. Special Forces killed Osama bin Laden, the al Qaeda leader who had directed the 9/11 terrorist attacks, in a raid in Pakistan.[61] A few months later, U.S. combat troops departed from Iraq, as negotiated between the United States and Iraq by the outgoing Bush administration in late 2008—though continuing conflict and the rise of the brutal Islamic State of Iraq and Syria (ISIS) terrorist group prompted the Obama administration to send U.S. troops back to Iraq in 2014, with some 5,000 military personnel there when Obama left office.[62] Apart from military action, in 2016, Obama signed the historic Paris Agreement on climate change, which set goals for countries to reduce their emissions.[63]

In many areas, the Obama administration either failed to follow through on foreign-policy promises or fell far short of their goals. Obama issued an executive order in his first week in office to close the Guantanamo Bay detention facility for suspected terrorists within one year; but when he left office in 2017, the prison remained open (albeit with a small number of prisoners), due to congressional resistance to bringing prisoners to the United States and the administration's inability to negotiate an agreement with Congress to resolve the situation.[64] Despite Obama's campaign pledges to prioritize diplomacy over military action, he ultimately ordered ten times as many drone strikes—remotely piloted aircrafts that are targeted to attack enemies, but in so doing may harm civilians as well—as his predecessor.[65]

The Obama administration's most contentious foreign policies were its inconsistent responses, both substantively and procedurally, to terrorist insurgences around the world. In 2011, the United States and North Atlantic Treaty Organization (NATO) allies conducted air strikes in Libya that led to the toppling of dictator Muammar al-Quaddafi; but the ensuring civil chaos raised questions about the military action, particularly following the tragic death of four Americans in an attack on the U.S. consulate in Benghazi in September 2012.[66] Members of Congress criticized the Obama administration for not seeking legislative authorization for the 2011 intervention, and Republicans were highly critical of

Secretary of State Hillary Clinton and U.S. Ambassador to the United Nations Susan Rice for their statements and actions following the 2012 attack.[67]

Public protests in the Middle East, known as the "Arab Spring," brought hope for the advancement of democracy in several states, but that optimism proved short-lived. In Iraq, as discussed earlier, the power vacuum and conflict that developed after U.S. troops departed in 2011 led to the rise of ISIS and the return of U.S. forces to Iraq in Obama's second term. In Syria, pro-democracy protests against the tyrannical rule of Bashar al-Assad led to civil war, and, in 2012, Obama pledged to take military action if the government crossed a "red line" of using chemical weapons against its people. When that happened the following year, however, the White House backed down, saying it would act only with congressional authorization, which was not forthcoming.[68]

In Iran, the Obama administration successfully negotiated a six-nation accord that imposed restrictions on Iran's development of nuclear weapons in return for the lifting of some economic sanctions. But the agreement was widely disputed in Congress, with strong opposition from Republicans and concerns raised by some Democrats as well.[69] While Obama largely followed through on his campaign promises to pursue U.S. priorities abroad by working with other nations, his policy choices and conflicts with Congress illustrated a lack of sustained executive leadership on key issues that likely will define his foreign-policy legacy.

Donald J. Trump

The early months of the Trump presidency demonstrated the same unpredictability and uncertainty in foreign affairs that defined Trump's unique and unexpected road to the White House. During the 2016 presidential race, Trump criticized the foreign policies of both George W. Bush and Obama, from the Iraq War to the Iran nuclear deal. In his inaugural address, Trump declared, "From this moment on, it's going to be America First."[70] After taking office, he issued numerous executive orders in a wide range of areas; in foreign policy, his temporary ban on travel from six Muslim-majority countries and refugee admission to the United States, and withdrawal of the United States from the Trans-Pacific Partnership for trade, were especially consequential.

For his foreign-policy team, Trump relied heavily on military and business leaders over Washington policy experts, and his initial inner circle of White House advisers sparked several controversies about expertise, conflicts of interest, and other matters. In April 2017, Trump decided to authorize air strikes against Syria in response to humanitarian atrocities there. But an overarching strategy to guide foreign-policy decision making was not evident in his first few months in office.

Conclusion

The role of the president in foreign policy has expanded greatly since the founding of the American republic, due to increased responsibilities of the United States as well as the evolution of the modern presidency. While the president is the primary representative of the United States to other nations, Congress has explicit constitutional duties in foreign affairs. Corwin's quotation at the beginning of this chapter about an "invitation to struggle" between the two branches of government in American foreign policy making becomes particularly significant in times of crisis. Both the legislative and executive branches bear responsibility for maintaining the constitutional system of sharing powers and checking each other. In the twenty-first century, cooperation between the branches of government may be as important as cooperation with other nations to pursue American interests in foreign affairs successfully.

Notes

1 Edward S. Corwin, *The President: Office and Powers, 1787–1984*, 5th rev. ed., eds. Randall W. Bland, Theodore T. Hindson, and Jack W. Peltason (New York: New York University Press, 1984), 201.

2 Clinton Rossiter, *The American Presidency: The Powers and Practices, the Personalities and Problems of the Most Important Office on Earth* (New York: Harcourt Brace, 1956), 16.

3 Richard E. Neustadt, *Presidential Power: The Politics of Leadership* (New York: John Wiley & Sons, 1960), 7.

4 Amy B. Zegart, *Flawed By Design: The Evolution of the CIA, JCS, and NSC* (Stanford, CA: Stanford University Press, 1999).

5 Richard E. Neustadt, *Presidential Power and the Modern Presidents: The Politics of Leadership from Roosevelt to Reagan* (New York: Free Press, 1990), 29.

6 U.S. Constitution.

7 Louis Fisher, *Presidential War Power*, 3rd ed. (Lawrence, KS: University Press of Kansas, 2013), 8–10.

8 For a counter-perspective, which contends that the framers intended to give the presidency primary authority in war powers, see John Yoo, *The Powers of War and Peace: The Constitution and Foreign Affairs After 9/11* (Chicago, IL: University of Chicago Press, 2005). Yoo states that Congress's power to declare war refers to a formal recognition of conflict between states, but that the president is responsible for all negotiations and decisions preceding such a declaration. Had the framers intended to restrict presidential war power, Yoo says, they would have done so explicitly, following the model of some state constitutions.

9 U.S. Constitution.

10 Fisher, *Presidential War Power*, 13.

11 *Federalist* 69, quoted in Fisher, *Presidential War Power*, 12.

12 Fisher, *Presidential War Power*, 12.

13 U.S. Constitution.

14 Sidney M. Milkis and Michael Nelson, *The American Presidency: Origins and Development, 1776–2014*, 7th rev. ed. (Washington, DC: CQ Press, 2016), 51.

15 Louis Henkin, "Foreign Affairs and the Constitution," *Foreign Affairs* (1987/88): 284–310.

16 "The Pacificus-Helvidius Letters," 1793, excerpted in *The Evolving Presidency: Landmark Documents, 1787–2014*, 5th ed., ed. Michael Nelson, (Washington, DC: CQ Press, 2015), 47–53.

17 "George Washington's Farewell Address," 1796, excerpted in *The Evolving Presidency*, ed. Nelson, 54–61.

18 Ibid.

19 "The Monroe Doctrine," 1823, in *The Evolving Presidency*, ed. Nelson, 68–71. Also see Fred I. Greenstein, *Inventing the Job of President: Leadership Style from George Washington to Andrew Jackson* (Princeton, NJ: Princeton University Press, 2009), 69–70.

20 Theodore Roosevelt, "Fourth Annual Message," December 6, 1904, *The American Presidency Project*, www.presidency.ucsb.edu/ws/index.php?pid=29545.

21 The intellectual and policy debates about a new international order that took place in the United States during and after World War I are discussed in Ross A. Kennedy, *The Will to Believe: Woodrow Wilson, World War I, and America's Strategy for Peace and Security* (Kent, OH: Kent State University Press, 2009).

22 Stephen C. Schlesinger, *Act of Creation: The Founding of the United Nations* (Boulder, CO: Westview, 2003), 108, 263–81.

23 Stephen E. Ambrose and Douglas G. Brinkley, *Rise to Globalism: American Foreign Policy since 1938*, 8th rev. ed. (New York: Penguin Books, 1997), 13–14.

24 John Lewis Gaddis presents a comprehensive analysis of containment during the Cold War in *Strategies of Containment: A Critical Appraisal of American National Security Policy during the Cold War*, rev. and expanded ed. (New York: Oxford University Press, 2005).

25 Zegart, *Flawed by Design: The Evolution of the CIA, JCS, and NSC.*

26 See, for example, Richard Tanner Johnson, *Managing the White House: An Intimate Study of the Presidency* (New York: Harper & Row, 1974); Cecil V. Crabb and K.V. Mulcahy, *Presidents and Foreign Policy Making: From F.D.R. to Reagan* (Baton Rouge, LA: Louisiana State University Press, 1987); John P. Burke and Fred I. Greenstein, *How Presidents Test Reality: Decisions on Vietnam, 1954 and 1965* (New York: Russell Sage Foundation, 1989); Patrick J. Haney, *Organizing for Foreign Policy Crisis: Presidents, Advisers, and the Management of Decision Making* (Ann Arbor, MI: University of Michigan Press, 1997); Jean A. Garrison, *Games Advisors Play: Foreign Policy in the Nixon and Carter Administrations* (College Station, TX: Texas A&M University Press, 1999); and William W. Newmann, *Managing National Security Policy: The President and the Process* (Pittsburgh, PA: University of Pittsburgh Press, 2003).

27 See Alexander L. George, "The Case for Multiple Advocacy in Making Foreign Policy," *American Political Science Review* 66 (1972): 751–85; George, *Presidential Decisionmaking in Foreign Policy: The Effective Use of Information and Advice* (Boulder, CO: Westview Press, 1980). For case studies of George's concept, see Alexander Moens, *Foreign Policy Under Carter: Testing Multiple Advocacy Decision Making* (Boulder, CO: Westview, 1990); and Meena Bose, *Shaping and Signaling Presidential Policy: The National Security Decision Making of Eisenhower and Kennedy* (College Station, TX: Texas A&M University Press, 1998).

28 Meena Bose, "Words as Signals: Drafting Cold War Rhetoric in the Eisenhower and Kennedy Administrations," *Congress & the Presidency* 25 (1998): 23–41.

29 On Eisenhower's national security decision making, see Fred I. Greenstein, *The Hidden-Hand Presidency: Eisenhower as Leader* (New York: Basic Books,

1982); Bose, *Shaping and Signaling Presidential Policy*; Robert R. Bowie and Richard H. Immerman, *Waging Peace: How Eisenhower Shaped An Enduring Cold War Strategy* (New York: Oxford University Press, 2000); Jean Edward Smith, *Eisenhower in War and Peace* (New York: Random House, 2012); and Evan Thomas, *Ike's Bluff: President Eisenhower's Secret Battle to Save the World* (New York: Little, Brown, 2012).

30 See transcripts from the meetings held by Kennedy and his advisers, known as the Executive Committee or "ExComm," during the Cuban missile crisis in Ernest R. May and Philip D. Zelikow, *The Kennedy Tapes: Inside the White House During the Cuban Missile Crisis* (Cambridge, MA: Belknap Press, 1997); and Sheldon M. Stern, *Averting the "Final Failure": John F. Kennedy and the Secret Cuban Missile Crisis Meetings* (Stanford, CA: Stanford University Press, 2003).

31 For an analysis of the evolution of the national security adviser position, see John P. Burke, *Honest Broker? The National Security Advisor and Presidential Decision Making* (College Station, TX: Texas A&M University Press, 2009).

32 Louis Fisher, "On What Legal Basis Did Truman Act?" *The American Journal of International Law* 89 (1995): 21–39; Gary R. Hess, *Presidential Decisions for War: Korea, Vietnam, the Persian Gulf, and Iraq*, 2nd ed. (Baltimore, MD: Johns Hopkins University Press, 2009).

33 Hess, *Presidential Decisions for War*; Robert Dallek, *Flawed Giant: Lyndon Johnson and His Times, 1961–1973* (New York: Oxford University Press, 1998). For transcripts of tape recordings that Johnson made of telephone conversations during his presidency, see *Taking Charge: The Johnson White House Tapes 1963–64*, ed. Michael R. Beschloss (New York: Simon & Schuster, 1997); and *Reaching for Glory: Lyndon Johnson's Secret White House Tapes 1964–65*, ed. Michael R. Beschloss (New York: Simon & Schuster, 2001).

34 Arthur M. Schlesinger, Jr., *The Imperial Presidency* (Boston, MA: Houghton Mifflin, 1973). Schlesinger's analysis is a mea culpa of his original support for Truman's decision to wage the Korean War without congressional approval. See Fisher, *Presidential War Power*, 101–102.

35 For the text of the War Powers Resolution and a detailed analysis of its implementation, see Richard F. Grimmett, "The War Powers Resolution: After Thirty-Six Years," *Congressional Research Service*, April 22, 2010.

36 Journalist Don Oberdorfer, who covered the four summit meetings for the *Washington Post*, evaluates the path to the end of the Cold War in the 1980s in *From the Cold War to a New Era: The United States and the Soviet Union, 1983–1991*, updated ed. (Baltimore, MD: Johns Hopkins University Press, 1998).

37 Mary Elise Sarotte examines the archival record in the United States and Europe on the fall of the Berlin Wall and the subsequent decision to reunify Germany in *1989: The Struggle to Create Post-Cold War Europe* (Princeton, NJ: Princeton University Press, 2009).

38 For a highly detailed explanation of the Iran-Contra negotiations, see Theodore Draper, *A Very Thin Line: The Iran-Contra Affairs* (New York: Hill and Wang, 1991). Also see the exhaustive report prepared by the independent counsel for the controversy, Lawrence E. Walsh, *Firewall: The Iran-Contra Conspiracy and Cover-up* (New York: W.W. Norton, 1997).

39 Edmund Muskie, Brent Scowcroft, and John Tower, *The Tower Commission Report: The Full Text of the President's Special Review Board* (New York: Bantam, 1987). Also see David M. Abshire, *Saving the Reagan Presidency: Trust is the Coin of the Realm* (College Station, TX: Texas A&M University Press, 2005).

40 George H.W. Bush and Brent Scowcroft, *A World Transformed* (New York: Knopf, 1998). Also see Meena Bose, "Who Makes U.S. Foreign Policy? Presidential Leadership in Gulf Wars I and II," in *The Presidency and the Challenge of Democracy*, ed. Michael A. Genovese and Lori Cox Han (New York: Palgrave Macmillan, 2006), 139–58.

41 The battle over U.S. dues to the U.N. in the late 1990s is discussed in Meena Bose, "Private and Public Diplomacy: The U.S. Permanent Representative to the U.N. in the Clinton Years," paper presented at "William Jefferson Clinton: The 'New Democrat' From Hope" Conference, Hofstra University, November 10–12, 2005. Also see Courtney B. Smith, "The Impact of Dues Withholding on the U.S.-U.N. Relationship," in *U.S. Presidential Leadership at the UN: 1945 to Present*, ed. Meena Bose, (Hauppauge, NY: Nova Science, 2014). For a broader assessment of Clinton's foreign-policy leadership, see Emily O. Goldman and Larry Berman, "Engaging the World: First Impressions of the Clinton Foreign Policy Legacy," in *The Clinton Legacy*, ed. Colin Campbell and Bert A. Rockman (New York: Chatham House, 2000).

42 107th Congress, Public Law 107-40, "To Authorize the Use of United States Armed Forces Against Those Responsible for the Recent Attacks Launched Against the United States," September 18, 2001.

43 White House, President George W. Bush, *The National Security Strategy of the United States of America*, September 2002, https://georgewbush-whitehouse.archives.gov/nsc/nss/2002/.

44 "The National Security Strategy," September 2002, Section V, "Prevent Our Enemies From Threatening Us, Our Allies, and Our Friends With Weapons of Mass Destruction."

45 An early evaluation of the George W. Bush administration's post-9/11 foreign-policy is Ivo H. Daalder and James M. Lindsay, *America Unbound: The Bush Revolution in Foreign Policy* (Washington, DC: Brookings, 2003).

46 107th Congress, Public Law 107-243, "Authorization for Use of Military Force against Iraq Resolution of 2002," October 16, 2002. Also see George W. Bush, *Decision Points* (New York: Crown, 2010), chapter 8, "Iraq."

47 See, for example, Richard N. Haass, *War of Necessity, War of Choice: A Memoir of Two Iraq Wars* (New York: Simon & Schuster, 2009); and David E. Sanger, *The Inheritance: The World Obama Confronts and the Challenges to American Power* (New York: Crown, 2009).

48 James P. Pfiffner evaluates the George W. Bush presidency's actions in each of these four areas, arguing that they "undermined the constitutional balance among the branches" (p. 4), in *Power Play: The Bush Presidency and the Constitution* (Washington, DC: Brookings, 2008).

49 Steven G. Calabresi and Christopher S. Yoo argue that the concept of the "unitary executive" dates back to the administration of George Washington, and has been applied in every subsequent presidency, in *The Unitary Executive: Presidential Power from Washington to Bush* (New Haven, CT: Yale University Press, 2008). They focus, however, on removal of executive branch appointees and direction of executive branch actions, not on foreign policy, and they explicitly note that "the classic vision of the unitary executive … had absolutely nothing to do with claims of implied, inherent presidential domestic and foreign policy power of the kind asserted by the [George W. Bush] administration" (p. 21). John Yoo, who served in the Department of Justice during George W. Bush's first term, makes the case for broad executive power in foreign affairs in *The Powers of War and Peace: The Constitution and Foreign Affairs After 9/11* (Chicago, IL: University of Chicago Press, 2005). For a critique of the "unitary executive" concept, see Robert J. Spitzer, *Saving*

the *Constitution from Lawyers: How Legal Training and Law Reviews Distort Constitutional Meaning* (Cambridge: Cambridge University Press, 2008).

50 Shirley Anne Warshaw, *The Co-Presidency of Bush and Cheney* (Stanford, CA: Stanford University Press, 2009); and Peter Baker, *Days of Fire: Bush and Cheney in the White House* (New York: Doubleday, 2013).

51 Scholarly analyses of the George W. Bush administration's legacy for executive decision making in foreign policy include Meena Bose, ed., *President or King? Evaluating the Expansion of Executive Power from Abraham Lincoln to George W. Bush* (Hauppauge, NY: Nova Science, 2012); Meena Bose, ed., *The George W. Bush Presidency*, 3 Volumes (Hauppauge, NY: Nova Science, 2016); James Mann, *George W. Bush: The 43rd President, 2001–2009* (New York: Times Books, 2015); and Jean Edward Smith, *Bush* (New York: Simon & Schuster, 2016).

52 George W. Bush, Address to a Joint Session of Congress and the American People, September 20, 2001, *The American Presidency Project*, www. presidency.ucsb.edu/ws/?pid=64731.

53 U.S. Department of Homeland Security website, "Creation of the Department of Homeland Security," www.dhs.gov/history.

54 Office of the Director of National Intelligence website, "Who We Are," www.dni.gov/index.php/who-we-are. For an analysis of pre-9/11 difficulties with intelligence sharing and post-9/11 efforts, see Amy B. Zegart, *Spying Blind: The CIA, the FBI, and the Origins of 9/11* (Princeton, NJ: Princeton University Press, 2007).

55 Statement by Norwegian Nobel Committee, "The Nobel Peace Prize for 2009," October 9, 2009, www.nobelprize.org/nobel_prizes/peace/laureates/2009/press.html.

56 President Barack Obama, "Inaugural Address," January 20, 2009, www. presidency.ucsb.edu/ws/index.php?pid=44.

57 Ibid.

58 President Barack Obama, "Remarks by the President on a New Beginning," Cairo University, Cairo, Egypt, June 4, 2009, https://obamawhitehouse. archives.gov/video/President-Obama-Speaks-to-the-Muslim-World-from-Cairo-Egypt#transcript.

59 President Barack Obama, "The New Way Forward," United States Military Academy at West Point, New York, December 1, 2009, https://obamawhitehouse. archives.gov/blog/2009/12/01/new-way-forward-presidents-address.

60 Christi Parsons and W.J. Hennigan, "President Obama, Who Hoped to Sow Peace, Instead Led the Nation in War," *Los Angeles Times*, January 13, 2017, www.latimes.com/projects/la-na-pol-obama-at-war/.

61 CNN Library, "Death of Osama bin Laden Fast Facts," April 23, 2017, www. cnn.com/2013/09/09/world/death-of-osama-bin-laden-fast-facts/index.html.

62 Scott Wilson and Karen DeYoung, "All U.S. Troops to Leave Iraq by the End of 2011," *Washington Post*, October 21, 2011, www.washingtonpost.com/world/national-security/all-us-troops-to-leave-iraq/2011/10/21/gIQAUyJi3L_story.html?utm_term=.bfa8604761e7; Ben Hubbard, Robert F. Worth, and Michael R. Gordon, "Power Vacuum in Middle East Lifts Militants," *New York Times*, January 4, 2014, www.nytimes.com/2014/01/05/world/middleeast/power-vacuum-in-middle-east-lifts-militants.html?_r=0; Mark Thompson, "Number of U.S. Troops in Iraq Keeps Creeping Upward," *Time*, April 18, 2016, http://time.com/4298318/iraq-us-troops-barack-obama-mosul-isis/.

63 White House, "President Obama: The United States Formally Enters the Paris Agreement," September 3, 2016, https://obamawhitehouse.archives. gov/blog/2016/09/03/president-obama-united-states-formally-enters-paris-agreement.

64 Connie Bruck, "Why Obama Has Failed to Close Guantanamo," *New Yorker*, August 1, 2016, www.newyorker.com/magazine/2016/08/01/why-obama-has-failed-to-close-guantanamo.

65 Steve Coll, "The Unblinking Stare: The Drone War in Pakistan," *New Yorker*, November 24, 2014, www.newyorker.com/magazine/2014/11/24/unblinking-stare; Jack Moore, "Drone Strikes Under Obama Killed Up to 117 Civilians Worldwide, Intelligence Report Claims," *Newsweek*, January 20, 2017, www.newsweek.com/strikes-during-obamas-presidency-killed-many-117-civilians-545080. For scholarly analyses of continuity in policy from the George W. Bush to Barack Obama administrations, see Meena Bose, ed., *Change in the White House? Comparing the Presidencies of George W. Bush and Barack Obama* (Hauppauge, NY: Nova Science, 2013).

66 Paul Richter and Christi Parsons, "U.S. Intervention in Libya Now Seen as Cautionary Tale," *Los Angeles Times*, June 27, 2014, www.latimes.com/world/middleeast/la-fg-us-libya-20140627-story.html; Sarah Aarthun, "4 Hours of Fire and Chaos: How the Benghazi Attack Unfolded," *CNN World*, September 13, 2012, www.cnn.com/2012/09/12/world/africa/libya-consulate-attack-scene/index.html.

67 Charlie Savage, "Attack Renews Debate Over Congressional Consent," *New York Times*, March 21, 2011, www.nytimes.com/2011/03/22/world/africa/22powers.html; Charlie Savage and Thom Shanker, "Scores of U.S. Strikes in Libya Followed Handoff to NATO," *New York Times*, June 20, 2011, www.nytimes.com/2011/06/21/world/africa/21powers.html; David M. Herszenhorn, "House Benghazi Report Finds No New Evidence of Wrongdoing by Hillary Clinton," *New York Times*, June 28, 2016, www.nytimes.com/2016/06/29/us/politics/hillary-clinton-benghazi.html.

68 Peter Baker and Jonathan Weisman, "Obama Seeks Approval by Congress for Strike in Syria," *New York Times*, August 31, 2013, www.nytimes.com/2013/09/01/world/middleeast/syria.html; Haley Bissegger, "Timeline: How President Obama Handled Syria," *The Hill*, September 15, 2013, http://thehill.com/policy/international/322283-timeline-of-how-president-obama-handled-syria-.

69 Michael R. Gordon and David E. Sanger, "Deal Reached on Iran Nuclear Program; Limits on Fuel Would Lessen With Time," *New York Times*, July 14, 2015, www.nytimes.com/2015/07/15/world/middleeast/iran-nuclear-deal-is-reached-after-long-negotiations.html; Jennifer Steinhauer, "Democrats Hand Victory to Obama on Iran Nuclear Deal," *New York Times*, September 10, 2015, www.nytimes.com/2015/09/11/us/politics/iran-nuclear-deal-senate.html; Jim Zarroli, "As Sanctions on Iran Are Lifted, Many U.S. Business Restrictions Remain," *National Public Radio*, January 26, 2016, https://news.wbhm.org/npr_story_post/2016/as-sanctions-on-iran-are-lifted-many-u-s-business-restrictions-remain/.

70 Donald J. Trump, "The Inaugural Address," January 20, 2017, www.whitehouse.gov/inaugural-address.

12 Presidents and Leadership

Justin S. Vaughn

Five days before Christmas in 1963, Lyndon Johnson was in a pickle. He had been president for less than a month, following John F. Kennedy's assassination. The all-important Farm Bill was working its way through Congress, but a clause had been added that the President adamantly opposed. It required presidents to publicly report to Congress on wheat sales to the Soviet Union, an act that would require waiving congressional restrictions and thus make the president—him—appear too chummy with the Soviets. Johnson needed the Farm Bill to pass—it had been a major fixture of domestic policy for nearly three decades at that point— but he also needed to win an election to office in his own right in less than a year against a Republican opponent who would salivate over the opportunity to paint Johnson as a friend of the Kremlin. To get himself out of this situation, the President needed to get the legislation changed so that it no longer included the offending clause. To do that would require something we demand of all our presidents—leadership.

In this instance, Johnson relied on his most familiar approach to leadership—a high-pressure beseeching of a key legislator to do the President's bidding that he utilized so often and to such effect that historians have since given the approach its own name: the Johnson Treatment. On this day, it was a fellow Democrat from Texas, Representative Albert Thomas, who was on the receiving end of the Johnson Treatment.[1] In less than two minutes, Johnson told Thomas he loved him, calling him a friend and a buddy, while they quibbled over the precise wording of the statute. The President also asked his fellow Texan if he thought he was a "damned idiot" and told him, in far crasser terms, not to tell him something he knew not to be true. By the time the call ended, Johnson had both buttered Thomas up and put him on the defensive, something the President was renowned for doing throughout his political career as a way to lead friends and foes alike to the solutions he preferred.

This one-on-one, emotionally charged wrangling over details and deals was Johnson's preferred approach to presidential leadership, one that fit his temperament and maximized his strongest political skills, and one that worked well in the historical moment when Congress was ripe for deal making and before television had come to dominate political communication in the United States. Of course, not all presidents engage in leadership in precisely this way. Presidential leadership takes many forms, formally as well as informally, and exists in many arenas. Leadership occurs when presidents speak to the people, telling them why they stand a particular way on a specific policy question, or explaining to the masses what a development means to the nation, whether it be successfully landing an astronaut on the moon or mourning the loss of several when a space shuttle explodes. Leadership is seen when a president publicly advocates congressional action on an upcoming roll call vote as well as when they use their veto pen to reject legislation both chambers of Congress have agreed upon. Leadership is seen when a president sends troops into harm's way but also when a president makes the choice to avoid military action and pursue diplomatic paths to peace. Leadership is also seen when a president fires an incompetent or otherwise unacceptable member of their administration, just as it is when they identify the need for centralized management and assign a trusted advisor to oversee the numerous bureaucrats involved in managing a policy problem. Leadership happens in all these examples and countless more.

The more you learn about the American presidency, the more you learn that there have been about as many different approaches to presidential leadership as there have been occupants of the Oval Office. Johnson's high-pressure approach, in fact, is rather unique among presidents, and few since then have attempted consistently such an intimate and physical style as they sought to get key political actors to do what they wished. For example, George W. Bush, a Republican from Texas, took a different approach in a different context. Almost exactly four decades after Johnson's phone conversation with Albert Thomas, Bush decided to travel the nation, visiting 60 American cities in as many days as he took a local approach to selling his plan for Social Security reform.[2] As he put it, having recently won reelection convincingly over Senator John Kerry (D-MA), he had earned political capital, and now he intended to spend it. On his trip throughout the country, Bush spoke with local papers, met with local leaders, and appealed to citizens who had voted both for and against him to contact their elected leaders in Congress and pressure them to support the President's reform proposal, which he had been campaigning on the previous year in his battle for reelection. For Bush, leadership in this instance meant communicating a preferred policy solution in a sustained way to as many people as possible, as directly as possible, and empowering them to then communicate their support for this solution to their congressional representatives.

Jimmy Carter, a Democrat from Georgia who governed a decade after Johnson, took a very different approach when he felt he needed to lead the American people to confront the energy crisis, along with other problems facing the nation, that wracked the nation in the summer of 1979. Carter gave a major address where he framed the challenges, which also included unemployment and inflation, as a national "crisis of confidence"—one that led to growing doubt about individuals' lives as well as declining unity of national purpose.[3] For Carter, presidential leadership meant creating a cerebral connection between the White House and Americans across the country, and challenging those Americans to think differently about the problems facing the nation.

Barack Obama, a Democrat from Illinois whose fast-rising political career catapulted him to the White House a mere 12 years after first being elected to the Illinois state legislature, took an approach not altogether different from Carter's intellectual oratorical effort, as he sought to get a different group to rethink their attitudes toward the United States. In this case, rather than connect with Americans, Obama was focused on convincing world leaders and the masses in their nations to reconsider their view of the United States. With many thinking the United States' global reputation had been damaged after the wars in Iraq and Afghanistan begun during the George W. Bush administration, Obama set a priority of counteracting that decline and communicating to leaders and the led alike in numerous countries that a new order had emerged in the United States and the changes he planned to effect with respect to how the United States would engage the world under his administration. In his first year as president, he traveled to more than two dozen countries, but one visit stood out. On June 4th, 2009, sandwiched between visits to Saudi Arabia and Germany, Obama went to Cairo, Egypt to deliver a major address titled "A New Beginning" at Cairo University.[4] The goal of the speech was to communicate not just with Egyptians, but the Islamic world more broadly. Obama sought to acknowledge mistakes made by the United States, celebrate Islamic contributions to global civilization, and reset the relationship between the country he now led and the region he was then visiting. In this situation, for Obama, leadership meant coming to a place where the relationship with the United States had become fraught, atoning for historical shortcomings while promising meaningful change, and having that message be disseminated throughout the world to convince members of an important group to reconsider the path they were on vis-à-vis the United States.

In these four instances, we see a wide range of leadership approaches, along with an equally diverse set of strategic objectives, which themselves represent the range of matters presidents are expected to lead on. These different approaches reflect not only different personal styles, but also different contexts. In each case, however, there is a commonality; presidents communicated their preferred outcome to the audience that was arguably most able to ensure that outcome. Johnson took his grievance over a clause in the Farm Bill to a close colleague in his party's congressional caucus who was also a high-ranking member of the legislature. If anyone would be both inclined and able to get Johnson's preferred excision made, it would be Thomas. George W. Bush also had an objective related to Congress but didn't need one man to make one minor change; he needed dozens of votes from cross-pressured members of Congress. To reach them, he went first to the voters who put them into office. To reach those voters, he went to where they lived—he visited their towns, he sat for interviews with their local media—rather than rely on a so-called Rose Garden strategy where he made speeches in Washington D.C. and hoped the thrust of those remarks would be clearly and correctly communicated by the mass media to voters at home. Carter wanted to reach American citizens as well, so he gave a major address designed to maximize exposure to as many Americans as possible. He wanted those Americans to think anew about the challenges the nation faced and their responsibilities involved in the United States overcoming them, so he delivered a high-profile message in which he framed the motivating problems in the way he hoped Americans would begin to see them. And finally, Obama went to the people he needed to communicate with in order to achieve his goal, which was not only initiating a new approach to the broader world in general and the Islamic world specifically, but also encouraging Muslims in the Middle East and beyond to reconsider how they viewed the United States.

Tellingly, these examples also have another notable commonality, which we will revisit later in this chapter: Each one of these leadership efforts failed. Despite his harangue, Johnson never got the clause he was so upset about removed from the Farm Bill. George W. Bush not only never got a chance to sign his Social Security reform bill, his "60 cities in 60 days" sales pitch tour proved so ineffective that support for his proposal actually *declined* by seven percentage points over the course of his effort.[5] Carter's attempt to inspire Americans to rethink their approach on the challenges of the day failed so badly that the speech, frequently referred to as the "malaise speech," has gone down in history as one of the worst political speeches of all time.[6] Voters did end up embracing a new approach to solving their political problems not long after, though not the way Carter hoped. Rather, the next year they chose to send Carter packing from the White House as they instead elected Ronald Reagan, who was essentially the polar opposite of Carter. And, finally, Obama's hope to reset American relations with the Islamic world not only proved to be unsuccessful, it also created a major political problem that became a primary theme in his reelection opponent's campaign against him a few years later. Critics of the president dubbed his trip to Egypt and elsewhere as an "apology tour" that disrespected the nation he was elected to lead.[7]

The fact that these leadership efforts failed was not exclusively the result of presidential error or weakness. Rather, these events reflect the fact that presidents operate in highly constrained environments and possess a limited number of political and policy tools with which to achieve their goals. The previous example aside, Johnson was a master negotiator with Congress—arguably among the best at this type of presidential leadership. George W. Bush's Social Security reform tour, although un-successful, was exceptionally well designed and executed. For years, po-litical scientists had been identifying factors that enhanced the likelihood that presidents would positively affect public opinion and had deter-mined that a sustained focus on a single topic while getting out of Wash-ington, DC and attempting to bypass national media for local outlets was the optimal approach. Bush's team put together all these ingredients in an unprecedented effort. The fact that it did not work is more a function of the impediments to leadership than anything else.

To gain a better understanding of presidential leadership prospects, we must first better understand what is meant when we hear the phrase "presidential leadership." The next section focuses on defining this con-cept. Subsequent sections discuss key presidential leadership qualities, the American public's expectations regarding presidential leadership and the obstacles that frequently plague leadership efforts.

What is Presidential Leadership?

To understand the dimensions of presidential leadership and how dif-ferent presidents compare with one another across them, we must first understand what presidential leadership is at the conceptual level. Doing so, however, is no small task, as many scholars have attested to over time. Rather, as Andrew B. Whitford and Jeff Yates have observed, the phrase "lends itself to competing definitions and meanings."[8] We know the great historical examples, of course, such as when Abraham Lincoln signed the Emancipation Proclamation in 1863 freeing all slaves held in rebellious states or, more recently, in September 2001, when George W. Bush took up a bullhorn amid the rubble where the World Trade Center stood only a few days before. Certainly, moments like these are extraordinary ex-emplars, but by virtue of their extraordinary nature not very helpful in helping us understand what presidential leadership is day in, day out. To develop that kind of understanding, we need to think more conceptually about the matter.

Most simply, presidential leadership can be understood as "the capacity of the president to make a difference."[9] Precisely what kind of difference, however, makes all the difference. In their text, *Presidential Leadership: Politics and Policy Making*, George C. Edwards III and Stephen J. Wayne focus directly and intently on the subject:

> Within the presidency, the president is clearly the chief. Executive officials look to the office for direction, coordination, and general guidance in the implementation of policy; members of Congress look to it for establishing priorities, exerting influence, and providing ser-vices; the leaders of foreign governments look to it for articulating positions, conducting diplomacy, and flexing muscle; the general

public looks to it for enhancing security, solving problems, and exercising symbolic and moral leadership—a big order, to be sure.[10]

Edwards and Wayne further refine the concept of leadership to two contrasting perspectives; both focus on change, with the difference being both the scope and consequences of presidential actions as well as whether the president is the director or facilitator of the change in question. According to them, "In the role of director, the president is out in front, establishing goals and encouraging others inside and outside of government to follow. Accordingly, the president is the moving force of the system and the initiator of change."[11] Conversely, the "less heroic" facilitator perspective emphasizes leadership as exploiting opportunities. "In the role of facilitator, the president reflects, and perhaps intensifies, widely held views and uses available resources to achieve his constituency's aspirations. Thus, the president prods and pushes the government, in which roles, responsibilities, and powers are shared."[12]

Essential Leadership Qualities

There are many paths to presidential leadership, depending not only on the context that a president operates in but also the various skills and qualities a president possesses personally. Fred Greenstein has identified six criteria that help determine whether a president will be an effective or ineffective leader: effectiveness as a public communicator, organizational capacity, political skill, vision, cognitive style, and emotional intelligence.[13] The first of these, *effectiveness as a public communicator*, is a fundamentally modern component of presidential leadership and becomes increasingly important as communication outlets continue to proliferate. Ironically, despite the major importance of public communication, many of our recent presidents have not been great communicators. Indeed, since the start of the broadcast era in the mid-twentieth century, only a few could be considered to be good communicators; the short list would likely include only Kennedy, Reagan, Clinton, and Obama, each of who had their own communicative shortcomings but were clearly superior to their peers. Communication skills alone are insufficient to achieve greatness, however—after all, of the aforementioned group, only Reagan was able to celebrate many major policy accomplishments. *Organizational capacity* is essential in contemporary presidential leadership—without the ability to build and manage a team, not to mention design institutional arrangements, a president will be unable to steer the ship of state or make informed decisions.

The president cannot rely just on their team, however, as they must possess their own *political skill*. Without the ability to build relationships and influence others at a high level, presidential agendas are destined to flounder. Of course, to even develop this agenda, a president must possess *vision.* This need not mean they have grand political philosophies—after all, George H.W. Bush disdained "the vision thing" and still put together an impressive series of victories while leading the United States capably during the early days of the post-Cold War era. But it does mean they understand the linkages between the policies they advocate and the goals they wish to achieve. Such understanding is linked to a president's *cognitive style*, as well. This refers to the way in which presidents think and perceive information, and can be considered both with respect to how they process information and how well they process it. Greenstein points out how Carter was an engineer who tackled problem solving by reducing issues to their component parts, whereas Clinton was an exceptional synthetic thinker who did not analyze problems but rather brought together numerous sources of information. Despite their cognitive differences, both processed information at a high level, especially compared to less intellectually talented presidents such as Reagan. Reagan, however, possessed far superior emotional intelligence than both Carter and Clinton. Defined as the ability to identify and manage your own emotions and the emotions of others, emotional intelligence is essential both to connecting meaningfully with the masses and approaching the profession of the presidency in a balanced and healthy manner.[14]

Greenstein's set of criteria cover a wide swath of the qualities related to presidential greatness but can be considered incomplete. Another expert, Michael Siegel, identifies four leadership traits in his book, *The President as Leader*.[15] These include vision, which overlaps with Greenstein's approach, but also the wherewithal to implement their vision, a focus on a few goals at a time, and effective decision making. Presidents who know and communicate their goals, make good strategic decisions, and pursue their agendas in manageable segments are more likely to accomplish their objectives than if they were directionless, disorganized, and ill or under informed and attempt to get everything they want accomplished all at once. Importantly, presidents must possess as many of these qualities that Greenstein and Siegel have identified, not just so that they can achieve their strategic goals, but also because the leadership that such qualities facilitate is exactly what the American people expect from their presidents.

Leadership Expectations

The American public not only expects presidents to "prod and push" to advance their agenda, they expect them to do so successfully. Today, presidential expectations are lofty, greater than ever before, and continuing to grow at a steady clip. Certainly, Donald Trump and Obama could commiserate on the shared burden of presidential expectations, but a pressure-packed Oval Office is nothing new. Although the list of what the public might expect from the American president might be endless, at the top of it are some heady responsibilities; Michael Genovese, for example, identifies a wide range of such expectations, including effectiveness, toughness, skill, authority, and agenda setting.[16] Edwards and Wayne have shown that, prior to Obama's inauguration, greater than four out of five Americans expected the 44th president to work effectively with Congress, manage the executive branch wisely, and fulfill the proper role of the nation in global affairs.[17] These figures were slight increases over similar expectations for Obama's predecessor, George W. Bush, who faced expectations not much different to some of his predecessors such as Reagan and Carter and others still before them.[18] As presidential aide Ray Price told his then boss, Richard Nixon, during the 1968 presidential campaign:

> People identify with a President in a way they do no other public figure. Potential presidents are measured against an ideal that's a combination of leading man, God, father, hero, pope, king, with maybe just a touch of the avenging Furies thrown in. They want him to be larger than life, a living legend, and yet quintessentially human; someone to be held up to their children as a model; someone to be cherished by themselves as a revered member of the family, in somewhat the same way in which peasant families pray to the icon in the corner. Reverence goes where power is.[19]

Price's dramatic phrasing conveys well the heroic nature of presidential expectations and gives some hints as to the sources of these outsized expectations. The president as leading man is a relatively modern development; after all, early American presidents had no such expectation to burden them. Richard Waterman, Robert Wright, and Gilbert St. Clair have pointed out that our first presidents, including some who are regularly considered to be among our finest, were not expected to be politically ambitious, to advance a legislative agenda, or to speak or campaign publicly.[20] Instead, for more than a century, American presidents avoided active leadership of the governing process; instead, they typically deferred to Congress and oversaw a small and reactive executive institution. As the United States saw "the expansion of the public space" as it entered the twentieth century, a series of trends coalesced to drive the presidency toward its more ambitious and proactive future; these trends included increasing industrialization, urbanization, technological proliferation, and an expanding role in global politics.[21]

As I have argued elsewhere with Jose Villalobos:

> These new realities called for energetic national leadership, and the vague and elastic contours of Article II of the U.S. Constitution provided a source of new federal authority for those executives seeking it. From Theodore Roosevelt's muscular embrace of executive

power to the rise of World War I and Woodrow Wilson's embrace of internationalism, presidents during the opening decades of the new century gradually answered the call for stronger leadership, in turn raising expectations for future presidential performance as the challenges facing the nation—and its leadership—grew in both scope and severity. Franklin Delano Roosevelt's administration, however, cemented the notion among members of the public that the president held the helm of the ship of state. During these years, Roosevelt's leadership helped the nation emerge from the depths of the Great Depression to wage and—under his successor, Harry S. Truman—ultimately win World War II and take its place as a global hegemon with its powerful economy, vaunted military, and growing global reach. Over the ensuing decades, Roosevelt's legacy would yield unprecedented expectations for presidential leadership as chief executives were assigned the tasks of managing the economy, ensuring employment, keeping the peace while pressing the nation's agenda abroad, and taking care of society's needs at home. Roosevelt's activist leadership, though controversial at the time, eventually primed the public to expect future presidents—all of them—to be extraordinary, a development referenced in the scholarly texts as alternately 'heroic' or 'Superman' presidencies.[22]

Of course, Superman only exists in fiction and "heroic" is almost always used in hyperbole, especially when it comes to presidents. Presidents have failed to achieve expectations so frequently and consistently that a social scientific concept exists to describe this fundamentally underwhelming phenomenon: the expectations gap. The underlying thesis holds that a gap exists between what presidents can accomplish and what their public expects of them. Scholars have been discussing this gap for decades, from Richard Neustadt in the final edition of his seminal text, *Presidential Power*,[23] to empirical analyses by scholars such as Jim Stimson,[24] Arvind Raichur, and Richard Waterman,[25] which show that trends of declining approval within and across multiple presidencies can be explained by the rise and expansion of the expectations gap. More recently, a project by Waterman, Hank Jenkins-Smith, and Carol Silva shows that the expectations gap affects not just presidential approval, but also incumbent support in reelection bids.[26] Today, presidents and scholars alike know that the expectations gap exists. The reasons why merit further discussion in the next section.

Leadership Obstacles and Forces of Constraint

Whether functioning as a director or a facilitator, a president engaging in leadership is primarily practicing the art of influencing others. As

Edwards wrote more recently, in an essay written for the 2016 White House Transition Project:

> Influencing others is central to most people's conception of leadership, including those most focused on politics. In a democracy, we are particularly attuned to efforts to persuade, especially when most potentially significant policy changes require the assent of multiple power holders.[27]

The difficulty gaining this assent cannot be understated. Numerous obstacles routinely present themselves in a president's path, frequently making successful direct leadership impossible and successful facilitation improbable. Although not an exhaustive accounting, some of the most important obstacles in a president's path to leadership include the structure of the American political system, the fragmented and often polarized nature of American public opinion, and the dynamics of key political conditions. Or, as Edwards and Wayne note, "The Constitution divides authority; institutions share power; and parties usually lack cohesion and a sustained policy thrust."[28]

The Constitutional Structure

Indisputably, the primary reason why presidents fail to satisfy public expectations for leadership ties directly to the basic characteristics of the American constitutional system. Crafted in 1787 and ratified the following year, the U.S. Constitution created a fundamentally weak chief executive, so weak that Genovese calls it an "antileadership" system of government, noting that a variety of "built-in roadblocks create an immunity system from leadership in all but the most extraordinary times."[29] The most prominent of these leadership roadblocks are the rule of law, separation of powers, and checks and balances.

Because the rule of law has such a profound role in American politics and policy making, presidential options are always restricted. A president is not a dictator, despite their occasional secret wishes and the more frequent allegations made by disaffected partisan opponents whenever a president they do not like does something bold. Thinking creatively, the framers of the Constitution separated three discrete sources of power into three distinct institutions. The legislative power was given to a bicameral legislature (i.e., Congress) while the judicial power was given to a Supreme Court (and, soon after, a broader federal judiciary created by Congress during its first legislative session in 1789). The executive power—that is, the ability to implement the laws passed by Congress and to manage the performance of the government itself—was assigned to the presidency. However, unlike the charge given to Congress in Article I of the Constitution—which was lengthy, specific, and dealt directly with precisely what powers the legislative body did and did not have—Article II was comparatively circumspect and vague. Presidents had the mandate to "take care" that the law be faithfully executed, but little clarity existed about not only what that meant, but also the means presidents had available to them to do so. Moreover, whatever powers the presidency did possess were checked by powers given to the other branches. For example, the president's power to nominate justices to the Supreme Court was checked by the requirement that these appointments be confirmed by the Senate. Similarly, presidential efforts to negotiate treaties were also subject to Senate ratification, and as the nation and its government would both expand, presidential ability to manage the growing bureaucracy would also prove subject to congressional oversight. Simply put, for a president to get what they want, they must have the tacit consent, if not full support, of the rest of the constitutional system.

Polarization

The United States today suffers from extreme partisan polarization, a concept that refers to the "vast and growing gap between liberals and conservatives, Republicans and Democrats."[30] The current polarized era began developing noticeably in the 1980s but has led to a severe split between the two dominant American political parties over the last two decades. Successive presidents, Republican and Democrat alike, have found it nearly impossible to lead in sustained and significant ways due to heightened obstruction from their partisan opposition, not to mention the increasing ideological purity of their own party's base. Persistent judicial nomination delays, frequent narrow party-line votes, and even impeachment are among some of the consequences for the presidency in the current polarized era.

Governing in a polarized era—particularly one where the polarization is as pronounced as it is in the United States today—constrains presidential opportunities to lead because it means the opposition party is both homogeneous in its policy preferences and that those preferences are typically diametrically opposed from the president's own party. As most moderates have been purged from both parties over recent decades, there are few, if any, leaders in the political center that presidents can broker deals with. Unified government is hardly panacea, either. For one thing, of the 19 congressional sessions since Reagan's election in 1980, only five have seen unified party control of both Congress and the White House: 1993–1994 and 2009–2010 when Democrats controlled the legislative and executive branch, and 2003–2004, 2005–2006, and 2017–2018 when Republicans held the same. Second, the president's partisan allies do not always live up to that description. Fellow partisans, after all, are sometimes the most difficult for presidents to negotiate with. For example, Senator Ben Nelson (D-NE) gave Obama fits as he tried to win passage of the Affordable Care Act in 2009–2010. More recently, members of the so-called Freedom Caucus—a group of right-wing Republicans in the House of Representatives—managed to take on Trump and Speaker of the House Paul Ryan in 2017 and successfully kill one bill designed to repeal and replace the Affordable Care Act, later getting a considerably more conservative version successfully through the chamber.

All in all, partisan polarization restricts a president's prospects for successful leadership. Without a sizeable group of moderates to negotiate with and left only with an opposition base typically starkly opposed to the president's agenda, presidents instead focus on leading their fellow partisans through an approach Brandon Rottinghaus has called "going partisan," where presidents focus not on persuading opponents but rather on keeping fellow partisans from leaving the fold.[31]

Political Conditions

Although the extremely polarized nature of the political environment is arguably the dominant characteristic of contemporary American politics, several other factors constrain presidential leadership opportunities. The list of such factors is long, but at the top are the president's own popularity, whether they are eligible for reelection, if it is a presidential or midterm election year, the size of their party's faction in Congress, what issues are most salient, and how the economy is performing. When most of these factors stack up positively, the president's leadership prospects are maximized, but when things are pointed in the wrong direction, already limited leadership capacity shrinks further.

Often the most critical factor in shaping presidential prospects for leadership, the president's popularity with the American people determines greatly both what presidents have the capital to pursue and the extent to which they will be willing to pursue bold and risky goals. For decades, political scientists have known that the president's standing with the public affected his bargaining leverage with members of Congress and other important elites in the American political system.[32] Unsurprisingly, scholarship also shows that presidents go to great lengths to pursue higher approval ratings, knowing that their prospects for leadership are greater the higher they are.[33] That said, one of the more fascinating, relatively recent discoveries among political scientists is that presidents pursue bold agendas (i.e., they do not just pander to popular positions) not only when they are popular, but also when they are unpopular. In other words, popular presidents possess the capital to lead, while unpopular presidents have little to lose by pressing for agenda items that might be inconsistent with popular will.[34] It is the president not clearly popular or unpopular that is most constrained by their approval rating.

This linkage between approval and leadership, however, can be tempered by time. Like members of Congress, presidents are primarily focused on seeking reelection. Because the 22nd Amendment to the Constitution limits them to two terms, however, there are often clear differences between what presidents are willing and able to pursue in their first term and, should they be fortunate enough to be reelected, their second term. First-term presidents simultaneously have more to prove and more to lose vis-à-vis their standing with the American electorate than second-term presidents, who tend to accomplish far less and quickly begin thinking about their legacies. The situation becomes particularly acute in election years, both when presidents themselves are up for reelection and the midterm elections, where the entire U.S. House of Representatives and one-third of the U.S. Senate are up for reelection. Little substantive policy development tends to happen during those years, with members of Congress loathe to alienate key members of their electoral coalitions by taking unpopular positions and often fellow partisans of the president running campaigns that stress their independence from their party's unofficial leader. With all these eyes on their respective electoral prizes, the opportunities for successful presidential leadership narrow.

Political dynamics within Congress matter all the time, however, and not just when elections draw nigh. While the presence of unified or divided government matters a great deal, this is a relatively blunt way of thinking about party control of the federal government. If the president's party has a +1 advantage in both chambers, they technically enjoy unified government. There are benefits to having even this most narrow of margins, such as control of the speakership and the ability to chair committees, but if you ask any president, they would say without a moment's hesitation that they would much rather have a much greater margin between their fellow partisans in Congress and their partisan opposition. Larger margins mean that not only is it easier to craft the majority (and occasionally super majority) coalitions necessary to move an agenda item through the legislature, but also that the president's party is closer in keeping with the public's preferences. After all, the public tends to elect candidates who best reflect their policy priorities—if there are significantly more members of one party in Congress than the other, it is a fair bet that the campaign messages they are carrying resonate more with the populace.

How important an issue is to the American people—or at least to a key subset of the American people—also shapes a president's leadership prospects. When an issue is salient, both the president and other political elites are more likely to act upon it. Conversely, when it is not salient, presidential leadership becomes more difficult. Over the past few decades, scholars have shown that presidents possess some limited and conditional ability to raise the salience of an issue with consistent prioritizing, but even then, leadership is an uphill endeavor. Similarly, the condition of the economy shapes a president's leadership prospects.

If the market is booming, revenues are up, and unemployment is down, a president will be better positioned to push for a wide range of expensive policy goals, ranging from tax cuts to new entitlements. However, if the market is down, jobless rates up, and consumer confidence rattled, presidential options will be limited.

Taken together, we can see that presidential capacity for leadership is always in flux—the absence or presence of various combinations of external factors, many of which the president has little control over, dramatically effect what presidents are both expected and able to do. Most presidents likely go to sleep each night dreaming of a scenario in which their approval is soaring, the public is demanding action on the issues they themselves prioritize, the Congress is disproportionately filled with fellow partisans eager to do the president's bidding, and no one is unwilling to take bold action on policy goals because a difficult election is looming. The reality, however, is that most mornings, presidents wake up to different situations. The result of these intersecting factors is the contemporary reality all presidents must face and, ironically, try to ignore and lead anyway—the Constitution sets up a governing context that is fundamentally hostile to presidential leadership. As Edwards notes:

> The American political system is not a fertile field for the exercise of presidential leadership. Most political actors, from the average citizen to members of Congress, are free to choose whether to follow the chief executive's lead; the president cannot force them to act. At the same time, the sharing of powers established by the Constitution's checks and balances not only prevents the president from acting unilaterally on most important matters but also gives other power holders different perspectives on issues and policy proposals.[35]

Nevertheless, presidents continue to attempt to lead, both because they are expected to and because many of them think that they have the talent and skill necessary to succeed where their predecessors have failed. Although they share the commonality of seeking to lead, virtually every president has their own unique approach to leadership.

Conclusion

As the previous pages have indicated, successful presidential leadership is both expected by the American people and difficult to come by for even the most talented and conscientious president. This challenge is perhaps even greater for Trump, who faces an intensely hyper-partisan political environment. In addition, having run as an anti-establishment outsider, Trump is already dealing with obstruction from not only his political opponents on the left, but from some establishment Republicans as well. The ability to identify and clearly communicate goals, accurately assess the context in which these goals must be pursued, navigate the myriad obstacles, and achieve set objectives is as limited as ever before and perhaps more so with Trump due to his political inexperience and the fact that he is not like any president who has come before him. Unfortunately, for future presidents the leadership task is likely to become even more pressing and difficult. The constitutional structure that hamstrings presidents will not soon change. Partisan polarization—in Congress, in the media, and in the electorate—shows no sign of abating. Politically, the nation continues to be not only polarized into warring partisan camps, but evenly divided such that the kind of large majority for either party necessary to make bold and sustained policy change seems indefinitely elusive. Meanwhile, the media environment continues to proliferate, making it ever more difficult for presidents to communicate effectively.

To be great leaders, future presidents will need to have bold yet achievable agendas that they pursue with equal parts strategy and wisdom. They will need to master the management of both their administration and an ever-evolving media ecosystem in a way that enables them to successfully transition from successful campaigning to successful governing. They must realize that the skills necessary to become president are not the same as those necessary to be a successful president. As Edwards notes:

> We should not infer from success in winning elections that the White House can persuade members of the public and Congress to change their minds and support policies they would otherwise oppose. The American political system is not a fertile field for the exercise of presidential leadership. Most political actors, from the average citizen to members of Congress are free to choose whether to follow the chief executive's lead; the President cannot force them to act. At the same time, the sharing of powers established by the Constitution's checks and balances not only prevents the presidents from acting unilaterally on most important matters, but also gives other power holders different perspectives on issues and policy proposals.[36]

For presidents to successfully lead in the years to come, they must internalize the fundamental limitations of the executive institution, and strategize around them. Doing so will require patience, humility, and wisdom, along with all the other qualities discussed previously in this essay. Those qualities are in short supply for most regular citizens, not to mention presidents. When the next person to possess them finally gets their time in the Oval Office, the nation's finest engineers and sculptors should dust off their blast caps, chisels, and mallets, for it will be time to add another face to Mount Rushmore.

Notes

1 The Miller Center at the University of Virginia has preserved online a recording of a portion of this call. To listen to Representative Albert Thomas get the Johnson Treatment, visit the following link: https://millercenter.org/the-presidency/educational-resources/albert-thomas-gets-the-johnson-treatment.

2 George C. Edwards III, "Changing Their Minds? George W. Bush and the Limits of Presidential Persuasion," *21st Century Society* 2 (2007): 25–48.

3 See Kevin Mattson, *"What the Heck are you Up to, Mr. President?" Jimmy Carter, America's "Malaise," and the Speech that Should Have Changed the Country* (New York: Bloomsbury, 2009).

4 Scott Wilson, "Obama Calls on Muslims for a 'New Beginning' with U.S., *Washington Post*, June 5, 2009, www.washingtonpost.com/wp-dyn/content/article/2009/06/04/AR2009060401024.html.

5 Dana Milbank, "No Light at the End of the Tour," *Washington Post*, April 30, 2005, www.washingtonpost.com/wp-dyn/articles/A27030-2005Apr30.html?nav=rss_politics/specials/socialsecurity.

6 Daniel Dale, "The Worst Speech of All Time," *Toronto Star*, July 19, 2009, www.thestar.com/news/insight/2009/07/19/the_worst_speech_of_all_time.html.

7 Karl Rove, "The President's Apology Tour," *Wall Street Journal*, April 23, 2009, www.wsj.com/articles/SB124044156269345357.

8 Andrew B. Whitford and Jeff Yates, *Presidential Rhetoric and the Public Agenda: Constructing the War on Drugs* (Baltimore, MD: Johns Hopkins University Press, 2009), 1.

9 Fred I. Greenstein, "The Person of the President, Leadership, and Greatness," in *The Executive Branch*, eds. Joel D. Aberbach and Mark A. Peterson (Oxford: Oxford University Press, 2005), 235.

10 George C. Edwards III and Stephen J. Wayne, *Presidential Leadership: Politics and Policy Making*, 7th ed. (Belmont, CA: Thomason Wadsworth, 2006), 1.

11 Ibid., 19.

12 Ibid., 20.

13 Fred I. Greenstein, *The Presidential Difference: Leadership Style from FDR to George W. Bush*, 2nd ed. (Princeton, NJ: Princeton University Press, 2004), 217–223.

14 "Emotional Intelligence," *Psychology Today*, www.psychologytoday.com/basics/emotional-intelligence.

15 See Michael E. Siegel, *The President as Leader* (New York: Routledge, 2011).

16 Michael A. Genovese, *Memo to a New President* (New York: Oxford University Press, 2008), 147.

17 George C. Edwards III and Stephen J. Wayne, *Presidential Leadership: Politics and Policy Making*, 8th ed. (Boston, MA: Wadsworth, 2008), 109.

18 Ibid., 107; George C. Edwards III, *The Public Presidency* (New York: St. Martin's, 1983), 189.

19 Michael Novak, *Choosing Our King: Powerful Symbols in Presidential Politics* (New York: Macmillan, 1974), 44.

20 Richard Waterman, Robert Wright, and Gilbert St. Clair, *The Image-is-Everything Presidency: Dilemmas in American Leadership* (Boulder, CO: Westview, 1999), 153.

21 Bert Rockman, *The Leadership Question* (New York: Praeger, 1984), 134.

22 Justin S. Vaughn and Jose D. Villalobos, *Czars in the White House: The Rise of Policy Czars as Presidential Management Tools* (Ann Arbor, MI:

University of Michigan Press, 2015), 23–24. See also Michael A. Genovese, "The Finitude of Presidential Power," in *Understanding the Presidency*, 2nd ed., eds. James Pfiffner and Roger H. Davidson (New York: Longman, 2000), 420–438.

23 Richard E. Neustadt, *Presidential Power and the Modern Presidents: The Politics of Leadership from Roosevelt to Reagan* (New York: Free Press, 1990), ix.

24 James A. Stimson, "Public Support for American Presidents: A Cyclical Model," *Public Opinion Quarterly* 40 (1976): 1–21.

25 Arvind Raichur and Richard W. Waterman, "The Presidency, the Public, and the Expectations Gap," in *The Presidency Reconsidered*, ed. Richard W. Waterman (Itasca, IL: Peacock, 1993), 1–21.

26 See Richard Waterman, Hank Jenkins-Smith, and Carol Silva, *The Presidential Expectations Gap: Public Attitudes Concerning the Presidency* (Ann Arbor, MI: University of Michigan Press, 2014); and Richard Waterman, Carol Silva, and Hank Jenkins-Smith, "The Expectations Gap Thesis: Public Attitudes Toward an Incumbent President," *Journal of Politics* 61 (1999): 944–966.

27 George C. Edwards III, "The Potential of Presidential Leadership," White House Transition Project, 2016, p. 1, https://ssrn.com/abstract=2753222.

28 Edwards and Wayne, *Presidential Leadership*, 2006, 1.

29 Genovese, "The Finitude of Presidential Power," 427, 429–431.

30 "Political Polarization," Pew Research Center, www.pewresearch.org/packages/political-polarization/.

31 Brandon Rottinghaus, "Going Partisan: Presidential Leadership in a Polarized Political Environment," *Issues in Governance Studies* 62 (2013): 1–15.

32 See Edwards, *The Public Presidency*.

33 See Paul Brace and Barbara Hinckley, *Follow the Leader: Opinion Polls and the Modern Presidents* (New York: Basic Books, 1992).

34 Brandice Canes-Wrone, *Who Leads Whom? Presidents, Policy, and the Public* (Chicago, IL: University of Chicago Press, 2006).

35 Edwards, "The Potential of Presidential Leadership," 2.

36 George C. Edwards III, "The Essence of Presidential Leadership," National Constitution Center, March 30, 2016, https://constitutioncenter.org/blog/the-essence-of-presidential-leadership/.

Selected Bibliography

Abraham, Henry J. 1999. *Justices, Presidents and Senators: A History of the U.S. Supreme Court Appointments from Washington to Clinton.* Lanham, MD: Rowman & Littlefield.

Abramowitz, Alan. 2011. *The Disappearing Center: Engaged Citizens, Polarization, and American Democracy.* New Haven, CT: Yale University Press.

Abramson, Paul, John Aldrich, and David Rohde. 2009. *Change and Continuity in the 2008 Elections.* Washington, DC: CQ Press.

Abshire, David M. 2005. *Saving the Reagan Presidency: Trust is the Coin of the Realm.* College Station, TX: Texas A&M University Press.

Adkins, Randall E. 2008. *The Evolution of Political Parties, Campaigns, and Elections: Landmark Documents, 1787–2008.* Washington, DC: CQ Press.

Adkins, Randall E., and Andrew J. Dowdle. 2000. "Break Out the Mint Juleps in New Hampshire? Is New Hampshire the 'Primary' Culprit Limiting Presidential Nomination Forecasts?" *American Politics Quarterly* 28: 251–269.

———. 2001a. "How Important Are Iowa and New Hampshire to Winning Post-Reform Presidential Nominations?" *Political Research Quarterly* 54: 431–444.

———. 2001b. "Is the Exhibition Season Becoming More Important to Forecasting Presidential Nominations?" *American Politics Research* 29: 283–288.

———. 2002. "The Money Primary: What Influences the Outcome of Pre-Primary Presidential Nomination Fundraising?" *Presidential Studies Quarterly* 32: 256–275.

———. 2009. "Change and Continuity in the Presidential Money Primary." *American Review of Politics* 28: 319–341.

Aldrich, John. 1980. *Before the Convention: Strategies and Choices in Presidential Nominations.* Chicago, IL: University of Chicago Press.

Allison, Graham, and Philip Zelikow. 1999. *Essence of Decision: Explaining the Cuban Missile Crisis.* New York: Addison-Wesley.

Alter, Jonathan. 2009. *The Promise: President Obama, Year One.* New York: Simon and Schuster.

Ambrose, Stephen E., and Douglas G. Brinkley. 1997. *Rise to Globalism: American Foreign Policy Since 1938*, 8th rev. ed. New York: Penguin Books.

Ambrosius, Lloyd. 1987. *Woodrow Wilson and the American Diplomatic Tradition: The Treaty Fight in Perspective.* New York: Cambridge University Press.

Andres, Gary, and Patrick J. Griffin. 2002. "Successful Influence: Managing Legislative Affairs in the Twenty-first Century." In *Rivals for Power: Presidential-Congressional Relations*, ed. James A. Thurber. New York: Rowman and Littlefield.

Andres, Gary, Patrick Griffin, and James Thurber. 2004. "Managing White House-Congressional Relations: Observations from Inside the Process." *Presidential Studies Quarterly* 30: 553–563.

Arceneaux, Kevin, and Martin Johnson. 2013. *Changing Minds or Changing Channels?* Chicago, IL: University of Chicago Press.

Arnold, Peri. 1998. *Making the Managerial Presidency: Comprehensive Reorganization Planning, 1905–96*, 2nd ed. Lawrence, KS: University Press of Kansas.

Ashby, Leroy, and Rod Gramer. 1994. *Fighting the Odds: The Life of Senator Frank Church*. Pullman, WA: Washington State University Press.

Azari, Julia R. 2014. *Delivering the People's Message: The Changing Politics of the Presidential Mandate*. Ithaca, NY: Cornell University Press.

Azari, Julia R., and Justin S. Vaughn. 2014. "Barack Obama and the Rhetoric of Electoral Logic." *Social Science Quarterly* 95: 523–540.

Azari, Julia, Lara Brown, and Zim Nwokora. 2013. "Between a Rock and a Hard Place." In *The Presidential Leadership Dilemma: Between the Constitution and a Political Party*, eds. Julia Azari, Lara Brown, and Zim Nwokora. Albany, NY: SUNY Press.

Baker, Peter. 2013. *Days of Fire: Bush and Cheney in the White House*. New York: Doubleday.

Baker, William F., and George Dessart. 1998. *Down the Tube: An Inside Account of the Failure of American Television*. New York: Basic Books.

Barber, James David. 2008. *The Presidential Character: Predicting Performance in the White House*, 4th rev. ed. New York: Prentice Hall.

Barilleaux, Ryan. 1988. *The Post-Modern Presidency: The Office after Ronald Reagan*. New York: Praeger.

Barilleaux, Ryan J., and Christopher S. Kelley, eds. 2010. *The Unitary Executive and the Modern Presidency*. College Station, TX: Texas A&M University Press.

Barilleaux, Ryan J., and Randall E. Adkins. 1993. "The Nominations: Process and Patterns." In *The Elections of 1992*, ed. Michael Nelson. Washington, DC: CQ Press.

Barrett, Andrew W. 2007. "Press Coverage of Legislative Appeals by the President." *Political Research Quarterly* 60: 655–668.

Barrett, Andrew W., and Jeffrey S. Peake. 2007. "When the President Comes to Town: Examining Local Newspaper Coverage of Domestic Presidential Travel." *American Politics Research* 35: 3–31.

Barrett, Andrew W., and Matthew Eshbaugh-Soha. 2007. "Presidential Success on the Substance of Legislation." *Political Research Quarterly* 60: 195–222.

Bartels, Larry M. 1988. *Presidential Primaries and the Dynamics of Public Choice*. Princeton, NJ: Princeton University.

Baum, Lawrence. 2007. *The Supreme Court*, 9th ed. Washington, DC: CQ Press.

Baum, Matthew A. 2003. *Soft News Goes to War: Public Opinion and American Foreign Policy in the New Media Age*. Princeton, NJ: Princeton University Press.

Baum, Matthew A., and Samuel Kernell. 1999. "Has Cable Ended the Golden Age of Presidential Television?" *American Political Science Review* 93: 99–114.

Baumgartner, Frank R., and Bryan D. Jones. 2009. *Agendas and Instability in American Politics*, 2nd ed. Chicago, IL: University of Chicago Press.

Baumgartner, Jody, and Jonathan S. Morris. 2006. "*The Daily Show* Effect: Candidate Evaluations, Efficacy, and American Youth." *American Politics Research* 34: 341–367.

Bawn, Kathleen, Martin Cohen, David Karol, Seth Masket, Hans Noel, and John Zaller. 2012. "A Theory of Political Parties: Groups, Policy Demands, and Nominations in American Politics." *Perspectives on Politics* 10: 571–597.

Beckmann, Matthew N. 2010. *Pushing the Agenda: Presidential Leadership in U.S. Lawmaking, 1953–2004*. New York: Cambridge University Press.

Behr, Roy L., and Shanto Iyengar. 1985. "Television News, Real World Cues, and Changes in the Public Agenda." *Public Opinion Quarterly* 49: 38–57.

Belco, Michelle, and Brandon Rottinghaus. 2009. "Proclamation 6920: Using Executive Power to Set a New Direction for the Management of National Monuments." *Presidential Studies Quarterly* 39: 605–618.

———. 2017. *The Dual Executive*. Stanford, CA: Stanford University Press.

Bennett, W. Lance. 1990. "Toward a Theory of Press-State Relations in the U.S." *Journal of Communication* 40: 103–125.

———. 2009. *News: The Politics of Illusion*, 8th ed. New York: Longman.

Bennett, W. Lance, Regina G. Lawrence, and Steven Livingston. 2007. *When the Press Fails: Political Power and the News Media from Iraq to Katrina*. Chicago, IL: University of Chicago Press.

Berman, Larry. 1979. *The Office of Management and Budget and the Presidency, 1921–1979*. Princeton, NJ: Princeton University Press.

Berry, Jeffrey M., and Sarah Sobieraj. 2011. "From Incivility to Outrage: Political Discourse in Blogs, Talk Radio, and Cable News." *Political Communication* 28: 19–41.

Beschloss, Michael, ed. 1997. *Taking Charge: The Johnson White House Tapes 1963–64*. New York: Simon & Schuster.

———. ed. 2001. *Reaching for Glory: Lyndon Johnson's Secret White House Tapes 1964–65*. New York: Simon & Schuster.

Binder, Sarah A. 2001. "The Senate as a Black Hole? Lessons Learned from the Judicial Appointments Experience." In *Innocent until Nominated: The Breakdown of the Presidential Appointments Process*, ed. Calvin MacKenzie. Washington, DC: Brookings.

Binder, Sarah A., and Forrest Maltzman. 2009. *Advice and Dissent: The Struggle to Shape the Federal Judiciary*. Washington, DC: Brookings.

———. 2013. "New Wars of Advice and Consent: Judicial Selection in the Obama Years." *Judicature* 97: 49.

Blumenthal, David, and James A. Morone. 2009. *The Heart of Power: Health and Politics in the Oval Office*. Berkeley, CA: University of California Press.

Blumenthal, Sidney. 1980. *The Permanent Campaign: Inside the World of Elite Political Operatives*. Boston, MA: Beacon Press.

Bolton, Alexander, and Sharece Thrower. 2016. "Legislative Capacity and Executive Unilateralism." *American Journal of Political Science* 60: 649–663.

Bond, Jon R., and Richard Fleisher. 1990. *The President in the Legislative Arena*. Chicago, IL: University of Chicago Press.

Bond, Jon R., Richard Fleisher, and B. Dan Wood. 2003. "The Marginal and Time-Varying Effect of Public Approval on Presidential Success in Congress." *Journal of Politics* 65: 92–110.

Borneman, Walter. 2008. *Polk: The Man Who Transformed the Presidency and America*. New York: Random House.

Borrelli, Stephen A., and Grace L. Simmons. 1993. "Congressional Responsiveness to Presidential Popularity: The Electoral Context." *Political Behavior* 15: 93–112.

Bose, Meena. 1998. *Shaping and Signaling Presidential Policy: The National Security Decision Making of Eisenhower and Kennedy.* College Station, TX: Texas A&M University Press.

———. 1998. "Words as Signals: Drafting Cold War Rhetoric in the Eisenhower and Kennedy Administrations." *Congress & the Presidency* 25: 23–41.

———. 2005. "Private and Public Diplomacy: The U.S. Permanent Representative to the U.N. in the Clinton Years." Paper presented at "William Jefferson Clinton: The 'New Democrat' From Hope" Conference, Hofstra University, November 10–12.

———. 2006. "Who Makes U.S. Foreign Policy? Presidential Leadership in Gulf Wars I and II." In *The Presidency and the Challenge of Democracy*, eds. Michael A. Genovese and Lori Cox Han. New York: Palgrave Macmillan.

———. ed. 2012. *President or King? Evaluating the Expansion of Executive Power from Abraham Lincoln to George W. Bush.* Hauppauge, NY: Nova Science.

———. ed. 2013. *Change in the White House? Comparing the Presidencies of George W. Bush and Barack Obama.* Hauppauge, NY: Nova Science.

———. ed. 2016. *The George W. Bush Presidency*, 3 Volumes. Hauppauge, NY: Nova Science.

Boulianne, Shelley. 2009. "Does Internet Use Affect Engagement? A Meta-Analysis of Research." *Political Communication* 26: 193–211.

Bowie, Robert R., and Richard H. Immerman. 2000. *Waging Peace: How Eisenhower Shaped an Enduring Cold War Strategy.* New York: Oxford University Press.

Brace, Paul, and Barbara Hinckley. 1992. *Follow the Leader: Opinion Polls and Modern Presidents.* New York: Basic Books.

Brams, Steven J. 1978. *The Presidential Election Game.* New Haven, CT: Yale University Press.

Brewer, Paul R., and Xiaoxia Cao. 2006. "Candidate Appearance on Soft News Shows and Public Knowledge about Primary Campaigns." *Journal of Broadcasting & Electronic Media* 50: 18–35.

Brody, Richard. 1991. *Assessing the President: The Media, Elite Opinion and Public Support.* Stanford, CA: Stanford University Press.

Brown, Lara M. 2010. *Jockeying for the American Presidency: The Political Opportunism of Aspirants.* New York: Cambria Press.

Brule, David J., and Wonjae Hwang. 2010. "Diverting Legislature: Executive-Legislative Relations, the Economy, and US Uses of Force." *International Studies Quarterly* 54: 361–379.

Burke, John P. 1992. *The Institutional Presidency.* Baltimore, MD: Johns Hopkins University Press.

———. 2000. *The Institutional Presidency*, 2nd ed. Baltimore, MD: Johns Hopkins University Press.

———. 2009. *Honest Broker? The National Security Advisor and Presidential Decision Making.* College Station, TX: Texas A&M University Press.

Burke, John P., and Fred I. Greenstein. 1989. *How Presidents Test Reality: Decisions on Vietnam, 1954 and 1965.* New York: Russell Sage Foundation.

Burnham, Jeffrey. 2010. "The President and the Environment: A Reinterpretation of Neustadt's Theory of Presidential Leadership." *Congress & the Presidency* 37: 302–322.

Burns, James MacGregor. 1963. *The Deadlock of Democracy: Four-Party Politics in America.* Upper Saddle River, NJ: Prentice-Hall.

———. 1978. *Leadership.* New York: Harper & Row.

Busch, Andrew E. 2005. *Reagan's Victory: The Presidential Election of 1980 and the Rise of the Right.* Lawrence, KS: University Press of Kansas.

———. 2011. "Domestic Policy from Campaigning to Governing." In *Governing at Home: The White House and Domestic Policymaking*, eds. Michael Nelson and Russell Riley. Lawrence, KS: University Press of Kansas.

Bush, George H.W., and Brent Scowcroft. 1998. *A World Transformed.* New York: Knopf.

Calabresi, Steven G., and Christopher S. Yoo. 2008. *The Unitary Executive: Presidential Power from Washington to Bush.* New Haven, CT: Yale University Press.

Cameron, Charles M. 2000. *Veto Bargaining: Presidents and the Politics of Negative Power.* New York: Cambridge University Press.

Campbell, Angus, Philip E. Converse, Donald E. Stokes, and Warren E. Miller. 1960. *The American Voter.* New York: Wiley.

Campbell, Karlyn Kohrs, and Kathleen Hall Jamieson. 1990. *Deeds Done in Words: Presidential Rhetoric and the Genres of Governance.* Chicago, IL: University of Chicago Press.

Canes-Wrone, Brandice. 2006. *Who's Leading Whom?* Chicago, IL: University of Chicago Press.

Canes-Wrone, Brandice, and Scott de Marchi. 2002. "Presidential Approval and Legislative Success." *Journal of Politics* 64: 491–509.

Canes-Wrone, Brandice, William G. Howell, and David E. Lewis. 2008. "Toward a Broader Understanding of Presidential Power: A Reevaluation of the Two Presidencies Thesis." *Journal of Politics* 70: 1–16.

Caplan, Lincoln. 1987. *The Tenth Justice: The Solicitor General and the Rule of Law.* New York: Random House.

Carol, Marty, David Karol, Hans Noel, and John Zaller. 2008. *The Party Decides: Presidential Nominations Before and After Reform.* Chicago, IL: University of Chicago Press.

Carpenter, Dan. 2005. "The Evolution of the National Bureaucracy in the United States." In *The Executive Branch*, eds. Joel D. Aberbach and Mark Peterson. New York: Oxford University Press.

Carter, Stephen L. 1995. *The Confirmation Mess: Cleaning Up the Federal Appointments Process.* New York: Basic Books.

Caruson, Kiki, and Victoria A. Farrar-Myers. 2007. "Promoting the President's Foreign Policy Agenda: Presidential Use of Executive Agreements as Policy Vehicles." *Political Research Quarterly* 60: 631–644.

Cater, Douglas. 1954. *Power in Washington.* New York: Vintage.

Chiou, Fang-Yi, and Lawrence S. Rothenberg. 2017. *The Enigma of Presidential Power: Parties, Policies, and Strategic Uses of Unilateral Action.* New York: Cambridge University Press.

Christenson, Dino P., and Douglas L. Kriner. 2015. "Political Constraints on Unilateral Executive Action." *Case Western Reserve Law Review* 65: 897–931.

Cobb, Roger W., and Charles D. Elder. 1972. *Participation in American Politics: The Dynamics of Agenda-Building.* Boston, MA: Allyn and Bacon.

Cohen, David, and John Wells. 2004. *American National Security and Civil Liberties in an Era of Terrorism.* New York: Palgrave Macmillan.

Cohen, Jeffrey E. 1995. "Presidential Rhetoric and the Public Agenda." *American Journal of Political Science* 39: 87–107.

———. 1997. *Presidential Responsiveness and Public Policy-Making: The Public and the Policies That Presidents Choose.* Ann Arbor, MI: University of Michigan Press.

———. 2008. *The Presidency in the Era of 24-Hour News.* Princeton, NJ: Princeton University Press.

———. 2010. *Going Local: Presidential Leadership in the Post-Broadcast Age.* New York: Cambridge University Press.

———. 2012. *The President's Legislative Policy Agenda, 1789–2002.* New York: Cambridge University Press.

———. 2013. "Everybody Loves a Winner: On the Mutual Causality of Presidential Approval and Success in Congress." *Congress & the Presidency* 40: 285–307.

Cohen, Jeffrey, and David Nice. 2003. *The Presidency.* New York: McGraw-Hill.

Cohen, Martin, David Karol, Hans Noel, and John Zaller. 2008. *The Party Decides: Presidential Nominations Before and After Reform.* Chicago, IL: University of Chicago Press.

Coleman, John J., and Paul Manna. 2007. "Above the Fray? Uses of Party System References in Presidential Rhetoric." *Presidential Studies Quarterly* 37: 399–426.

Conley, Richard S. 2000. "Divided Government and Democratic Presidents: Truman and Clinton Compared." *Presidential Studies Quarterly* 30: 222–244.

Cooper, Phillip J. 2001. "Presidential Memoranda and Executive Orders: Of Patchwork Quilts, Trump Cards, and Shell Games." *Presidential Studies Quarterly* 31: 126–141.

———. 2002. *By Order of the President: The Use and Abuse of Executive Direction Action.* Lawrence, KS: University of Kansas Press.

———. 2005. "George W. Bush, Edgar Allan Poe, and the Use and Abuse of Presidential Signing Statements." *Presidential Studies Quarterly* 35: 515–532.

Cornwell, Elmer E. Jr. 1965. *Presidential Leadership of Public Opinion.* Bloomington, IN: Indiana University Press.

Corrado, Anthony. 2011. "The Regulatory Environment of the 2008 Elections." In *Financing the 2008 Election*, eds. David Magleby and Anthony Corrado. Washington, DC: Brookings.

Corrado, Anthony, and Molly Corbet. 2009. "Rewriting the Playbook on Presidential Campaign Financing." In *Campaigning for President 2008*, ed. Dennis W. Johnson. New York: Routledge.

Corwin, Edward S. 1949. "The Presidency in Perspective." *The Journal of Politics* 11: 7–13.

———. 1984. *The President: Office and Powers, 1787–1984*, 5th rev. ed., eds. Randall W. Bland, Theodore T. Hindson, and Jack W. Peltason. New York: New York University Press.

Covington, Cary R., J. Mark Wrighton, and Rhonda Kinney. 1995. "A 'Presidency-Augmented' Model of Presidential Success on House Roll Call Votes." *American Journal of Political Science* 39: 1001–1024.

Crabb, Cecil V., and Kevin V. Mulcahy. 1987. *Presidents and Foreign Policy Making: From F.D.R. to Reagan*. Baton Rouge, LA: Louisiana State University Press.

Cronin, Thomas E. 1984. "Thinking and Learning about Leadership." *Presidential Studies Quarterly* 14: 22–34.

Cronin, Thomas E., and Michael A. Genovese. 1998. *The Paradoxes of the American Presidency*. New York: Oxford University Press.

Daalder, Ivo H., and James M. Lindsay. 2003. *America Unbound: The Bush Revolution in Foreign Policy*. Washington, DC: Brookings.

Dahl, Robert A. 1957. "The Concept of Power." *Systems Research and Behavioral Science* 2: 201–215.

Dallek, Robert. 1998. *Flawed Giant: Lyndon Johnson and His Times, 1961–1973*. New York: Oxford University Press.

Deering, Christopher J. 1987. "Damned if You Do and Damned if You Don't." In *The In-And-Outers: Presidential Appointees and Transient Government in Washington*, ed. G. Calvin Mackenzie. Baltimore, MD: Johns Hopkins University Press.

Deering, Cristopher J., and Forrest Maltzman. 1999. "The Politics of Executive Orders: Legislative Constraints on Presidential Power." *Political Research Quarterly* 52: 767–783.

Diamond, Edwin, and Stephen Bates. 1993. *The Spot: The Rise of Political Advertising on Television*, 3rd ed. Cambridge, MA: MIT Press.

Dickinson, Matthew J. 1996. *Bitter Harvest: FDR, Presidential Power and the Growth of the Presidential Branch*. New York: Cambridge University Press.

———. 2005. "The Executive Office of the President: The Paradox of Politicization." In *The Executive Branch*, eds. Joel D. Aberbach and Mark Peterson. New York: Oxford University Press.

———. 2014. "The President and Congress." In *The Presidency and the Political System*, 10th ed., ed. Michael Nelson. Washington, DC: CQ Press.

Dickinson, Matthew J., and Jesse Gubb. 2016. "The Limits to Power without Persuasion." *Presidential Studies Quarterly* 46: 48–72.

Dickinson, Matthew J., and Kathryn D. Tenpas. 2002. "The Revolving Door at the White House: Explaining Increasing Turnover Rates among Presidential Advisers, 1929–1997." *Journal of Politics* 64: 434–448.

Dominguez, Casey Byrne Knudsen. 2010. "Is It a Honeymoon? An Empirical Investigation of the President's First Hundred Days." *Congress & the Presidency* 32: 63–78.

Dowdle, Andrew J., Randall E. Adkins, Karen Sebold, and Patrick A. Stewart. 2013. "Financing the 2012 Presidential Election in a Post-Citizens United World." In *Winning the Presidency 2012*, ed. William J. Crotty. Boulder, CO: Paradigm.

Dowdle, Andrew J., Randall E. Adkins, and Wayne P. Steger. 2009. "The Viability Primary: What Drives Mass Partisan Support for Candidates before the Primaries?" *Political Research Quarterly* 62: 77–91.

Downs, Anthony. 1972. "Up and Down with Ecology: The Issue-Attention Cycle." *Public Interest* 28: 38–50.

Draper, Theodore. 1991. *A Very Thin Line: The Iran-Contra Affairs*. New York: Hill and Wang.

Edwards, George C. III. 1983. *The Public Presidency*. New York: St. Martin's.

———. 1989. *At the Margins: Presidential Leadership of Congress*. New Haven, CT: Yale University Press.

———. 1997. "Aligning Tests with Theory: Presidential Influence as a Source of Influence in Congress." *Congress & the Presidency* 24: 113–130.

———. 2003. *On Deaf Ears: The Limits of the Bully Pulpit*. New Haven, CT: Yale University Press.

———. 2007. "Changing Their Minds? George W. Bush and the Limits of Presidential Persuasion." *21st Century Society* 2: 25–48.

———. 2007. *Governing by Campaigning: The Politics of the Bush Presidency*. New York: Longman.

———. 2009. *The Strategic President: Persuasion and Opportunity in Presidential Leadership*. Princeton, NJ: Princeton University Press.

Edwards, George C. III, and Andrew Barrett. 2000. "Presidential Agenda Setting Congress." In *Polarized Politics: Congress and the President in a Partisan Era*, eds. Jon R. Bond and Richard Fleisher. Washington, DC: CQ Press.

Edwards, George C. III, and B. Dan Wood. 1999. "Who Influences Whom? The President, Congress, and the Media." *American Political Science Review* 93: 327–344.

Edwards, George C. III, and Stephen J. Wayne, eds. 1983. *Studying the Presidency*. Knoxville, TN: University of Tennessee Press.

———. 2006. *Presidential Leadership: Politics and Policy Making*, 7th ed. Belmont, CA: Thomason Wadsworth.

———. 2008. *Presidential Leadership: Politics and Policy Making*, 8th ed. Boston, MA: Wadsworth.

Edwards, George C. III, Andrew Barrett, and Jeffrey Peake. 1997. "The Legislative Impact of Divided Government." *American Journal of Political Science* 41: 545–563.

Edwards, George C. III, John H. Kessel, and Bert A. Rockman. 1993. *Researching the Presidency: Vital Questions, New Approaches*. Pittsburgh, PA: University of Pittsburgh Press.

Edwards, George C. III, William Mitchell, and Reed Welch. 1995. "Explaining Presidential Approval: The Importance of Issue Salience." *American Journal of Political Science* 39: 108–134.

Eisinger, Robert. 2003. *The Evolution of Presidential Polling*. New York: Cambridge University Press.

Eisinger, Robert, and Jeremy Brown. 1998. "Polling as a Means toward Presidential Autonomy: Emil Hurja, Hadley Cantril and the Roosevelt Administration." *International Journal of Public Opinion Research* 10: 237–256.

Ellis, Richard J., ed. 1998. *Speaking to the People: The Rhetorical Presidency in Historical Perspective*. Amherst, MA: University of Massachusetts Press.

———. 2012. *The Development of the American Presidency*. New York: Routledge.

Ellis, Richard J., and Stephen Kirk. 1995. "Presidential Mandates in the Nineteenth Century: Conceptual Change and Institutional Development." *Studies in American Political Development* 9: 117–186.

Elsea, Jennifer K. 2003. "Presidential Authority to Detain 'Enemy Combatants.'" *Presidential Studies Quarterly* 33: 568–601.

Epstein, Lee, and Jack Knight. 1998. *The Choices Justices Make*. Washington, DC: CQ Press.

Epstein, Lee, and Jeffrey Segal. 2005. *Advice and Consent: The Politics of Judicial Appointments.* New York: Oxford University Press.

Eshbaugh-Soha, Matthew. 2003. "Presidential Press Conferences over Time." *American Journal of Political Science* 47: 348–353.

———. 2005. "The Politics of Presidential Agendas." *Political Research Quarterly* 58: 257–268.

———. 2010a. "The Politics of Presidential Speeches." *Congress & the Presidency* 37: 1–21.

———. 2010b. "The Tone of Local Presidential News Coverage." *Political Communication* 27: 121–140.

———. 2013. "Presidential Leadership of the News Media: The Case of the Press Conference." *Political Communication* 30: 548–564.

———. 2015. "Traditional Media, Social Media, and Different Presidential Campaign Messages." In *Controlling the Message: New Media in American Political Campaigns,* eds. Victoria A. Farrar-Myers and Justin S. Vaughn. New York: New York University Press, pp. 136–154.

———. 2016. "Presidential Agenda-Setting of Traditional and Nontraditional News Media." *Political Communication* 30: 1–20.

Eshbaugh-Soha, Matthew, and Jeffrey S. Peake. 2005. "Presidents and the Economic Agenda." *Political Research Quarterly* 58: 127–138.

———. 2006. "The Contemporary Presidency: 'Going Local' to Reform Social Security." *Presidential Studies Quarterly* 36: 689–704.

———. 2008. "The Presidency and Local Media: Local Newspaper Coverage of President George W. Bush." *Presidential Studies Quarterly* 38: 606–627.

———. 2011. *Breaking through the Noise: Presidential Leadership, Public Opinion, and the News Media.* Stanford, CA: Stanford University Press.

Farnsworth, Stephen J., and Robert S. Lichter. 2006. *The Mediated Presidency: Television News and Presidential Governance.* New York: Rowman & Littlefield.

Farrar-Myers, Victoria A. 1998. "Transference of Authority: The Institutional Struggle over the Control of the War Power." *Congress & the Presidency* 25: 183–197.

———. 2007. *Scripted for Change: The Institutionalization of the American Presidency.* College Station, TX: Texas A&M University Press.

Fine, Jeffrey A., and Adam L. Warber. 2012. "Circumventing Adversity: Executive Orders and Divided Government." *Presidential Studies Quarterly* 42: 256–274.

Fiorina, Morris. 1992. *Divided Government.* New York: Longman.

———. 2009. *Disconnect: The Breakdown of Representation in American Politics.* Norman, OK: University of Oklahoma Press.

Fisher, Louis. 1995a. "On What Legal Basis Did Truman Act?" *The American Journal of International Law* 89: 21–39.

———. 1995b. *Presidential War Power.* Lawrence, KS: University of Kansas Press.

———. 1998. *The Politics of Shared Power: Congress and the Executive,* 4th ed. College Station, TX: Texas A&M University Press.

———. 2004. *Presidential War Power,* 2nd rev. ed. Lawrence, KS: University Press of Kansas.

———. 2013. *Presidential War Power,* 3rd ed. Lawrence, KS: University Press of Kansas.

Foote, Joe S. 1988. "Ratings Decline of Presidential Television." *Journal of Broadcasting and Electronic Media* 32: 225–230.

Francis, Megan Ming. 2014. *Civil Rights and the Making of the Modern American State*. New York: Cambridge University Press.

Franklin, Daniel P., and Michael P. Fix. 2016. "The Best of Times and the Worst of Times: Polarization and Presidential Success in Congress." *Congress & the Presidency* 43: 377–394.

Frederickson, Kari. 2001. *The Dixiecrat Revolt and the End of the Solid South, 1932–1968*. Chapel Hill, NC: University of North Carolina Press.

Gaddis, John Lewis. 2005. *Strategies of Containment: A Critical Appraisal of American National Security Policy during the Cold War*, rev. ed. New York: Oxford University Press.

Galanter, Marc. 1974. "Why the 'Haves' Come Out Ahead: Speculations on the Limits of Legal Change." *Law and Society Review* 9: 98.

Galvin, Daniel J. 2009. *Presidential Party-Building: Dwight D. Eisenhower to George W. Bush*. Princeton, NJ: Princeton University Press.

———. 2012. "Presidential Partisanship Reconsidered: Eisenhower, Nixon, Ford, and the Rise of Polarized Politics." *Political Research Quarterly* 66: 46–60.

———. 2012. "The Dynamics of Presidential Policy Choice and Promotion." In *Building Coalitions, Making Policy: The Politics of the Clinton, Bush, and Obama Presidencies*, eds. Martin A. Levin, Daniel DiSalvo, and Martin M. Shapiro. Baltimore, MD: Johns Hopkins University Press.

Gans, Herbert. 1980. *Deciding What's News: A Study of CBS Evening News, NBC Nightly News, Newsweek, and Time*. New York: Vintage Books.

Garrison, Jean A. 1999. *Games Advisors Play: Foreign Policy in the Nixon and Carter Administrations*. College Station, TX: Texas A&M University Press.

Gelman, Jeremy, Gilad Wilkenfeld, and E. Scott Adler. 2015. "The Opportunistic President: How U.S. Presidents Determine Their Legislative Programs." *Legislative Studies Quarterly* 40: 363–390.

Gelpi, Christopher, and Joseph Grieco. 2015. "Competency Costs in Foreign Affairs: Presidential Performance in International Conflicts and Domestic Legislative Success, 1953–2001." *American Journal of Political Science* 58: 440–456.

Genovese, Michael A. 2000. "The Finitude of Presidential Power." In *Understanding the Presidency*, 2nd ed., eds. James Pfiffner and Roger H. Davidson. New York: Longman.

———. 2008. *Memo to a New President*. New York: Oxford University Press.

George, Alexander L. 1972. "The Case for Multiple Advocacy in Making Foreign Policy." *American Political Science Review* 66: 751–785.

———. 1980. *Presidential Decisionmaking in Foreign Policy: The Effective Use of Information and Advice*. Boulder, CO: Westview.

Gerhardt, Michael J. 2003. *The Federal Appointment Process: A Constitutional and Historical Analysis*. Durham, NC: Duke University Press.

Gilberg, Sheldon, Chaim Eyal, Maxwell McCombs, and David Nicholas. 1980. "The State of the Union Address and the Press Agenda." *Journalism Quarterly* 57: 584–588.

Gilliam, Franklin D. Jr., and Shanto Iyengar. 2000. "Prime Suspects: The Influence of Local Television News on the Viewing Public." *American Journal of Political Science* 44: 560–573.

Gillman, Howard. 2001. *The Votes that Counted: How the Court Decided the 2000 Presidential Election*. Chicago, IL: University of Chicago Press.

Gilmour, John B. 2002. "Institutional and Individual Influences on the President's Veto." *The Journal of Politics* 64: 198–218.

Goldman, Emily O., and Larry Berman. 2000. "Engaging the World: First Impressions of the Clinton Foreign Policy Legacy." In *The Clinton Legacy*, eds. Colin Campbell and Bert A. Rockman. New York: Chatham House.

Goldman, Sheldon. 1997. *Picking Federal Judges: Lower Court Selection from Roosevelt through Reagan*. New Haven, CT: Yale University Press.

Goldman, Sheldon, Elliot Slotnick, and Sara Schiavoni. 2011. "Obama's Judiciary at Midterm: The Confirmation Drama Continues." *Judicature* 94: 262–301.

———. 2013. "Obama's First Term Judiciary: Picking Judges in the Minefield of Obstructionism." *Judicature* 97: 7–47.

Graber, Doris A. 2006. *Mass Media and American Politics*, 7th ed. Washington, DC: CQ Press.

Graber, Doris A., and Johanna Dunaway. 2015. *Mass Media and American Politics*, 9th ed. Washington, DC: CQ Press.

Greenburg, Jan Crawford. 2007. *Supreme Conflict: The Inside Story of the Struggle for Control of the United States Supreme Court*. New York: Penguin Press.

Greenstein, Fred I. 1982. *The Hidden-Hand Presidency: Eisenhower as Leader*. New York: Basic Books.

———. 2004. *The Presidential Difference: Leadership Style from FDR to George W. Bush*, 2nd ed. Princeton, NJ: Princeton University Press.

———. 2005. "The Person of the President, Leadership, and Greatness." In *The Executive Branch*, eds. Joel D. Aberbach and Mark A. Peterson. Oxford: Oxford University Press.

———. 2009. *Inventing the Job of President: Leadership Style from George Washington to Andrew Jackson*. Princeton, NJ: Princeton University Press.

———. 2009. *The Presidential Difference: Leadership Style from FDR to Barack Obama*, 3rd ed. Princeton, NJ: Princeton University Press.

Groeling, Tim, and Samuel Kernell. 1998. "Is Network News Coverage of the President Biased?" *The Journal of Politics* 60: 1063–1087.

Gronke, Paul, and Brian Newman. 2003. "FDR to Clinton: Mueller to ?: A Field Essay on Presidential Approval." *Political Research Quarterly* 56: 501–512.

Grossman, Michael Baruch, and Martha Joynt Kumar. 1981. *Portraying the President: The White House and the News Media*. Baltimore, MD: Johns Hopkins University Press.

Haass, Richard N. 2009. *War of Necessity, War of Choice: A Memoir of Two Iraq Wars*. New York: Simon & Schuster.

Hacker, Jacob, and Paul Pierson. 2006. *Off Center: The Republican Revolution and the Erosion of American Democracy*. New Haven, CT: Yale University Press.

Hagen, Michael G., and Kathleen Hall Jamieson. 2000. "Do Newspaper Endorsements Matter? Do Politicians Speak for Themselves in Newspapers and on Television?" In *Everything You Think You Know about Politics and Why You're Wrong*, ed. Kathleen Hall Jamieson, New York: Basic Books.

Hager, Gregory L., and Terry Sullivan. 1994. "President-Centered and Presidency-Centered Explanations of Presidential Public Activity." *American Journal of Political Science* 38: 1079–1103.

Halperin, Mark, and John Heilemann. 2013. *Double Down: Game Change 2012.* New York: Penguin Press.

Hamilton, James. 2003. *All the News That's Fit to Sell: How the Market Transforms Information into News.* Princeton, NJ: Princeton University Press.

Hamilton, Lee H., and Jordan Tama. 2002. *A Creative Tension: The Foreign Policy Roles of the President and Congress.* Princeton, NJ: Woodrow Wilson Center Press.

Hammond, Thomas H., and Jeffery S. Hill. 1993. "Deference of Preference? Explaining Senate Confirmation of Presidential Nominees to Administrative Agencies." *Journal of Theoretical Politics* 5: 23–59.

Han, Lori Cox. 2001. *Governing From Center Stage: White House Communication Strategies during the Television Age of Politics.* Cresskill, NJ: Hampton Press.

———. 2011. *A Presidency Upstaged: The Public Presidency of George H.W. Bush.* College Station, TX: Texas A&M University Press.

Han, Lori Cox, and Diane J. Heith. 2018. *Presidents and the American Presidency,* 2nd ed. New York: Oxford University Press.

Haney, Patrick J. 1997. *Organizing for Foreign Policy Crisis: Presidents, Advisers, and the Management of Decision Making.* Ann Arbor, MI: University of Michigan Press.

Hargrove, Erwin C., and Michael Nelson. 1984. *Presidents, Politics, and Policy.* New York: Knopf.

Hart, Gary. 2006. *The Shield and the Cloak.* New York: Oxford University Press.

Hart, Roderick P. 1987. *The Sound of Leadership: Presidential Communication in the Modern Age.* Chicago, IL: University of Chicago Press.

Hart, Roderick P., Jay P. Childers, and Colene J. Lind. 2013. *Political Tone: How Leaders Talk and Why.* Chicago, IL: University of Chicago Press.

Heclo, Hugh. 1977. *A Government of Strangers.* Washington, DC: Brookings.

———. 1977. *Studying the Presidency: A Report to the Ford Foundation.* New York: Ford Foundation Press.

———. 1978. "The Executive Establishment." In *The New American Political System,* ed. Anthony King. Washington, DC: American Enterprise Institute.

———. 1983. "One Executive Branch or Many?" In *Both Ends of the Avenue,* ed. Anthony Kind. Washington, DC: American Enterprise Institute.

———. 2000. "Campaigning and Governing: A Conspectus." In *The Permanent Campaign and Its Future,* eds. Norman Ornstein and Thomas Mann. Washington, DC: Brookings.

———. 2011. "Whose Presidency Is It Anyway?" In *The Oxford Handbook of the American Presidency,* eds. George C. Edwards and William G. Howell. New York: Oxford University Press, 2011.

Heith, Diane J. 2003. *Polling to Govern: Public Opinion and Presidential Leadership.* Stanford, CA: Stanford University Press.

———. 2012. "Obama and the Public Presidency: What Got You Here Won't Get You There." In *The Obama Presidency: Appraisals and Prospects,* eds. Bert A. Rockman, Andrew Rudalevige, and Colin Campbell. Washington, DC: CQ Press.

———. 2013. *The Presidential Road Show: Public Leadership in an Era of Party Polarization and Media Fragmentation.* Boulder, CO: Paradigm.

Henkin, Louis. 1987/88. "Foreign Affairs and the Constitution." *Foreign Affairs*: 284–310.

Hersman, Rebecca K. C. 2000. *Friends and Foes: How Congress and the President Really Make Foreign Policy.* Washington, DC: Brookings.

Hess, Gary R. 2009. *Presidential Decisions for War: Korea, Vietnam, the Persian Gulf, and Iraq*, 2nd ed. Baltimore, MD: Johns Hopkins University Press.

Hetherington, Marc J., and Thomas J. Rudolph. 2015. *Why Washington Won't Work: Polarization, Political Trust, and the Governing Crisis.* Chicago, IL: University of Chicago Press.

Hinckley, Barbara. 1990. *The Symbolic Presidency: How Presidents Portray Themselves.* New York: Routledge.

———. 1994. *Less Than Meets the Eye: Foreign Policy Making and the Myth of the Assertive Congress.* Chicago, IL: University of Chicago Press.

Hindman, Michael. 2005. "The Real Lessons of Howard Dean: Reflections on the First Digital Campaign." *Perspectives on Politics* 3: 121–128.

Holbrook, R. Andrew, and Timothy G. Hill. 2005. "Agenda-Setting and Priming in Prime Time Television: Crime Dramas as Political Cues." *Political Communication* 22: 277–295.

Hollibaugh, Gary E. Jr. 2015. "Vacancies, Vetting, and Votes: A Unified Dynamic Model of the Appointments Process." *Journal of Theoretical Politics* 27: 206–236.

———. 2017. "Presidential Appointments and Policy Priorities." *Social Science Quarterly* 98: 162–184.

Hollibaugh, Gary E. Jr., Gabriel Horton, and David E. Lewis. 2014. "Presidents and Patronage." *American Journal of Political Science* 58: 1024–1042.

Hollibaugh, Gary E. Jr., and Lawrence S. Rosenberg. 2017. "The When and Why of Nominations: Determinants of Presidential Appointments." *American Politics Research* 45: 280–303.

Howell, William G. 2003. *Power without Persuasion: The Politics of Direct Presidential Action.* Princeton, NJ: Princeton University Press.

———. 2005. "Unilateral Powers: A Brief Overview." *Presidential Studies Quarterly* 35: 417–439.

Howell, William G., and Jon Pevehouse. 2003. "Presidents, Congress and the Use of Force." *International Organization* 59: 209–232.

———. 2007. *While Dangers Gather: Congressional Checks on Presidential War Powers.* Princeton, NJ: Princeton University Press.

Howell, William G., and Jon C. Rogowski. 2013. "War, the Presidency, and Legislative Voting Behavior." *American Journal of Political Science* 57: 150–166.

Howell, William G., and Kenneth Mayer. 2005. "The Last One Hundred Days." *Presidential Studies Quarterly* 35: 533–553.

Hull, Christopher C. 2007. *Grassroots Rules: How the Iowa Caucus Helps Elect American Presidents.* Stanford, CA: Stanford University Press.

Hult, Karen M., and Charles E. Walcott. 2004. *Empowering the White House: Governance under Nixon, Ford, and Carter.* Lawrence, KS: University Press of Kansas.

———. 2011. "Domestic Policy Development in the White House." In *Governing at Home: The White House and Domestic Policymaking*, eds. Michael Nelson and Russell Riley. Lawrence, KS: University Press of Kansas.

Iyengar, Shanto. 1991. *Is Anyone Responsible?* Chicago, IL: University of Chicago Press.

Iyengar, Shanto, and Donald R. Kinder. 1987. *News That Matters: Television and American Opinion.* Chicago, IL: University of Chicago Press.

Iyengar, Shanto, Mark D. Peters, and Donald R. Kinder. 1982. "Experimental Demonstrations of the 'Not-So-Minimal' Consequences of Television News Programs." *American Political Science Review* 76: 848–858.

Jacobs, Lawrence R., and Robert Y. Shapiro. 1995. "The Rise of Presidential Polling: The Nixon White House in Historical Perspective." *Public Opinion Quarterly* 59: 163–195.

———. 2000. *Politicians Don't Pander: Political Manipulation and the Loss of Democratic Responsiveness.* Chicago, IL: University of Chicago Press.

Jacobson, Gary. 2015. "Barack Obama and the Nationalization of Electoral Politics in 2012." *Electoral Studies* 40: 471–481.

Jamieson, Kathleen Hall, and Bruce W. Hardy. 2009. "Media, Endorsements, and the 2008 Primaries." In *Reforming the Presidential Nomination Process,* eds. Stephen S. Smith and Melanie J. Springer. Washington, DC: Brookings.

Johnson, Loch K. 1998. *A Season of Inquiry: Congress and Intelligence.* Chicago, IL: Dorsey Press.

Johnson, Richard Tanner. 1974. *Managing the White House: An Intimate Study of the Presidency.* New York: Harper & Row.

Johnson, Robert David. 2006. *Congress and the Cold War.* New York: Cambridge University Press.

Jones, Charles O. 1994. *The Presidency in a Separated System.* Washington, DC: Brookings.

———. 1999. *Separate but Equal Branches: Congress & the Presidency,* 2nd ed. New York: Chatham House.

Kelley, Christopher S., and Bryan W. Marshall. 2008. "The Last Word: Presidential Power and the Role of Signing Statements." *Presidential Studies Quarterly* 38: 248–267.

Kennedy, Ross A. 2009. *The Will to Believe: Woodrow Wilson, World War I, and America's Strategy for Peace and Security.* Kent, OH: Kent State University Press.

Kernell, Samuel. 1978. "Explaining Presidential Popularity." *American Political Science Review* 72: 506–522.

———. 1986. *Going Public: New Strategies of Presidential Leadership.* Washington, DC: CQ Press.

———. 1997. *Going Public: New Strategies of Presidential Leadership,* 3rd ed. Washington, DC: CQ Press.

———. 2007. *Going Public: New Strategies of Presidential Leadership,* 4th ed. Washington, DC: CQ Press.

Kernell, Samuel, and Laurie L. Rice. 2011. "Cable and the Partisan Polarization of the President's Audience." *Presidential Studies Quarterly* 41: 693–711.

Kessel, John H. 2001. *Presidents, the Presidency, and the Political Environment.* Washington, DC: CQ Press.

Ketcham, Ralph. 1987. *Presidents above Party: The First American Presidency, 1789–1829.* Chapel Hill, NC: University of North Carolina Press.

Kettl, Don. 2014. *System Under Stress: Homeland Security and American Politics,* 3rd ed. Washington, DC: CQ Press.

Kiewiet, D. Roderick, and Matthew D. McCubbins. 1985. "Appropriations Decisions as a Bilateral Bargaining Game between President and Congress." *Legislative Studies Quarterly* 10: 181–210.

King, Gary, and Lyn Ragsdale. 1988. *The Elusive Executive: Discovering Statistical Patterns in the Presidency.* Washington, DC: CQ Press.

Kingdon, John W. 1995. *Agendas, Alternatives, and Public Policies.* Boston, MA: Little, Brown.

———. 2011. *Agendas, Alternatives, and Public Policies*, 2nd ed. Boston, MA: Longman.

Klinghard, Daniel P. 2005. "Grover Cleveland, William McKinley, and the Emergence of President as Party Leader." *Presidential Studies Quarterly* 35: 736–760.

Klinkner, Philip A., and Rogers Smith. 2002. *The Unsteady March: The Rise and Decline of Racial Equality in America.* Chicago, IL: University of Chicago Press.

Koenig, Louis W. 1996. *The Chief Executive*, 6th ed. New York: Harcourt Brace.

Kolko, Gabriel. 1963. *The Triumph of Conservatism: A Reinterpretation of American History, 1900–1916.* New York: Free Press of Glencoe.

Krause, George A., and Jeffrey E. Cohen. 2000. "Opportunity, Constraints and the Development of the Institutional Presidency: The Issuance of Executive Orders, 1939–1996." *Journal of Politics* 62: 88–114.

Krehbiel, Keith. 1998. *Pivotal Politics: A Theory of U.S. Lawmaking.* Chicago, IL: University of Chicago Press.

Kriner, Douglas L. 2010. *After the Rubicon: Congress, Presidents, and the Politics of Waging War.* Chicago, IL: University of Chicago Press.

Kriner, Douglas L., and Eric Schickler. 2016. *Investigating the President: Congressional Check on Presidential Power.* Princeton, NJ: Princeton University Press.

Krosnick, Jon A., and Donald R. Kinder. 1990. "Altering the Foundations of Support for the President through Priming." *American Political Science Review* 84: 497–512.

Kumar, Martha Joynt. 2007. *Managing the President's Message: The White House Communications Operation.* Baltimore, MD: Johns Hopkins University Press.

Lammers, William W. 1982. "Presidential Attention-Focusing Activities." In *The President and the Public*, ed. Doris Graber. Philadelphia, PA: Institute for the Study of Human Issues.

Lammers, William W., and Michael A. Genovese. 2000. *The Presidency and Domestic Policy: Comparing Leadership Styles, FDR to Clinton.* Washington, DC: CQ Press.

Landy, Marc, and Sidney M. Milkis. 2000. *Presidential Greatness.* Lawrence, KS: University Press of Kansas.

Laracey, Mel. 2002. *Presidents and the Public: The Partisan Story of Going Public.* College Station, TX: Texas A&M University Press.

LaRocca, Roger T. 2002. *The Presidential Agenda: Sources of Executive Influence in Congress.* Columbus, OH: Ohio State University Press.

Lawrence, Regina G. 2015. "Campaign News in the Time of Twitter." In *Controlling the Message: New Media in American Political Campaigns*, eds. Victoria A. Farrar-Myers and Justin S. Vaughn. New York: New York University Press.

Lebo, Matthew J., and Andrew J. O'Green. "The President's Role in the Partisan Congressional Arena." *Journal of Politics* 73: 718–734.

Lee, Frances E. 2008. "Dividers Not Uniters: Presidential Leadership and Senate Partisanship 1981–2004." *The Journal of Politics* 70: 914–928.

———. 2009. *Beyond Ideology: Politics, Principles and Partisanship in the U.S. Senate.* Chicago, IL: University of Chicago Press.

———. 2016. *Insecure Majorities: Congress and the Perpetual Campaign.* Chicago, IL: University of Chicago Press.

Leighley, Jan E. 2003. *Mass Media and Politics: A Social Science Perspective.* Boston, MA: Houghton Mifflin.

Leuchtenberg, William E. 1963. *Franklin D. Roosevelt and the New Deal: 1932–1940.* New York: Harper and Row.

Levin, Martin A., Daniel DiSalvo, and Martin M. Shapiro, eds. 2012. *Building Coalitions, Making Policy: The Politics of the Clinton, Bush, and Obama Presidencies.* Baltimore, MD: Johns Hopkins University Press.

Lewis, David E. 2003. *Presidents and the Politics of Agency Design.* Stanford, CA: Stanford University Press.

———. 2008. *The Politics of Presidential Appointments: Political Control and Bureaucratic Performance.* Princeton, NJ: Princeton University Press.

Lewis-Beck, Michael S., and Peverill Squire. 2009. "Iowa: The Most Representative State?" *PS: Political Science & Politics* 42: 39–44.

Light, Paul C. 1982. *The President's Agenda: Domestic Policy Choice from Kennedy to Carter.* Baltimore, MD: Johns Hopkins University Press.

———. 1995. *Thickening Government: Federal Hierarchy and the Diffusion of Accountability.* Washington, DC: Brookings.

———. 1999. *True Size of Government.* Washington, DC: Brookings.

Lockerbie, Brad, Stephen Borrelli, and Scott Hedger. 1998. "An Integrative Approach to Modeling Presidential Success in Congress." *Political Research Quarterly* 51: 155–172.

Loomis, Burdett. 2001. "The Senate: An 'Obstacle Course' for Executive Appointments?" In *Innocent until Nominated: The Breakdown of the Presidential Appointments Process*, ed. Calvin Mackenzie. Washington, DC: Brookings.

Lowande, Kenneth. 2014. "After the Orders: Presidential Memoranda & Unilateral Action." *Presidential Studies Quarterly* 44: 724–741.

Lowi, Theodore J. 1985. *The Personal President.* Ithaca, NY: Cornell University Press.

McCarty, Nolan. 2004. "The Appointments Dilemma." *American Journal of Political Science* 48: 413–428.

McCarty, Nolan, and Rose Razaghian. 1999. "Advice and Consent: Senate Responses to Executive Branch Nominations, 1885–1996." *American Journal of Political Science* 43: 1122–1143.

McCombs, Maxwell E., and Donald L. Shaw. 1972. "The Agenda-Setting Function of the Mass Media." *Public Opinion Quarterly* 36: 176–187.

McConnell, Grant. 1966. *Private Power and American Democracy.* New York: Alfred Knopf.

McGauvran, Ronald J., and Matthew Eshbaugh-Soha. 2017. "Presidential Speeches Amid a More Centralized and Unified Congress." *Congress & the Presidency* 44: 55–76.

Mackenzie, G. Calvin. 1981. *The Politics of Presidential Appointments.* New York: Free Press.

———. 2001. "The State of Presidential Appointments." In *Innocent until Nominated: The Breakdown of the Presidential Appointments Process*, ed. Calvin G. Mackenzie. Washington, DC: Brookings.

Maltese, John Anthony. 1994. *Spin Control: The White House Office of Communications and the Management of Presidential News*, 2nd rev. ed. Chapel Hill, NC: University of North Carolina Press.

Mann, James. 2015. *George W. Bush: The 43rd President, 2001–2009.* New York: Times Books.

Mattson, Kevin. 2009. *"What the Heck Are You Up to, Mr. President?" Jimmy Carter, America's "Malaise," and the Speech that Should Have Changed the Country.* New York: Bloomsbury.

May, Ernest R., Philip D. Zelikow. 1997. *The Kennedy Tapes: Inside the White House during the Cuban Missile Crisis.* Cambridge, MA: Belknap Press.

Mayer, Kenneth R. 1999. "Executive Orders and Presidential Power." *Journal of Politics* 61: 445–466.

———. 2001. *With the Stroke of a Pen: Executive Orders and Presidential Power.* Princeton, NJ: Princeton University Press.

———. 2009. "Thoughts on 'The Revolution in Presidential Studies.'" *Presidential Studies Quarterly* 39: 781–785.

Mayer, William G. 2004. "From the End of the Nomination Contest to the Start of the National Conventions: Preliminary Thoughts on a New Period in Presidential Campaign Politics." *The Forum* 2(2): Article 1.

Mayer, William G., and Andrew E. Busch. 2004. *The Front-Loading Problem in Presidential Nominations.* Washington, DC: Brookings.

Mayhew, David R. 1991. "Divided Party Control: Does it Make a Difference?" *PS: Political Science and Politics* 24: 637–640.

———. 2005. *Divided We Govern: Party Control, Lawmaking, and Investigations, 1946–2002.* New Haven, CT: Yale University Press.

Meernik, James. 1995. "Congress, the President and the Commitment of the U.S. Military." *Legislative Studies Quarterly* 20: 377–392.

Michaels, Judith E. 1997. *The President's Call: Executive Leadership from FDR to George Bush.* Pittsburgh, PA: University of Pittsburgh Press.

Mickey, Robert. 2015. *Paths Out of Dixie: The Democratization of Authoritarian Enclaves in America's Deep South, 1944–1972.* Princeton, NJ: Princeton University Press.

Milkis, Sidney M. 1995. *The President and the Parties: The Transformation of the American Party System since the New Deal.* New York: Oxford University Press.

Milkis, Sidney M., Jesse H. Rhodes, and Emily J. Charnock. 2012. "What Happened to Post-Partisanship? Barack Obama and the New American Party System." *Perspectives on Politics* 10: 57–76.

Milkis, Sidney M., and Michael Nelson. 2016. *The American Presidency: Origins and Development, 1776–2014*, 7th ed. Washington, DC: CQ Press.

Miller, Joanne, and Jon Krosnick. 2000. "News Media Impact on the Ingredients of Presidential Evaluations: Politically Knowledgeable Citizens Are Guided by a Trusted Source." *American Journal of Political Science* 44: 301–315.

Miroff, Bruce. 2016. *Presidents on Political Ground: Leaders in Action and What They Face.* Lawrence, KS: University Press of Kansas.

Moe, Terry M. 1985. "The Politicized Presidency." In *The New Direction in American Politics*, eds. John E. Chubb and Paul E. Peterson. Washington, DC: Brookings.

Moe, Terry M., and William G. Howell, 1999. "Unilateral Action and Presidential Power: A Theory." *Presidential Studies Quarterly* 29: 850–873.

Moens, Alexander. 1990. *Foreign Policy under Carter: Testing Multiple Advocacy Decision Making.* Boulder, CO: Westview.

Monroe, Dan. 2003. *The Republican Vision of John Tyler.* College Station, TX: Texas A&M University Press.

Mueller, John E. 1970. "Presidential Popularity from Truman to Johnson." *American Political Science Review* 64: 18–34.

———. 1973. *War, Presidents and Public Opinion.* New York: John Wiley.

Murray, Kathleen Shoon, and Peter Howard. 2000. "Variation in White House Polling Operations: Carter to Clinton." *Public Opinion Quarterly* 66: 527–558.

Murray, Robert K., and Tim H. Blessing. 1994. *Greatness in the White House: Rating the Presidents from George Washington through Ronald Reagan*, 2nd ed. University Park, PA: Pennsylvania State University Press.

Muskie, Edmund, Brent Scowcroft, and John Tower. 1987. *The Tower Commission Report: The Full Text of the President's Special Review Board.* New York: Bantam.

Nathan, Richard P. 1975. *The Plot That Failed: Nixon and the Administrative Presidency.* New York: John Wiley.

———. 1983. *The Administrative Presidency.* New York: John Wiley.

Nemacheck, Christine L. 2007. *Strategic Selection: Presidential Nomination of Supreme Court Justices from Herbert Hoover through George W. Bush.* Charlottesville, VA: University of Virginia Press.

Neuman, W. Russell. 1986. *The Paradox of Mass Politics: Knowledge and Opinion in the American Electorate.* Cambridge, MA: Harvard University Press.

Neustadt, Richard E. 1960. *Presidential Power and the Modern Presidents.* New York: John Wiley.

———. 1990. *Presidential Power and the Modern Presidents: The Politics of Leadership from Roosevelt to Reagan.* New York: Free Press.

Newmann, William W. 2003. *Managing National Security Policy: The President and the Process.* Pittsburgh, PA: University of Pittsburgh Press.

Nichols, David K. 2010. *The Myth of the Modern Presidency.* University Park, PA: Pennsylvania State University Press.

Nokken, Timothy P., and Brian R. Sala. "Confirmation Dynamics: A Model of Presidential Appointments to Independent Agencies." *Journal of Theoretical Politics* 12: 91–112.

Norrander, Barbara. 1992. *Super Tuesday: Regional Politics and Presidential Primaries.* Lexington, KY: University Press of Kentucky.

———. 1993. "Nomination Choices: Caucus and Primary Outcomes, 1976–1988." *American Journal of Political Science* 37: 343–364.

———. 2000. "The End Game in Post-Reform Presidential Nominations." *Journal of Politics* 62: 999–1013.

———. 2006. "The Attrition Game: Initial Resources, Initial Contests and the Exit of Candidates During the US Presidential Primary Season." *British Journal of Political Science* 36: 487–507.

Novak, Michael. 1974. *Choosing Our King: Powerful Symbols in Presidential Politics*. New York: Macmillan.

Oberdorfer, Don. 1998. *From the Cold War to a New Era: The United States and the Soviet Union, 1983–1991*, updated ed. Baltimore, MD: Johns Hopkins University Press.

O'Brien, David M. 2003. *Storm Center: The Supreme Court in American Politics*, 6th ed. New York: Norton.

———. 2008. *Storm Center: The Supreme Court in American Politics*, 8th ed. New York: W.W. Norton.

Pacelle, Richard L. Jr. 2003. *Between Law and Politics: The Solicitor General and the Structuring of Race, Gender and Reproductive Rights Litigation*. College Station, TX: Texas A&M University Press.

Page, Benjamin I., and Jason Barabas. 2000. "Foreign Policy Gaps between Citizens and Leaders." *International Studies Quarterly* 44: 339–364.

Page, Benjamin I., and Robert Y. Shapiro. 1992. *The Rational Public: Fifty Years of Trends in Americans' Policy Preferences*. Chicago, IL: University of Chicago Press.

Parkin, Michael. 2010. "Taking Late Night Comedy Seriously: How Candidate Appearances on Late Night Television Can Engage Viewers." *Political Research Quarterly* 16: 3–15.

Peake, Jeffrey S. 2001. "Presidential Agenda Setting in Foreign Policy." *Political Research Quarterly* 54: 69–86.

Peake, Jeffrey S. and Matthew Eshbaugh-Soha. 2008. "The Agenda-Setting Impact of Major Presidential TV Addresses." *Political Communication* 25: 113–137.

Peterson, Mark A. 1990. *Legislating Together: The White House and Capitol Hill from Eisenhower to Reagan*. Cambridge, MA: Harvard University Press.

Pfiffner, James P. 1996. *The Strategic Presidency: Hitting the Ground Running*, 2nd ed. Lawrence, KS: University of Kansas Press.

———. 2008. *Power Play: The Bush Presidency and the Constitution*. Washington, DC: Brookings.

Pika, Joseph A., John Anthony Maltese, and Andrew Rudalevige. 2017. *The Politics of the Presidency*, 9th ed. Washington, DC: CQ Press.

Poen, Monte. 1979. *Harry S. Truman versus the Medical Lobby*. Columbia, MO: University of Missouri Press.

Polsby, Nelson. 2004. *How Congress Evolves: Social Bases of Institutional Change*. New York: Oxford University Press.

Polsky, Andrew J. 2012. *Elusive Victories: The American Presidency at War*. New York: Oxford University Press.

———. 2015. "Shifting Currents: Dwight Eisenhower and the Dynamic of Presidential Opportunity Structure." *Presidential Studies Quarterly* 45: 91–109.

Ponder, Daniel E. 2012. "Presidential Leverage and the Politics of Policy Formulation." *Presidential Studies Quarterly* 42: 300–323.

Powell, Richard J. 1999. "'Going Public' Revisited: Presidential Speechmaking and the Bargaining Setting in Congress." *Congress & the Presidency* 26: 153–170.

Prakash, Saikrishna B., and Michael D. Ramsey. 2001. "The Executive Power of Foreign Affairs." *Yale Law Journal* 231: 231–356.

Prior, Markus. 2009. "Improving Media Effects Research through Better Measurement of News Exposure." *Journal of Politics* 71: 893–908.

Provine, Doris Marie. 1980. *Case Selection in the United States Supreme Court.* Chicago, IL: University of Chicago Press.

Ragsdale, Lyn. 2009. *Vital Statistics on the Presidency: George Washington to George W. Bush*, 3rd ed. Washington, DC: CQ Press.

Raichur, Arvind, and Richard W. Waterman. 1993. "The Presidency, the Public, and the Expectations Gap." In *The Presidency Reconsidered*, ed. Richard W. Waterman. Itasca, IL: Peacock.

Rapoport, Ronald B., Walter J. Stone, and Alan I. Abramowitz. 1991. "Do Endorsements Matter? Group Influence in the 1984 Democratic Caucuses." *American Political Science Review* 85: 193–203.

Reeves, Andrew, and Jon C. Rogowski. 2016. "Unilateral Powers, Public Opinion, and the Presidency." *Journal of Politics* 78: 137–151.

Resh, William G. 2015. *Rethinking the Administrative Presidency: Trust, Intellectual Capital, and Appointee-Careerist Relations in the George W. Bush Administration.* Baltimore, MD: Johns Hopkins University Press.

Rhode, David W., and Harold J. Spaeth. 1976. *Supreme Court Decision Making.* San Francisco, CA: Freeman.

Rhodes, Jesse H. 2014. "Party Polarization and the Ascendance of Bipartisan Posturing as a Dominant Strategy in Presidential Rhetoric." *Presidential Studies Quarterly* 44: 120–142.

Rhodes, Jesse H., and Zachary Albert. 2015. "The Transformation of Partisan Rhetoric in Presidential Campaigns, 1952–2012: Partisan Polarization and the Rise of Bipartisan Posturing among Democratic Candidates." *Party Politics.* DOI: 10.1177/1354068815610968.

Ridout, Travis N., and Brandon Rottinghaus. 2008. "The Importance of Being Early: Presidential Primary Front-Loading and the Impact of the Proposed Western Regional Primary." *PS: Political Science & Politics* 41: 123–128.

Ripley, Randall B., and James M. Lindsay. 1993. *Congress Resurgent: Foreign and Defense Policy on Capitol Hill.* Ann Arbor, MI: University of Michigan Press.

Rockman, Bert A. 1984. *The Leadership Question: The Presidency and the American System.* New York: Praeger.

———. 2000. "Reinventing What for Whom? President and Congress in the Making of Foreign Policy." *Presidential Studies Quarterly* 30: 133–156.

Rose, Richard. 1991. *The Postmodern President*, 2nd ed. Chatham, NJ: Chatham House.

Rosenfeld, Sam. 2014. *A Choice, Not an Echo: Polarization and the Transformation of the American Party System.* Doctoral Dissertation, Harvard University.

Rossiter, Clinton. 1956. *The American Presidency: The Powers and Practices, the Personalities and Problems of the Most Important Office on Earth.* New York: Harcourt Brace.

Rottinghaus, Brandon. 2013. "Going Partisan: Presidential Leadership in a Polarized Political Environment." *Issues in Governance Studies* 62: 1–15.

Rottinghaus, Brandon, and Chris Nicholson. 2010. "Counting Congress In: Patterns of Success in Judicial Nomination Requests by Members of Congress to the President." *American Politics Research* 38: 691–717.

Rottinghaus, Brandon, and Daniel E. Bergan. 2011. "The Politics of Requesting Appointments: Congressional Requests in the Appointment and Nomination Process." *Political Research Quarterly* 64: 31–44.

Rottinghaus, Brandon, and Elvin Lim. 2009. "Proclaiming Trade Policy: Presidential Unilateral Enactment of Trade Policy." *American Politics Research* 37: 1003–1023.

Rottinghaus, Brandon, and Jason Maier. 2007. "The Power of Decree: Presidential Use of Executive Proclamations, 1977–2005." *Political Research Quarterly* 60: 338–343.

Rudalevige, Andrew. 2002. *Managing the President's Program: Presidential Leadership and Legislative Policy Formation.* Princeton, NJ: Princeton University Press.

———. 2005. *The New Imperial Presidency: Renewing Presidential Power after Watergate.* Ann Arbor, MI: University of Michigan Press.

———. 2012. "Executive Orders and Presidential Unilateralism." *Presidential Studies Quarterly* 42: 138–160.

———. 2013. "Presidential Authority in a Separated System of Governance." In *New Directions in American Politics*, ed. Raymond J. La Raja. New York: Routledge.

Saeki, Manabu. 2004. "Override Propensity in the U.S. Congress: Veto Challenge and Override Vote by the Two Chambers." *Journal of Legislative Studies* 10: 70–83.

Salokar, Rebecca Mae. 1992. *The Solicitor General: The Politics of Law.* Philadelphia, PA: Temple University Press.

———. 1995. "Politics, Law and the Office of the Solicitor General." In *Government Lawyers: The Federal Legal Bureaucracy and Presidential Politics*, ed. Cornell Clayton. Lawrence, KS: University Press of Kansas.

Sanger, David E. 2009. *The Inheritance: The World Obama Confronts and the Challenges to American Power.* New York: Crown.

Sarotte, Mary Elise. 2009. *1989: The Struggle to Create Post-Cold War Europe.* Princeton, NJ: Princeton University Press.

Savage, Sean. 2004. *JFK, LBJ, and the Democratic Party.* Albany, NY: SUNY Press.

Scala, Dante J. 2003. *Stormy Weather: The New Hampshire Primary and Presidential Politics.* New York: Palgrave Macmillan.

Schickler, Eric. 2016. *Racial Realignment: The Transformation of American Liberalism, 1932–1965.* Princeton, NJ: Princeton University Press.

Schier, Steven, ed. 2000. *The Postmodern Presidency: Bill Clinton's Legacy in U.S. Politics.* Pittsburgh, PA: University of Pittsburgh Press.

Schlesinger, Arthur Jr. 1973. *The Imperial Presidency.* Boston, MA: Houghton Mifflin.

Schlesinger, Stephen C. 2003. *Act of Creation: The Founding of the United Nations.* Boulder, CO: Westview.

Schubert, Glendon. 1965. *The Judicial Mind.* New York: Free Press.

Scigliano, Robert. 1981. "The War Powers Resolution and the War Powers Act." In *The Presidency and the Constitutional Order*, eds. Joseph M. Bessette and Jeffrey K. Tulis. Baton Rouge, LA: Louisiana State University Press.

Segal, Jeffery A., and Harold J. Spaeth. 2002. *The Supreme Court and the Attitudinal Model Revised.* New York: Cambridge University Press.

Seidman, Harold, and Robert Gilmour. 1986. *Politics, Position and Power*, 4th ed. New York: Oxford University Press.

Shesol, Jeff. 2010. *Supreme Power: Franklin Roosevelt vs. The Supreme Court.* New York: W.W. Norton.

Shull, Steven A. 1993. *A Kinder, Gentler Racism? The Reagan-Bush Civil Rights Legacy.* New York: Routledge.

———., ed. 1999. *Presidential Policymaking: An End-of-Century Assessment.* Armonk, NY: M.E. Sharpe.

———. 2006. *Policy by Other Means: Alternative Adoption by Presidents.* College Station, TX: Texas A&M University Press.

Siegel, Michael E. 2011. *The President as Leader.* New York: Routledge.

Sinclair, Barbara. 2000. "Hostile Partners: The President, Congress and Law-making in the Partisan 1990s." In *Polarized Politics*, eds. Jon R. Bond and Richard Fleisher. Washington, DC: CQ Press.

———. 2003. "Legislative Cohesion and Presidential Policy Success." *Journal of Legislative Studies* 9: 41–56.

———. 2012. "Doing Big Things: Obama and the 111th Congress." In *The Obama Presidency: Appraisals and Prospects*, eds. Bert A. Rockman, Andrew Rudalevige, and Colin Campbell. Washington, DC: CQ Press.

Skinner, Richard M. 2008. "George W. Bush and the Partisan Presidency." *Political Science Quarterly* 123: 605–622.

Skowronek, Stephen. 1982. *Building a New American State: The Expansion of National Administrative Capacities, 1877–1920.* New York: Cambridge University Press.

———. 1993. *The Politics Presidents Make: Leadership from John Adams to George Bush.* Cambridge, MA: Belknap Press.

———. 1997. *The Politics Presidents Make: Presidential Leadership from John Adams to Bill Clinton.* Cambridge, MA: Belknap Press.

———. 2011. *Presidential Leadership in Political Time: Reprise and Reappraisal.* Lawrence, KS: University Press of Kansas.

Slotnick, Elliot, Sara Schiavoni, and Sheldon Goldman. 2016. "Writing the Book of Judges, Part II: Confirmation Politics in the 113th Congress." *Journal of Law and Courts* 4: 187–242.

Slotnick, Elliot, Sheldon Goldman, and Sara Schiavoni. 2015. "Writing the Book of Judges, Part I: Obama's Judicial Appointments Record after Six Years." *Journal of Law and Courts* 3: 331–367.

Smith, Courtney B. 2014. "The Impact of Dues Withholding on the U.S.-U.N. Relationship." In *U.S. Presidential Leadership at the UN: 1945 to Present*, ed. Meena Bose. Hauppauge, NY: Nova Science.

Smith, Jean Edward. 2012. *Eisenhower in War and Peace.* New York: Random House.

———. 2016. *Bush.* New York: Simon & Schuster.

Snyder, Susan K., and Berry R. Weingast. 2000. "The American System of Shared Powers: The President, Congress and the NLRB." *Journal of Law Economics & Organization* 16: 269–305.

Sobel, Richard. 2001. *The Impact of Public Opinion on U.S. Foreign Policy since Vietnam.* New York: Oxford University Press.

Sollenberger, Michael. 2008. *The President Shall Nominate: How Congress Trumps Executive Power.* Lawrence, KS: University of Kansas Press.

Spitzer, Robert J. 2008. *Saving the Constitution from Lawyers: How Legal Training and Law Reviews Distort Constitutional Meaning.* New York: Cambridge University Press.

———. 2013. "Comparing the Constitutional Presidencies of George W. Bush and Barack Obama: War Powers, Signing Statements, Vetoes." *White House Studies* 12: 125–146.

Steger, Wayne P., Andrew J. Dowdle, and Randall E. Adkins. 2004. "The New Hampshire Effect in Presidential Nominations." *Political Research Quarterly* 57: 375–390.

Stern, Sheldon M. 2003. *Averting the "Final Failure": John F. Kennedy and the Secret Cuban Missile Crisis Meetings.* Stanford, CA: Stanford University Press.

Stimson, James A. 1976. "Public Support for American Presidents: A Cyclical Model." *Public Opinion Quarterly* 40: 1–21.

Strickler, Jeremy. 2016. "Visions of National Strength: The Modern Presidency and the Politics of Linkage." Paper presented at the annual meeting of the American Political Science Association, Philadelphia, PA, September 1–4.

Stuckey, Mary E. 1991. *The President as Interpreter-in-Chief.* Chatham, NJ: Chatham House.

———. 2005. "Doing Diversity across the Partisan Divide: George H. W. Bush, Bill Clinton, and American National Identity." In *In the Public Domain: Presidents and the Challenges of Public Leadership*, eds. Lori Cox Han and Diane J. Heith. Albany, NY: SUNY Press.

Sullivan, Terry, and Scott de Marchi. 2011. "Congressional Bargaining in Presidential Time: Give and Take, Anticipation, and the Constitutional Rationalization of Dead Ducks." *Journal of Politics* 73: 748–763.

Sundquist, James L. 1986. *Constitutional Reform and Effective Government.* Washington, DC: Brookings.

Tenpas, Kathryn Dunn. 1997. *Presidents as Candidates: Inside the White House for the Presidential Campaign.* New York: Garland.

———. 2003. "Campaigning to Govern: Presidents Seeking Reelection." *PS: Political Science and Politics* 36: 199–202.

Tenpas, Kathryn Dunn, and Jay McCann. 2007. "Testing the Permanence of the Permanent Campaign: An Analysis of Presidential Polling Expenditures, 1977–2002." *Public Opinion Quarterly* 71: 349–366.

Thomas, Evan. 2012. *Ike's Bluff: President Eisenhower's Secret Battle to Save the World.* New York: Little, Brown.

Tichenor, Daniel J. 2014. "The Presidency and Interest Groups: Allies, Adversaries, and Policy Leadership." In *The Presidency and the Political System*, 10th ed., ed. Michael Nelson. Washington, DC: CQ Press.

Toobin, Jeffrey. 2007. *The Nine: Inside the Secret World of the Supreme Court.* New York: Doubleday.

Troy, Gil. 2007. *Morning in America: How Ronald Reagan Invented the 1980s.* Princeton, NJ: Princeton University Press.

Truman, Harry S. 1956. *Memoirs, Volume Two: Years of Trial and Hope.* Garden City, NY: Doubleday.

Tulis, Jeffrey K. 1987. *The Rhetorical Presidency.* Princeton, NJ: Princeton University Press.

Vaughn, Justin S., and Jose D. Villalobos. 2011. "White House Staff." In *New Directions in the American Presidency*, ed. Lori Cox Han. New York: Routledge.

————. 2015. *Czars in the White House: The Rise of Policy Czars as Presidential Management Tools.* Ann Arbor, MI: University of Michigan Press.

Vieira, Norman, and Leonard Gross. 1998. *Supreme Court Appointments: Judge Bork and the Politicization of Senate Confirmations.* Carbondale, IL: Southern Illinois University Press.

Walcott, Charles E., and Karen M. Hult. 1995. *Governing the White House.* Lawrence, KS: University Press of Kansas.

————. 1999. "White House Staff Size: Explanations and Implications." *Presidential Studies Quarterly* 29: 638–656.

Walsh, Lawrence E. 1997. *Firewall: The Iran-Contra Conspiracy and Cover-up.* New York: W.W. Norton.

Wanta, Wayne, Mary Ann Stephenson, Judy VanSlyke Turk, and Maxwell E. McCombs. 1989. "How Presidents State of Union Talk Influenced News Media Agendas." *Journalism Quarterly* 66: 537–541.

Warber, Adam L. 2006. *Executive Orders and the Modern Presidency: Legislating from the Oval Office.* Boulder, CO: Lynne Rienner.

Warshaw, Shirley Anne. 1997. *The Domestic Presidency: Policy Making in the White House.* Boston, MA: Allyn and Bacon.

————. 2000. *The Keys to Power: Managing the Presidency.* New York: Longman.

————. 2009. *The Co-Presidency of Bush and Cheney.* Stanford, CA: Stanford University Press.

Waterman, Richard. 1989. *Presidential Influence and the Administrative State.* Knoxville, TN: University of Tennessee Press.

Waterman, Richard, Carol Silva, and Hank Jenkins-Smith. 1999. "The Expectations Gap Thesis: Public Attitudes toward an Incumbent President." *Journal of Politics* 61: 944–966.

Waterman, Richard, Hank Jenkins-Smith, and Carol Silva. 2014. *The Presidential Expectations Gap: Public Attitudes Concerning the Presidency.* Ann Arbor, MI: University of Michigan Press.

Waterman, Richard, Robert Wright, and Gilbert St. Clair. 1999. *The Image-is-Everything Presidency: Dilemmas in American Leadership.* Boulder, CO: Westview.

Wattenberg, Martin P. 1991. *The Rise of Candidate-Centered Politics: Presidential Elections in the 1980s.* Cambridge, MA: Harvard University Press.

Wayne, Stephen J. 1978. *The Legislative Presidency.* New York: Harper & Row.

Weingast, Berry R. 2006. "Caught in the Middle: The President, Congress, and the Political-Bureaucratic System." In *The Executive Branch*, eds. Joel D. Aberbach and Mark A. Peterson. New York: Oxford University Press.

Weissert, Carol S., and William G. Weissert. 1996. *Governing Health: The Politics of Health Policy.* Baltimore, MD: Johns Hopkins University Press.

Weko, Thomas J. 1995. *The Politicizing Presidency: The White House Personnel Office, 1948–1994.* Lawrence, KS: University of Kansas Press.

Whitford, Andrew B., and Jeff Yates. 2009. *Presidential Rhetoric and the Public Agenda: Constructing the War on Drugs.* Baltimore, MD: Johns Hopkins University Press.

Wildavsky, Aaron. 1961. "The Two Presidencies." *Trans-Action* 4: 7–14.

Wilson, James Q. 1975. "The Rise of the Bureaucratic State." *The Public Interest* 41: 77–79.

Witcover, Jules. 1977. *Marathon: The Pursuit of the Presidency, 1972–1976*. New York: Viking Press.

Wood, B. Dan. 2007. *The Politics of Economic Leadership: The Causes and Consequences of Presidential Rhetoric*. Princeton, NJ: Princeton University Press.

Wood, B. Dan, and Jeffrey S. Peake. 1998. "The Dynamics of Foreign Policy Agenda Setting." *American Political Science Review* 92: 173–184.

Wroe, Andrew. 2008. *The Republican Party and Immigration Politics: From Proposition 187 to George W. Bush*. New York: Palgrave Macmillan.

Yalof, David A. 1999. *Pursuit of Justices: Presidential Politics and the Selection of Supreme Court Nominees*. Chicago, IL: University of Chicago Press.

Yoo, John. 2005. *The Powers of War and Peace: The Constitution and Foreign Affairs after 9/11*. Chicago, IL: University of Chicago Press.

Zaller, John. 1992. *The Nature and Origins of Mass Opinion*. New York: Cambridge University Press.

Zegart, Amy B. 1999. *Flawed by Design: The Evolution of the CIA, JCS, and NSC*. Stanford, CA: Stanford University Press.

———. 2007. *Spying Blind: The CIA, the FBI, and the Origins of 9/11*. Princeton, NJ: Princeton University Press.

Index